MAP OF THE NORTH WESTERN FRONTIER OF INDIA
SHOWING THE PAMIR REGION AND PART OF AFGHANISTAN

A NIGHT MARCH IN THE GOBI DESERT.

THE
HEART OF A CONTINENT:

A NARRATIVE OF TRAVELS IN MANCHURIA,
ACROSS THE GOBI DESERT, THROUGH THE HIMALAYAS,
THE PAMIRS, AND CHITRAL.
1884–1894.

BY

CAPTAIN FRANK E. YOUNGHUSBAND, C.I.E.,

INDIAN STAFF CORPS,
GOLD MEDALLIST, ROYAL GEOGRAPHICAL SOCIETY.

> "Make me feel the wild pulsation that I felt before the strife,
> When I heard my days before me, and the tumult of my life;
> Yearning for the large excitement that the coming years would yield,
> Eager-hearted as a boy when first he leaves his father's field,
> And his spirit leaps within him to be gone before him then,
> Underneath the lights he looks at, in among the throngs of men:
> Men, my brothers, men the workers, ever reaping something new,
> That which they have done but earnest of the things that they shall do."
>
> TENNYSON.

LONDON:
JOHN MURRAY, ALBEMARLE STREET.
1896.

LONDON:
PRINTED BY WILLIAM CLOWES AND SONS, LIMITED,
STAMFORD STREET AND CHARING CROSS.

TO THE MEMORY OF

MY MOTHER,

THROUGH WHOM, AS THE SISTER OF ROBERT SHAW,

I INHERITED THE SPIRIT OF EXPLORATION;

AND TO WHOSE KEEN INTEREST IN ALL MY PLANS,

AND THE

SELF-DENYING ENCOURAGEMENT SHE GAVE ME IN THEIR EXECUTION,

I OWE SO MUCH OF WHAT SUCCESS HAS ATTENDED MY WORK,

I DEDICATE

THIS RECORD OF MY TRAVELS.

PREFACE.

THE first thing a man who travels from London to Scotland wants to do is to describe to his friends at the end of his journey his experiences on the way—whether the train was crowded or not, what the weather was like, and how perfect or imperfect the arrangements of the railway company were. It is the same general instinct of wishing to tell out to others the experiences one has had that is now acting in me. To do this in conversation is, in my case, a hopeless task—because, for one thing, my experiences of travel have now accumulated so heavily; and, for another, I find insuperable difficulties in giving by word of mouth accounts of travels in strange lands unfamiliar to the hearer. At the same time I am always experiencing the wish that my friends should be able to share with me, as much as it is possible to do so, the enjoyment I have felt in looking upon Nature in its aspects wild, in distant unfrequented parts of the earth, and in mixing with strange and little-known peoples, who, semi-barbarians though they may be, have often more interesting traits of character than others in a higher scale of civilization.

I have, therefore, been year by year impelled to write out my experiences in a collected form, and in such a way as may be accessible, not only to those with whom I am personally acquainted, but also, I hope, to many another kindred spirit, who shares with me that love for adventure and seeking out the unknown which has grown up within me. The great pleasure in writing is to feel that it is possible, by this means, to reach such men; to feel that I can speak to them just as they, by their books and by their works, have spoken to me, and that I may, in some slight degree, be passing on to others about to start on careers of adventure, the same keen love of travel and of Nature which I have received from those who have gone before.

There are others, too, whom I hope my book may reach—some few among those thousands and thousands who stay at home in England. Amongst these there are numbers who have that longing to go out and see the world which is the characteristic of Englishmen. It is not natural to an Englishman to sit at an office desk, or spend his whole existence amid such tame excitement as life in London, and shooting partridges and pheasants afford. Many consider themselves tied down to home; but they often tie themselves down. And if a man has indeed the spirit of travel in him, nothing should be allowed to stand in the way of his doing as he wishes. And one of the hopes I have as I write this book is, that it may tempt some few among the stay-at-homes to go out and breathe a little of the pure fresh air of Nature, and inhale into their beings some of the revivifying force and heightened power of enjoyment of all that is on this earth which it can give.

My book cannot claim to be scientific, nor to be written in any correct literary style, but I have endeavoured to speak out, as clearly and impressively as I can, what I saw, what I did, and what I felt in the little-known, and sometimes unknown, regions which I have visited, and to give the impressions which formed themselves in my mind of the various peoples whom I met. Some portion of this will, I hope, prove of value to others besides the general reader; but it has been a ceaseless cause of regret to me that I had never undergone a scientific training before undertaking my journeys. During the last year or two I have done what I can by myself to supply this deficiency; but amongst the Himalaya mountains, in the desert of Gobi, and amid the forests of Manchuria, how much would I not have given to be able to exchange that smattering of Greek and Latin which I had drilled into me at school for a little knowledge of the great forces of Nature which I saw at work around me!

With these few remarks of introduction, and with the hope that there may be some among my readers to whom the spirit in which it has been written may appeal; that there may be among the busy crowds in England some to whom it may give an hour's change of scene, and a momentary glimpse into the great world of Nature beyond our little isle; and that there may be some among my countrymen scattered over the world to whom this description of still other lands than those they have so far seen may give pleasure, I send out this story of a wanderer's doings, of the scenes which he has witnessed, and of the feelings which have moved him.

> "Where rose the mountains, there to him were friends;
> Where roll'd the ocean, thereon was his home;
> Where a blue sky, and glowing clime, extends,
> He had the passion and the power to roam;
> The desert, forest, cavern, breaker's foam,
> Were unto him companionship; they spake
> A mutual language, clearer than the tome
> Of his land's tongue, which he would oft forsake
> For Nature's pages glass'd by sunbeams on the lake.
>
> . . . . .
>
> "Perils he sought not, but ne'er shrank to meet:
> The scene was savage, but the scene was new;
> This made the ceaseless toil of travel sweet,
> Beat back keen winter's blast, and welcom'd summer's heat."
>
> BYRON.

NOTICE.

THE appearance of this volume has been delayed by a variety of unforeseen causes. Before the manuscript was completed, the author was suddenly called upon to go to Chitral, during the campaign which was being carried out in that country in 1895. Again, last December, when but a few pages were in print, he was unexpectedly summoned to a distant part of the world at a few hours' notice.

Before leaving, he requested me to see the work through the press. This task has been an unusually interesting and agreeable one, but has been attended by some little difficulty, for some of the places named are not to be found on any existing maps, while, inasmuch as many of the incidents described are known to the author alone, the process of verification, when any uncertainty arose, was in some instances impossible.

In these circumstances, I must ask the reader not to hold the author responsible for any inaccuracies which may be found in these pages.

Captain Younghusband's achievements as a traveller and explorer, which won for him a very distinguished place among the Gold Medallists of the Royal Geographical Society, are too well known to call for many words of introduction to this record of his principal expeditions.

In 1886 he visited Manchuria, and penetrated to the summit of Chang-pai-shan, the "Ever-White Mountain," in company with Mr. James of the Indian Civil Service.

Returning thence to Peking, he started, in 1887, on his adventurous journey through the heart of Asia, across the

Gobi Desert and Chinese Turkestan to Kashgar and Yarkand, and from that point crossed the Himalayas by the Mustagh Pass to Srinagar.

In 1889 he was sent to investigate the circumstances of the Kanjuti or Hunza raids on the Kirghiz territory, in the course of which he descended the valley of the Yarkand River, explored the Saltoro and Shimshal Passes, and, after reaching the Taghdumbash Pamir, visited Safder Ali, the chief of the Hunzas, at his head-quarters at Hunza.

In 1890 Captain Younghusband made his famous expedition to the Pamirs, at the close of which he was peremptorily ordered off territory claimed by Russia. The officer conveying this message was Colonel Yonoff, with whom Captain Younghusband, but a few hours before, had been encamping on the most friendly terms. For this act the Russian Government subsequently apologized.

In 1892, after the brilliant little campaign in which Safder Ali was subdued, he was sent to Hunza, where a British representative was established; but early in the following year was suddenly summoned to Chitral, on the outbreak of disturbances consequent upon the death of the ruler, Aman-ul-Mulk. When peace was restored, and the succession of the Mehtar, Nizam-ul-Mulk, was secured, Captain Younghusband was for some months stationed at the capital as British representative, and during this time he became thoroughly acquainted with a country which was destined, soon afterwards, to attract much interest in England. In this work will be found a full account of Chitral and her people, and of the unfortunate ruler whose death was the immediate cause of the expedition of 1895.

The account of that expedition, already published by Captain Younghusband, forms an episode in the record of his experiences, of which this volume gives the first connected narrative.

JOHN MURRAY.

CONTENTS.

CHAPTER I.

THE EVER-WHITE MOUNTAIN.

My first journey to Dharmsala—Robert Shaw—Preparations for an extended journey—Mr. H. E. M. James—Decision to go to Manchuria—Arrival at Newchwang—"The Ever-White Mountain"—To Mukden—Chinese inquisitiveness—Tomb of Nurhaden—To the Yalu River—Want of milk and butter—Industry of Chinese colonists—We enter the great forest—Mosquitoes—Sable hunters—The Sungari River—Its sources—I reach the summit of the "Ever-White Mountain"—Kirin—Chinese dinners—Chinese manners ... 1

CHAPTER II.

MANCHURIA TO PEKING.

Start for Tsi-tsi-har—The Sungari again—Luxury of milk and cream—The Mongolian and Chinese frontier—Return to cultivation—Hulan—Torturing of Père Conraux—Pei-lin-tzu—A pattern mission station—Sansing—A Chinese fort and guns—Ninguta—Chinese carts and carters—The Russian frontier—Hunchun—Transport of Krupp guns—General I—A Russian frontier post—Cossacks—Colonel Sokolowski—Russian hospitality—Novo-kievsk—The Corean frontier—England and Russia 22

CHAPTER III.

BACK TO PEKING.

We turn our faces homewards—Kirin—Hsiao Pa-chia-tzu—The Roman Catholic mission—To Mukden—14° below zero—Winter traffic—Mongolian ponies—A frozen mist—The Scottish mission at Mukden—Its medical work—Return to Newchwang—My indebtedness to Mr. James—Remarks on Manchuria—Its products and people—Christmas Day in a Chinese inn—Shan-hai-kuan—The Great Wall of China—Compared with the Pyramids—Kaiping—A procession of corpses—British navvies—The Kaiping coal-mine—Mr. Kinder—How he constructed his locomotives—The first Chinese railway—Native superstitions and prejudices—Feng-shui—Tientsin—Ice-boat sailing—New Year's visits—Peking 42

CHAPTER IV.

PEKING TO KWEI-HWA-CHENG.

Arrival of Colonel Bell—Preparations for an overland journey to India—Our different routes—Fascination of planning a journey—Start from Peking—My servant—Liu-san—The Great Wall at Kalgan—American medical mission—Views on opium-smoking—M. Ivanoff—A Chinese ex-naval officer—Chinese ignorance of geography—Agreements with carters—In the valley of the Yang-ho—The winds from the Mongolian plateau—Formation of cart-roads in the loess—Mules—We enter the "Land of Gog and Magog"—On the Mongolian plain—Yurts—Kindliness of the Mongols—Partridges—Chinese supplanting Mongols—Rapid changes of temperature—Arrival at Kwei-hwa-cheng—The China inland mission—Their system and hardships—How Chinese troops are levied—Mr. Clarke—Kwei-hwa-cheng—Its diminishing trade—Its temples—Mongol bazaar—Caravan-men—Preparations for crossing the Gobi Desert—Finding an auspicious date—My equipment 58

CHAPTER V.

ACROSS THE GOBI DESERT.

My company—The guide—His extraordinary memory for wells—Ma-te-la—We start—The In-shan Mountains—Mongolian pastures—Encroachments of Chinese and Russians—Messrs. Collins & Co. of Tientsin—The Mongolian camel—Warnings of robbers—Liu-san and his revolver—Deer and the mode of killing them—Mongol temples—Aggressive ravens—Approaching the Sheitung-ula Mountains—A local tradition—The Ho-lai-Bu stream—Deceptive distances—The heart of the Gobi Desert—Monotonous marches—Characteristics of the desert—Temperature and winds—Extracts from diary—Wild ponies—Elm trees—The Galpin Gobi—Hurricane and darkness—Partridges—The Hurku Hills—Bortson well—On Prjevalsky's track—A trading caravan—Uses of a Mongol boot—Valuable gifts—Mongol customs—A dust-storm—Curious sandhills—Their origin—Wind-formed sand—Mr. Barosakbai—The mountain system—Preparing for attack—A glass of sherry—Man-chis-tol—A "general hit out"—Slow progress—Glimpses of snow—Wild camels—Wild mules—The Altai Mountains—Refractory camels—Ma-te-la bolts home—A strange sunset—Mongol agriculture—Ula-Khutun—Origin of sloping gravel plains—*Ovis argali*—A glimpse of the Tian-shan—Desert of Zungaria—*Ovis poli* horns—Difficulties of Chinese language—A period of depression—A scorching wind—We enter Turkestan—Its inhabitants—Turki women—We cross the Tian-shan Mountains—An oasis—Last stage of desert journey—Arrival at Hami ... 78

CHAPTER VI.

THROUGH TURKESTAN TO YARKAND.

Inquiries for Colonel Bell—Bazaar at Hami—A Russian merchant—I hire carts—A satisfactory arrangement—Start from Hami—A poor inn—Eurh-pu—The desert again—Tombs of mandarins—A dreary land—A cart as a bedroom—Chinese soldiers and their ways—"The great English nation"

—We lose our way—Shi-ga-tai—Bad inns of Kashgaria—Pi-chan—A pleasant oasis—Curious holes—A Turki inn—Wells of Chinese soldiers—Arrival at Turfan—An Afghan merchant—A cross-examination—The Andijanis—The shops and wares—A Hajji—His experiences and his influence—Kokhandees—Living in holes—Description of Turfan—Toksun—A hard day's work—Kumesha—Karashar—Tunganis—Kalmak encampments—The Turks—Purchasing a pony—A rescued Mongol lady—Fords, ferries, and swamps—Hospitable Turks—Mosquitoes again—The worst carter in Asia—The art of cart-driving—Korlia—A reorganization—Doolans—Kuché—Soldier thieves—A regular horse-dealer—Traces of Yakoob Beg—Kizil—Cultivated land—Aksu—Travelling merchants—Rahmat-ula-Khan—Ush Turfan—Memories of Robert Shaw—A Kirghiz encampment—Curious companions—Darning my stockings—Balls of curds—The Kara-kara Pass—The Syrt country—A captive eagle—Riding down eagles—Hostile Kirghiz—Rahmat-ula-Khan's diplomacy—His opinions on Russians and English—First sight of the Pamir Mountains—Artysh—Arrival at Kashgar—The Afghan aksakal—"Ropert"—MM. Petrovsky and Hendriks—Arrival and welcome at Yarkand 123

CHAPTER VII.

INTO THE HEART OF THE HIMALAYAS.

Chinese Turkestan—Chiefly desert—Oases—A land of extremes—A people of imperturbable mediocrity—A suggestion from Colonel Bell—Preparations for the Mustagh Pass—Dalgleish's house—His characteristics—Robert Shaw—His career and fate—Chinese officials—Courtesy of the Amban—A sumptuous feast—My guide Wali—Start from Yarkand—Market days—Kugiar—Tupa Dawan Pass—The Pakhpu—Chiraghsaldi Pass—Danger of Kanjuti robbers—The Yarkand River—Karash-tarim—Raskam district—Disused smelting furnaces—Khoja Mohammed gorge—Surakwat stream—A bad day's march—Foretaste of severe cold—Elation of difficulty—The Aghil Pass—"The other side of the hill"—A stupendous scene—A precarious descent—The Oprang River—The Karakoram—Suget Jangal—K.2 170

CHAPTER VIII.

THE MUSTAGH PASS.

A discouraging start—A precipice blocks the way—My Ladaki servant refuses descent of the precipice—Mountains of solid ice—My first glacier—Ice-caves—Scarcity of supplies—Difficulties of the ponies—A possible way out—My last pair of boots—In a sea of ice—The two Mustagh passes—A choice of evils—A critical stage—Intense cold at night—On the summit of the pass—Advantages of silence—A perilous ice-slope—Drogpa gives in—A sheer precipice to pass—Courage of my men—The last to descend—In safety once more—A glorious night scene—Crevasses—My last bottle of brandy broken—Baltoro Glacier—Suffering from want of boots—A ducking—We reach Askoli—Inhospitable reception—Start for the New Mustagh Pass—Superstitious dread of the mountains—Cornered between two glaciers—The Punmah Glacier—A rope bridge—Wali's fear—The Braldo River—The Shigar valley—Baltistan—The Baltis—A subject race—I take leave

xiv   CONTENTS.

                                                                    PAGE
of Wali—M. Dauvergne—M. Notovitch—The Zoji-la Pass—The Sind and
Kashmir valleys—Arrival at Srinagar—I try to civilize myself—Meeting
with Captain Ramsay—Congratulations of Sir F. Roberts—To Murree
and Rawal Pindi—Arrival of Liu-san and the ponies   188

CHAPTER IX.

THE KANJUTI RAIDS.

Return of the exploring fever—Disappointment—Sudden order to go to Hunza
—Hunza or Kanjut—A race of raiders—Sir Mortimer Durand—Abbottabad
—I inspect my Gurkhas—Murree—Gurkhas are not horsemen—The Sind
valley—Cheeriness of the Gurkhas—Zoji-la—We enter Ladak—Buddhist
monasteries—Arrival at Leh—An old friend—Shukar Ali—Captain
Ramsay—Kashmir sepoys—Baltis—A goatskin raft—Difficulties of transport—Coolies—Ponies—Donkeys—Camels decided on—Supplies—Start
again—Khardung Pass—Mountain sickness—Nubra valley—Saser Pass—
Depsang Plains—Karakoram Pass—Absence of snow—Dalgleish's murder
—Suget Pass—Shahidula—A deputation of Kirghiz—Account of a Kanjuti
raid—Characteristics of the Kirghiz   214

CHAPTER X.

AMONG THE GLACIERS.

Waiting for the subsidence of the river—Bound for an unknown region—The
Shimshal and Saltoro passes—Supplies arrive—Preparations for exploration
—Start for Shahidula—Khal Chuskun—Sokh-bulak Pass—Kirghiz Jangal
—Kulanuldi—In the valley of the Yarkand River—A swollen ford—Ruins
at Karash-tarim—Minerals—Bazar Darra stream—Information about the
Kuen-lun Mountains and their drainage—A climb to reconnoitre—Karul
on the Surakwat—Tradition of Khoja Mohammed—The Aghil Pass—On
new ground—In search of the Saltoro Pass—The Oprang valley—A wall
of ice—View of Gusherbrum—Among the glaciers—Peculiar snow-clouds
—Baffled—We reach the Saltoro Pass—A heavy snowstorm—An avalanche
—A narrow escape—Forced to return to camp—The Sarpo Laggo valley—
I lose the caravan—Magnesium-wire signals—Suget Jangal—In search of
the Shimshal Pass—Mode of ascending glaciers—Very bad crevasses—A
cul de sac—Comfortless quarters—Return to camp—Beautiful ice-forms—
Glacier scenery—Crevasse Glacier—Return to Suget Jangal   230

CHAPTER XI.

A KANJUTI STRONGHOLD.

Death of my pony—The Oprang River—Want of maps—We lose our bearings
—Constant fordings—The pluck of the Gurkhas—Chang Jangal—A post at
last—News from Hunza—Arrival of Turdi Kol at last—To Darwaza—A
robbers' stronghold—The Gurkha naik claims his privilege—Plan of
approach—A precarious position—A curious group—A peaceful ending—
We advance—Hardships of the Hunza men—We cross the Shimshal Pass
—A "pamir"—A letter from Safder Ali—We return to the Yarkand
River   254

CHAPTER XII.

BY THE SKIRTS OF THE PAMIRS TO HUNZA.

The Raskam River—Letters from Lieutenant Bower and Major Cumberland—
I dispose of my ponies—Captain Grombtchevsky—His equipment—The
Cossacks—Russian soldiers and their work—Inspection of my Gurkhas—
Gurkhas and Cossacks—A pleasant incident—Kurba Pass—Taghdumbash
Pamir—Ilisu—Kuch Mohammed Bey—I go to Tashkurgan—Major Cumberland and Lieutenant Bower—The Sarikolis—Fugitives from Shignan—
The Taghdumbash Pamir—To the Khunjerab Pass—*Ovis poli*—Curious
shining particles—A stalk—To the Mintaka Pass—Chinese official—Offended
dignity—Dismissing my Kirghiz—Their greediness—We cross the Mintaka
—Across the Indus watershed—An interesting valley—Misgah—A Hunza
Arbap—His greed—Gircha—Visit from the Prime Minister, Wazir Dadu—
Gulmit—A state reception—Safder Ali—I take a seat—A business interview
—Safder Ali and Alexander the Great—The right to raid—A heated discussion—Firing exercises—An undignified ruler—I leave Gulmit—The fate
of Safder Ali—Gilgit—Return to Kashmir—I take leave of my Gurkhas ... 266

CHAPTER XIII.

TO THE PAMIRS—1890.

Previous travellers in the Pamirs—My companion, Mr. George Macartney—Leh
—Messrs. Beech and Lennard—We reach Yarkand—Unchanging character
of Central Asian cities—Arrival of Captain Grombtchevsky—A curious
dinner-party—We start for the Roof of the World—Tashkurgan—The
Neza-tash Pass—The Little Pamir—Characteristics of a Pamir—Vegetation
—Severity of the cold—The Kirghiz—Aktash—Across the Little Pamir—
The Istigh River—Alichur Pamir—Ak-chak-tash—Hot springs—*Ovis poli*
—Somatash—The inscribed stone at Bash Gumbaz—Scene of the conflict
between the Russians and Afghans in 1892—Routes to the Alichur Pamir
—The valley of the Aksu—Sarez—Murghabi—Russian outposts—The Ak-
baital—Rang-kul—The mysterious Lamp Rock—The mystery explained—
To the Kara-kul Lake—Kizil Jek Pass—Kara-art Pass—Down the
Markan-su to Opal—Arrival in Kashgar—Winter quarters—Chinese gongs
—M. Petrovsky 291

CHAPTER XIV.

A WINTER IN KASHGAR.

Official visits—The Chinese Taotai and general—A Chinese opinion of European
civilization—General Wang—The barracks—Discipline and occupations of
the soldiers—Rifle practice—Cosmopolitan Kashgar—Central Asian traders
—Opinions of the Afghan Amir of British and Russian rule—Impressions
of Russian power—Effects of our retirement from Afghanistan in 1881—
M. Petrovsky—His views about England—About treatment of natives in
India—About the Crimea—Russian carelessness about learning languages
—M. Blanc—Dr. Sveyn Hedin—M. Dutreuil de Rhins—Subsequently

xvi   CONTENTS.

PAGE

murdered in Tibet—Père Hendriks—His accomplishments and privations—Arrival of Messrs. Beech and Lennard—A Christmas dinner—Monotony of life—Arrival of a post—Bad news and good—I am made a C.I.E.—Permission to return to India—Arrival of Lieutenant Davison—His adventures—We start together—A misunderstanding 306

CHAPTER XV.

KASHGAR TO INDIA.

I take leave of Macartney—Departure from Chinese Turkestan—Its murky atmosphere—Pilgrimages to Mecca—The Gez defile—A temporary lake—Bulun-kul—I part from Lieutenant Davison—Little Kara-kul—A remarkable lake—A grand view—Tagarma plain—Tashkurgan again—Reports of Russian force on the Pamirs—Wakhjrui Pass—Bozai-Gumbaz—A party of Cossacks—Colonel Yonoff arrives—His mission—Tent of Russian officers—Compared with my own—A dinner-party—Surveying work done by the Russians—The Khora Bhort Pass—Exchange of information—Departure of the Russians—Colonel Yonoff returns to order me away—I consent under protest—Subsequent apology of Russian Government—I go to the Kukturuk valley—Lieutenant Stewart arrives with escort—Return of Lieutenant Davison—His treatment by the Russians—Among the mountains again—The watershed of the Indus and Oxus—The heart of Central Asia—The Panja River—Back to Bozai-Gumbaz—How to return to India?—We find a pass—A snowstorm—A glacier—Instinct of the yak—An icy blast—Rough descent—The Karumbar River—Gilgit—Heavy snow on the Burzil Pass—A detachment of Gurkhas snowed up—Frostbite—The Tragbal Pass—The valley of Kashmir—End of another journey—Death of Davison 322

CHAPTER XVI.

CHITRAL AND HUNZA.

State of Hunza—Expedition against Safder Ali in 1892—I am sent to relieve Captain Stewart—British power in Border States—The policy of "punish and retire" not the best—Pacification of Hunza—British suzerainty—The true mode of dealing with petty chiefs—Loyalty of Hunza—Mohammed Nazim, successor of Safder Ali—My return to the country—Rakapushi Peak—Nilt, the scene of the gallant affair in 1892—Baltit—Meeting with Mohammed Nazim—Characteristics of the people—Winter preparations—Turning swords into ploughshares—News of trouble in Chitral—Death of the Mehtar—I am summoned by Colonel Durand—Account of Chitral—Aman-ul-Mulk and his sons—Rival claimants—Sher Afzul's successful attack—Nizam-ul-Mulk defeats him—Application for British aid—Our advance from Gilgit—Shandur Pass—Ghiza—Frost-bites—Mastuj—Description of Nizam-ul-Mulk—A popinjay—The Chitralis—Life in Chitral—The coming of spring—Excursions—Lessons in mountaineering—A mountain view—Characteristics of the country 341

CHAPTER XVII.

CHITRAL AND HER RULERS.

Departure of Mr. Robertson and Lieutenant Bruce—The Mehtar and his associates—Illiterate but intelligent—Ideas and interests of the Chitralis—Travellers' tales—The Mehtar's visit to India and its effects—His system of government—Daily durbars—Summary justice—Meals—Conversational trials—The Mehtar's wonderful knowledge of his subjects—The Adamzadas—Federation of chiefs—Ignorant opposition to British rule—General Council of State—Absence of all secrecy—Progressive and reactionary parties—Governors of provinces—Rapid mode of administration—Compared with cumbrous methods of British Government—Living among the people—The Mehtar's love of sport—Desire to visit England—Reception in villages—Opinion of British officers—Impulsiveness of Chitralis—Ignorance of value of money—Hatred of work—I am removed to Mastuj, and leave Chitral—The death of Nizam-ul-Mulk 357

CHAPTER XVIII.

THE MISSIONARY QUESTION IN CHINA.

Interest in the question of missions in China—Admirable work done by missionaries—Not all of equal merit—True and false missionaries—Statistics of converts no true test—Conversion—Growing and expanding work of Christianity—The Armenian atrocities and Asiatics—Spirit of Christianity and Asiatics—Fanatic missionaries—Elements of good in heathen religions—Universality of religion—Belief in a Great Spirit—Influence of personal character—Progress must be slow 377

CHAPTER XIX.

IMPRESSIONS OF TRAVEL.

Impressions and reflections produced by travel—Nature's most important messages—Life in the Gobi Desert—Manifestations of Nature—Men's ideas influenced by their surroundings—Hunza—Conjectures of other worlds—The stored knowledge of civilization—Impressions produced by mountains—Their comparative sizes—The forests of Manchuria—The crowded haunts of men—Asiatic races—The goal of man's progress—Intellectual power of different races—Moral superiority—Dealings of Englishmen with natives—The power of sympathy—Tenacity of purpose—Lieutenant Fowler at Reshun—Development of man as a social being—Conclusion 387

LIST OF ILLUSTRATIONS.

	TO FACE PAGE
A Night March in the Gobi Desert	*Frontispiece.*
Courtyard of a Chinese Inn	8
Manchurian House	32
Our Party in Manchuria	48
Sandhills in the Gobi Desert	98
Farm in the Tian Shan Mountains	120
A Bazaar in Chinese Turkestan	124
Robert Shaw and His Attendants, before leaving for Kashgar, 1874	156
An Oasis in Chinese Turkestan	170
In the Himalayas	180
Camp on the Glacier, Mustagh Pass	192
Crossing an Ice-slope on the Mustagh Pass	196
Rope Bridge, near Askoli	206
In the Sind Valley	218
Kashgar	312
Valley in the Hindu Kush	354
Nizam-ul-Mulk, Mehtar of Chitral	358
Night Scene in the Gobi Desert	388

MAPS.

Map of Manchuria	56
Map to illustrate Journey from Peking to Yarkand	168
Map of Asia, showing Captain Younghusband's Various Journeys	*at end*
Map of the Northern Frontier of India, prepared by Messrs. Constable and Doubleday	*in pocket at end*

THE HEART OF A CONTINENT.

CHAPTER I.

THE EVER-WHITE MOUNTAIN.

WHAT it was that first started me off on wanderings, which during the last ten years have led me over so large a portion of Asia, it is difficult to say exactly. But I think the first seeds of the divine discontent at staying still were sown in the summer of 1884, when I had obtained a few months' leave from my regiment, the King's Dragoon Guards, then stationed at Rawal Pindi, in the Punjab, and made use of them to tour through some of the lower ranges of the Himalayas.

My instinct first led me to Dharmsala, for many years the home of my uncle Robert Shaw, who with Hayward was the first Englishman to push his way right through the Himalayas to the plains of Turkestan beyond. Here I found many of his old pensioners—men who had accompanied him on his several journeys to Yarkand and Kashgar—and books too, and maps, and old manuscripts. I was among the relics of an explorer, at the very house in which he had planned his explorations, and from which he had started to accomplish them. I pored over the books and maps, and talked for hours with the old servants, till the spirit of exploration gradually entered my soul, and I rushed off on a preliminary tour on foot in the direction of Tibet, and planned a great journey into that country for the following year.

That first wild wandering through the Himalayas is one on which I look back with almost keener enjoyment than on any other journey I have subsequently made. I had been in Switzerland and seen snow-mountains before, but only as a boy, when I was not able to wander as I would. Now I was free, and in all the pride and keenness of twenty-one. One march a day was not enough for me; I made two regularly, and sometimes three, and I wanted to go everywhere in the two months which was all I then had available. The scenery of such valleys as those of Kangra and Kulu was enchanting, and then came the excitement of preparing to cross my first snow-pass. I had pictured to myself every imaginable horror from descriptions in books (written, of course, as I afterwards understood, from experiences at exceptional seasons), and I can still recall my disappointment at finding that all these horrors had degenerated into simple heart-breaking plodding through soft deep snow hour after hour, with an icy wind blowing, and the sun striking down on the top of my head and combining with the rarefaction of the air to give me as bad a headache as I ever had. Then, too, the feeling of disgust and despair at the sight of those utterly bare brown mountains which lie beyond the first forest-clad zone of the Himalayas, their cold and almost repellant appearance,—all this I remember well, and the rawness and inexperience of the whole of my arrangements, and the discovery that I could not march for twenty or thirty miles a day, as I had imagined I should be able to do, with just about enough food for the whole day as would form a decent breakfast for a man in hard work. And yet there was a delicious sense of satisfaction as each long day's march was over, as each pass was crossed, each new valley entered, and the magnificent health and strength which came therewith inspired the feeling of being able to go anywhere and do anything that it was within the powers of man to do.

From this first tour through the Himalayas I came back with the exploring fever thoroughly on me, and I plunged incessantly into books of travel. Very fortunately, too, just a few months later on in the cold weather of the same year I found some small scope for my superabundant energies in a three months' reconnaissance which I was sent to make upon the Indus and towards the Afghan frontier; and then, after being attached for some weeks to the Quarter-Master General's department under the present Sir William Lockhart, for the durbar in honour of the Amir of Afghanistan, I was sent to Simla as an *attaché* in the Intelligence Department, and ordered to revise the "Gazetteer" of the Kashmir frontier. Here was most congenial work, for it dealt with all the approaches to that mysterious land of Yarkand and Kashgar which had so fascinated me at Dharmsala, and of which I had so often heard in connection with my uncle, the explorer. The fine library of books of travel in every part of Asia which was now at my disposal was yet another incentive to exploration, and many were the schemes which I revolved in my mind that summer of 1885 at Simla.

But the immediate cause of my first big journey was Mr. James.* It was by the greatest piece of good fortune that we came together. We met first at a dinner-party, and the conversation between us turned on Yarkand and Kashgar. (I would beg my readers thoroughly to impress upon their minds the position of these places, for their names will frequently be mentioned throughout this book.) I naturally waxed eloquent on the subject, and a week or two afterwards we again met at dinner, and again talked about the same places. And then, after a few days, on one Sunday afternoon Mr. James walked into my house and asked me if I would go a journey with him. Nothing was said as to where we

* Mr. H. E. M. James, of the Indian Civil Service, then Director-General of the Post-Office in India, now Commissioner in Sind.

should go; but to go a journey anywhere was enough for me, and of course I said "Yes." I remember sitting that afternoon in church at Simla and looking up the rows of people, thinking how every man amongst them would wish to be in my place, if he only knew what I was going to do; for at that time I thought that everybody must necessarily want to make a journey if he could only get the chance, and that to do so must be the very highest ambition of a man.

Mr. James, it appeared, had originally intended to travel with Mr. Carey, the well-known explorer of Tibet, who was just then starting on his travels. But there had been difficulty about Mr. James's leave, and so he had had to postpone his journey till the following spring, and, being without a companion, had asked me to join him wherever he might go. This act of kindness is one for which I shall ever be grateful, and I shall always feel that it was to Mr. James that I owe the first start on my career of travel.

Both of us had an inclination towards China, and we at once decided in a general way that to China we should go. It so happened that in my leisure hours I had read up a number of books about Manchuria, Mongolia, and North China, and compiled itineraries from them. I was therefore able to give my chief, Sir Charles Macgregor, then Quarter-Master-General in India, some little proof that I was serious in the matter, and he promised to help me and do what he could to smoothe over difficulties about my leave. Then followed a month or two with my regiment, during which we marched some three hundred miles to a camp of exercise, and took part in manœuvres such as we have in India only, and in which two armies of twenty thousand men each were started off from bases over one hundred miles apart, and told to find and fight each other how and when and where they could; and at the close of these manœuvres in the spring of 1886 I obtained my leave, and was able to join Mr. James at Calcutta.

Our plans had now shaped themselves into a journey round Manchuria. It was a country of many interests, and it was but little known. It was the cradle of the present ruling dynasty of China; and the few travellers who had been there had described its lovely scenery, its noble rivers, its fertility and natural resources, and the healthiness of its climate. Reading all this in the heat of India, we were fascinated by it; and as its proximity to Russian territory on the one hand and Japan on the other gave it military and political interests also, we felt that time spent in such a country would not be wasted.

On March 19, 1886, we left Calcutta, and in due course found ourselves at Newchwang, the treaty port of Manchuria. This was to be the base of operations, and we were fortunate enough to be joined here by Mr. H. Fulford, of the Chinese Consular Service, an officer who spoke Chinese thoroughly well, knew all the customs of the country, and was able to give us that assistance which as strangers in the land we so much needed. It is not, however, my intention to give a full detailed account of our journey in Manchuria, for that has already been done by Mr. James, in his book, "The Long White Mountain," in which will be found not only a description of our travels, but a fund of information about the history, the religion, and the customs of the people. I shall merely supplement his work with a few of the impressions which were left upon myself.

Our first objective point was a mountain well known in Chinese legends—the Chang-pai-shan, or "Ever-White Mountain." This fabulous mountain had, it is true, been visited in 1709 by one of those enterprising Jesuit surveyors, who seem to have pushed their way everywhere, and compiled a wonderfully accurate map of the Chinese empire. But no European had subsequently visited the mountain to corroborate their accounts, and much romantic mystery still attached itself to it. By the Manchus especially the mountain was held in the deepest reverence, and I quote from Mr. James's book a translation of a poem by the Emperor Kieulung regarding it—

"To ascend to the primitive source of our August Race, which has founded our Tai-tsing (Great-dear dynasty), we must carry ourselves to that mountain, distinguished in like fashion (with the dynasty) for the size and for the colour with which it shines. The famous lake Tamoun occupies part of its summit; the rivers Yalu, Hun tung, and Ai hu' arise from its bosom, carrying fertility over the fields which they water; and the fragrant mists which for ever rise in this charming spot are, without contradiction, those of true glory and solid happiness. On this blessed mountain, a celestial virgin, a daughter of heaven, tasted a fruit to which she was attracted by the brightness of its colour above all others, ate, conceived, and became the mother of a boy, heavenly like herself. Heaven itself gave him the name of Kioro, to which it added, by way of distinction, that of the precious metal, and ordained that he should be called Aisin Kioro, or Golden Kioro."

The Ever-White Mountain was reported to be situated in the heart of an immense forest, to be of enormous height (the name itself suggesting a snow-clad peak), and to have an unfathomable lake at its summit. We were accordingly fired with enthusiasm to penetrate its mystery and ascend its summit, and on May 19 we left the treaty port of Newchwang with this object in view.

We now had our first taste of Chinese travel, and it proved on the whole by no means unpleasant. In the first place, the climate was perfect—mild and soft, like an English summer. The country was everywhere richly cultivated, and was dotted over with well-built, pent-roofed farmhouses, not at all unlike those which one sees in England. We travelled in carts—the small carts so often described in books on China—with two mules each, driven tandem, the baggage piled up inside and behind, and ourselves seated at the base of the shafts alongside the drivers, with our legs dangling over the side. In the summer months, when the roads are soft and muddy, the pace is not rapid, and the traveller can jump off, walk alongside, and jump on again as he likes. But in the winter, when the roads are frozen and worn down by the heavy traffic almost as smooth as an asphalte roadway, these carts trundle along at a good five or six miles an hour, and with a thousand or twelve hundred pounds of goods will do their thirty miles a day without any difficulty.

Everywhere along the road are found inns where accommodation for man and beast can be obtained. The first plunge from European civilization—which in our case was represented by the house of Mr. Allen, the British Consul at Newchwang—into a Chinese inn is not agreeable; but when once one has settled down to the inevitable roughness of travel, one finds many advantages in it. As a rule a private room can be obtained, all the necessaries of life are procurable, and fodder for the animals is always ready. These inns are generally well-built houses, and are a real boon to the native travellers and merchants. There is usually one long room, with a low platform on either side and a passage down the middle. On these platforms, or *kangs*, which can be warmed underneath, the guests recline or squat at the low tables which are placed on them, eating their meals and chatting volubly. At night the travellers sleep in long rows cheek by jowl along the platforms. The great drawback to these inns is their dirt, inside and around, and we often longed for the cleanliness of those Japanese inns which Fulford used to describe to us.

At 120 miles from Newchwang we reached Mukden, the capital of Manchuria, and at one time the seat of government for the present reigning dynasty of China. Our reception there was not a pleasant one, and as we rode through the streets in search of an inn, we were followed even into the house by a hooting, yelling crowd. A Chinaman has no regard for privacy, and these men showed considerable annoyance because we would not let them into our private room, and allow them to stare at us, examine everything we possessed, feel our clothes to see what sort of cloth they were made of, and question us unendingly about our ages, where we had come from, how long we meant to stay, and where we were going Even when we had cleared our room, they did not desist from pestering us, but, while we were undressing, poked holes with their fingers in the paper windows of our room, and then applied their eyes to these easily made peep-holes. Looking up in the middle of our ablutions, we would see a mass of eyes—just the eyes, with nothing else visible—peering at us. The effect was peculiarly irritating, and we would dash out with furious remonstrance; but as soon as we were inside again they would come back exactly as before, and we had eventually to resign ourselves to the inevitable.

But these are the ordinary experiences of every traveller in China, and I am only repeating what has been described a hundred times before. We were kept a week at Mukden, making up a caravan of mules to take us into the mountains. We accordingly had time to see the sights of the place, and go some excursions in the neighbourhood. Of these the most interesting was to the tomb of Nurhachu, the founder of the present dynasty. These Manchus have high ideas as to the fitting resting-places for their great men, and there are few more impressive tombs than this of the simple mountain chief who raised his clan from perfect obscurity to be the rulers of the most populous empire the world has ever seen. Situated in the country, away from the din of city life, in the midst of a park of sombre cypresses and pines many miles in extent, and surrounded by a wall, at the massive gateway of which guards are placed to prevent any

COURTYARD OF A CHINESE INN.

but Manchus of pure descent from entering, it impresses the imagination with a sense of dignified repose, in truest keeping with its object.

In Mukden, too, and its neighbourhood there are many temples, but of the ordinary Chinese type, and of no special interest. In the matter of temples, indeed, the Chinese are singularly unsuccessful in inspiring interest. I did not see a single temple in China that really impressed me—not one to compare with those which may be seen all over India. With but very few exceptions, they are tawdry and even flimsy, and one never seems to meet with evidence of that immense amount of care and labour and thought in their construction, or of that sense of the beautiful, which characterizes the great temples of India. The wooden pillars, often plain, and the grotesquely painted walls which one mostly sees in China, are a poor substitute for the stately marble pillars and exquisite carvings of an Indian temple.

On May 29 our caravan was complete, and we left Mukden to travel eastward to the Yalu river, on the borders of Corea. We soon entered a hilly country, and the scenery became perfectly lovely—hillsides covered with woods of a thoroughly English type, oaks and elms such as we never see in India. The valleys were filled with thriving little villages and hamlets, and on the streams and rivers were glimpses of wonderful beauty. The quantity of flowers and ferns, too, was extraordinary. Mr. James was making a botanical collection, and in one day we found five different kinds of lily of the valley, maidenhair ferns of various forms—one especially lovely, in shape like a kind of spiral bowl—lilies, violets, anemones, and numbers of other English flowers. It was a perfect little country that we were in, and we revelled in the beauties about us.

One of the valleys we passed through was that from which the founder of the Manchu dynasty had started on his career of conquest—a peaceful-looking little valley in which were some avenues of magnificent elm trees. At this stage we were much impeded by rain. Almost daily now it rained heavily. We fortunately always had either inns or farmhouses in which to put up at night, but we constantly got wet through on the march, and the going was often very heavy. We had work, too, to get over the ground at the rate we wanted. We used to rise at 4.30 or 5 every morning, pack up our things, have our breakfast, and then hang about for two dreary hours whilst the lazy mule-men were loading up their animals. On the march we had to keep constant watch over the mules to help them over bad places and prevent their wandering. At mid-day we halted for a couple of hours to feed ourselves and our animals, and then went on again till six or seven. More than once on the march I remember being so tired that I lay down on a fallen log, propped myself up against some branch, and went off fast asleep in spite of the rain. What I felt particularly, too, at this period was the want of milk and butter. The Chinese and Manchus never milk their cows. They seem to think it disgusting to drink milk. They will eat rats and dogs, but they will not drink milk, or at any rate they don't. And we missed this simple necessary very much, and eventually had to take large quantities of oil with our food in its place.

The heavy rain naturally swelled the rivers, and a dozen miles from its source a stream would be unfordable. When that is the case, the traveller has either to cross in one of the native "dug-outs"—mere logs of wood with a hollow scooped out down the centre—or wait several days till there is a lull in the flood. This last is what we had to do on more than one occasion, and in some ways I was glad; for it gave us a little rest and time to overhaul and repair our kit. On such occasions we put up in some farmhouse near the river, and here out in the country, away from the crowds of the towns, we could examine John Chinaman at leisure. All the part we were now in has been colonized by pure Chinese, who are taking the place of the original Manchus. These latter were few in numbers, and had been drafted off with their families to garrison the towns of China proper, and now the Chinese immigrants from the over-populated or famine-stricken districts of China were flowing into these Manchurian valleys, clearing away the forest, and bringing year by year more of it under cultivation. They were, in fact, doing here exactly what our colonists have been doing for so many years in Canada. The amount of work they got through was, I thought, marvellous. At the first streak of dawn they rose, had a good meal, and then set to at that heart-breaking work, clearing land of the stumps of trees which they had felled. Hour after hour they would work away, hacking and hewing at these, and some of them digging up the ground and preparing it for a crop, and at mid-day they would stop and have another square meal; then return to the same old wearing task till darkness set in, when they would come trooping in for their evening meal. They were for the most part strong, hard men, with enormous appetites. Millet porridge, vegetable stews, and soups were their chief food, which they ate out of bowls in huge quantities. Their houses were often comfortable, well-built, and roomy, the roofs being the especial feature, as they are in all Chinese houses, on account of their great strength and solidity. The houses were not always as clean as they might have been, but still were on the whole far better homes than one would expect to find in the backwoods of a colony. And I was a good deal struck with the energetic spirit which these colonists showed in pushing their way through the forests. A Chinaman is always known to be industrious, but here was good tough vigour in addition.

At length we reached the Yalu, the natural boundary between Corea and Manchuria. It was a noble river where we struck it—three hundred yards or so broad, and ten to fifteen feet deep. Its sides were covered down to the water's edge with forests, and at intervals, where the ground was flatter, were patches of cultivation and a few farmhouses, or meadows covered with flowers of every description—often with masses of stately lilies, some specimens of which measured six inches across, or with waving sheets of purple irises and columbines. Then gliding noiselessly across the scene would come a raft drifting quietly down the river, and sadly tempting us to do the same, instead of laboriously plodding our way through the forest up the stream.

But we were now approaching the Ever-White Mountain, and the interest of getting there would, we well knew, repay all our exertions. As we neared it, however, our difficulties gradually increased. At Mao-erh-shan, on the Yalu, two hundred and eighty miles from Mukden, where we had expected to get all ordinary supplies, we found hardly anything. For a day or two before reaching this place, we had been living upon very short rations, and had been looking forward to getting a good square meal of meat when we arrived there. But only some uneatable pork was to be had, and we were obliged to content ourselves, in the meat line, with an egg curry, made of salted eggs six months old, and only eatable at all with the aid of a very strong curry.

We now had to leave the valley of the Yalu and plunge into the heart of the forest which surrounded the White Mountain. Day after day we ascended the ridges which run down from it—up one side of the ridge and down the other, then up again, and so on unendingly. We never saw anything but the trunks of the trees. Even from the summits of the ridges nothing was to be seen; we were simply swamped in forest, and could not see out of it. I know of nothing more depressing than this, to struggle on, forcing a way for the mules through the undergrowth, and hauling and shoving them up the slopes and rocky gullies, and then to arrive at the top and find ourselves still hedged in by trunks of trees, and able to see nothing whatever beyond. We were, too, afflicted by a scourge of mosquitoes and midges. In no part of India have I felt them so much. In the daytime we had the midges driving us wild with their irritating pricks, and at nights the mosquitoes in clouds. By simply closing the hand a dozen of them could be caught at any time. Of course we had to wear veils the whole day long, and keep our hands in our pockets or wrapped round with cloth whenever we could; but even then we suffered badly, and washing was a positive torture. Gad-flies were another form of torture invented for these parts. They would attack us pretty constantly, but it was chiefly to the poor animals that they directed their attention, and the wretched mules were often covered with blood and driven wild by their attacks.

At night we would put up in a sable-hunter's hut. These are met with every twelve or fifteen miles, and each is the head-quarters of a party of hunters who trap sables and also seek the ginseng root—the root of a plant upon which the Chinese set great store for medicinal purposes. These huts were suitable enough for the small parties who ordinarily inhabited them, but when our large party came in addition they were crammed tight. We had to sleep in them, for to sleep outside amongst the swarms of mosquitoes and in the damp of the forest was almost impossible. We therefore packed ourselves into the huts, and were sometimes so tightly squeezed in the row on the kang, that we had to lie heads and tails with the Chinamen, to get ourselves all in. We had also to keep a fire burning to raise smoke for the purpose of driving off the mosquitoes; so the heat on a summer's night and the state of the atmosphere inside may be imagined! We, of course, got quite inadequate rest, and that period of our journey was a very trying one.

These hunters received us, as a rule, very well, but theirs

was not an existence which we could envy. The sable-hunters had a certain amount of excitement. They would set their traps all over the forest, go their rounds to examine them, and now and then, at rare intervals, find they had caught something. But the ginseng plant seekers would wander through the forest day after day and all day long, and if they found one plant in the season they would be content. This plant would be worth perhaps £15, for the Chinese believe the genuine wild plant to have the most wonderful properties.

A remarkable point about these men is the strict code of honour they have amongst themselves. At one place, for instance, we noticed a clearing made in the undergrowth of the forest round a small plant not far from the track. This proved to be one of these much-sought-after plants. It had been discovered by a man, but as it was not fully grown, it had been left there to mature, and the standard of honour was so strict among these people, that, in spite of the value of the plant and the ease with which it might have been carried away, no one would touch it.

Travelling on through the forest, we reached one of the branches of the great Sungari river—an affluent of the river Amur, and, at its junction, of even greater volume than that river. This stream we now ascended, as it was said to flow down from the Ever-White Mountain we were in search of; but after two days' travelling we were brought to a standstill, as regards mule-carriage, by a bog, through which it was impossible to take any animal. One man for carrying loads was all we could secure, and so we had to reduce our baggage to its very minimum, and each one carry his own, while the one porter carried such supplies as we should be unable to obtain on ahead; for though we heard of there being one or two sable-hunters' huts, the owners of these were said to be almost starving themselves for want of food, there having been some hitch about the arrival of the fresh stock of provisions for the year. Shouldering our loads, we pushed our way through the incessant bogs which now filled up the valley, and at night put up in the huts. This was the hardest piece of work we had done, for we covered from fifteen to twenty miles a day, and that through ground where we frequently sank up to our knees and never felt sure of our footing, and with a load on our backs to make it still more wearisome. Added to this was the further trial that we had to place ourselves on half-rations. Ever since we had entered the forest we had found a difficulty in obtaining supplies; flour was very scarce, so that we had to live principally upon millet porridge, and meat was not forthcoming as often as we should have liked after our hard work. But now, as we approached the mountain, supplies became scarcer still, and after we had left the mules, and consequently while we were doing our hardest work, we were on fare which made me at least so ravenous that I more than once went round to the hunters' cooking-pot and scraped out all I could from the inside after they had finished their meal. On three separate occasions I remember James, Fulford, and myself all sitting down to dine off one partridge between us; this, with a little palatable soup and a scone was all we had after our trying march.

We had, however, the satisfaction of knowing that we now really were approaching the mysterious White Mountain. As we climbed higher the forest began to open out, and on the fourth day after leaving the mules we found ourselves at its base, and saw it rising up above the forest. It was with a sigh of infinite relief that we looked upon it, but I cannot say that, here in its solid reality, it inspired us with awe commensurate with the mystery which had been attached to it. It certainly rose high above all the surrounding forest-clad hills, and perhaps in the British Isles would pass muster as a mountain; but it was not the snow-clad monarch we had expected to see, and it afterwards proved to be but eight thousand feet in height.

Still, here the mountain was, and what it lacked in grandeur was made up for in beauty, for its sides were covered with the most exquisite meadows and copses. In Kashmir there are many beautiful meadows, but none to compare with those of the Ever-White Mountain. These were such as I have never seen equalled. Masses of colour, flowers of every kind, whole meadows of irises and tiger-lilies and columbines, and graceful, stately fir trees scattered about to relieve any excess of colour and add to the beauty of the whole. And, looking closer, we found ferns of the most delicate tracery, deep blue gentians, golden buttercups, azaleas, orchids, and numbers of other flowers of every type of beauty, all in their freshest summer bloom.

The following day we visited some springs which form one of the sources of the Sungari, and on the next we ascended the mountain. The trees became fewer and fewer, and we emerged on to open slopes covered with long grass and dwarf azaleas, heather, yellow poppies, and gentians. Except the steepness there was no difficulty in the ascent, and we made for a saddle between two rugged peaks which crowned the mountain. We pressed eagerly on to reach this, as from it we hoped to look out beyond, far away over Corea on the opposite side. At last we reached the saddle, and then, instead of the panorama we had expected, we looked down in astonishment on a most beautiful lake in a setting of weird, fantastic cliffs just at our feet. We were, in fact, on an extinct volcano, and this lake filled up what had once been its crater. The waters were of a peculiarly deep clear blue, and situated here at the very summit of a mountain, and held in on every side by rugged precipitous cliffs, this lake was particularly striking. We tried to descend to its brim, but could find no way down the cliffs; so, after boiling a thermometer to ascertain the altitude, I set out to ascend the highest of the rocky peaks which formed a fringe around it. The climb was a stiff one, but I succeeded in reaching the summit—the very top of the Ever-White Mountain—and from there I looked out over a billowy expanse of forest-clad hills stretching away on every side, as far as the eye could reach in the direction of Manchuria, and as far as one could see over Corea; nothing but forest, except where the lake lay below me like a sapphire in a setting of rock, and it was only by this and by occasional glints of the river that the monotonous green was broken.

But the lake was the saving feature. It appeared to be about six or seven miles in circumference, and at its farther end was an outlet, from which flowed the main branch of the Sungari. This, then, was the source of that noble river which, a few hundred miles lower down, we afterwards found to be over a mile broad, and which has claims, indeed, to be considered the main branch of the great Amur—a magnificent river excelled in size and grandeur by few others in the world.

I rejoined my companions, and we set off rapidly down the mountain-side, delighted at having successfully achieved the object of our journey, and with the feeling that all our toil had not been in vain. The Ever-White Mountain was not white with snow, and therefore not as lofty as we had been led to expect; it was white, or partially white, with pumice-stone from the old volcano. But it was a satisfaction to have established this fact, and the beauty of its flower-covered slopes and of the meadows at its base, and the solitude of the wonderful lake at its summit, were ample compensation for our disappointment in its height.

Three days later we were back at the place where we had left our mules, and we ravenously devoured some eggs which we managed to secure there. It is said to be good to rise from a meal with an appetite. In those days we always rose from our meals with magnificent appetites. It was the greatest relief, however, not to have to carry a load any longer, and, happiness being merely a relative quality, we felt thoroughly happy on the following day as we trudged along beside the mules, with no weight on our backs to crush the heart out of us.

Our intention now was to descend the Sungari to Kirin, one of the principal towns of Manchuria, and situated about three hundred miles from the source of the river, near where it enters the more open part of the country. We had still many days of weary plodding through the forest, climbing ridge after ridge, crossing and recrossing tributary streams, one of which we had to ford twenty-four times in the course of a single march, and everywhere waist-deep. But at length, and very suddenly, we found ourselves clear of the forest, and in a populous district of extraordinary fertility. The soil—all reclaimed from the forest—was almost black, and, judging from the crops, must have been wonderfully rich. The houses were all new, large, and well built, and provisions could be obtained in plenty. After rough travelling in uninhabited parts, one really appreciates being amongst men again and seeing active life all round; and here, as before, we were impressed by the vigour and prosperity of these Chinese colonists breaking through the forest. In Asia one sees plenty of the old age-worn life, but on that continent it is only in very few places that one can see the fresh young life of a colony pushing vigorously ahead.

On August 12 we reached Kirin, and the first round of our journey was completed. Kirin is a large town of from eighty to one hundred thousand inhabitants, very picturesquely situated among wooded hills, on a bend of the Sungari, here, only three hundred miles from its source, a majestic stream a quarter of a mile broad and twenty feet deep. But it rained incessantly while we were there, and the filth and smells of the place, increased in consequence of this, prevented us from enjoying as we should have done all its natural beauties.

Three weeks we remained here, paying off the mule-men who had brought our baggage from Mukden, and arranging for carts to continue our journey round Manchuria. The chief attraction we found in the place was an arsenal recently set up here entirely by Chinamen, and managed by them alone, without any European guidance or supervision whatever. Here we found magazine rifles, gatling guns, and field-guns being turned out in a very creditable fashion. We called on the manager, who himself conducted us round the workshops. It was he who had started the place, and we were fairly astonished to find such a really creditable establishment in the heart of Manchuria, many hundreds of miles from the coast, and in a country where there were neither railways nor waterways, nor even good roads for the carriage of the heavy and delicate machinery. Mr. Sung, the manager, had something more than mere imitative genius; he had also some notion of invention and adapting. Having brought up an initial plant of machinery, he had with that made more; and he had himself invented a magazine rifle. Coal he obtained in the neighbourhood, and a certain amount of iron too, but most of the latter had to be imported. He was very civil to us, and invited us to dinner, where we met some other officials of the place.

Chinese dinners are of the most elaborate description, and this one was no exception. Course after course was served up, till we must have had between thirty and forty of them, including such delicacies as sea-slugs, sharks' fins, and birds-nest soup. The Chinese are remarkably good cooks, and, though the dishes are often served in a way which is not very palatable to Europeans, there is no doubt that the actual cooking is excellent. There were, for instance, little suet dumplings, so beautifully cooked and so light that they almost melted in the mouth like jelly. Some of the dishes of vegetables were also extremely good, and I especially recall a plate of stewed young celery. He may differ from us as to the means of doing it, but it is evident that the Celestial has a very good idea of the way to look after the inner man. I cannot say, however, that I can bestow much praise on his liquor department. Warmed spirit distilled from rice is not good, and taken as incessantly as a Chinese expects you to take it, and as most Chinamen do take it, it is apt to make you decidedly heavy, if not more, and sick as well. But the point in which the Chinese most excel in these social gatherings is in their duties as hosts. They are perfect hosts, full of attention to their guests, of cheery *bonhomie*, and of conversation. There is elaborate politeness, and a good deal of etiquette is observed, but no stiffness is apparent; every one is cheery, and every one talks incessantly. It was a revelation, indeed, to us to find what good fellows these Chinamen could be amongst themselves. Seeing only the lower classes, the mule-men, the loafers of the streets, and the frequenters of the inns, one is apt to form a very unfavourable impression of the Chinese, and to regard them as a rude, coarse, and unmannerly race, who hate strangers, and take little trouble to disguise their feelings. But when one can see the Chinese gentlemen at home, one modifies this impression very considerably; and personally, from this and other occasions on which I afterwards had opportunities of meeting Chinese gentlemen, I saw much to admire and even to like in them. I liked their never-failing politeness to one another, which seemed to me too incessant and sustained to be mere veneer, and to indicate a real feeling of regard for one another. Chinamen have little regard for strangers, but I think they have for one another. Then, again, their cheeriness amongst themselves is a trait which one likes. The general impression among Europeans is that Chinamen are cold, hard creatures who have not a laugh in them. As a matter of fact, they have plenty of heartiness and joviality when they care to indulge in it. I should say, too, that their conversation is good; it is certainly bright, and it is very natural and well sustained. Of course, in conversation with Europeans they do not excel; they are lamentably ignorant of geography, for instance, and they generally annoy the stranger by asking if his country is tributary to China. But in the conversation carried on amongst themselves there seem to be many topics quite as good as geography and the weather, and one hears long, well-thought-out, and well-expressed arguments on philosophic and moral subjects, freely interspersed with quotations from their classics. A Chinaman is perhaps rather too celestial, rather too much up in the clouds and above ordinary mortals, and certainly shows too little interest in the common everyday affairs of this world; but he is an interesting man to meet at home, and, mingled with the irritation which his superciliousness so often inspires, I often had a feeling of real regard for a man who can aspire to such a lofty standpoint as the Chinaman does, and in his case I felt that it was not all simple self-conceit, for he had in him the pride of belonging to an empire which has stood intact for thousands of years, and which was approaching civilization when we ourselves were steeped in barbarism.

CHAPTER II.

MANCHURIA TO PEKING.

*"Epirus' bounds recede, and mountains fail;
Tired of up-gazing still, the wearied eye
Reposes gladly on as smooth a vale
As ever Spring yclad in grassy dye :
Ev'n on a plain no humble beauties lie,
Where some bold river breaks the long expanse,
And woods along the banks are waving high,
Whose shadows in the glassy waters dance,
Or with the moonbeam sleep in midnight's solemn trance."*

ON September 3, after a three weeks' rest, we set out once more on our travels, heading this time towards Tsi-tsi-har. The roads were to be comparatively level and good, so we were able to return to the use of carts, and travel over twenty-five miles or so daily. But the season was bad, rain had been falling constantly, and in consequence the roads—of course, none of them metalled—were simply quagmires. Even just outside Kirin we stuck for a couple of hours in a hopeless mass of mud, and delays more or less lengthy were constant. But we had three mules to each cart, and when one was badly stuck we harnessed on a team from another to help, and in this way managed to get over more ground each day than the state of the roads would have led one to believe possible. At about twenty-four miles from Kirin we crossed the Sungari by a ferry, and kept along the right bank of the river. The hills became lower and lower and the valleys wider as we proceeded, till we soon found ourselves in open undulating country, very richly cultivated and thickly inhabited. The crops, now in full ear, were extraordinarily heavy; the millet especially, both the large and the small, being unusually heavy in the ear. The villages, too, were all of a considerable size and numerous. But separate farmhouses or small hamlets were seldom seen —probably on account of the brigandage, which was very rife all over North Manchuria. We heard frequent tales of carts being attacked on the road, and of villages and even towns being pillaged. We had, however, no personal experience of these brigands, and this part of our journey, though interesting as lying through a populous and thriving district, was lacking in incident and excitement.

Just beyond Petuna we again struck the Sungari, at the point where the Nonni joins it from the north. Here in the swamps by the river we had an experience of mosquitoes which quite eclipsed all former records. Thinking the marsh looked a likely place for snipe, we went down into it. We heard a suppressed kind of roar, like that of the distant sea, and we thought it must come from the river. But it was nothing but mosquitoes. For a foot or two above the marsh they were in myriads. For a short time we tried snipe-shooting, for there were a number of snipe about; but the mosquitoes bit right through our breeches and gloves, and drove us so mad we had to leave hurriedly.

The Sungari was here spread out in many channels to a width of some ten miles. We crossed it by a ferry, and on the opposite side we soon entered the open rolling steppes of Mongolia. The cultivation ceased, and with it the villages, so that we now only passed an occasional hut inhabited by Mongols, and entered on a quite new phase of our journey. Scarcely a tree was to be seen, and for mile after mile we passed over rolling downs covered with rich grass and exquisite flowers. In the hollows were often lakes of very considerable size, some of them several miles in length. And these were covered with swarms of water-fowl—thousands and thousands of duck and geese. Indeed, these lakes must have been the breeding-ground of the water-fowl, which, in the cold weather, find their way down to the warmer parts of the continent. Large numbers of bustard, too, we saw, and many herds of antelope.

The chief attraction for us, however, at this period of our journey, was the milk and cream we could obtain. What a treat it was, after nearly four months without milk or any of its products, to drink some of the rich delicious stuff which these Mongols brought us! At one time in the forest, when I had been out of sorts, I had been allowed a glass of condensed milk from our stores as a medical comfort; it was such a luxury to get even this, that I was sorely tempted to feign sickness for another day to obtain more. But here was the pure article in any quantity, and as rich and thick with cream as any from Devonshire. These Mongols made, too, a sort of cream cheese which was most delicious. It was a kind of solidified Devonshire cream, which they made by simmering milk for about twenty-four hours, and then removing the cake of cream formed at the top, drying it, and rolling it up like a pancake. It was rather less thick than a cream cheese, but thicker than Devonshire cream, and it tasted exactly like the latter. The advantage of it was that we could roll it up in a piece of paper, and eat it in alternative bites with a piece of bread on the line of march. And plenty of it we did eat in this way.

Of the Mongols we saw very little. They were probably removed from the main line of traffic, and kept well clear of it and of the shady characters who might frequent it. We only came across two of the felt yurts which are their characteristic abodes, and those Mongols whom we did meet lived in houses, and were more or less tamed and settled.

At length, on September 20, we reached Tsi-tsi-har, a large town of about forty or fifty thousand inhabitants, and the seat of government of the province of the same name, which fills up the whole of North Manchuria. But there was little to see beyond the ordinary shops, the dirty streets, and tumble-down temples of every Chinese town. This was our most northern point. Winter was approaching, and already we had had some touches of frost. We had yet much ground to get over, and so we struck off back again towards the Sungari, making this time for Hulan. We passed over some more of the Mongol steppes, and now, as the rainy season had ended and the roads were dry, we could take our carts along at a trot, and would often cover over thirty miles in the day. The country was rolling prairie as before, and covered with rich grass, on which we often saw large herds of ponies feeding —fine, strong little ponies, like miniature cart-horses, and very hardy.

Suddenly one day we drove right into cultivation. We had crossed the boundary-line between the Mongol and Chinese territory. It is a purely artifical line laid across the downs, but up to that line the Chinese cultivate the land; beyond it the Mongols hold sway, and no attempt to reducing the land to cultivation is made. Consequently, the boundary-line between Chinese territory proper and that which the Chinese still allow to the Mongols is formed by rows of millet and wheat.

Hulan, situated at about two hundred miles from Tsi-tsi-har, we found to be a new and thriving town only recently built, and surrounded with a strong masonry wall. The shops were excellent, and there was a busy, bustling air about the whole place. This town had in the previous year been attacked by a band of brigands, who had sought out the principal merchants, levied black-mail from them, and then decamped. It was here, too, that a French missionary, Père Conraux, had been most cruelly tortured and almost killed in the year previous to our visit.

From this point we turned northward again to visit another

new town named Pei-lin-tzŭ, where we had heard a Roman Catholic Mission was established. We were unfortunate, however, in finding that M. Card, the priest in charge, was not at home. So we turned southward again to Pa-yen-su-su, another mission station, where we found both its own director and M. Card from Pei-lin-tzŭ. It was indeed a pleasure to see these men, and to have that warm, heartfelt greeting which one European will give to another, of whatever nationality, in the most distant corners of the world. Except the French consul who had been sent to inquire into the outrage on Père Conraux in the previous year, no European had ever before visited these distant mission stations, and we, on our part, had not met a European for several months now, so the delight of this meeting may be well imagined. But, apart from that, we were very deeply impressed by the men themselves. Few men, indeed, have ever made a deeper impression on me than did these simple missionaries. They were standing, transparent types of all that is best in man. There was around them an atmosphere of pure genuine goodness which made itself felt at once. We recognized immediately that we were not only with *good* men, but with *real* men. What they possessed was no weak sentimentality or flashy enthusiasm, but solid human worth. Far away from their friends, from all civilization, they live and work and die; they have died, two out of the three we met in those parts, since we left. When they leave France, they leave it for good; they have no hope of return; they go out for their whole lives. They may not make many converts, but they do good. No man, Chinaman or European, who came in contact for five minutes with M. Raguit, M. Card, or M. Riffard, whom we afterwards met, could help feeling the better for it. Their strong yet gentle and simple natures, developed by the hardships of their surroundings and the loftiness of their ideals, and untainted by the contact with worldly praise and glamour, impressed itself on us at once, and, as we saw evidenced in the people around, had affected the Chinese likewise.

> "Great deeds cannot die;
> They, with the sun and moon, renew their light
> For ever, blessing those that look on them."

Others may bring discredit on the missionary cause, and produce the feeling of hostility to it which undoubtedly exists, but these are the men who are a true light in the world, and who will spread the essence of Christianity—the doing of good to others—abroad.

This remote mission station—established here where no other Europeans had penetrated—was a source of the greatest interest to us, and fulfilled our highest ideal of such a station. There was here no elaborate costly house, no air of luxury, such as may be seen in many missionary establishments elsewhere, but everything was of the most rigorous simplicity. There was merely a plain little house, almost bare inside, and with stiff, simple furniture. Under such hard conditions, with such plain surroundings, and shut off for ever from intercourse with the civilized world, it might be supposed that these missionaries would be dull, stern, perhaps morbid men. But they were precisely the contrary. They had a fund of simple joviality, and were hearty and full of spirits. They spoke now and then with a sigh of "la belle France," but they were evidently thoroughly happy in their lives, and devoted to their work.

From these simple hospitable mission stations we made our way to Sansing. Every day now it was becoming colder, and at one place we were delayed for a day by a very heavy snowstorm. We had to hurry along, for the missionaries had assured us that in winter the thermometer fell to over 40° below zero Fahrenheit, and had showed us a thermometer which they had used, on which they had seen the mercury fall to $-47°$ Centigrade. The country we passed through was now hilly, and covered with copses of wood—oak and birch. Nothing could have been more like an English country scene, and on the edges of these copses we regularly found some excellent pheasant-shooting. All day long, too, flock after flock of geese flew by us overhead, making towards the south. Usually these were a long way out of shot, but on a windy day they would often be forced down so as just to top the hills, and then from the summit we would get a shot at them as they flew over.

We once more crossed the Sungari, and on October 13 reached Sansing, an older town than those we had recently passed through, and with much less life and bustle about it. Very good furs, however, were to be obtained here, and, as hard winter might be on us any day now, we fitted ourselves out with long loose sheepskin coats, reaching well down to the ankles. Sansing is the furthest inhabited place of any importance in the direction of the Amur. The Sungari is here quite navigable for boats of considerable size, and consequently the Chinese had erected near by some fortifications of considerable strength. We rode out to see them, and I was astonished to find a fort constructed of earthwork, and planned on the most approved European lines, and armed with Krupp guns of six or seven tons' weight. We walked straight into the fort, looked all round it, found a Chinese soldier walking inoffensively about, and asked him to unlock the doors of the magazine, which he proceeded to do; and then, having finished our inspection of the fort, we were going quietly away, when the colonel of the regiment stationed in it sent out and begged us to come in to tea. He was most kind and hospitable, but in the middle of the tea came a messenger who had ridden in hot haste from Sansing, with an order from the general there to say that we were on no account to be allowed inside the fort. This was most embarrassing. And, having seen all that was to be seen, we assured our host, with every mark of sincerity, that, these being the orders of the general, nothing should detain us for a single moment, and that we would leave the fort instantly. The hospitable old colonel, however, insisted upon our finishing our tea, and I hope he never got into trouble owing to the slackness of discipline of his men in letting us into the fort.

This fort would absolutely bar the passage of the Sungari if the guns could be trusted, for they were of far larger calibre than any which would be likely to be brought against them; and I marvelled at the perseverance and energy which the Chinese must have shown in bringing them up here, for they had had to be transported some hundreds of miles by land, and over hilly country. Field guns and even siege battery guns might have been transported fairly easily; but it must have been a very heavy task indeed to carry these huge pieces of ordnance, six or seven tons in weight, right across Manchuria. But with the Chinese there is always a doubt as to whether their guns will go off at the critical time, for they are so utterly careless with them and with the delicate machinery connected with them, and allow it all to go to rust and ruin with such perfect disregard for consequences, that one can never be sure that at the hour of need the guns which they must have brought up with so great an amount of labour will not fail them entirely.

After a couple of days' rest at Sansing, we turned southward and ascended the Hurka river to Ninguta. The road was execrable. We still had our carts, and how we, or rather the drivers, managed to get them along a road really fit only for pack-animals was a marvel. There was a constant series of ascents and descents of spurs running down to the river. These were nearly always steep, and the road narrow and rocky. More than once our carts fell down the side, and on one occasion a cart and its team turned two complete somersaults as it rolled down the hillside. And yet, when we had unpacked it and hauled it up on to the road again, we found no serious damage done to either it or the mules. The top covering of the cart was rather knocked about, but the main part of it was still all sound; and the mules merely shook themselves and then stared stonily ahead, as if it were all in the day's work and not to be wondered at. Both Chinese carts and Chinese mules are astonishing products. The carts are beautifully built, and made strong without being too heavy; and the mules are as hard as can be, and as a rule really very docile. A Chinese carter seldom drives them by the reins, but guides them entirely by voice and cracks of the whip. In this way they struggle along till the cart bumps up against some very big rock, and then they roll, cart and all, down the hillside, or until they run into a mass of bog and quagmire, when an additional team is harnessed on from the cart behind. Even in this latter case the fate of these mules is not always a happy one; and on one occasion when, after struggling vainly with a single team to pull a cart through, we had harnessed on another team and then set to work, the shaft mule managed in some way to get clear of the shafts, and got under the wheels of the cart, and in this position was dragged along for a hundred yards or so before the other mules could be stopped. We thought he must be dead—suffocated with mud if nothing else. But he got up, shook himself, stared stolidly about with an aggrieved expression, as if it were really rather harder luck than usual, and then allowed himself to be put in the shafts again and go on with the rest of the day's work. These bogs occurred constantly in the hollows between the spurs, and we had frequently immense difficulty in getting through them. Small villages were only occasionally met with, and the country was far less well populated than that we had recently come through. The hills were covered with woods of oak and birch, and their summits with pines. Amongst them, it was said, there were gold-mines, which, however, it was only permissible for government to work, as the Chinese think that indiscriminate gold-mining only leads to fighting and quarrelling and trouble, and the emperor therefore forbids it to his subjects entirely. We crossed numerous side streams, and these, as well as the Hurka itself, swarm with fish, mostly salmon. The natives form dams across the side streams, and catch them in hundreds. So at this time, what with pheasants, ducks, geese, and salmon, we were living very comfortably, and making up for our privations in the forests of the White Mountain.

As we neared Ninguta the valley opened up into a wide plain, which was well cultivated and populated, and on October 26 we reached Ninguta, a flourishing place of nearly twenty thousand inhabitants. Here we found a telegraph station just opened. The Chinese attach considerable importance to this frontier, touching as it does on Russian territory, and the construction of this telegraph line was one of the signs of the interest they took in it. The line was well and stoutly constructed under the supervision of a Danish gentleman. But the office was manned entirely by Chinese, and the language in use was English. Every clerk spoke English, and it was a pleasure to us to meet any one who spoke our native tongue.

We halted here a couple of days, and then started for Hunchun, a garrison post of some importance, situated on the extreme frontier, and just at the point where Russian, Chinese, and Corean territory meet. Winter was creeping on apace now. The thermometer on the morning we left Ninguta was at 11° Fahrenheit, so we had to push on hard to get to our furthest destination, which we hoped might be on the sea, at the Russian port just beyond Hunchun, and then back to our original starting-point at Newchwang, before the severest part of the Manchurian winter overtook us. The road was terribly bad, again crossing over ridges fifteen hundred to two thousand feet in height, passing over heavy bogs and morasses, and through forests of pine, birch, and oak. On November 5 we struck the Tumen river, which we had expected to find a fine stream, like the Sungari near Kirin; but it proved to be only about a hundred yards wide, and not deep enough to cover the rocks and boulders, which showed up everywhere. No doubt it is fuller in the summer, but it can at no season be navigable, as it was at one time supposed to be.

Hunchun we found to be simply a garrison town. There were here about three thousand troops, and the small town there was served for little else than to supply their wants. But we discovered in it a number of European articles which had been imported from the Russian station close by. Clocks, sweets, soap, canned fruits, and many other luxuries were to be obtained here, and at a very reasonable price. We bought a can of Singapore pineapples for a shilling.

Hunchun is situated in a plain at the foot of some low hills, and round it in the direction of the Russians—here only ten miles distant—are some strong forts mounted with heavy Krupp guns. I was sufficiently astonished to see these Krupp guns at Sansing, to which place they could have been brought from Kirin by water, and between Kirin and the coast there are only comparatively low hills; but how the Chinese could possibly have managed to drag these enormous guns over the range upon range which separate Hunchun from Kirin, and through all the morasses and forests we had seen on the way, puzzled me much. Mr. James found that they had placed the guns on gigantic sledges, and then brought them over in the depth of winter, when the ground and bogs and everything else were frozen hard. Yet even then they must have had extraordinary difficulty, for in winter in these parts the snowfall is very heavy; and these guns at Hunchun

MANCHURIAN HOUSE.

remain a standing evidence of what can be done by sheer hard labour, without the aid of modern machinery and appliances. I fear, though, that this is the only good purpose they will serve; for, as I remarked before, the Chinese have no notion of looking after these delicate pieces of mechanism when they have got them.

At Hunchun was stationed the lieutenant-general in charge of the frontier—a person of considerable importance—and on the day after arrival we proceeded to call on him. He received us after dark at his official residence in some state. Every official residence in China has a number of gateways, more or fewer of which are opened according to the rank of the visitor. In our case every gateway was opened; the courtyards were lined with soldiers, and the whole place was lighted up with Chinese lanterns, which, as the residence was newly built, and large and spacious, made the scene very bright and picturesque. General I (pronounced Ee) was a dignified, fine-looking old soldier, who had done much good service in the Taeping rebellion. He was very polite and courteous, treated us to some champagne, and talked to us in an intelligent and interesting manner. Nobody can be ruder than a common Chinaman, and nobody can be more polite and refined than a Chinese gentleman when he wishes.

From Hunchun Mr. James had written to the commander of the Russian post across the frontier, saying that we were unprovided with passports to travel in Russian territory; but that, if he would give us permission to do so, we should like very much to visit Novo-kievsk. We then started off towards Russian territory. At about ten miles from Hunchun, on the summit of a hill, we saw a tall sort of obelisk with an inscription on it, which we found to be the boundary-pillar set up only a few months before by the Chinese imperial commissioner sent in conjunction with a Russian commissioner to define the frontier in this direction. Just beyond we descried a couple of horsemen trotting towards us, and as they drew near we saw that they were unmistakably Cossacks. Neither of us had seen a mounted Cossack before; but their resemblance to all the pictures one sees of them in illustrated papers and books was evidence enough who they were. There was the same rough, shaggy-looking grey sheepskin cap, long overcoats, high boots, whip, and rifle slung over the back, that we knew so well from pictures. They saluted, and gave Mr. James a letter from Colonel Sokolowski, who commanded the Russian post. The colonel said he would be most happy to allow us to cross the frontier, and that he hoped that we would visit his post and "accept the cordial but frugal hospitality of a Cossack." We rode on, therefore, and at about three miles from the frontier came across the Russian station of Swanka, situated among some low rather bare hills. There were stationed here at the time of our visit about three hundred Cossacks. Some low rough barracks had just been constructed for them, and small cottages for the officers were dotted about all round. The colonel's house was larger and better built, but all of them were of the rough simple description one would expect to find at a distant frontier outpost.

Here we were most cordially received by the Russian colonel. Russians never err in want of cordiality—to Englishmen especially—and in this remotest part of Asia, thousands of miles from either St. Petersburg or London, we met, uninvited guests as we were, with real warmth of reception. The colonel's house had about it no superfluity of luxury. It had glass windows and a stove—which are luxuries the Russian would not have met with if he had visited my own head-quarters in the Chitral frontier during last year—but the walls and the floors were quite bare, and the furniture of the very simplest. There was only one room, a part of which was partitioned off into a bedroom and dressing-room, and the whole place was crowded up with military stores—for a Russian colonel seems to be his own quarter-master and storekeeper—and all about the room were piles of saddlery, racks of arms, and heaps of miscellaneous articles of Cossack equipment.

We had some light refreshment, and then the colonel took us round to see the barracks. Here the Cossacks were still hard at work, completing the building before winter set in. They were hard, strong-looking men, fair in complexion, with cheery good-natured faces; and there was about them a workmanlike air, which gave one the idea that they could and would turn their hands to anything. An English soldier is perfectly right when he has shaken down on active service, but in barracks he produces the impression that his dress is his main interest in life. A Cossack, on the other hand, wherever one meets him, looks as if he were ready to buckle to and fight there and then; and certainly dress or appearance is the last thing in the world he would trouble his head about. The barracks they had just constructed were rough but clean, and about as good as those of our native troops in India. They were inferior to those of the Chinese troops over the way at Hunchun, but they were evidently of a temporary description. The rations of the Cossacks consisted principally of black bread, and they received also an allowance of soup-like stew or stew-like soup; but the whole ration was decidedly inferior to what the British soldier gets. Their pay is twenty roubles—about fifty shillings—a month, which would be very liberal if they had not out of it to pay for the whole of their equipment. The amount which actually reaches their pocket was, according to the colonel, about a halfpenny a day! It must indeed require conscription to induce men to go through all a Cossack does for this ludicrous remuneration.

In the evening the colonel had a small dinner-party, when three of the officers of the post and a Chinaman, who spoke

Russian, and acted as interpreter between the Russian and Chinese officials, came in. After eating some small dishes, such as sardines and salmon chips, at a side table, and washing them down with a glass or two of vodka, which the colonel informed us was a quite necessary proceeding, to clear our throats for the dinner that was coming, we sat down to the main business. First of all, a great soup-tureen was placed on the table, filled with a good substantial soup. "No ceremony, gentlemen; *je mange énormement*," said the colonel. And he proceeded to ladle himself out a good helping, and every one round the table then did the same. Each of us had at his side six bottles of wine and beer, and these we were expected to attack indiscriminately. "You're drinking nothing," shouts out the colonel, as he stretches across the table and fills your glass with claret—a very excellent sort of claret, he said, they got from the Crimea. Before that was finished, another officer would fill your glass—the same glass!—with sherry. Then the colonel would insist upon you trying the beer. Meanwhile course after course of the most substantial dishes were being served up. Each one helped himself from them, but in addition one or other of the officers would cut off a huge slice and put it down in one of our plates. The hospitality was genuine and most hearty; but how we got through that evening was a marvel to us. We had been leading a hard, healthy life lately, so had good appetites, and were able to keep fairly well in line with the Russians in the eating way. But the drinking was terrible. If we had been allowed to keep at one liquor we might possibly have survived; but the mixture of port and beer, and sherry and claret, and Guinness's stout and vodka, backwards and forwards, first one and then the other, was fatal.

In the middle of dinner a jingling of bells was heard, and up drove a tarantass. The door opened, and in came a young Russian officer. He had arrived with his wife. "Just in time for dinner," said the colonel. "Make room over there, will you?" and down the officer sat, while his wife went to her house. The dinner went on without any break, and the new arrival was treated as if he had been expected for dinner, and had merely come in a little late. Yet he and his wife were new to the post, and had just travelled for three weeks through Siberia, across those awful roads! No question seemed to be asked of the lady whether she was tired or not after her journey, and it never seemed to strike anybody that she possibly could be.

Meanwhile the Chinaman was making himself thoroughly at home. There is seldom any need to tell a Chinaman not to be shy, and there certainly was not in this case. Before dinner, he had arrived while the colonel was out, and had proceeded without any compunction into the Russian's dressing-room, and made every use of his washing and dressing things. And now at dinner he was equally free and easy. He never had to be pressed to take some more to eat, or to fill up his glass; and he talked away incessantly the whole of dinner. Nor did he think it necessary, though the guest of the Russians, to refrain from telling stories very detrimental to them. He thought, I suppose, that these stories would please us; but, coming from such a shifty gentleman, we were able to put them at their real value, and beg him not to trouble to continue.

Colonel Sokolowski had served in the Russo-Turkish war, and was very bitter on the subject of it. "Just look at all we went through," he said. "All the thousands of men we lost, and the hardships we had to undergo; and what was the result of it all? What good did we get from it? Nothing; absolutely nothing!" He was now in charge of this portion of the frontier, and had under him, I understood, a regiment of cavalry, a battery of artillery, and a battalion of infantry. He was obliged, also, as the chief of a frontier, to speak two languages besides his own (and, as being especially useful on the Chinese frontier, he spoke French and German). Yet, on comparing notes, we found that I, as a subaltern in a British cavalry regiment in India, was drawing more pay than he was. And as for Mr. James, he could with his pay have bought up a dozen—literally a dozen—of these frontier commandants. Where, however, the Russian had the advantage over us was in the matter of climate. It takes a great deal of money indeed to make up for the sickening weariness of hot weather in the plains of India. All these Russian officers about us were strong, robust men, bursting with health. Between them and a set of Englishmen in the plains of India in the months of July and August there was a difference which is but poorly compensated for by a few additional rupees.

After we had eaten and drunk and talked for some hours, the other officers went off, and the colonel said to us, "I don't know quite where you will sleep. There is a sofa for one of you; the other two had better sleep on the floor." This we proceeded to do, and so passed our first night in Russian territory. The colonel had spoken of his Cossack hospitality being rough but cordial. It was both.

On the following day we started off for the larger station of Novo-kievsk, fifteen miles distant, and situated on the coast. On the way we met the commissaire, or chief civil official. He spoke English, and was very polite to us, and volunteered to allow us to go to Vladivostok—a trip which we should very much like to have made, but we could not spare the time for it. The fact of this Russian official being so civil to us, though we had no passports, was another proof of the friendly disposition of the Russians towards us. Novo-kievsk was a small place with a garrison of a battalion of infantry, a battery of artillery, and about a hundred mounted Cossacks. There were very few buildings besides the barracks. The roadways were unmetalled, and the whole place had a dreary uncared-for appearance. We could discover no Russian hotel or inn of any description, and had to put up at a Chinese inn. There were two Russian and four Chinese shops. The latter were the best, and were about equal to a second-rate Parsee shop in an Indian cantonment. The barracks and cottages of the married officers and men were very small, and whitewashed, and extremely cold and dreary in appearance. The whole place, barracks, shops, church, and everything, was not so large, and certainly not so well built, as the barracks of my regiment in India. The absence of life, too, was particularly striking. In the afternoon, at any rate, we expected to see the officers and their wives coming out for some sort of amusement and exercise. But nobody appeared. The officers seem to spend their spare time in smoking, drinking, and playing cards; and the wives, I conclude, in looking on, for there did not appear to be much else for them to do.

There was a hill just by the town, and of course we climbed it. We afterwards met the commissaire again, and he told us that he had often heard that it was characteristic of Englishmen that whenever they saw a hill they immediately craved to go up it, and he was immensely tickled at hearing we actually had climbed this hill. He said he had scarcely known a single Russian in the place ascend it; but here, directly an Englishman arrives, he immediately proceeds to do so. From the top we obtained a view over Possiet Bay, on which this little station of Novo-kievsk is situated, and on the opposite side of the water, about two miles distant, we could make out the small settlement of Possiet, consisting of thirty or forty houses.

On descending the hill, we found a squad of recruits hard at work drilling. They carried a knapsack and the great-coat in a roll round it and over the body. They were being taught to march with the leg kept very stiff and straight, and a smart little adjutant was dancing about up and down the line, every now and then catching some man, who was out of step or dressing, a tremendous punch on the nose! The men were small—I should not say they averaged more than five feet five inches or five feet six inches—but they were thick-set and robust-looking, and as hard as all Cossacks seem to be.

We were close here to the Corean frontier, so there were numbers of Coreans about. Many are settled in this valley, and seem to flourish and to be looked upon with favour by the Russian authorities. They always appeared to me to be rather a dull, insipid race, but they are said to be quiet and orderly, and as the Russians want population to cultivate and improve the land, so much of which is now merely run to waste, they are welcomed to Russian territory to carry out the work which the Russians themselves seem incapable of. Colonel Sokolowski told us that his government were extremely anxious to have all this Eastern Siberia colonized by Russians. They would, and did, give every encouragement they could to settlers; they gave them free farming implements, horses, and cattle, and brought them out from Russia free of expense; but the settlers had no energy or vigour; they accepted all that was given them, and set to work to produce enough to live on, but nothing beyond. "If you English," said the colonel, "had had this country, you would have made a magnificent place of it by now; but our Russians have none of that colonizing spirit you have, and the country is only very slowly opened up." Since that time, however, the Siberian railway has been taken in hand. The Russians are waking up in earnest, and a great future ought to lie before these magnificently fertile tracts of Eastern Siberia. What the Chinese colonists have been able to do on their side of the border is a type of what the Russians could do also. And with a railway to aid in its development, all these regions about the Amur and its tributaries ought to equal the most thriving parts of Canada.

We only stayed one day in Novo-kievsk, and then returned to our friend Colonel Sokolowski's post, dining with him there again, and meeting there the commissaire. The talk turned on the subject of English encroachments. These two Russian officials said people were always talking of English designs against Russian territory, and it was curious to find here the same kind of alarmist rumours and suspicions of hyper-crafty designs and deep-laid schemes of aggression that we are so accustomed to in India. The British fleet had only a few weeks before visited Possiet Bay, and immediately all the cacklers had set to work to find a hidden object for this. The English intended, they supposed, to bombard Possiet and seize a port here in Eastern Siberia as they had just done at Port Hamilton. Fortunately for Mr. James and myself, both the military and civil officials in charge on this frontier were more wide-minded, even-tempered men, and, as I have shown, treated us with marked civility and without any sign of suspicion, so that we were enabled to carry out a most interesting little visit.

CHAPTER III.

BACK TO PEKING.

WE now turned our faces homewards. We had reached the limit of our journey, and now had to hurry back to the coast at Newchwang. Mr. James went by a short cut to Kirin, while Fulford and I, with the carts, travelled round by Ninguta to meet a man whom we expected with letters. On November 11 we left Hunchun, and now winter had regularly set in. The thermometer was at zero or a degree or two above or below it, and snow was beginning to fall. At Ninguta we found the river, which we had three weeks before crossed in a ferry, and which was about one hundred and fifty yards broad and with a by no means slow current, now frozen over so completely that we could run our heavily laden carts over on the ice. Here at Ninguta we met our man, and at last received letters. We had not received a single batch since we had started on our journey six months before, and, after all the hardships and the frequent *ennui* of travel, the delight of getting in touch again with one's friends and inhaling one soft breath of air from our native land was intense and almost bewildering. It made us forget all the hard part we had gone through; that all seemed a dream now, and just that touch from outside put enough new energy into us to have started us contentedly on another fresh journey if need had been.

Fulford and I met with no incident on our road to Kirin, though we passed the body of a man who had on the previous day been murdered by brigands; and on November 26 we rejoined Mr. James at Kirin. The great Sungari was now frozen over hard. The ice was more than a foot thick on it, and we were able to trot our carts smoothly across a river three hundred yards wide and twenty feet deep.

From Kirin we did not proceed direct to the coast, as we were anxious to visit the head-quarters of the Roman Catholic mission in North Manchuria, at a village named Hsiao Pa-chia-tzu, about twenty miles from Kuan-cheng-tzu. On approaching this place, we saw from far away over the plain the tower of a church—a remarkable innovation in a Manchurian landscape. On our arrival we were cordially welcomed by the two priests—Père Litot and Père Maviel—and introduced to the bishop, a noble-looking, kindly gentleman, who had lived for over thirty years in the country, and has since died there. A noticeable feature in this mission was that the whole village was Christian. The missionaries had begun by educating and training children as Christians. These had grown into men, and had sent their children in their turn, and in the course of time the whole village had become Christian. We attended the service on Sunday, and were very much struck by the really sincere and devout character of these converts. Brought up from their childhood as Christians, and under the kindly, genial influence of these good priests, the people of this little village seemed like a different race from the cold, hard Chinamen around them.

We could only stay one day, and the next we pushed on to Mukden. The cold was now becoming intense. On account of the heavy traffic on the road, we had to make very early starts in the morning so as to secure places at the inns in the evening. We rose at two or three every morning, had a good plate of porridge and some tea, and then started off. For the first hour or two it would, of course, be dark. Snow covered the ground, and the thermometer would read anything from zero to 14° Fahrenheit below zero, which was the coldest we registered. But though it was so cold, I do not remember suffering very much from it. The air was generally still, and we had the advantage of starting from a warm house with something warm inside us, and at the end of our day's march, we again found a good warm room to go to. It was afterwards, on the Pamirs and in the Himalayas, that I really felt the cold, for there, instead of a warm room to start from, I only had a small tent, and sometimes no tent at all, nor sufficient firewood for a fire, and the high altitudes, by causing breathlessness and bringing on weakness, added to my discomfort. Here in Manchuria, unless it happened to be windy—and then, of course, it was really trying—the cold affected us very little. The roads were frozen hard and the snow on them well beaten down by the heavy traffic, and we trundled along a good thirty miles a day.

The traffic in this winter season was wonderful. I counted in a single day's march over eight hundred carts, all heavily laden and drawn by teams, or at least two and many of them nine animals, ponies or mules. A main road in Manchuria in the winter is a busy scene, and these strings of carts going along on the frosty morning, with the jingling bells on the teams, and the drivers shouting at their animals, were signs of life and animation which we had hardly expected to see after our first experience on the heavy, muddy roads in the summer. The inns were numerous and crowded, and as a string of carts passed by the inn, men would come running out, proclaiming the advantages of their particular hostelry, and trying to persuade the carters to come in. Then, when the carts stopped, the inn men would bustle about, fetching grain and fodder for the animals and food for the men, and there was as much bustle and activity as in a market town in England. I remarked, too, how very well the carters fed their animals. These Manchurian, or rather Mongolian, ponies and mules are never allowed any blankets or clothing of any description, and stand out quite bare all night in a cold so great that I have even seen the hoar frost lying thick on an animal's back in the morning. But they are fed enormously while they are in work. They are given in the day as much as sixteen pounds of grain, besides bran and chopped millet-stalks. When they are not at work they are eating, and the eating and the work together occupy so much time that I could never discover when they slept. The programme for these animals was to start an hour or two before daybreak in the morning. At midday, or somewhat before, they would halt, and the instant they had stopped they would be put to a trough, which would then be piled up with a feed of barley or millet mixed up with bran and chopped millet-stalks or straw. This and watering would occupy them the greater part of the two hours' halt. They would then start off again for the rest of the day's journey, and halt for the night at dusk. Immediately on arrival they would be given another of these enormous feeds, and in the middle of the night a third. Then the next morning they would be off again before daylight. Grain, of course, was very cheap and plentiful, but in no other part of Asia have I seen animals so well fed as in Manchuria, and the result was that their owners could get the fullest amount of work out of them, so that two animals would draw their twelve hundred pounds of goods for thirty miles a day without any difficulty.

The country we passed through was very pretty even in winter, and must have been really beautiful in summer. It was undulating, well covered with trees, and intersected with many little streams and rivers. At this season it was all under snow, but we saw one morning one of the most perfectly lovely sights I have ever seen. I have never seen a similar sight, either before or since. It was a *frozen* mist. As the sun rose we found the whole air glittering with brilliant particles sparkling in the rays of the sun—and the mist had encrusted everything, all the trunks of the trees and all the delicate tracery of their outlines, with a coating like hoar frost. The earth, the trees, and everything in the scene was glistening white, and the whole air was sparkling in the sunlight. It lasted but a short time, for as the sun rose the mist melted away, but while it could be seen one seemed to be in a very fairyland.

We passed through many villages and thriving little towns, and at length, after covering the last ninety miles in two days, we arrived at Mukden and found ourselves among our own countrymen again. We drove up to the Scottish mission established here, the members of which had been particularly kind to us on our previous visit to Mukden, and had pressed us to stay with them on our return. Messrs. Ross and Webster and Dr. Christie came running out of the house as they saw us driving up in the cart, and it was only as we were shown into a cosy drawing-room, where the ladies were having tea, that we realized how rough we had grown on the journey. We had each of us developed a beard, which, as well as our hair, now, in the light of civilization, seemed very unkempt. Our faces were burning red from the exposure, and our clothes—especially our boots—were worn out and torn with the rough wear they had undergone. We had had many trials on the journey, but this facing a ladies' tea-party in a drawing-room in our disreputable condition was the hardest of them all. As soon as, by the light of comparison, we had discovered our unpresentable state, we begged to be allowed to go and do the best we could for ourselves. Mr. Webster then produced every manner of luxury for us—clean white shirts and, what to me was most acceptable of all, some socks. For some time past my own had been worn to shreds, and as my boots too, as well as a pair which Mr. James had very kindly given me, were all in pieces, my feet had been sadly galled and blistered.

Then we made our way back to the drawing-room, and as the novelty of a return to civilization wore off, we felt more and more the genial influences around us. The Scottish are always hospitable, but few even of them could have exceeded in hospitality these missionaries at Mukden. Mrs. Webster was incessantly at work devising some fresh form of comfort for us—at one time making up a cosy room for each of us, at another producing every kind of clothing, and at another bringing out the most astonishing variety of Scottish cakes and scones and muffins.

This Scottish mission is established with a special object, and on lines different from most other missions. The object is to try and get at the Chinese officials and gentry; to preach to the lower classes as well, but to make an especial attempt to get in touch with the gentry and upper classes of society. With this object, highly trained men are sent out, and the mission is established with some "style," though I use this word not to imply any particularly luxurious surroundings, but rather to impress the difference from the extremely simple and plain establishment of other missions which I have seen. It is recognized that Chinese officials are reluctant to mix freely with men who live in very humble houses and dress indifferently, and it is thought that men who adopt a higher style of living and dress will have more chance of meeting with these sensitive Chinamen. It is, moreover, considered by the heads of this mission that men will work better in a distant land if they are accompanied by their wives to cheer and encourage them and help on the mission work by teaching children. It is part, too, of the general line of action that at each mission station there should also be a missionary doctor, through whom first access may be gained to men who might otherwise never be approachable.

This class of mission does not inspire the same amount of

enthusiasm, as, for instance, that of the French missionaries we had met in Northern Manchuria; but it may be quite as effective, and for the immediate object, that of gaining access to the higher classes, it is probably much better suited. The medical part of the mission, especially, is eminently practical, and likely to be appreciated by the people. As we ourselves saw, high Chinese officials did make use of the services of Dr. Christie, and, though it cannot be expected that, because a man is cured of an illness, he should straightway become a Christian, it is evidently an advantage to both the Chinaman and the missionary that they should have had the opportunity of coming in contact with one another. Something of the strong earnest character of the medical missionary must be reflected on to the Chinaman, and the missionary on his side will have been able to learn something of the prejudices and difficulties of the educated classes of the Chinese.

We could only spare one full day's halt at Mukden, and we then pushed on to Newchwang, where we arrived on December 19, just seven months after we had left it. Here Mr. James lodged with Mr. Allen, the consul, while I was most hospitably entertained by Mr. Edgar, the commissioner of Chinese customs. It is a well-authenticated and pleasing fact that wherever you meet Englishmen on the borders of civilization, even though you may be utter strangers to them, you will be treated as if you were their most intimate, lifelong friend. This happens all over the world, and it is an unmistakable proof that the true feeling of men towards each other is one of good-will. Men are at heart sociable and anxious to know each other and attach themselves to one another, and the coldness and restraint of intercourse in civilized parts is merely the product of civilization—an outward veneer only—covering the real warmth of heart which every man has, and which immediately becomes apparent when he leaves the centres of civilization.

OUR PARTY IN MANCHURIA.

At Newchwang our party broke up; Mr. James went off to Port Arthur and thence to Japan, while Mr. Fulford and I proceeded to Peking. After these years I feel strongly how much I owe to Mr. James. It was through him that I had thus gained my first experience of real travelling, and, though I did not appreciate it at the time, afterwards, when I had myself to head an expedition, I realized what sterling qualities of steady, dogged perseverance he must have possessed to lead our party successfully through the forests to the mysterious Ever-White Mountain. I have always wondered that a man, who had held high offices in India and been accustomed to the luxurious style of camp life of an Indian civil officer, should in his holiday-time choose to rough it as Mr. James did. As I used to see him marching sturdily along through the forest, the marshes, and especially when he had to carry his kit on his back, I used to marvel. To a young subaltern the thing was natural, but when a high Indian official of more than twenty years' standing did it, there must have been in him a wonderful amount of "go" and pluck, and this Mr. James undoubtedly possessed.

The Manchurian journey was completed, but some general words about the country may be interesting. Those who wish for full information can find it in Mr. James's "Long White Mountain." In the first place, it will have been gathered from the narrative that the country is one of extraordinary fertility. Both in this respect and in its climate it seems to resemble the best parts of Canada. It is mostly land formerly covered with forest, and consequently the soil has all the richness which the accumulation of decaying vegetation through many ages gives. A very large proportion of the country is, indeed, even now under forest, though every year the Chinese colonists eat further into it. The climate is severe in winter. At Newchwang, on the coast, the thermometer falls to 10° or 12° below zero Fahrenheit;

and in the north, when the full force of winds which sweep across two continents is felt, the thermometer, according to the French missionaries, falls, as I have already mentioned, to more than 40° below zero Fahrenheit. The summers are warm, but not hot, the maximum temperature being from 90° to 95° Fahrenheit. The springs are said to be very beautiful, and the autumns are crisp and bright. The rainfall, judging from our experiences, must be considerable, and the country receives the full benefit in that respect of its proximity to the ocean.

Of the mineral products of the country it is impossible for me to give an accurate account, but we met with a coal-mine, an iron-smelting furnace, and a small silver-mine within twenty miles of each other, and gold is found in many parts of the country. In what quantity these minerals are obtainable I am unable to say. The country must be thoroughly explored by some competent mineralogist before even an approximate estimate can be given.

The vegetable production includes, besides timber (fir, oak, elm, and walnut), wheat, beans, hemp, poppy, tobacco, and rice. The people cultivate the land with great industry, and, assisted by nature, extract the most plentiful crop from it. Large quantities of beans and bean oil are brought down to the coast for exportation to other parts of China.

Of the people some account has already been given. Mr. Taylor Meadows, a former consul at Newchwang, and Mr. James calculate the population at from twenty to twenty-three millions; but of these not one million are real Manchus, and the remainder are Chinese immigrants. Manchuria is therefore populated by Chinamen, and not by Manchus. These Chinese colonists, like Chinese everywhere, are hard-working and industrious, and the country flourishes and develops in spite of the bad administration and of the brigandage so rife in all parts, and especially in the north. The people are well housed, well fed, and well clothed. Food is plentiful and cheap, and the excellence of the winter roads makes it possible to import goods readily from the coast. The character of the people will have been gathered from the previous narrative. They are certainly not attractive to strangers, and at the end of a journey one leaves them without regret; but they have this good quality of industry—they are persevering in their efforts at colonization, and thrifty in their habits.

Two days before Christmas, Fulford and I had to start for Tientsin. It was rather a wrench to have to leave our friends just before Christmas in this way, but I thought it possible that we might just reach Tientsin before the river was closed, and so be able to get away down the coast at once. Christmas Day we spent in a Chinese inn. We, of course, had a plum-pudding, which had been presented to us by our friends, and some wine in which to drink the health of those at home, and certainly it had been a great satisfaction to me to have been able to telegraph home from Newchwang our safe return from our journey, so that now at Christmas-time they might feel no uneasiness on my account.

We passed nothing of interest till we reached Shan-hai-kuan, the point where the Great Wall of China begins, or ends, in the sea. This was a sight really worth seeing. A line of hills between two or three thousand feet in height, stretched from inland close down to the seashore; and all along these heights, as far as the eye could reach, ran this wonderful wall, going down the side of one hill, up the next, over its summit and down the other side again, and then at the end coming finally down and plunging right into the sea till the waves washed the end of it. It was no trumpery little wall, nor such a wall, for instance, as one sees round a modern prison, but a regular castle wall, such as they built in the Middle Ages round their strongest castles, thirty or forty feet high, of solid stone, and fifteen feet or so thick, wide enough for two carriages to drive abreast on it, with towers every few hundred yards. This was the Great Wall of China at its commencement, and it is, I think, almost more wonderful than the Pyramids. I have seen both. Both astounded me by their evidence of colossal industry; but the Great Wall of China, pushing straight over the mountains, regardless of height and distance, is, perhaps, the most impressive of the two. There are points, however, in which the Pyramids excel the Great Wall. The Pyramids are perfect throughout. Not a flaw can be found. Each huge block is laid with absolute precision, and there is no sign inside or out of anything less enduring than these immense blocks of stone being employed. The Great Wall, on the other hand, though it runs for hundreds of miles in the magnificent state I have described, dwindles down eventually to a mere mud wall, and, moreover, even in the best parts, the inside of it is only rubbish. It is not perfect throughout its entire length, nor solid right through. The Pyramids will remain when the Great Wall has run to ruin.

At Shan-hai-kuan we found several modern forts constructed and armed with Krupp guns—a curious contrast to the antiquated wall of defence by which they lay. An instructor to the Chinese in the use of these guns, a German non-commissioned officer, was stationed here. He spoke very disparagingly about the interest the Chinese took in their duties. It was impossible, he said, to get them to look after their guns properly. They could not be made to see the necessity of it, and costly, highly finished guns were going to ruin for want of proper care. This defect is seen everywhere in Chinese naval and military officers.

From here we went to Kaiping. On the way we passed cart after cart laden with coffins, and with a cock in a cage at the top of each. A Chinaman dislikes being buried outside the Great Wall, and as soon as his relatives can afford it, they bring him home inside it again. These were the bodies of colonists who had died in Manchuria, and were being brought back to their homes again. The cock was intended, by his crowing, to keep the spirit awake while passing through the Great Wall; otherwise, it was feared, the spirit might go wandering off somewhere and forget the body, and the body might be brought in and the spirit left behind.

As we neared Kaiping we were surprised to see two British navvies walking along the road, and there was not the slightest mistake who they were, for as we passed, one said to the other, "I wonder who the —— —— that is, Bill?" They were miners employed in the colliery at this place. The Kaiping coal-mine was in the charge of Mr. Kinder, who very kindly gave us a room for the night, and the next day showed us round the mine. At the time of our visit it was nine hundred feet deep, and could turn out five hundred tons of coal a day. Now, however, it can turn out its thousand or one thousand five hundred tons without difficulty. Mr. Kinder, who is still in charge, is a man of surprising energy and enterprise. Employed by a Chinese company, over whom, however, I fancy, he has a considerable influence, he first of all got this coal-mine into working order. Then he ran a small tramway down the coast, for the purpose of carrying the coals to a port. The waggons on this were at first drawn by ponies, but after a time Mr. Kinder made up a little engine, which he called the "Rocket," to do the work. This engine he showed us with great pride. It was entirely constructed by himself on the spot, and the only parts which had been imported were the wheels, which had been brought from Hong-kong—the remnants of an old tramway service. The Chinese had been afraid of a whole engine being imported by a "foreign devil," but a machine made on the spot aroused no fears. In the course of time another more powerful engine was made and the tramway enlarged. Then, as the Chinese grew accustomed to seeing steam-engines, Mr. Kinder was able to introduce the idea of having engines from abroad instead of making inferior ones on the spot. The ice had been broken. The first prejudice had been overcome, and railways in China had been started. Engines, rolling-stock, and rails were now imported, and a railway towards Tientsin was commenced. This, Mr. Kinder, with only one European assistant to supervise the mine, was now constructing. A year or two afterwards it reached Tientsin, and has now been extended eastward to Shan-hai-kuan. Its extension to Manchuria will be the next move, and then the whole of that magnificently rich country will be opened up. If any one deserves the credit of having introduced railways into China, I think Mr. Kinder must be the man.

Mr. Kinder had many stories of his intercourse with Chinese which amused us. He was called at one time before some very high Manchu prince who had never seen a European. The prince eyed the Englishman suspiciously for a time, and then began stroking him down, at the same time saying that the gentleman was quite tame, and did not apparently bite nor kick. He had been made to believe that Europeans really were, as they are always called by the Chinese, devils, and he had expected to find a sort of wild animal brought before him. This is one of the prejudices a European, dealing with the Chinese, has to overcome.

Another sort of prejudice which often stood very much in Mr. Kinder's way, was that of "Feng-shui." This is a prejudice connected with the spirit world. The living, the Chinese consider, must conform to certain rules, or the evil spirits will enter the house, and harm will come to all connected with it. A stranger in China is surprised to notice a wall, ten, twenty, or fifty yards long, according to the size of the house, placed a few yards off straight in front of the gateway. This wall stands out by itself, and fulfils no apparent object. It is really intended to prevent evil spirits entering the houses. Evil spirits, according to the Chinese, can only go straight ahead; they cannot turn a corner. So if a wall is built straight in front of the gateway, the spirits run up against that and are unable to enter the house. This is only one instance of the superstition of Feng-shui. It has many similar prejudices with which the construction of a railway through the country was likely to interfere. For instance, it was objected by the Chinese, that if the railway was raised the spirits might go along the top of the carriages and look down into their houses. "But then," said Mr. Kinder, "just look at the embankment and think how many devils that will keep out, running for miles and miles as it does, right in front of your doorways." Much of this sort of diplomacy was needed to overcome prejudice after prejudice, but Mr. Kinder was as good at diplomacy as he was at engineering, and railways in China are now an accomplished fact.

From Kaiping we proceeded to Tientsin, passing over a dead level plain, and reaching that place on New Year's Day, 1887. The Peiho river had just been frozen over, and steamer communication with the south was blocked till the spring. At Tientsin I was very hospitably entertained by the consul, Mr. Byron Brenan, and his wife, with whom Mr. James and I had stopped on our previous visit. There is generally plenty going on in the little foreign community at Tientsin, and besides a mounted paper-chase, organized by the French, we had ice-boat sailing and skating. The ice-boat was a great attraction, and with full sails set we went skimming along at a good thirty miles an hour over the flooded plains. This ice-boat was built upon runners like magnified skates, it had sails like a yacht, and of course a rudder. The pace was tremendous, for there is little friction and no resistance such as a ship has to encounter at sea. For the same reason it could be turned in an instant in any direction, and the only difficulty was to keep a firm enough hold as the boat whisked round. On one occasion a lady did not do so, and was sent off at a tangent, skimming gracefully along over the ice in one direction, while the boat went off thirty miles an hour in another! Any other form of yachting is tame in comparison with this ice-boat sailing, and its only disadvantage is the cold. Flying through the air with the thermometer not far off zero is very cold work, and necessitates good heavy furs.

During my stay in Tientsin, the Russian New Year fell, and Mr. Brenan took me a round of visits to the Russian consul and the Russian merchants in the place. With them the New Year is observed with great ceremony. At each house we found substantial refreshment laid out on a side-table, and were pressed to drink good luck to the coming year in champagne. The Russians in Tientsin are mostly tea-merchants, and some of them are extremely rich, and live in very luxuriously furnished houses. They all of them had that warm, hearty, cordial manner which is the characteristic of Russians.

After this I went on to Peking, and was entertained in the British Legation, first by Mr. Walter Hillier, then Chinese Secretary, now Consul-General in Corea, and afterwards by Sir John and Lady Walsham. I trespassed far too long on their hospitality, but they were so kind in their reception of me, and it was such a relief to be settled in comfortable home-like surroundings after the rough life I had been leading, that I was unable to break myself away till the spring had come on, and so I was with them for nearly three months. And here, of course, I learnt a great deal about the Chinese which I should certainly never have been able to learn by myself. Mr. Hillier was known to be a fine Chinese scholar, and to have a very intimate knowledge of the Chinese. Conversations with him were therefore especially interesting, and in my subsequent journeys I was able to profit much by the advice he gave me.

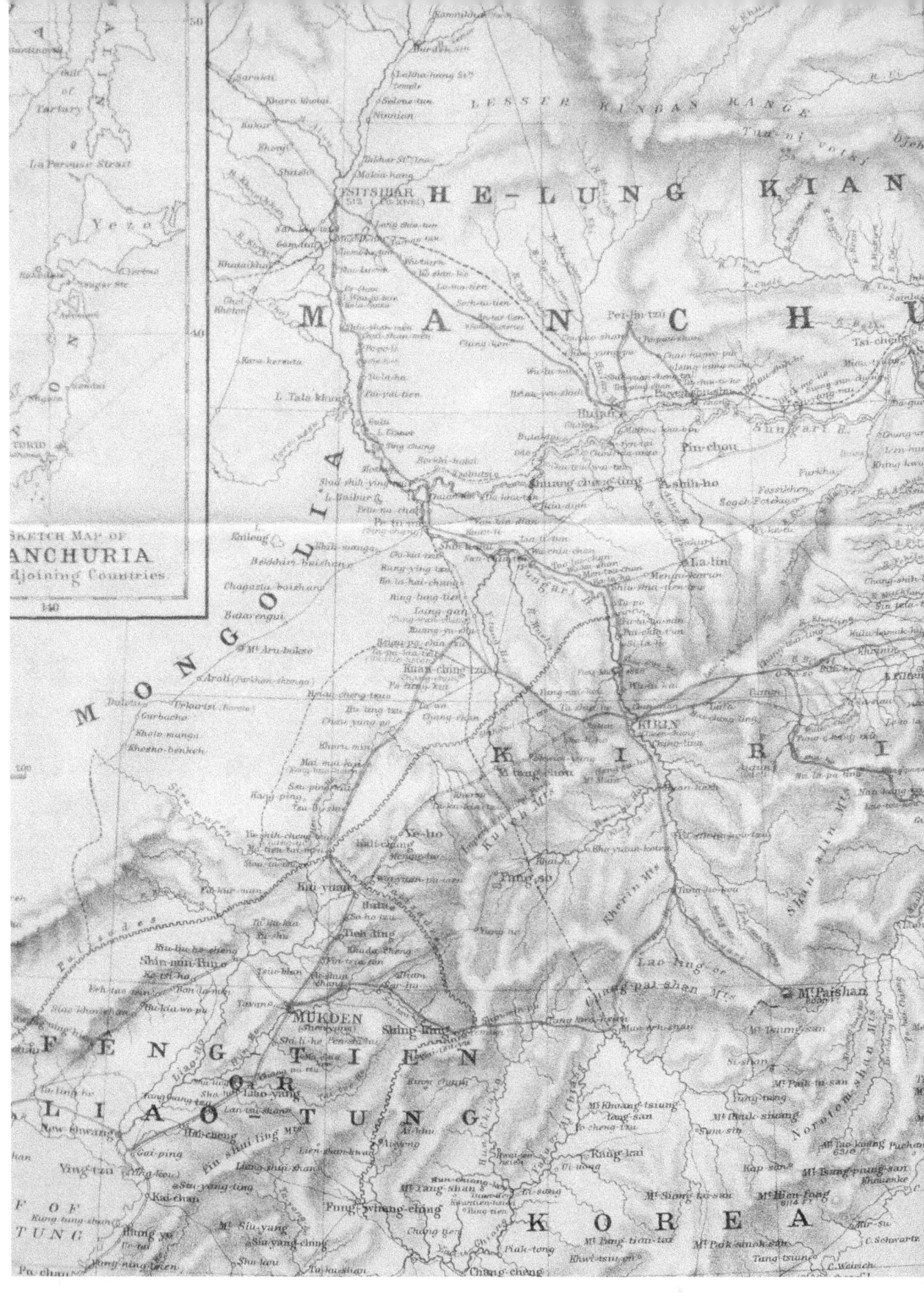

Peking has been described so often that it is unnecessary to do so once more. The only striking things about it are the size of its walls and its gateways, the filth of its streets, and the utter disregard for decency of its inhabitants. One could not stir outside the Legation without going through the most disgusting filth, and the practical result of this is, that the members of the foreign legations go out as little as possible. They entertain among themselves, though, very considerably, and during the winter there was a constant succession of dinner-parties and dances, and every afternoon we used to meet at the skating-rink, a covered-in enclosure with natural ice, flooded over and frozen fresh every day. The British Legation entertainments were of course very brilliant, for the house is an old palace with unusually large, fine, well-decorated rooms, and these Lady Walsham had just had newly furnished from home. At an entertainment there, surrounded with the most beautiful furniture, and every sort of modern comfort, and with people of every European nationality talking around one, it was hard to realize that this was all in the very capital of one of the most seclusive countries in the world, and that it is only in the last thirty of the three thousand years during which the Chinese Empire has existed that such a thing has been possible.

CHAPTER IV.

PEKING TO KWEI-HWA-CHENG.

"And o'er him many changing scenes must roll,
Ere toil his thirst for travel can assuage."

WHILE I was waiting in Peking, news arrived that Colonel M. S. Bell, V.C., of the Royal Engineers, was to come there and travel straight through to India. I knew Colonel Bell, having served under him in the Intelligence Department in India, so I immediately decided upon asking him to allow me to accompany him. Here was the opportunity for which I had longed. Here was a chance of visiting that hazy mysterious land beyond the Himalayas, and actually seeing Kashgar and Yarkand, with whose names I had been acquainted since I was a boy through letters from my uncle, Robert Shaw. A journey overland to India would take us through the entire length of Chinese Turkestan, the condition of which was still unknown since the Chinese had re-conquered it by one of those long-sustained efforts for which they are so remarkable. We should be able to see these secluded people of Central Asia, dim figures of whom I had pictured in my mind from reading the accounts of the few travellers who had been amongst them. Then, too, there was the fascination of seeing the very heart of the Himalayas, as we should have to cross their entire breadth on the way to India. And all combined was one grand project—this idea of striking boldly out from Peking to penetrate to India—that of itself inspired enthusiasm and roused every spark of exploring ardour in me. No excitement I have ever experienced has come up to that of planning out a great journey. The only drawback in such a life is the subsequent reaction when all is over, and the monotonous round of ordinary existence oppresses one by its torpidity and flatness in comparison. The project before me was a journey in length nearly as great as one across Central Africa and back again, and, to me at least, far more interesting than any African travel—a journey through countries varying from the level wastes of the Gobi desert, to the snow-clad masses of the Himalayas; passing, moreover, through the entire length of an empire with a history of three thousand years, and still fresh in interest to the present day. And with the chance of making such a journey, who could help feeling all the ardent excitement of travel rising in him, and long to be started on it.

Colonel Bell arrived in Peking towards the end of March, and said he would be only too glad to allow me to accompany him; but he thought that it would be rather a waste of energy for two officers to travel together, so we arranged to follow different routes.

There were, of course, some initial difficulties to be overcome —the chief one being leave of absence from my regiment. But Sir John Walsham, for whose kindness on this occasion I could never feel too grateful, overcame this by telegraphing direct to Lord Dufferin, and that difficulty—generally the greatest which military explorers have to encounter—was at once removed.

The telegram having been despatched, Colonel Bell and I spread out our maps and discussed operations. He was anxious to see the populous parts of China, so decided upon going through the provinces inside of the Great Wall to Kansu, and then striking across the Gobi desert to Hami, following throughout the main route between Peking and Chinese

Turkestan. To my lot fell the newer and more purely exploring work, and it was determined that I should follow the direct road across the Gobi desert, and, if possible, meet Colonel Bell at Hami.* Colonel Bell then left Peking, after fixing a date on which we should meet at Hami, and my friends in the Legation said that, judging from the general style of his movements, they thought it extremely improbable that he would wait for me there more than three-quarters of an hour. As it turned out, we never met again till we arrived in India, and then Colonel Bell told me that he really had waited for me a whole day in Hami—this place in the middle of Central Asia, nearly two thousand miles from our starting-point—and, astonished at finding I had not turned up to date, had proceeded on his way to India.

Meanwhile, I had to remain in Peking to await the reply of the telegram to the Viceroy, and occupy myself in sundry preparations and in the search for an interpreter. A favourable reply arrived, and then Sir John Walsham, with his usual kindness, interested himself in procuring for me the best passport it was possible to obtain from the Chinese, and that having been obtained, April 4, 1887, was fixed as the date of my departure from Peking.

The evening preceding my departure was one which it will be hard indeed to forget, and I think I realized then for the first time clearly what I was undertaking. Lady Walsham asked me after dinner to mark on a map for her the route I proposed to follow, and to tell her exactly what I hoped to do. Then, as I traced out a pencil line along the map of Asia, I first seemed to appreciate the task I had before me. Everything was so vague. Nowhere in Peking had we been

* This route had never previously, nor, as far as I am aware, has it since been, traversed by a European. It lies midway between the high-road to Chinese Turkestan and the route which Mr. Ney Elias followed in 1872 on his way from Peking to Siberia, and for the exploration of which he obtained the Gold Medal of the Royal Geographical Society.

able to obtain information about the road across the desert. I had never been in a desert, and here were a thousand miles or so of one to be crossed. Nor had we any information of the state of the country on the other side of the desert. It was held by the Chinese, we knew, but how held, what sort of order was preserved in the country, and how a solitary European traveller would be likely to fare among the people, we knew not. Lastly, at the back of all, looming darkly in the extremest distance, were the Himalayas, to cross which had previously been considered a journey in itself.

All the terrible vagueness and uncertainty of everything impressed itself on me as I traced that pencil line on the map. It was a real plunge into the unknown I was about to make, and, however easy the route might afterwards prove to future travellers, I felt that it was this first plunging in that was the true difficulty in the matter. Had but one traveller gone through before me; had I even now with me a companion upon whom I could rely, or one good servant whom I could trust to stand by me, the task would have seemed easy in comparison. But all was utterly dark before me, and the journey was to be made alone with the Chinese servant whom I had found in Peking.

That last night in safety and civilization all these difficulties and uncertainties weighed heavily upon me. But with the morning they were forgotten, and they never troubled me again. The start was to be made, and the real excitement begun, and an unalterable conviction came over me that somehow or other I should find myself in India in a few months' time.

Sir John and Lady Walsham and all the members of the Legation collected at the gateway to bid me good-bye, and, as they did so, I tried to thank them for all the many kindnesses they had shown me, and for the good-will and interest they had taken in my plans. There are many things one looks back to on a journey, but few things cheered me so much in my more dejected moments as the vivid recollection I used to keep of what I felt were the sincerely meant good wishes of the friends I was just leaving.

Then I rode out of the gateway and beyond the walls of Peking, and was fairly launched on my journey. Just a few pangs of depression and a few spectres of difficulties appeared at first, and then they vanished for good; and, as the hard realities of the journey began to make themselves felt, I braced myself up and prepared to face whatever might occur without thinking of what was behind.

With me at starting was one Chinese servant who had accompanied Mr. James through Manchuria, and who was to act as interpreter, but who afterwards gave up when we came to the edge of the desert; and a second, Liu-san, who eventually travelled with me the whole way to India, acting in turn as interpreter, cook, table-servant, groom, and carter. He served me well and faithfully, and he was always hard-working and willing to face the difficulties of the road. And when I think of all that depended on this, my single servant and companion, I cannot feel too grateful for the fidelity he showed in accompanying me.

For the first two weeks, as far as Kwei-hwa-cheng, the baggage was carried in carts, while I rode. The day after leaving Peking we passed through the inner branch of the Great Wall at the Nankon gate, and a couple of days later at Kalgan I saw the outer branch. It is a wonderful sight, this Great Wall of China. I had previously seen it at its commencement in the sea at Shan-hai-kuan,* and I passed through it again a march or two west of Kalgan. When I passed through it at this spot, it had dwindled down to very insignificant proportions. I describe it in my diary as a "miserable structure, bearing no resemblance to the gigantic

* See above, p. 51.

edifice near Peking. It is about twenty feet high, made of mud, crumbling to pieces, and with large gaps. At intervals of from half a mile to a mile there are mud-built towers."

At Kalgan I found a little missionary colony of Americans, among whom Mr. Sprague was most kind in giving me assistance and trying to obtain information about this route across the desert from Kwei-hwa-cheng which I would have to follow. Besides Mr. Sprague, there was Mr. Williams and two lady doctor missionaries, Miss Diament and Miss Murdock, who seemed to me to do much good. A medical missionary has a great pull. He (in this case she) can show charity and good-will in a clear, tangible, practical form, which is, generally speaking, much appreciated. These lady doctors appeared to go in specially for opium cures. They, like most of the missionaries one meets in China, had a great deal to say against the habit of opium-smoking, and described very vividly its evil consequences and the difficulty of getting rid of the habit when once acquired. This, in fact, seems to be one of the greatest objections to it. A man who has once acquired the habit cannot get out of it. Miss Murdock described to me how men affected in this way used to come and implore her to cure them; but her only effectual method was to confine them. She would make them pay for their food, and also produce a surety who would be responsible, if the patient died, for the removal of the body. In this stern way she had effected many cures, though she was disappointed at times in finding her patient going back to the habit again when temptation was thrown in his way.

M. Ivanoff, a Russian tea-merchant, was another of the Europeans I met at Kalgan. It is always a pleasure to meet a Russian. He is invariably so frank and hearty. No one would ever accuse a Russian of not being warm-hearted, and to a stranger in a strange land this Russian merchant was particularly so. He at once produced maps and books to look up information for me, and insisted upon presenting me with a new map, and a particularly good one, which was afterwards of the utmost service to me. I like to record these little acts of kindness and consideration which I have received from Russians individually, because I believe there are no two nations that would take to each other more than the Russians and ourselves, if the opportunity were forthcoming, and the more the members of each nation know each other the better it would be for us both.

Another of the acquaintances I made at Kalgan was the ex-captain of a Chinese gunboat which had been engaged in the action at Foochow during the Franco-Chinese war. His was a curious story. The Chinese have a principle that in a battle a commander must either be victorious or else die. This man's vessel had been moored at some distance from the French fleet, and had consequently escaped the fate of the rest of the Chinese ships, and had not been blown out of the water. The captain, seeing the day was lost, and not being able to do anything to retrieve the disaster with his little gunboat, had run ashore and escaped. The Chinese Emperor, however, considered this a most ignominious proceeding. If the French had not killed him, he ought to have killed himself, and, as he had not done so, he was ordered into exile for life to the Mongolian border, and told to think himself fortunate that he had not been executed. And here the poor little gentleman was—very sore against his own government, but lively and cheery withal, and certainly most useful to me. He used to accompany me for hours through the bazaars, trying to get things which I wanted, or to obtain information about the road.

Kalgan has some very good shops, and I even bought a watch there. It does an immense trade with the Mongols, and with the caravans which start from there northwards across the desert to Siberia. But even here we could learn nothing about the route across the desert from Kwei-hwa-cheng. It is extraordinary how devoid the Chinese are of anything like an instinct for geography. Anything beyond a man's own town or the road he works on has no interest for him, and he knows nothing of. Caravans start regularly from Kwei-hwa-cheng across the desert to Hami. Kwei-hwa-cheng is only a week's journey from Kalgan, and Kalgan is a great trading centre, and yet nowhere in the place was information to be obtained of the route by which we had to go. How different all this is from what one sees in the bazaars of Central Asia, where the merchants—some from India, some from Turkestan, some from Afghanistan—meet and talk over the countries they have travelled over and the state of the roads, and where a traveller can always obtain a fair general idea of any caravan route now in use!

A feature of travelling in China is the elaborate agreement which has to be made with the carters. Before leaving Peking, Mr. Hillier, who in such matters was one of the most obliging and careful men I have met, had drawn up a document which appeared as comprehensive as a royal proclamation or a lawyer's deed. But even in that the carters found a flaw, and Mr. Sprague informed me that unless I paid some more money they would not land me on the date mentioned. So this was rectified, and on April 10 I started from Kalgan.

We now left the great caravan route from Peking to Siberia, and ascended the broad valley of the Yang-ho. Here each village was walled, and towers were scattered over the country—speaking of troublous times and predatory bands. The fields were poorly cultivated, and the people less well-to-do. Although we were well into April, the weather was still cold, and streams were covered with ice in the morning. No leaves were on the trees yet, and, although I was wearing a leather coat, cardigan jacket, flannel shirt, and vest, I still felt it cold riding along beside the carts.

We used, too, to have very cold winds blowing from the northward—from the direction of the high plateau of Mongolia. These blew with great force, and clouds of gritty, sandy dust from the desert and from the bare hill ranges which border it were carried along with them. This well accounts for the dull, hazy atmosphere so common at Peking, which is seen also in Chinese Turkestan. It was this wind which had produced the loess formation, which is met with in many parts of Northern China. It carries down all the dust of the desert and deposits it layer upon layer, till in some places it reaches a thickness of several hundred feet upon the plains of China. Counter winds meet the desert wind, and from that and other causes it is brought to a standstill, and down fall the particles of dust it has been hurrying along with it on to the ground below. In this way large tracts of China to the south of the desert are covered with the loess formation. It makes a light, very friable kind of soil, which crumbles away on the least pressure being put on it, and has a tendency to cleave vertically. In consequence of this, the roads through a loess formation present a very remarkable appearance. A cart passes over the loess. The soil breaks away, the wind blows off the dust thus formed, and a deep track is the result. Other carts follow, more loess is broken up, more dust blown away, the track gets deeper and deeper, till in the course of centuries a road is made one or two hundred feet below the level of the surrounding country; and this road is bounded on each side by perpendicular cliffs, for, as mentioned above, the loess has a vertical cleavage.

In the valley of the Yang-ho, which we were now ascending, we passed along roads of this description. They are only wide enough for the passage of one cart, and consequently, before entering the defile, we had to send on a man to shout and stop any cart coming from the opposite direction.

Donkeys I note as having been particularly fine in this

district; but a circumstance that struck me very much in North China was, that the mules produced by a cross between the donkeys and ponies of the country are very much larger than either. In Peking one used to see magnificent mules in the carts belonging to the high officials. I was told that from fifty to a hundred pounds were sometimes given for the highest class of mules; and these animals were frequently 14·2 to 15 hands in height, and fully a hand or a hand and a half higher than the ponies they were bred from.

On April 12 we passed through the Great Wall, and entered what Marco Polo calls the land of Gog and Magog. The gate of the Great Wall was not imposing, consisting as it did merely of a rough framework of wood, near which was a low hut, in which dwelt a mandarin with a small guard, and in front of which were two small cannons fastened on to a piece of timber. On either side of the gateway were large gaps in the wall—here only of mud—which carts or anything else might pass through.

On the 14th, after starting at three in the morning, we emerged on to the broad, open plain of Mongolia proper. It was a lovely morning, with a faint blue haze over the low hills, which edged the plain on each side and in the far distance; and an extraordinary bounding sense of freedom came over me as I looked on that vast grassy plain, stretching away in apparently illimitable distance all round. There was no let or hindrance—one could go anywhere, it seemed, and all nature looked bright, as if enticing us to go on. We were on a rolling plain of grass. Here and there in the distance could be seen collections of small dots, which, as we came nearer, proved to be herds of camels and cattle. Numbers of larks rose on every side and brightened the morning with their singing. Small herds of deer were frequently met with; bustard too were seen, while numbers of geese and duck were passing overhead in their flight northward.

Away across the plains we had seen some black spots with faint columns of blue smoke rising from them in the morning air. These were the yurts, or felt tents, of the Mongols, towards which we were making. On reaching them I found them to be very much what books of travel had led me to expect—dome-shaped, with a hole in the roof, made of a framework of lattice, with felt bound round on the outside. The inhabitants of one of them made room for me. A felt was spread out to lie on, and a couple of small tables placed by my side. All round the sides of the tent boxes and cupboards were neatly arranged, and at one end were some vases and images of Buddha. In the centre was the fireplace, situated directly beneath the hole in the roof. I was charmed with the comfort of the place. The Chinese inns, at which I had so far had to put up, were cold and draughty. Here the sun came streaming in through the hole in the top, and there were no draughts whatever. There was no dust either; and this being the tent of a well-to-do Mongol, it was clean and neatly arranged.

The whole family collected to see my things, and pulled my kit to pieces. The sponge was a great source of wonder; but what attracted them most of all was a concave shaving-mirror, which magnified and contorted the face in a marvellous way. They shrieked with laughter at it, and made the young girls look at their faces in it, telling them they need not be proud of their good looks, as that was what they were really like.

It was a pleasure getting among these jolly, round-faced, ruddy-cheeked Mongols, after living amongst the unhealthy-looking Chinese of the country we had been travelling through lately, who showed little friendliness or good-humour, and always seemed to cause a bad taste in the mouth. These first Mongols whom I met happened to be an unusually attractive lot. They were, of course, better off than those whom

I afterwards met with far away in the desert, and this perhaps accounted for their ever-cheery manner, which left such an agreeable impression on me.

Another attraction of this first day in Mongolia was the milk and cream—thick and rich as one could get anywhere; and here, again, was a pleasing contrast to China, where, as I have said, the cows are never milked, and none is therefore procurable.

Altogether this was one of those bright days which throw all the hardships of travel far away into the shade, and make the traveller feel that the net result of all is the highest enjoyment. The shadows have only served to show up the light, and bring out more clearly the attractions of a free, roaming life.

On the following day we entered some hilly country again. On the road we saw some partridges, which allowed the carter to walk right up to them so that he was able to hit one with his whip, and even then the others did not go, till they also were hit with the whip. At the end of the march we came upon country cultivated by Chinamen, who here, as nearly all along the borders of Mongolia, are encroaching on the Mongols, and gradually driving them out of the best country back to the desert. The slack, easy-going Mongol cannot stand before the pushing, industrious Chinaman; so back and back he goes. It is the old story which is seen all through nature—the weak and lazy succumbing to the strong and vigorous. The observer's sympathies are all with the Mongol, though, and he feels regret at seeing the cold, hard-natured Chinaman taking the place of the open-hearted Mongol.

A point to be noticed at this time of year was the rapid changes of temperature. It may be quite mild in the morning, with a soft balmy feeling in the air. Then suddenly a bitter wind will spring up, and the thermometer will instantly fall ten degrees. The inhabitants appeared to suffer much from this cause, and fevers and sickness are common at this season.

As we neared Kwei-hwa-cheng, which we reached on April 17, the country became more and more thickly populated—entirely with Chinamen, though, properly speaking, the district is part of Mongolia—and an increasing amount of traffic was met with on the roads. Numbers of the small description of carts were seen, crammed full of goods inside and out, and frequently carrying as much as 1000 catties (1380 lbs.), and the long heavy carts laden with hides. The number of Tungles was also noticeable, and sometimes in the hills would be seen the cave-houses cut into the loess.

On arrival at Kwei-hwa-cheng, I called on Mr. and Mrs. G. W. Clarke of the China Inland Mission, to whom I had a letter of introduction. I met with that warm reception which is characteristic of missionaries; a room was prepared for me, and the most real hospitality shown me. Mr. Clarke had been established here for two years now, and was, I believe, the first permanent missionary to reside in the place. I had not before met a member of the China Inland Mission in his home, and consequently was especially interested in hearing Mr. Clarke's account of his work. The zeal and energy which this mission shows is marvellous. Its members dress as Chinamen, live right away in the interior, in the very heart of China, and make it their endeavour to get really in touch with the people. They receive no regular pay, but as money comes in to the mission, enough is sent them to cover the bare expenses of living. Often, through the lack of funds, they are on the point of starving, and Mrs. Clarke told me how, upon one occasion, she had been for two or three weeks with literally no money and no food, so that she had to beg her way and sell her clothes to raise money as best she could till funds arrived from head-quarters.

The mission takes in laymen, as well as ordained ministers, and followers of varying persuasions; and there is an excellent rule that, for a year or two after coming to China, the recruits need not belong permanently to the mission; but, if they find that they are not suited for the work, can return to England. The wisdom of this rule any one can readily understand, who has seen what work in the interior of China really means, and how different it is from any conception of it which can be formed in England. It must be a stern, true heart indeed which can stand the dreary years spent almost—sometimes quite—alone in a remote Chinese town, far away from all the glamour and catching enthusiasm of a missionary meeting at home, and surrounded by cold-blooded, unemotional Chinamen who by instinct *hate* you. No comfort about you, nothing but what you have within you to keep up your enthusiasm; but, on the contrary, everything to quench it. To keep up your work under these circumstances, you must have an inexhaustible fund of zeal within you. And it is because the directors of the mission recognize that many who come out raw from England cannot have such a vast reserve of zeal, that they have wisely given every one the chance of returning. Another good principle, as I learnt from Mr. Clarke, was laid down by Mr. Hudson Taylor, the founder and director of the mission—not to appeal to the British minister or consul for assistance, except when it was absolutely necessary.

Mr. Clarke had travelled for sixteen thousand miles in China during his long sojourn as a missionary in that country, and had resided in nearly every part of it. During the Franco-Chinese war he was in Yunan, and he gave me some amusing details of the way in which troops were raised there. When the nation is at war, one would naturally suppose the standing army would be used first. But the Chinese in this, as in most other things, do precisely the opposite to every one else. The regulars said, "We must not go away from our town to fight. Our business is to defend the town. If any one attacks that, we will keep it to the last, but we must not leave it." So when the Chinese had to fight the French in Tonquin, they were obliged to send out to the farms and villages, offering men who would fight rather higher wages than they would get in ordinary civil life. In this way the generals of a district would raise a certain number of men, say a couple of thousand. These would be sent off to the war under four colonels, who would receive from government the pay for each man. But the colonels had to feather their nests, so they would give a certain number of men a premium to go off home again, and then they (the colonels) would go on drawing the pay of the absentees from government, and put it all into their own pockets. Thus, out of the two thousand who were originally sent off, probably about one thousand only would reach the seat of war, while the colonels would pocket the pay of the other thousand. So there were not half the number of troops in Tonquin that were reported to have been there.

Then the numbers of the French troops which Chinese generals reported to Peking as having been opposed to them is marvellous. I had an opportunity once of reading, side by side, the despatches of the Chinese commander (published in the *Peking Gazette*) and the despatches of the French general (published by the French Government) about the same battles. It was most instructive reading. The Chinese reported to the emperor, and the emperor, I suppose, solemnly believed, that the French had from ten to twenty times the number they really had; and the slaughter these gallant Chinese soldiers effected beats everything previously recorded in history. According to the *Peking Gazette*, no less than 1,800,000 Frenchmen were actually killed in the Tonquin war; and, according to the same authority, Admiral Courbet was killed on forty-six separate occasions.

While our preparations were in progress, Mr. Clarke and I took many walks through Kwei-hwa-cheng. It is a curious town, and seems to have outgrown itself on two separate occasions. Originally enclosed within walls about three hundred yards square, which are still remaining, it outgrew these, and an outer wall was built all round about a mile square. This also it outgrew, and large numbers of houses have been built beyond the second wall. At the time of my visit, however, the population was falling off, and the place was losing a great deal of its former importance as a depôt of trade with Mongolia. Mr. Clarke said that there were two reasons for this: firstly, because the tea, which used formerly to be brought up from Hankow to this place, and then taken across the Gobi desert to Kiakhta, is now carried by steamers to Tientsin, and thence by Kalgan to Kiakhta and Siberia; and, secondly, because the war in Kashgaria and the Tungan rebellion had almost stopped trade for some years, and it had never since revived.

Kwei-hwa-cheng used originally to be a Mongol town. It is even now included in Mongolia, and there is a Mongol prince resident in the place; but no one would believe that it was not Chinese, for it is occupied almost exclusively by Chinamen, and the Mongols are relegated to the outskirts. There are, however, some fine Buddhist temples and a large number of Mongol lamas in the city. These, Mr. Clarke says, are much less sincere in their Buddhism than the Chinese Buddhist priests. Neither ought, strictly speaking, to eat meat, and the Chinese priests as a rule do not; but the Mongols have more lax ideas, and are not above eating flesh occasionally. The scene in the Mongol bazaar, on the north side of the inner city, is very interesting. Here are seen the weather-beaten, ruddy-faced Mongols from the desert, with their huge foxskin caps and dirty sheepskin coats, coming in to buy a few necessaries, which they are unable, or rather too lazy, to make for themselves, and they bargain at the stalls, with the astute Chinese stall-keepers, for leather boots, whips, pipes, caps, and various other things. And there are the Chinese caravan-men buying up requisites for marching in the desert—camel pack-saddles, water-casks, sacks for provisions, ropes, and all the odds and ends which have to be taken. Apart from their general sunburnt and weather-beaten appearance, there is an unmistakable look about these caravan-men by which they can always be distinguished. They invariably have a peculiar slouch, a bend-over from the hips, and a stoop about the shoulders, acquired from riding night after night during those long dreary desert marches, bent over on the back of a camel, or trudging along by their side in the listless, half-sleepy way one cannot help indulging in on those monotonous plains.

The retail trade of Kwei-hwa-cheng seems to be almost entirely in articles required by travellers and by the Mongols. Good coal is obtainable within two days.

Preparations for crossing the Gobi desert to Hami had now to be made. Kwei-hwa-cheng was the last town in this direction, and the starting-point of caravans for Eastern Turkestan. Carts, or rather the mules or ponies which drew them, could go no further, so I had to discharge them and look out for camels. Sallying forth to the town on the day after my arrival, I went with Mr. Clarke to visit the establishment of one of the great firms which trade with Turkestan. Here in the yards we saw rows of neatly bound loads of merchandise, brick tea, cotton goods, silk, china, and ironmongery, all being made up ready for a caravan which was about to start for Guchen, a town some seven marches beyond Hami in the direction of Kulja. Full information about the route was now at last forthcoming, and I looked with the profoundest interest on men who had actually been to these mist-like towns of Central Asia. It appeared that there was a recognized route across the desert, and that during the winter months a caravan would start about once a month. But Guchen was the place to which the caravans ordinarily went, and Hami was only occasionally visited by them. The road to the latter place branched off at about ten marches from Hami. We were told that these caravans took from eighty to ninety days to reach Guchen, and some ten days less to Hami. Dried apricots from Hami and raisins from Turfan were apparently all that was brought back in return from Turkestan. The ordinary charge for carriage from Kwei-hwa-cheng to Guchen, I was told, was 16 taels (about £4) for a camel-load of 240 lbs. This track across the desert is, however, only used for merchants' caravans, and the official track from Kwei-hwa-cheng to Hami is by Uliasutai and Kobdo, the one followed by Mr. Ney Elias in 1872. Soldiers returning from Zungaria do so by Kiakhta and across the Gobi to Kalgan.

We did not at first succeed in finding a man who was willing to hire out camels to go on such a long journey with so small a party as ours would be. Men had no objection to travelling in large caravans, but they did not like the idea of starting across the desert with a party of only four. But I could not wait for the caravan which was about to start. By doing so I might be detained in one way and another for some weeks, and as I had the whole length of Chinese Turkestan to traverse, and to cross the Himalayas before winter closed in, I could not afford such a delay. It was fortunate for me that at this juncture I had the aid and experience of Mr. Clarke at my disposal. He was indefatigable in his search for a man, and eventually found a Chinese native of Guchen who undertook to hire me out five camels, to carry 300 lbs. each, for 180 taels (about £45), and to provide a guide to accompany my party across the desert to Hami. A solemn agreement was then drawn up, and it was stipulated that, for the above sum, we were to be landed at Hami in sixty days.

To consult a Chinese almanac for an auspicious day on which to start was the next thing to be done. The guide was very particular about this, as he said it would never do to start in a casual way on a journey like this. We must be most careful about the date of starting. The 23rd, 24th, and 25th of April were all in turn rejected, for one reason after another, and the 26th was finally settled upon as being suitable in all respects.

In the meanwhile there was plenty of work to be done, laying in provisions and providing ourselves with every possible necessary. Nothing would be procurable on the way except perhaps a sheep here and there, so we had to buy up supplies of all kinds sufficient to last the party for two months. Some people think that on a journey it is absolutely necessary to make themselves as uncomfortable as possible. But I had learnt by experience to think otherwise, and determined to treat myself as well as circumstances would permit, so that, when it should become really necessary to rough it (as it afterwards did during the passage of the Himalayas), I should be fit and able to do it. So, besides a couple of sacks of flour, a sack of rice, and thirty tins of beef, which were to be our main stand-by, I had also brought from Peking such luxuries as a few tins of preserved milk, butter, and soup; and here in Kwei-hwa-cheng I procured some dried apricots and raisins, a sack of Mongolian mushrooms, which gave a most excellent relish to the soup, another sack of potatoes, a bag of dried beans, which Mr. Clarke gave me, and lastly some oatmeal. All these luxuries added very little really to the total amount of baggage, and even if they had made an extra camel-load, it would not have hindered the journey in any way, while they added very considerably to my efficiency.

A tent was made up in the town on what is known in India as the Kabul pattern; but, as it afterwards turned out, this was, for travelling in the desert, about the very worst description of tent possible. The violent winds so constant there catch the walls of it and make it almost impossible to keep the tent standing. What I would recommend for future travellers is a tent like my guide's, sloping down to the ground at the ends as well as on each side, and with no straight wall anywhere to catch the wind.

Rather unusual articles of equipment were two water-casks, which we filled with water daily on the march, so that if, as sometimes happened, we lost our way and missed the well, or found it choked with sand, we should always have something to fall back on.

CHAPTER V.

ACROSS THE GOBI DESERT.

> "But here—above, around, below,
> On mountain or on glen,
> Nor tree, nor shrub, nor plant, nor flower,
> The weary eye may ken."
>
> SCOTT.

THE auspicious day, April 26, having at length arrived, I had reluctantly to say good-bye to my kind and hospitable friends—the last of my countrymen I should see for many a month to come—and take my plunge into the Gobi and the far unknown beyond. It was like going for a voyage; all supplies were taken, and everything made snug and ready. Ours was a compact little party—the camel-man, who acted as guide, a Mongol assistant, my Chinese "boy," eight camels, and myself. Chang-san, the interpreter, had gone back to Peking, feeling himself unable to face the journey before us, and so I was left to get on as best I could, in half-English, half-Chinese, with the boy, Liu-san. The guide was a doubled-up little man, whose eyes were not generally visible, though they sometimes beamed out from behind his wrinkles and pierced one like a gimlet. He was a wonderful man, and possessed a memory worthy of a student of Stokes. The way in which he remembered where the wells were, at each march in the desert, was simply marvellous. He would be fast asleep on the back of a camel, leaning right over with his head either resting on the camel's hump, or dangling about beside it, when he would suddenly wake up, look first at the stars, by which he could tell the time to a quarter of an hour, and then at as much of the country as he could see in the dark. After a time he would turn the camel off the track a little, and sure enough we would find ourselves at a well. The extraordinary manner in which he kept the way surpasses anything I know of. As a rule no track at all could be seen, especially in the sandy districts; but he used to lead us somehow or other, generally by the droppings of the camels of previous caravans, and often by tracks which they had made, which were so faint that I could not distinguish them myself even when pointed out to me. A camel does not leave much of an impression upon gravel, like a beaten-down path in a garden; but the guide, from indications here and there, managed to make out their tracks even in the dark. Another curious thing about him was the way he used to go to sleep walking. His natural mode of progression was by bending right forward, and this seemed to keep him in motion without any trouble to himself, and he might be seen mooning along fast asleep. He had, however, one failing—he was a confirmed opium-smoker; directly camp was pitched he would have out his opium pipe, and he used to smoke off and on till we started again. I was obliged occasionally to differ in opinion from this gentleman, as will be seen further on; but, on the whole, we got on well together, and my feelings towards him at parting were more of sorrow than of anger, for he had a hard life of it going backwards and forwards up and down across the desert almost continuously for twenty years; and his inveterate habit of opium-smoking had used up all the savings he ought to have accumulated after his hard life.

The Mongol assistant, whose name was Ma-te-la, was a careless, good-natured fellow, always whistling or singing, and bursting out into roars of laughter at the slightest thing, especially at any little mishap. He used to think it the best possible joke if a camel deposited one of my boxes on to the ground and knocked the lid off. He never ceased wondering at all my things, and was as pleased as a child with a new toy when I gave him an empty corned-beef tin when he left me. That treasure of an old tin is probably as much prized by his family now as some jade-bowls which I brought back from Yarkand are by mine.

Poor Ma-te-la had to do a most prodigous amount of work. He had to walk the whole—or very nearly the whole—of each march, leading the first camel; then, after unloading the camels, and helping to pitch the tents, he would have to scour the country round for the argals or droppings of camels, which were generally the only thing we could get for fuel. By about two in the morning he could probably get some sleep; but he had to lie down amongst the camels in order to watch them, and directly day dawned he would get up and take them off to graze. This meant wandering for miles and miles over the plain, as the camels are obliged to pick up a mouthful of scrub, here and there, where they can, and consequently range over a considerable extent of ground. He would come into camp again for a short time for his dinner, and then go off again, and gradually drive the camels up to be ready for the start; then he would have to help to load them, and start off on the march again. It used to seem to me fearfully hard work for him, but he never appeared any the worse for it, and was always bright and cheery. I gave him a mount one day on one of my camels, but he would never get up again, as he said the guide would give him no wages if he did.

There were eight camels. I rode one myself, four others carried my baggage and stores, and my servant rode on the top of one of these baggage camels; of the remaining three, one carried the water, one was laden with brick tea, which is used in place of money for buying things from the Mongols, and the third was loaded with the men's things. The total weight of my baggage, with the two months' stores, servant's cooking things, camp equipage, etc., was 1416 lbs.

We left Kwei-hwa-cheng by the north gate of the town, and,

after passing for some five miles over a well-cultivated plain, began to ascend the great buttress range on to the Mongolian plateau. This range, called the In-shan, is, as it were, a support to the highlands of Mongolia, and forms the step up on to them. Crossing these mountains the following day, we afterwards entered an undulating hilly country, inhabited principally by Chinese. Villages were numerous, cart-tracks led in every direction, and the valleys were well cultivated. There were also large meadows of good grass, where immense flocks of sheep were feeding; but I was astonished to see that, although we were now in Mongolia, the largest and best flocks were tended by and belonged to Chinese, who have completely ousted the Mongols in the very thing which, above all, ought to be their speciality. It is really a fact that the Chinese come all the way from the province of Shantung to these Mongolian pasture-lands to fatten sheep for the Peking market. Here is another instance of the manner in which the pushing and industrious Chinaman is forcing his way, and gradually driving back the less persevering inhabitants of the country on which he encroaches; and it seems probable that the Chinese from the south, and the Russians from the north, will, in course of time, gradually force the poor Mongols into the depth of the desert.

Seeing all these flocks of sheep, it occurred to me that it might be worth while for some of our merchants to set up a wool-trade. There is a large amount of excellent grazing ground in Southern Mongolia, and it would only be a question whether the cost of carriage to Tientsin would make it possible to compete with the Australian.

Messrs. G. W. Collins and Co., of Tientsin, have already set up a trade in camels' wool, which they obtain from this part of Mongolia through their agent who lives at Kwei-hwa-cheng. A beautifully soft warm cloth is made from this camel-wool, than which nothing could be better for wear in winter.

The Mongolian camel* has very long hair in winter, which it sheds in summer. A few years ago a European merchant travelled through Southern Mongolia and established a trade in this wool, so that now the Mongols and Chinese caravan-men save it up instead of wasting it, as formerly, and bring it in for sale at Kwei-hwa-cheng.

I was warned to look out for robbers about here. Some uncanny-looking gentlemen came prowling about my camp one day, and the guide told me to keep my eye well on them and have my revolver ready. I was in some anxiety about my Chinese boy, Liu-san. He knew I must have a lot of money with me, though he did not know exactly where, for I hid it away in all sorts of places; one lump of silver in a sack of flour, another in an empty beef-tin, and so on. So I was at first afraid that if a loaded revolver were given him, he might make it very unpleasant for me one day in the wilds. So, to inspire awe of our party in outsiders, I gave him an unloaded revolver; but afterwards, thinking that doing things by halves was little good, I loaded it for him, and told him that I had the most complete trust in him. He and I must be true to each other; I would look after him, and he must look after me. The plan answered admirably; he used to swagger about with the revolver, showed it to everybody he met, and told the most abominable lies about the frightful execution he could do with it. Nobody can lie with such good effect as a Chinaman, and as he told the gaping Mongols and Turkis, that though he could only bowl over about twenty men at a time with his weapon, I was bristling all over with much more deadly instruments, they used to look upon me with the greatest awe, and I never had the semblance of a disturbance on the whole of my journey.

* I refer my readers to a most excellent description of this camel, its habits and peculiarities, given by Prjevalsky in his book "Mongolia," translated by Mr. Delmar Morgan.

Liu-san's propensity for fibbing was not always so fortunate, and he used to annoy me considerably at times by telling people that I was a man of great importance, with the object, of course, of enhancing his own. I used to see him button-hole a grave old Turki, and tell him in a subdued whisper, with mysterious glances at me, that I was "Yăng-ta-jên," the great man Young(husband), an influential envoy from Peking, and that the utmost respect must be shown to me. Then he would pretend to be very obsequious to me, and bow and kow-tow in the most servile manner. It was hard to know whether to be angry with him or to laugh over it; he was always so very comical about it. There would be a twinkle in his eye the whole time, and now and then, while all this was going on, he used to say to me in English (*his* English), "I think master belong big gentleman; no belong small man." He thought I was a big gentleman quite off his head, though, to go wandering about in such out-of-the-way places, instead of staying comfortably at home; and he used to say, "I think master got big heart; Chinese mandarin no do this."

In this part of the country we used to see a great many herds of deer—the Chinese huang-yang—and the Mongol hunters have a very curious way of shooting them. They set up a long row of big stones, placed at intervals of about ten yards apart, across the usual track of the deer; the deer, as they come along over the smooth plain, are so surprised at such an extraordinary sight that they pause and have a look at the curious phenomenon. Then the wary Mongol hunter, crouching behind one of these stones, applies the slowmatch to the flash-pan of his matchlock and shoots the nearest deer.

We passed several Mongol temples and Lamaseries, white-washed and clean looking. On the top of a mound near one of our camping-grounds I saw a peculiar small temple or tomb, which I examined more closely; it was a rough heap of stones, and contained a tablet inside a niche. I was looking at this, when I was driven off with ignominy by some ravens which had their nest in it. They screeched and hovered about within a few inches of my eyes in such an unpleasant way that I, having no stick, beat a hasty retreat to camp.

On May 7 we emerged from the undulating hilly country, and, after crossing a small stream called the Moli-ho, came on to an extensive plain bounded on the north, at a distance of five or six miles, by a barren, rugged range of hills, at the foot of which could be seen some Mongol yurts, and a conspicuous white temple; while to the south, at a distance of about twenty miles, were the Sheitung-ula Mountains (called by the Chinese, the Liang-lang-shan, or Eurh-lang-shan), which lie along the north bank of the Yellow river, and were explored in 1873 by Prjevalsky. My guide had a tradition about these mountains that, five or six hundred years ago, a Chinese force of five thousand men was besieged on a hill by a Mongol force. They had been enticed into these deserts by the Mongols, who knew where all the water was to be found, while the Chinese, being unable to procure any, suffered terribly, and only a thousand survived; ever since the Chinese emperor has paid money to the Mongol prince to keep quiet.

A caravan from Guchen passed us on the 8th. There were about a hundred and fifty camels, mostly unladen, but several carried boxes of silver. This was the only caravan we met coming from the west; it had left Guchen sixty days previously.

The following day we passed close by a spur from the northern range of hills, which appeared to be of volcanic origin. The range presented a most fantastic appearance, rising in sharp rugged peaks. It consists of a series of sharp parallel ridges with intervening strips of plain, perhaps a quarter of a mile wide. In Manchuria we had also found indications of old volcanoes in the Chang-pei-shan, or Long White Mountain, and the river of lava between Kirin and Ninguta, while signs of volcanic action are to be seen in the Tian-shan Mountains, as was first noticed by Humboldt, and afterwards confirmed by Russian travellers.

A small stream—here a few inches deep only, flowing over a wide pebbly bed—runs down from these hills. My guide called it the Ho-lai-liu, and it is probably identical with the stream which Prjevalsky crossed on the southern side of the Sheitung-ula.

We encamped near it on the 10th, in a spot bounded on the south by a low round range of hills, or rather undulations. During the morning I set off to look at this, thinking it was a couple of miles or so distant, but the distances are most deceptive here, and I found myself at the top in ten minutes; it was merely an undulation. A few days previously I had strolled out casually to a hill which appeared to be about five minutes' walk off, but was obliged to walk fast for half an hour before I got there. There is nothing to guide the eye—no objects, as men or trees, to judge by; only a bare plain and a bare smooth hillside are to be seen in front, and it is hard to say whether a hill is half a mile or two miles distant. On this occasion I was glad to find it was only half a mile, as I had more time to examine the country round. We were between two parallel ranges. The intervening country is undulating, the depressions being generally sandy, while the slopes are of alluvial deposit, covered with a reddish clay, which supports a scanty crop of coarse grass and scrubby plants. A few flowers of stunted growth appear occasionally, but they evidently have a hard struggle for existence with the severe climate of these deserts. The flower that flourishes most in this region is the iris, which does not, however, attain a greater height than six or eight inches, though occasionally it is seen in clumps growing to a height of one or one and a half feet. In the next march I climbed a small rocky hill, on which I found wild peach in full bloom, growing luxuriantly in the clefts, and also yellow roses. Later on, among the lower ridges of the Altai Mountains, I found white roses.

We were now gradually approaching the heart of the Gobi, and the aspect of the country became more and more barren; the streams disappeared, and water could only be obtained from the rough wells or water-holes dug by former caravans. No grass could be seen, and in its place the country was covered with dry and stunted plants, burnt brown by the sun by day and nipped by the frost by night. Not a sound would be heard, and scarcely a living thing seen, as we plodded along slowly, yet steadily, over those seemingly interminable plains. Sometimes I would strike off from the road, and ascend some rising ground to take a look round. To the right and left would be ranges of bare hills, very much resembling those seen in the Gulf of Suez, with rugged summits and long even slopes of gravel running down to the plain, which extended apparently without limit in front of me. And there beneath was my small caravan, mere specks on that vast expanse of desolation, and moving so slowly that it seemed impossible that it could ever accomplish the great distance which had to be passed before Hami could be reached.

Our usual plan was to start at about three in the afternoon, and travel on till midnight or sometimes later. This was done partly to avoid the heat of the day, which is very trying to the loaded camels, but chiefly to let the camels feed by daylight, as they cannot be let loose to feed at night for fear of their wandering too far and being lost. Any one can imagine the fearful monotony of those long dreary marches seated on the back of a slow and silently moving camel. While it was light I would read and even write; but soon the sun would set before us, the stars would appear one by one, and through the long dark hours we would go silently on, often finding our way by the aid of the stars alone, and marking each as it sank below the horizon, indicating how far the night was advanced. At length the guide would give the signal to halt, and the camels, with an unmistakable sigh of relief, would sink to the ground; their loads would quickly be taken off; before long camp would be pitched, and we would turn in to enjoy a well-earned sleep, with the satisfaction of having accomplished one more march on that long desert journey.

Camp was astir again, however, early in the morning, and by eight I used to get up, and after breakfast stroll about to see what was to be seen, then write up my diary, plot out the map, have dinner at one or two, and then prepare for the next march. And so the days wore on with monotonous regularity for ten whole weeks.

But though these marches were very monotonous, yet the nights were often extremely beautiful, for the stars shone out with a magnificence I have never seen equalled even in the heights of the Himalayas. Venus was a resplendent object, and it guided us over many a mile of that desert. The Milky Way, too, was so bright that it looked like a bright phosphorescent cloud, or as a light cloud with the moon behind it. This clearness of the atmosphere was probably due to its being so remarkably dry. Everything became parched up, and so charged with electricity, that in opening out a sheep-skin coat or a blanket a loud cracking noise would be given out, accompanied by a sheet of fire. A very peculiar and unlooked-for result of this remarkable dryness of the atmosphere was the destruction of a highly cherished coat of mine which Sir John Walsham had given me just before I left Peking, saying that it would last me for ever; and so it would have done anywhere else but in the Gobi Desert. It was made of a very closely woven canvas material, and to all appearance was indestructible, but it is a fact that before a month was over, that coat was in shreds. From the extreme dryness it got brittle, and wherever creases were formed, it broke in long rents. The outside bend of the elbow of the sleeve was as sound as on the day it was bought, but the inside of the bend was cut to pieces, and split wherever it had been creased by the elbow.

The temperature used to vary very considerably. Frosts continued to the end of May, but the days were often very hot, and were frequently hottest at nine or ten in the morning, for later on a strong wind would usually spring up, blowing sometimes with extreme violence, up till sunset, when it generally subsided again. If this wind was from the north, the weather was fine but cold. If it was from the south, it would be warmer, but clouds would collect and rain would sometimes fall; generally, however, the rain would pass off into steam before reaching the ground. Ahead of us we would see rain falling heavily, but before it reached the ground it would gradually disappear—vanish away—and when we reached the spot over which the rain had been falling, there would not be a sign of moisture on the ground.

The daily winds, of which I have just spoken, were often extremely disagreeable. It was with the greatest difficulty that we could keep our tents from being blown down, and everything used to become impregnated with the sand, which found its way everywhere, and occasionally we had to give up our march because the camels could not make any head against the violence of the wind.

After crossing the connecting ridge between Sheitung-ula and the mountains, we passed through some very dreary country—a plain between parallel ranges of hills. The soil was either sandy or covered with small pebbles, and was dotted over with clumps of furze, which flowered almost exclusively on the southern side, the cold blast of the north wind nipping the flowers in the bud on the northern side. Extracts from my diary will best illustrate the description of country we now passed through.

May 13.—A very disagreeable windy day. The sand penetrates everywhere; you do not see the sand in the air, but everything in the tent gradually gets covered with a coating of it. The country is extremely dreary looking—nothing but sandhills everywhere, and the air hazy with the particles of sand. Every evening about five we see herds and flocks slowly wending their way over the plain and converging on the water near the camp, but only the sheep seem to be attended by any one, and there is scarcely ever a yurt in sight.

The ponies go about in a semi-wild state, in troops of about twenty mares, under the guardianship of one or more stallions, who drive them about from place to place seeking something to graze on. They are entirely free, and every evening at sunset they march slowly back to the Mongol yurt. The Mongols have great difficulty in getting hold of one when they want it. They chevy the selected pony, riding after him with a long pole having a noose at the end, which they at last succeed in throwing over his head.

On the 13th we passed through some low hills, and then descended a valley in which were some gnarled and stunted elm trees—the first trees I have seen in Mongolia. They were about thirty feet high, and evidently very old. We then passed over a sandy, barren waste, the beginning of the Galpin Gobi, the very worst part of the whole desert. We met a small caravan of Mongols, and passed the encampment of a large caravan going from Bautu to Guchen.

May 14.—A very strong wind sprang up E. by N. in the morning and blew all day, and in the evening it was too strong to march, so we halted to-day. There is no mistake about the desert now—a sandy waste in every direction, with scrub in patches; irises are very common in small clumps.

May 15.—A very strong wind again to-day. I waited

till nearly sunset for it to abate, but it only seemed to increase. However, I started. Before long dark clouds gathered, it blew harder, and finally began to rain heavily. It was now pitch dark, and the guide was literally feeling the way with his hands; so we halted and camped, only having accomplished about three miles. The caravan from Bautu did not attempt to march.

In my diary I apparently have merely recorded the fact that we halted and camped, but I remember well how hard it was to camp that night. The darkness was so great that we could not see a yard in front of us, a regular hurricane was blowing, and heavy bursts of drenching rain kept falling at intervals. The lantern could not be lighted, on account of the violence of the wind, and we had to grope about amongst the camels, get the loads off, feel for the tent, and then get that up as best we could—which was no easy matter, for the wind blowing against it nearly blew us off our legs, and it was all we could do to prevent the whole thing from being carried away.

The following day we continued over the Galpin Gobi, and it was most difficult to find our way, as the previous day's storm had obliterated all tracks. The guide, however, found the well in the most wonderful manner.

May 17.—We continued over the plain, which was covered with scrub, but there were a few tufts of coarse grass. A good many herds of camels were seen, and some ponies and sheep. Quantities of partridges rose from the scrub—many so tame that I used to chevy them running along the ground. They were generally in couples.

At eight o'clock a terrific wind blew up and dark clouds gathered, so that after trying to push on a bit we were obliged to halt, as it threatened to rain very heavily. Putting up a tent in a sandstorm is one of the most irritating things I know of. No sooner do you hammer a peg in than it is pulled up again by the force of the wind; the sand gets driven into your eyes as you kneel to drive in the pegs; and to add to it all, it was pitch dark, and heavy spurts of rain would come driving down at intervals. Tents with walls are not fit for this hard work, as the walls offer too much resistance to the wind.

May 18.—A fearful wind blew the whole day, with sand and occasional bursts of rain. Two Mongols encamped with us. They slept in a makeshift tent of felts supported by sticks, leaving just room enough for the men to lie down with a fire between them.

The guide wanted to halt on account of the wind, but I objected, and we started at 6.30 p.m., travelling on towards the range of hills in a westerly direction. The wind subsided at sunset, and it was a fine night; but the sand had been blown over the track, so that we lost our way and were compelled to halt at 11.30 p.m. in the middle of the plain, without sign of water.

May 19.—Luckily we had brought a little water in our water-casks, and so had enough for breakfast; but we had to start afterwards, as we could not remain without water.

We started at 11 a.m., and soon found the track, as we had the range to guide us, and at five miles reached a well; but after watering the camels we pushed on for the next well, gradually ascending the range, which I now found to be the eastern extremity of the Hurku Hills, the highest part of which was 700 feet above the plain, the track crossing it at 630 feet. We can realize how deceptive the distances are here. Some days ago we first saw this range, and I thought that we should reach it at the end of that march, but we have taken four days to do so. We passed over a plateau at the top of the range for three and a half miles, and then descended very gradually to the plain again, camping at 7.10 p.m. near a well.

The hills are very barren, but have a few low bushes scattered over their surface, which serve as food for the camels which roam among them. They present a jagged outline, the prominences being of bare igneous rock, but the depressions are filled with gravel of a grey colour.

May 20.—A really delightful morning. The desert is not so dreary after all; for no artist could wish for a finer display of colouring than the scene presents this morning. Overhead is a spotless, clear blue sky, and beneath it the plain has lost its dull monotonous aspect, fading away in various shades of blue, each getting deeper and deeper, till the hills are reached; and these again, in their rugged outline, present many a pleasing variety of colour, all softened down with a hazy bluish tinge; while the deceitful mirage makes up for the absence of water in the scene, and the hills are reflected again in what appear to be lovely lakes of clear, still water.

For two marches we kept gradually ascending towards a watershed, connecting the Hurku with a similar but somewhat lower range running parallel to the road, eight or ten miles to the south. Crossing this connecting ridge, we arrived at the Bortson well in the early hours of the morning of the 22nd.

There were a few Mongol yurts here on the banks of some small trickles of water, running down from the Hurku Hills to the north. Here I crossed Prjevalsky's track. In his first, and also in his third journey, he had crossed the Galpin Gobi from the south, and passed through this place on his way northward to Urga. The description he gives of the Galpin Gobi is not cheerful. He says, "This desert is so terrible that in comparison with it the deserts of Northern Tibet may be called fruitful. There, at all events, you may find water and good pasturage in the valleys: here there is neither, not even a single oasis—everywhere the silence of the Valley of Death. The Hurku Hills are the northern definition of the wildest and most sterile part of the Gobi."

The Galpin Gobi, where I crossed it to the Hurku Hills, could be seen extending as far as the eye could reach to the N.E. Where Prjevalsky crossed it its width was eighteen miles only, and it was 3570 feet above the sea. The Mongols there told him that it extended to the east and to the west for twenty days' march. It forms a marked depression in the great Mongolian plateau, and is a distinct dividing-line between the Altai and the In-shan mountain systems, for I will show presently that the Hurku Hills may be regarded as the prolongation of the former mountains.

On the 22nd we continued along the southern base of the Hurku Hills, passing over an almost level plain of an extremely desolate appearance. It was composed of a grey gravel, and was covered with small tufts of plants perfectly scorched up. What little there had been of spring green is already disappearing, and the young grass and plants which have had the courage to show themselves are withering, and all is brown and bare.

On the 22nd we had the misfortune to lose one of our camels; he shied at something, broke loose, threw his load (luckily), and disappeared into the darkness. He was never heard of again, although we hunted most of the night and all the next day till the evening.

After this we crossed some low hills running down from the Hurku range, and arrived on the banks of a delightful small stream, about a foot wide and a few inches deep, with some patches of green grass on its margin. Here we halted for three days to buy a couple of new camels. There were several Mongol yurts about here, and we had visits from some of the men. They are very fine-looking, tall, strong, muscular fellows, more like what one would expect of the descendants of Chenghiz Khan than any other Mongols. They were, however, very childish, amused at everything, and very rough in their manners.

The caravan from Bautu which was passed on the road on the 13th, caught us up here and pitched camp close by.

There were a hundred and forty camels, carrying made-up clothes and leathern boots to Guchen. Their camp looked very neat. The packs were arranged in long parallel lines, and were very neatly done up, and everything looked brand new. When it threatened rain, each pack was covered with a white felt, which was tied round it. The coolies had one big tent, and the agent a smaller one. The former were smart fellows, and did their work wonderfully quickly and well. They were Chinamen from Kwei-hwa-cheng. The agent in charge came over to visit me, and we had a long talk, for I had begun to pick up a certain amount of Chinese from my nightly conversations with Liu-san. This agent had been to Tientsin, and had bought there a few Remington and Martini-Henry rifles, and also a Gatling gun for the general at Urumchi. He said that from Ili (Kueldja) the usual road to Peking was by Kobdo, Uliassutai, and Kiakhta. It is one hundred and ten stages by the road— a distance which he says he rode in twenty-eight days upon one occasion, when taking an important despatch, at the time of the retrocession of Kueldja to China by Russia.

Two new camels having been purchased, we set out again on the 28th, in spite of the violent wind that was blowing; but we did not get far, and had to halt again the whole of the next day on account of the wind. Although it was now the end of May, the cold at night was still considerable, and I have noted that in bed I wore two flannel shirts and a cardigan jacket, lying under two thick blankets. It was the wind that made it cold, blowing from the W.N.W. and N.W.

On May 31 we passed over an undulating country covered with coarse grass. Several flocks and herds were seen, and to the south there appeared to be good grass-land in the depression between the Hurku Hills and a parallel range, ten or twelve miles to the south. According to a Mongol who visited us, there is some land cultivated by Mongols four miles to the south at Huru-su-tai. At seven and a half miles we passed a small stream of good water.

In the next few days we passed along a plain lying between the Hurku Hills and the southern parallel range, for which I could get no name. We saw a peak of the Hurku Hills, which my Mongol called Baroso-khai, and in some clefts, near the summit, we could see patches of snow.

We passed several Mongol encampments, and one day a Mongol official came to visit me. He was an old man, and not interesting, showing no signs of ordinary intelligence. He had bad eyes, and I gave him some of Calvert's carbolic ointment to rub on the eyelids, for which he did not appear at all thankful. He fished about in the leg of his long boot, and produced from it a miscellaneous collection of articles—a pipe, a small piece of string, some camel's wool, a piece of paper, and various odds and ends, and eventually my ointment was done up in a suitable packet to his satisfaction, and stowed away again in the leg of his boot.

The Mongols carry about half their personal effects in their boots, and my man, Ma-te-la, one day produced from his boots every little scrap that I had thrown away during the march, such as bits of paper, ends of string, a worn-out sock, and numerous other trifles. Everything is so precious to these Mongols in the desert that they never waste anything, and I soon learnt the value they put on every little article.

Liu-san one day took me to task severely for giving away an old lime-juice bottle to an ordinary Mongol. He said such valuable gifts ought to be reserved for the big men. So the next "swell" I came across was presented with a lime-juice bottle with great state, and he was given to understand that he was not likely to get such gifts as that every day in the week, and that he was lucky to have come across such a generous gentleman as myself.

As we passed Mongol encampments, men used to come

galloping over the plain to know if we had anything for sale, and to beg some tobacco of us. The Chinese guide would never give them any, although he had plenty; but poor Ma-te-la always used to give them a pinch or two, or, at any rate, a piece of brown paper—which he would produce from his boot, and which was probably a relic of something I had thrown away. Liu-san never smoked or drank—he said he was a teetotaller, and was afraid even of my lime-juice.

The ponies about here are very good, stout, sturdy little animals, up to any amount of work, but more fit for riding purposes than the miniature cart-horses which we had seen in the extreme eastern end of Mongolia, on the steppes near Tsi-tsi-har in Manchuria. Those were wonderful little animals, and were always used by the Chinese carters to put in the shafts, although they were never more than thirteen hands high—while the cart used to carry a load of sometimes two tons, being dragged along by six or seven animals (ponies and mules) in front, but with only this one sturdy little animal in the shafts.

On June 3, just as we were preparing to start, we saw a great dark cloud away in the distance over the plain. It was a dust storm coming towards us. Where we were it was quite still, and the sky was bright overhead, and perfectly clear, but away to the west we saw the dark clouds—as black as night. Gradually they overspread the whole sky, and as the storm came nearer we heard a rumbling sound, and then it burst upon us with terrific force, so that we were obliged to lie at full length on the ground behind our baggage. There was fortunately no sand about—we were on a gravel plain—but the small pebbles were being driven before the wind with great velocity, and hurt us considerably. The storm lasted for half an hour, and it was then as calm and bright as before, and much cooler.

We still marched over this steppe country. There are

SANDHILLS IN THE GOBI DESERT.

ranges of hills on either hand, about fifteen miles distant on the north and ten miles on the south, and the plain occupies the space between them, which is not quite flat, however, but slopes gradually up to the hills on either hand. The distances, as usual, are most deceptive; the ranges look quite close, as if you could get up to them easily in an hour, and the mountains ahead appear comparatively close, but you travel on and on and don't seem to get any nearer to the distant hills, while the peaks on your right and left are only very slowly left behind.

On the 4th we reached a Mongol encampment, called Tu-pu-chi. This is the most thickly populated part I have seen in the Gobi, as there were several other yurts scattered over the plain. The guide had left a large supply of flour and rice here on a previous trip, and now replenished the stock he had with him. The Mongols looked very poor, thin, and badly fed, and were miserably dressed. Their flocks of sheep, though, were in first-class condition, and were collected round the different yurts. We continued on about another six miles, and then halted by some more yurts, where a new Mongol joined our party to look after the camels.

On the following day we crossed a ridge connecting the Hurku Hills with the southern range, and descended a wide valley or plain between those two ranges on the western side of the connecting ridge. Between us and the southern range was a most remarkable range of sandhills, called by my guide Hun-kua-ling. It is about forty miles in length, and is composed of bare sand, without a vestige of vegetation of any sort on it, and I computed it in places to be as much as nine hundred feet in height, rising abruptly out of a gravel plain. With the dark outline of the southern hills as a background, this white fantastically shaped sand-range presents a very striking appearance. It must have been formed by the action of the wind, for to the westward is an immense sandy tract, and it is evident that the wind has driven the sand from this up into the hollow between the Hurku Hills and the range to the south, thus forming these remarkable sandhills. Tradition corroborates this supposition, for the Mongols say that a large force had been collected, and was preparing to march to China, when a mighty wind arose, blowing the sand of the desert against them and burying them all together, with several villages and temples. At the present time a stream runs along the northern foot of the range; this stream has some patches of meadow land on its banks, on which are pitched several groups of Mongol yurts.

The country we passed through was undulating, sloping downwards towards the range. In parts the soil was firm gravel, and in parts very loose sand—much more loose than ordinary sand. It seems to me that this is sand formed by wind, and not by water; it is finer and more gritty. The actual surface is very thinly coated with grey gravel, but this is so thin that each footstep leaves a mark in white from the underlying sand.

After passing the end of the sand-range, we entered a country different from any we had yet gone through. In origin it was probably a plain of sand, but the wind's action has broken it up into sandhills and depressions, making up a scene which, for its extreme wildness and desolation, surpasses anything I have ever seen. The elements of the air seem to have fought with and rent the very surface of the land, and the scene is one of indescribable confusion. To add to the weirdness of the spectacle, the country was covered with tamarisk bushes, the roots of which had been laid bare by the wind blowing the sand away. There they stood, with their gnarled and contorted roots exposed to view. The sandhills were sometimes very quaint and curious in shape, but they usually ran in long ridges, cutting into one another from every direction. They rise in the most sudden manner out of a level piece of ground, sometimes to a height of a hundred feet or even more.

This is a general section of them. At A the sand drops suddenly at a slope of ¼. A is a little below the highest point

of the hillock, and the edge it represents runs in an absolutely straight line through the length of the sandhill. The line of intersection with the ground (if the ground is level) is also absolutely straight, so that, looking towards the steep side, the sandhill presents the appearance of a well-constructed fortification. Every bush and piece of scrub on the plain has hillocks of sand on the leeward side. This is conspicuous, as the sand is white and the surroundings dark gravel. It seems to me that the sandhills are formed thus: A strong wind blows from the west, say, forming hillocks to the east of the bushes. At places where the bushes are close together, one hillock runs into another, several thus forming one big hillock. In the case of big ranges, I think it must have been started by a number of trees* growing on the stretch of fertile ground, or perhaps by a village, or a number of temples, as tradition says. The sand-range does not rest against any solid range, but occupies a position by itself between two ranges from fifteen to twenty miles apart, thus—

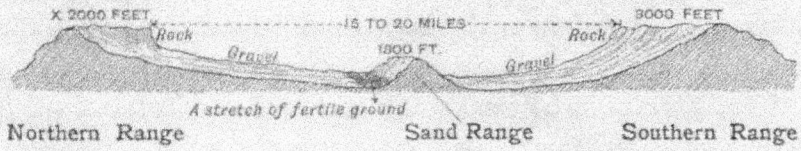

The plain between these two ranges is of gravel, underneath

* There are trees now growing in the neighbourhood to a height of twelve or fifteen feet, and these are sometimes in clumps of forty or fifty.

which is sand. Near Pidjan I saw a similar though lower range, and Prjevalsky mentions seeing one near Sachow.

The Hurku Hills come to an end here, and we could see before us across the plain, at a distance of eighty miles, the outlying spurs of the Altai Mountains; but though the former terminated here as a continuous range, yet they are connected to a certain extent, by a series of isolated hills to the north, with the Altai Mountains. This connection may, perhaps, be best illustrated by supposing the country to be flooded to a height of about four thousand feet above ordinary sea-level. Then on the west would be seen the great headlands of the Altai Mountains; on the east two capes (the Hurku Hills and the southern range) running out into the ocean. To the north would be a series of islands, stepping-stones as it were, forming the connection between the Hurku Hills and the Altai Mountains. To the south would be the open sea.

The Hurku range has an extreme length of about two hundred and twenty miles. It is highest in the western end, where it presents rather the appearance of a string of elongated ridges than of a continuous range, as it does further east. Its highest point is the prominent mountain, for which I obtained the name Barosakhai, but which I have not the slightest doubt is identical with the mountain called by the Russian traveller Pevstof, Gourbaun-Seikyn.* The height of this mountain is probably about eight thousand feet above the sea, and it had slight snow on it in the middle of June.

The ridges to the west of this have a height of about seven thousand feet; while to the east, where Prjevalsky crossed the range, it was 6120 feet above sea-level, and from that point it still diminishes in height to the eastward—at its termination having an approximate height of five thousand feet. Its width, where Prjevalsky crossed, is seven miles. Throughout it pre-

* I found it very hard to get at the proper pronunciation from the Mongols. The *n*'s are scarcely heard, and it is possible I may not have caught them.

sents a bare, sterile appearance, though a few plants mentioned by Prjevalsky, including the peach, may be found in places.

The range which runs parallel to the Hurku Hills, almost throughout their entire length, is very similar in general character, but is usually at a lower elevation—the difference in height varying from four or five hundred to a thousand feet. At the western extremity, however, the southern is the more elevated of the two by about eight hundred or a thousand feet.

On June 8, towards dark, after passing through the sand-hills, we approached a low range of hills. The guide halted here and told me to take out my revolver, as, he said, the hills were a favourite resort of robbers. So I dismounted and went on ahead of the caravan, revolver in hand; the boy and the guide (the latter armed with a tent-pole) each took a flank. We took the bell off the camel, and approached the hills in dead silence. It was most sensational, as it was now quite dark, and we could see nothing but the black outline of the hills against the sky, while the absence of the "tingle-tingle" of the bell made the death-like silence of the desert still more impressive.

When we got close up to the range, the guide said we had better wait till daylight, as the robbers had a nasty habit of rolling big stones down upon caravans going through the pass. So we put on our sheepskins, and lay down on the ground till day broke, taking it in turns to watch.

The Mongol said he had seen a horseman riding to the hill while it was dusk, and my boy occasionally conjured up images of others riding about, and let off his revolver twice; but nothing happened, and we resumed our march at 3.30, still on the defensive, with our revolvers in our hands, as the hills we now entered had plenty of suitable hiding-places for brigands. Nothing could be wilder or more desolate than these hills—utterly devoid of vegetation, and covered with a dark gravel.

On the summit of each little knoll was a heap of stones, which, in the dark, we should inevitably have mistaken for men, and probably have wasted a lot of ammunition on them, as the guide was careful to tell me that if I did not shoot any man I saw sharp, he (the brigand, not the guide) would shoot me. We halted at 6.30, near a small water-hole in the valley.

We started again soon after four in the afternoon, and an hour later reached the dry bed of a river flowing south, one hundred feet below the camp, and the lowest point I have yet reached in the Gobi (probably two thousand eight hundred feet). Here there was one very large cairn of stones and a lot of smaller ones, marking the place where a large caravan carrying silver was attacked five years ago, nine men being killed, the silver carried off, and the remainder of the men left to continue their way as best they could on foot across this awful desert.

For three miles further we passed through low hills. At every hundred yards or so was a small pile of stones, to which our two Mongols used regularly to add one or two. At the point where the hills ended were two large cairns, one on each side of the road. To these the Mongols added more stones, carefully building them up, and giving a sigh of relief as we left the hills and entered an open plain again.

At dusk we approached a hollow, in which was some water. The guide fearing that brigands might be encamped near this, we repeated the stage-conspirator performance, advancing noiselessly with revolvers in hand. Nobody appeared, however, and when we got on the open plain again, we resumed our former peaceful demeanour. It was a very disagreeable march, very dark, sultry, and oppressive, and we got along very slowly, as Mongols and camels were both very tired.

We camped at midnight, with no water within twelve miles. I opened the second bottle of sherry which I had brought from Peking, and which I had reserved for the worst part of the Gobi. I felt as if I were a regular tippler in the delight with which I heard the pop of the cork, and saw the wine gurgling out into the tumbler. It was not improved by the jolting of the journey and the heat, but was uncommonly good for all that.

The following day we continued over the plain, on which we passed two or three herds of wild asses, and on the 11th we reached a large Mongol encampment named Man-chin-tol, in a plain at the foot of the first spurs of the Altai Mountains, on the higher points of which we could see slight traces of snow. Water was plentiful, being found in small pools all over the plain. It had, however, a brackish taste, and there was soda efflorescence on the margin of the pools.

During the morning a small caravan of twenty camels from Su-chow pitched camp near us. It belonged to a Chinese merchant trading amongst the Mongols. We bought some black beans for the camels, and shiau-mi (small millet) for porridge for myself.

I had a general hit out all round to-day. On asking the guide how many days it was to Hami, he said twenty, but only thirteen remain to make up the sixty, which is the contract time. I told my boy to explain this to him, and tell him that he would not get eighteen taels for the half camel extra. He muttered something about having lost a camel and being delayed in buying new ones, and about the rain and the wind. But I explained to him that I was paying a high price, and had taken light loads to go quickly, and that fifty days was the time in which I ought to get to Hami, but that sixty days was put in the contract to cover all risks of rain, etc.; and finally I told him that I had a passport from the Tsung-li-yamen, and that all the mandarins had been written to, to give me help, so that when I arrived at Hami, and told the Yamen how he had delayed me on the road, there would be a row. But I am afraid all this talking won't get me to Hami any the quicker, because the camels are not capable of doing it. They are miserable creatures, old and broken down.

I saw this at Kwei-hwa-cheng, but the guide said he was going to change them for better ones in Mongolia. This he has not done, although I have been at him several times about it. Truth is, it is not all his fault; those scoundrels at Kwei-hwa-cheng are to blame. They made me give the whole money in advance (I protested against it, but it was the only thing to be done). With this they bought the camels—which were scarce at the time, as a large caravan was just about to start for Guchen—and sent the guide off with one hundred-weight of brick tea and no money. The consequence is that he cannot change the camels, and I had to advance him thirty-eight taels to buy two new ones, to replace the one that had run away and another gone sick. Of course he has got the whip hand of me, but *que voulez vous?* If I had not advanced the money, we should not have been even as far as we are now. My only guarantee is in his honesty, which is doubtful, and in the willingness of the Yamen at Hami to take up the matter, which is also problematical.

I had a fling at Liu-san too; he had begun explaining to me how bad the camel-men at Kwei-hwa-cheng were, and how Mr. Clarke's man had squeezed a part of the money I paid for the camels. Now, I happened to know that he had also squeezed ten taels of that, but I had purposely avoided telling him that I knew, in order not to complicate matters. Now I did tell him, looking him full in the face to see the effect. But a Chinaman is inscrutable. There was no sign of guilt. His face changed instantly from the highly moral expression which it had worn, to one of indignant defiance, and, turning to the guide, he said (in Chinese), "Yang-laya" (myself) "says that I squeeze money—I, a Tientsin man—in a place like Kwei-hwa-cheng!" and a lot more in the same strain. It was all I could do to keep from laughing at the way they both kept their countenances, because the arrangement had been between the two; but the guide's face did not move a muscle, except to express supreme astonishment at my audacity in even supposing such an honest boy as mine was capable of squeezing me. I said no more to my boy. His manner, however, has very much changed for the better, and he is evidently trying to get into my good books again. In the afternoon he told me a long yarn about how good and honest his father was, and how honest he knew himself to be—all of which I was very glad to hear, but did not offer any remarks on the subject. These rows will happen in the best-regulated families, but they are a nuisance. I limit them to once a fortnight, when possible, as one cannot be always "nagging" at the unfortunate guide. We started at 4.15, and continued over the plain, passing several yurts and many flocks of sheep and goats and some ponies.

June 13.—A north wind, slight rain in the morning, and very cloudy. It cleared at eleven, and away on the northern range was *snow*—quite low down, too—most delightful to look at. By two it had all cleared away, except on the highest ridge.

I suggested to the guide that we should halt for a day when we came to a good grazing-ground, to let the camels pick up, and then make a renewed effort; but he says that if they were to halt for one day, they would not go on at all the next—the only thing is to keep them at it. Rather like the cab-horse in "Pickwick," which had to be kept in harness for fear of it falling down!

To the north, at a distance of twenty-five miles, are the Altai Mountains, rising to about nine thousand feet above the sea. There was slight snow on the summit before to-day's fall. They are entirely bare, and the southern slopes are steep, but not precipitous. In the centre of the range is said to be a plateau of grass land to which the wild camels resort.

The guide says they keep away from the caravan tracks and stay up in the mountains. The Mongols follow them and catch their young, which they use for riding only, as they will not carry a pack. The guide says they will travel eight hundred li in a day—probably an exaggeration. Their legs are thin, and the hair smooth. At three years old they are said to be of the size of a horse; at five years, the size of a small tame camel.

The guide also says that there are wild horses and mules about here and westward. On to-day's march I saw some of what the guide calls wild mules, through my telescope. They are the kyang of Ladakh and Tibet, and are in size about thirteen or fourteen hands, and in colour a light bay, being brightest under the belly. The head and tail were like a mule's, the neck thick and arched. They trotted fast, with a free, easy motion. The guide says the horses go about in troops of two or three hundred.

We started at 3.45, and passed over a gravel plain in a west-by-south direction. This plain is bounded on the south by a range at a distance of about eight miles. The range runs in a general easterly by westerly direction, and is about six hundred feet high on the average.

We camped at twelve amongst some low hills, with water three miles to westward. The camels are very poor; one of the new ones has gone lame, and another can hardly move along with a very light load.

June 14.—A fine, bright day. The sun was very hot, but a cool breeze blew from the east.

We started at 4.20, still passing over the plain, and at ten entered some low hills. I had a long conversation with my boy in Chinese, helped out occasionally by English. His brother is an importer of racing ponies to Shanghai, and he says they all come from Jehol-Lamamian. They are driven down to Tientsin and shipped in foreign steamers at fifteen dollars a head, or three ponies with a man for thirty-six dollars. He has been a riding-boy himself at Shanghai, and is a pretty smart fellow at times, when he likes, and on the whole is a satisfactory boy for the trip. His English has improved a good deal, and, with my small knowledge of Chinese, we manage to understand each other all right. Now and then I am astonished to hear him come out with a choice selection of English swearing, to supplement his stock of Chinese oaths, when he is having a row with the guide.

We camped at 11.35 at Liang-ko-ba, a collection of four Mongol yurts on the plain, round a patch of green.

June 15.—Cloudy, with a few drops of rain. I could see the rain falling all round, but it passed off in steam without reaching the ground.

We changed two camels here; one had gone lame, and the other could scarcely move. I bought a sheep for three bricks of tea for which I had paid a tael in Kwei-hwa-cheng. There were some ponies feeding about. They were strong, well-shaped animals, but in bad condition. I rode one which a Mongol had ridden to our tent. It was very different from the clumsy ponies of Peking. We started at 4.40, and still passed over gravelly plain, keeping along the edge of a low range of hills parallel to the road on the right.

June 16.—Wind westerly, in violent gusts; fine, but cloudy; snow falling on Altai Mountains. In the morning I climbed a hill and had a fine view of the country round for about eighty miles in every direction. The main range of the Altai Mountains is not at all of a uniform height, but, on the contrary, consists of distinct high ridges connected by lower hills. To the eastward I could see the snow-capped ridge which forms the butt end of the Altai Mountains. It is about twenty-five miles in length, and north-west of it is a second ridge, which also had some slight snow on it. In the space between the two ridges—fifty or sixty miles—is a succession of lower hills, rising about one thousand feet above the plain. The two ridges rise abrupt and clear from the surrounding hills. Between my route and the Altai Mountains is a succession of low, narrow ridges with intervening plains running in a south-easterly direction. All are perfectly bare; there are no signs of bushes, and even grass is extremely scanty. To the south the same succession of ridges and plains extends. The ridges are from three hundred to five hundred feet in height, and five or six miles apart. On the next march we followed down the gravelly bed of a stream which appeared occasionally in a small trickle above the surface, and the margin of which was covered thickly with the soda efflorescence which seems invariably to mark the presence of water in the Gobi.

On the 17th we emerged from the hills again, on to another great plain running between two parallel ranges of bare hills. On this plain we saw some more wild asses or horses, which I had good opportunity of examining with my telescope. They have large heads and ears, and thick, rather short, full, round bodies, legs well in proportion to their bodies, long tails reaching nearly to the ground, and thin like a mule's or donkey's. As far as I can see, they have no mane, or only a very short one. The guide calls them mules, and says they are from wild she-asses.

The following day we continued over the plain, but after sunset it became extremely dark, the sky being covered with heavy rain-clouds. About eleven the camels began floundering about, and we found we were in a bog. There had been heavy rain here during the day; the soil was a very slimy clay, and the ground broken up into hillocks. The guide was with difficulty persuaded to light a lantern, as he says that it frightens the camels, and they see their way better without it.

When it was lighted, the position did not look cheerful. The camels were each perched up on a little hillock, separated from each other by pools of water and slimy clay. The guide, the two Mongols, and my boy were pulling away at their nose-strings, till I thought their whole noses would be pulled off, but they would not budge. Beating them behind was next tried, but that also failed. At last they tried pulling them backwards, and this had the desired effect—they were started, and once they were in motion they were kept going, although they nearly fell or split themselves up at every step. But now the path had disappeared, it began to rain, and I thought we were in for a night on the swamp, which would probably have been our fate had not my compass shown that we were going off in the wrong direction, there being no signs of a star for the guide to follow. At last we came upon sand, found a path, and very soon after a patch of gravel, on which we pitched camp.

We had to halt the next day, because the camels would not be able to get through the wet clay soil which surrounded us, in spite of what the guide had said about their getting stiff if they halted a day. We started the next morning, and for a few days continued along the plain between the two parallel ranges, that to the north rising some one thousand five hundred feet, and the one to the south about eight hundred feet above the plain. Both ranges, like all the other hills which I saw in crossing the Gobi, were absolutely bare.

One evening Ma-te-la, the Mongol assistant, was suddenly seen to shoot ahead at a great pace, and, on asking, I found he was going home. On he went, far away over the plain, till he became a mere dot in the distance, and I could not help envying him. In the same direction, and with nothing apparently between me and it but distance, was my home, and I felt myself struggling to pierce through space, and see myself returning, like Ma-te-la, home. But the dull reality was that I was trudging along beside a string of heavy, silent, slow-going camels, and on I had to go, for hour after hour through the night with monotonous regularity.

Suddenly, after travelling for nine hours, the gravel plain ended, and we passed over a stretch of grass and halted by a small stream. Close by were pitched four tents (yurts), and this was Ma-te-la's home.

He came to me the next day, saying the guide could not pay him all his wages, and asked me to lend the guide four taels, which I did. He has served the guide for two years, and the guide has now given him only fifteen taels (£3 15s.). That guide is a regular scoundrel. Poor Ma-te-la had to work night and day, collect fuel, fetch water, look after the camels grazing, and then have to walk the whole march. In spite of this he was always perfectly happy, and used to sing and whistle the whole march, and would laugh at everything—if you even looked at him you saw a grin overspread his whole countenance. And now, for all his two years of hard work in this frightful desert, in the arctic cold of winter and the tropical heat of summer, he got fifteen taels—about a penny a day.

Started at 3.10 p.m., and passed over the gravelly plain again. The sunset was most wonderful. Even in the Indian hills during the rains I have never seen such a peculiar red tinge as the clouds had to-night. It was not red, it was not purple, but a mixture between the two—very deep, and at the same time shining very brightly. I have seen at Simla and in Switzerland more glorious sunsets, with richer diffusion of colours, but never one of such a strange colouring as this. An hour and a half later, when it was nearly dark, a very light, phosphorescent-looking cloud hung over the place of sunset.

Camped at 1.30 a.m. in a hollow among some low hills, in which was a small stream of water.

June 23.—The gravel plain gradually gave way to a light clay soil, with plenty of bushes; and a little further we came on a regular meadow, with herds of cattle, sheep, and ponies, and several Mongol tents. We even saw patches of cultivation and trees, and water was plentiful, and was led on to the fields by irrigation ducts. Wheat was the only crop grown. The Mongol is evidently not fitted for agriculture, for the plots of cultivation were in the most untidy state. There were no signs of furrows, and the seed had evidently been thrown broadcast over the land; in some places it was very thick, and in others very thin. This was the first real oasis we had come across. It is in a depression between the range of hills, the ground gently sloping down to it from every side.

The name of this oasis is Ya-hu. It is about five miles in extent from west to east, and rather more from north to south. Some twelve miles to the west is a remarkable hill, called by the guide Ho-ya-shan. It rises very abruptly out of the plain to a height of about two thousand feet, and is a perfectly solid mass of rock of a light colour. There is said to be water on the summit, possibly in the crater of an old volcano, as in the Pei-shan in Manchuria.

On June 25 we reached Ula-khutun, where the road to Hami leaves the road to Guchen. It is merely a camping-ground, situated in a stony plain, surrounded by low mounds or heaps of gravel, at the southern base of a branch from the main range of the Altai Mountains, from which it is separated by a gravelly plain about twenty miles in width—the extension westward of the same plain in which Ya-hu is situated. The height of this southern ridge must be considerable, for a heavy snowstorm was falling on it even so late in the year as this (June 25), and the snow seemed to remain there.

A peculiarity common to all the mountains which I had seen in the Gobi—the long, even, sloping gravel plains which run down from their summits till they join the corresponding sloping plains of a parallel range or merge in the broad desert—had long puzzled me. But here, among the lower ridge of the Altai Mountains, I had better opportunities of examining the rocks, and it seems to me that the following is the true cause of the formation of these sloping plains.

The hills in the Gobi, as has been noted several times, are perfectly bare, and in such an extremely dry climate, exposed to the icy cold winds of winter and the fierce rays of the summer sun, and unprotected by one atom of soil, the rocks first decompose, and then crumble away to a remarkable extent, and there being no rainfall sufficient to wash away the *débris*, the lower features of a range gradually get covered with a mass of *débris* falling from the upper portions, and in the course of time a uniform slope is created, often thirty or forty miles in length, and it is only for a few hundred feet at the top that the original jagged rocky outline is seen.

In the smaller features the process of decomposition could be seen actually going on. The rocks are all cracked and give way at a touch,* while occasionally masses spontaneously detach themselves. The general effect, then, that is being produced on these mountains by the combined action of the heat of the sun and the winter frosts, is the same as would be produced by heat upon a rugged mass of ice. In the course of time (for the one, a few million years—for the other, a few minutes) both would be modified into round smooth masses.

From Ula-khutun we passed through some low hills, and on the march came across the horn of an *Ovis argali*. It was lying in the middle of the path. On measuring it, I found it was fifty inches round the curve and seventeen inches in circumference at base—an immense horn. The

* The rocks used actually to become sunburnt. On the side exposed to the sun and the weather they would become dark brown and shining, while on the side unexposed to the sun they were of a dull light-brown colour.

Mongols say there are plenty in the Tian-shan—they called it *arhgǎll*—and say it has a white breast (see Prjevalsky). The kuku-yamen, they say, is also found about here.

We camped at 6.30 by a spring and some good grass, which the camels have not had for some time. I climbed one of the highest hills to have a look round. There were plenty of white soft clouds about, but suddenly my eye rested on what I felt sure was a great snowy range. I had out my telescope, and there, far away in the distance, were the real Tian-shan, only just distinguishable from the clouds. My delight was unbounded, and for long I feasted my eyes on those "Heavenly Mountains," as the Chinese call them, for they marked the end of my long desert journey.

Our next march, however, was the most trying of all, for we had to cross the branch of the Gobi which is called the desert of Zungaria, one of the most absolutely sterile parts of the whole Gobi. We started at eleven in the morning, passing at first through the low hills, which were perfectly barren, but the hollows had a few tufts of bushes, and one hollow was filled with white roses. After seven and a half miles we left the hills, and entered a gravel plain covered with coarse bushes, but no grass. There was no path, and we headed straight for the end of the Tian-shan range. After passing over the plain for fifteen miles, we struck a path and followed it along till 11.30 p.m., when we halted to cook some food and rest the camels. It was of no use pitching camp, for there was neither water, fuel, nor grass; not a bush, nor a plant, nor a blade of grass—absolutely nothing but gravel. I lay down on the ground and slept till Liu-san brought me some soup and tinned beef. We started again at 4 a.m., and marched till 3.15 p.m. through the most desolate country I have ever seen. Nothing we have passed hitherto can compare with it —a succession of gravel ranges without any sign of life, animal, or vegetable, and not a drop of water. We were gradually descending to a very low level, the sun was getting higher and higher, and the wind hotter and hotter, until I shrank from it as from the blast of a furnace. Only the hot winds of the Punjab can be likened to it. Fortunately we still had some water in the casks, brought from our last camping-ground, and we had some bread, so we were not on our last legs; but it was a trying enough march for the men, and much more so for the camels, for they had nothing to eat or drink, and the heat both days was extreme. We at last reached a well among some trees. The guide called the distance two hundred and thirty li, and I reckon it at about seventy miles. We were twenty-seven hours and three-quarters from camp, including the halt of four and a half hours. We had descended nearly four thousand feet, and the heat down here was very much greater than we had yet experienced. We were encamped on the dry bed of a river, on the skirts of what looked like a regular park—the country being covered with trees, and the ground with long coarse grass. It was most striking, as on the other bank of the river there was not a vestige of vegetation.

We had taken on a Mongol guide, and I had told him to keep a look-out for *Ovis poli*. Shortly after we left our last camp among the low hills, he gave a shout, and darted off at a heap of sticks, and extricated two pairs of *Ovis poli* horns. One a magnificent pair which measured fifty-two and fifty-four inches respectively. These I took on, and left the other pair, which measured only forty-three inches. The large pair measured nineteen inches round the base—as thick as my thigh. The Mongol guide said this was a hiding-place for the hunters. It was placed fifty yards from some water, where the animals came to drink. I asked the guide if he had seen wild camels about here; he said, "Any amount," and that he had some young ones at his yurt, and also some skins. What a chance I had missed! for his tent was only ten miles off our camp at Ula-khutun. Further on in the desert of

Zungaria we passed a track which he said was that of a wild camel. It was smaller than the tame camel's footprint, and, as it was a single track and leading straight across our line of march right up the desert of Zungaria—from nowhere to nowhere—and miles from any camping-spot, it was not likely to have been anything else but that of a wild camel.

During this march my Chinese rather came to grief. I had been walking, and wanted to ride, so I said to the guide, "Yau chi" ("Want to ride"). The guide was eating some bread, and laughed at me, shaking his head. I got rather angry at this, and repeated, "Yau chi," at which he shook his head again and pointed to my camel. My boy now shouted out to him, and he then at once dismounted and seated my camel for me. It then struck me that "chi" also means "to eat," and he had thought I meant I wanted some of his bread, and had pointed to my saddle-bags, where I had my own. I ought to have said "Yau chi" in a surprised tone, whereas (not being in my usual amiable state of mind) I had said it in an angry tone, and the meaning was immediately altered from "I want to ride" to "I want to eat." Such are some of the intricacies of the Chinese language.

After this long and trying march we (or I, at any rate) scarcely got a wink of sleep, for the heat was stifling, without a breath of air, and I was lying on the ground in a Kabul tent, pestered by a plague of sandflies, which got into my eyes, nose, and everywhere. That was the most despairing time of my whole journey, and many times that night I accused myself of being the greatest fool yet created, and swore by all the gods I would never go wandering about the wild places of the earth again. These periods of depression must occur to every traveller. He cannot help asking himself now and then, "What's the good of it all?" But 'tis always darkest before the dawn, and I could just see the first glimmering of awakening day—the snowy summits of the "Heavenly Mountains" were rising above me. There was still some hard and trying work to be done, though. As the sun rose next morning a breeze sprang up which drove away the sandflies, but the heat became intense. In spite of it we had to start at 1.30 in the afternoon, and march till three the next morning.

For nearly two miles we passed through a country well covered with trees, and patches of coarse grass and bushes. The soil was partly clay and partly sand. This ended as suddenly as it had begun, and we passed over the gravel desert again, where there was no vestige of grass or scrub. The hot wind blowing off this seemed absolutely to scorch one up; but yesterday's order of things were now reversed—we were ascending while the sun was descending, and it gradually became cooler.

About ten at night we suddenly found ourselves going over turf, with bushes and trees on either side, and a shrill clear voice hailed us from the distance. We halted, and the guide answered, and the stranger came up and turned out to be a Turki woman, who led us through the bushes over some cultivated ground to a house, the first I had seen for nearly a thousand miles.

It was the first sign that I had entered a new land—Turkestan—the mysterious land which I had longed for many a day to see. Flowing by the house was a little stream of the most delicious water. It was scarcely a yard broad, but it was not a mere trickle like the others we had passed in the Gobi, but was flowing rapidly, with a delightful gurgling noise, and was deep enough for me to scoop up water between my two hands. I gulped down mouthful after mouthful of it, and enjoyed such a drink as I had not had for many a long day, and as I lay down on the grass on its bank while the water-casks were being filled, I thought the trials of the desert journey were nearly over. But they were not quite; hardly fifty yards from the stream the vegetation disappeared, and we were again on gravel desert, and we had still to travel for five hours, gradually ascending as before—at twelve passing through a gorge two and a half miles long, in a range of little hills running parallel to the slope. We halted as the day was dawning, on a part of the slope where there was enough scrub for fuel and for the animals to eat. No water.

Next day we continued to ascend the long lower slopes of the Tian-shan, gradually rounding the eastern extremity of these mountains. We passed a cart-track leading from Barkul to Hami, which makes this detour round the Tian-shan to avoid crossing them. The going was bad on account of the stones, and because the whole slope was cut up by dry watercourses. These were seldom more than a foot deep, but the slope was covered with them. They were formed by the natural drainage from the mountains, which, instead of running in deep valleys, spreads over the slope. The whole country was still barren, being covered with scrub only; but in the depression at the foot of the slope was a small Turki village, surrounded with trees and cultivation.

That night we encamped near a Turki house called Morgai, surrounded with fields of wheat and rice, watered from a small stream which appeared above the surface just here, and which, lower down, spread out and was swallowed in the pebbly slopes of the mountain.

The following morning I, for the first time, had an opportunity of examining more closely one of this new race of people through whose country I was about to travel for fifteen hundred miles or so. The men were tall and fine-looking, with more of the Mongol caste of feature about them than I had expected. Their faces, however, though somewhat round, were slightly more elongated than the Mongols, and there was considerably more intelligence about them. But there was more roundness and less intelligence, less sharpness in the outlines than is seen in the inhabitants of the districts about Kashgar and Yarkand.

In fact, afterwards, in the bazaar at Hami, I could easily distinguish a Kashgari from an inhabitant of the eastern end of Turkestan.

As I proceeded westward I noticed a gradual, scarcely perceptible change from the round of a Mongolian type to a sharper and yet more sharp type of feature. Whether this is accidental, or whether it is brought about by the commingling of separate races, I know not; but I think I am not wrong in stating that the further east one goes, the rounder and broader are the faces of the inhabitants, and the further west one goes the longer and narrower they become.

This may perhaps be accounted for in this way. As is well known, Mongolia was formerly occupied to a large extent by Turks (Uigars), but these were driven out by the Mongols, who finally, under Chingiz-Khan and his successors, overspread the whole of Turkestan and the countries to the west. Manchuria, however, the original home of the Tartars, was never inhabited by Turks; and in Eastern Mongolia we see the truest type of Tartar feature. In Western Mongolia the features are somewhat (though not very much) longer and narrower. In the eastern part of Turkestan there is a decided change towards the Turanian type, but still the round, broad Tartar features are very prominent; and then as we proceed westward, and get further away from Mongolia into the lands where the Mongols, or Moghuls, as they are also called, and Turks have lived together, and are now merged into one race, we notice that their faces become gradually longer and narrower; and further west still, among some of the inhabitants of Afghan Turkestan, numbers of whom may be seen in Kashgar and Yarkand, we see that the Tartar or Mongol type of feature is almost entirely lost.

Here at Morgai, too, I saw the Turki women. Very different they were from the doll-like Chinese women, with painted faces, waddling about on contorted feet; from the sturdy, bustling

Manchu women, and from the simple, silly Mongol girls with their great red cheeks and dirty, unintelligent faces. These Turkis were fine, handsome women, with complexions not much darker than Greeks or Spaniards. They had good colour on their cheeks, and their eyes were dark and full. Their whole appearance was most picturesque, for they had a fine, dignified bearing, and were dressed in a long loose robe not confined at the waist, their long black tresses allowed to fall over their shoulders, only fastened at the ends into two thick plaits; on their head, slightly inclined backwards, they wore a bright red cap, which set off their whole appearance very effectively.

They stared with great astonishment at the sudden appearance of a white man (though I fancy at that time my face was not quite as white as an Englishman's generally is). But we had not much time to examine each other's charms, for I had that day to cross the Tian-shan.

Starting early, we ascended the stream, but it soon disappeared again, and we saw nothing more of it. The hillsides were at first rather bare, but the higher we got the greener they became; and after five or six miles were covered with rich green turf, most delightful to look upon after the bare hills of the Gobi; while here and there through an opening in the hills we could catch a glimpse of the snowy peaks above. There are, however, no trees nor even bushes, either on the hills or in the valleys. I was told we should probably see some *Ovis argali*, so I went on ahead with my carbine and telescope. By the roadside we passed several horns of the *Ovis argali*, and two other kinds of wild sheep or goat, *Ovis argali* being the most common.

In the bed of the stream I found a magnificent *Ovis argali* head, measuring fifty-six inches and put it in triumph on a camel; but a few miles further on I rejected it with scorn, when, lying on a rock, I saw a huge head, one horn of which measured sixty-two inches. Both horns were in almost perfect condition, and were still on the skull, so that I had the whole thing complete. The guide said it was as big a one as was to be got.

All the *Ovis argali* horns I saw to-day were different from those which I saw on the Altai Mountains. The latter were thicker at the base (nineteen inches round as against sixteen), and they were more rounded, and not so much twisted. The Mongol says the sheep are the same.

We crossed the range at a height of eight thousand feet. Except the last half-mile the ascent was not steep, but led gradually up a narrow valley. The last mile or two was over soft green turf, and near the summit there was a perfect mass of flowers, chiefly forget-me-nots; and I am sure I shall not forget for a very long time the pleasure it was, seeing all this rich profusion of flowers and grass, in place of those dreary gravel slopes of the Gobi Desert. The sun had now set, and I climbed a neighbouring peak as a last hope of seeing an *Ovis argali*, but there was not a sign of one. There was no great view from the summit, as higher peaks rose all round, and I could only just catch a glimpse of the plain to the south, which was covered with a distant haze.

There were still no trees to be seen, and a curious characteristic of these hills is that there is absolutely no water. For twelve miles from Morgai to the summit of the pass we had not seen a drop of water. From this absence of water the valleys were not deep—not more than five or six hundred feet below the summit of the hills on either side—nor were the hill-sides remarkably steep, as in the Himalayas. They are grassy slopes with rocks cropping out at their summits, and here and there on their sides. Five miles on the southern side a small stream appeared, and the valley bottom was partitioned off into fields, round which irrigation ducts had been led; but these were all now deserted, and the water was wasted in flowing over uncultivated fields. Trees now began to appear near the stream, and at 11.10 p.m. we pitched camp on a little grassy

FARM IN THE TIAN SHAN MOUNTAINS.

plot near a stream of cold clear water, and under a small grove of trees. It really seemed the height of bliss—a perfect paradise, and the desert journey a terrible nightmare behind me. The singing of the birds, too, struck me very much; for in the Gobi there was always a death-like silence, and so I noticed the continued twitter which the birds kept up. Trees were more numerous now, and on the northern slopes of some of the hills I even saw some patches of pine forests.

I was hoping, after crossing the Tian-shan, to come upon a comparatively well-populated country, with a fair extent of cultivated land; but was disappointed at finding the same barren desert as before, with, however, a small oasis every fifteen or twenty miles. The inhabitants were principally Tunganis and Chinese, and looked very poor; but the Turkis were all fine, healthy-looking men.

On July 22 we passed a small square-walled town called Ching-cheng, surrounded by fields of wheat and some good grass land, but when these ended the desert began again directly.

A long way off over the desert we could see a couple of poplar trees rising out of the plain. These poplars are very common all over Chinese Turkestan, and they make excellent landmarks. We reached these at twelve at night, and found a few soldiers stationed there, who said that Hami was still a long way off. Now, as my constant inquiry for the last month had been, "How far are we from Hami?" and as the guide for the last few days had each time said we were only sixty miles off, I was rather exasperated to find that, instead of having ten or twenty miles more to get over, there was still a good fifty. So on striking camp at two the following afternoon, I told my men that my tent would not be pitched again till Hami was reached, so they had better prepare themselves for a good march. We travelled on all through the afternoon—a particularly hot one; then the sun set before us, and still we went on and on through the night till it rose again behind us.

We halted for a couple of hours by the roadside to ease the camels, and then set out again. At eight o'clock the desert ended, and we began to pass through cultivated land, and at last we saw Hami in the distance, and after traversing a tract of country covered with more ruined than inhabited houses, we reached an inn at 11 a.m., and it was with unspeakable relief that I dismounted from my camel for the last time.

My desert journey was now over, and I had accomplished the 1255 miles from Kwei-hwa-cheng in just seventy days; in the last week of which I had travelled 224 miles, including the crossing of the Tian-shan Mountains.

CHAPTER VI.

THROUGH TURKESTAN TO YARKAND.

My first inquiries after arrival were as to whether Colonel Bell had arrived. I had reached here some weeks later than the appointed date on which we were to have met, but still he had had a long round to travel, and might have been late too. I was told that he had passed through about three weeks before, and it was a marvel to me how he had managed to travel so quickly. But there is probably no faster or better traveller than Colonel Bell. He has travelled in Persia, Asia Minor, Beluchistan, Burma, and China, besides this present journey that he was engaged in; and those who have read the accounts of these travels know that there are few, if any, Europeans who have seen and done and recorded more than Colonel Bell.

My next inquiries were as to the means of reaching Kashgar, and the time it would take to get there. Difficulties, of course, arose at first. It was the hot season, and carters would not hire out their carts. In any case it would take seventy days to reach there, and this would bring us to the end of September, with the whole of the Himalayas to cross before winter.

In the evening I took a stroll through the town, and found all the bustle of life customary to a small trading centre. Hami is a small town of perhaps five or six thousand inhabitants. There are fairly good shops, and a busy bazaar, where one sees people of many nationalities meeting together—

Chinese, Mongols, Kalmacs, Turkis, and others. Large heavily laden travelling carts would come lumbering through, and strings of camels from across the desert.

I was looking out for a shop where it was said Russian goods could be bought. When I found it, I noticed Russian characters above, and on looking behind the counter was both surprised and delighted to see a Russian. He shook hands very heartily with me, and asked me to come inside. He spoke neither Chinese nor English, but only Russian and Mongol, and as I could speak neither of those languages, we had to communicate with each other through a Chinaman, who spoke Mongol. This Russian lived in a Chinese house, in Chinese fashion, but was dressed in European clothes. On the walls of his room I noticed a flaring picture entitled, the "Prince of Wales in India," in which everybody had a vermilion complexion, and was dressed in a most gorgeous and impossible uniform. He told me that trading at this place was not very profitable. He sold chiefly cotton goods and iron-ware, such as pails, basins, knives, etc. There had been five Russian merchants here, but two had gone to Kobolo, and two were engaged in hunting down Chinese mandarins, to try and get money which was owing to them.

The next evening I invited the Russian round to my inn to dinner. Conversation was difficult, but we managed to spend a very pleasant evening, and drank to the health of our respective sovereigns. I held up my glass and said, "Czar," and we drank together. Then I held it up again and said, "Skobeleff," and so on through every Russian I had heard of. My guest, I am sorry to say, knew very few Englishmen, but he had grasped the fact that we had a queen, so at five-minute intervals he would drink to her Majesty.

Three years later, when I was at Kashgar, I heard that two Russian merchants residing at Hami had been imprisoned by the Chinese authorities, and treated in the most terrible

A BAZAAR IN CHINESE TURKESTAN.

manner by them. A European in the employ of the Chinese heard of this, brought it to the notice of the Russian minister at Pekin, and I believe their release was obtained, but not before they had undergone the most fearful sufferings from hunger and imprisonment in foul, pest-stricken dungeons. I have often wondered whether my hearty, good-natured guest was one of them.

Besides the native town of Hami, there is also a Chinese walled town, about six hundred yards square, with four gateways, each surmounted by a massive tower.

Sir Henry Howorth, the author of the "History of the Mongols," asked me on my return whether I had noticed any old ruins at Hami. All the country round Hami is covered with ruins, but mostly of mud-constructed buildings, the age of which it is impossible to conjecture. I did not look out for anything special, and the only remarkable ruins I remember were those of what appeared to be an old temple with a dome of green glazed tiles.

We halted four days at Hami, and made a new start for Kashgar—the second great stage of the journey—on July 8. It appeared that carts could be taken the whole way, so camels were no longer required, and I was fortunate in being able to effect an excellent arrangement with my "boy" Liu-san, by which he engaged to land me at Kashgar by contract on a certain date. I was to be regarded as a piece of merchandise to be carted from one place to the other, and he was to undertake the whole of the arrangement. He was to land me and my baggage at Kashgar in forty days, and was to be paid seventy taels (about £17 10s.) here at Hami, and thirty taels more if we reached Kashgar in that time. He was to receive two taels extra for every day in advance of that time, and two taels would be deducted for every day more than the forty days. This arrangement fully answered my expectations. The money which was to be made for transport went into my "boy's," and not into some outsider's pocket, so that he at once became directly interested in the journey. And, in order to get along quickly, instead of having to go through all that irritating and irksome process of perpetually nagging away at the servants and pony-men, which utterly destroys all the charm of travel, I could go about with my mind at rest, well assured that my "boy" would be worrying at *me* to get up early in the morning, not to delay at starting, and to go on for another few miles instead of halting at a tempting place in the evening. I became an impassive log, and enjoyed myself immensely. It was quite a new sensation to be able to lie lazily on in bed while breakfast was being got ready; at the end of breakfast to find everything prepared for the start; and all the way through to have an enthusiastic and energetic servant constantly urging me to go on further and quicker.

The "boy," with the advance he had received from me, bought up a cart and four animals (two mules and two ponies), and this carried all the baggage and supplies of the party, while I rode a pony. The cart was of the description known in Turkestan as an araba, a large covered cart, with only one pair of very high wheels. One animal was in the shafts, and three tandem fashion in front. The weight of the baggage, supplies, etc. (including a certain amount of grain for the animals), which the cart carried, was one thousand five hundred catties (two thousand pounds).

Our start from Hami was made at eight in the evening. For half an hour we passed through cultivated lands, and then were in the dead desert again. Away on our right were the Tian-shan Mountains, but they looked quite bare, and no snowy peaks were visible; to the left all was desert. At about twenty miles we passed a small village called Ta-pu-ma, with the ruins of some barracks; and halted at 4.20 on the following morning at Eurh-pu, a pretty little village surrounded with orchards, the trees of which were covered with apples.

There were so many ruined houses that it is hard to say how many inhabited dwellings there were—probably about twenty. The inhabitants were both Chinese and Kalmaks. The inn was a very poor one, the rooms being low and dirty, with no windows or doors, and only an open doorway. The kang was very dirty and made of mud, and not even covered with matting. The roof was composed of grass laid across beams of wood, which let both rain and sun through.

Cloudy day and slight rain during the night of 7–8th. Thermometer—max., 90°; min., 66°.

July 9.—Started at 2.30. A thunderstorm delayed us for half an hour. The desert began again almost immediately after leaving Eurh-pu, but it is not so bad as the Gobi. There was a fair amount of grass and scrub, but it was unfitted for cultivation. Nearer the mountains there appeared to be villages, and, after going a few miles, we saw on the left a small green plain, with a fair-sized village and several streams running down towards it.

At forty li we passed the village of S'an-pu, which also had the ruins of a barracks, and on the western side were two tombs of Chinese military mandarins, who had died in the war. They were not handsome tombs, but they were very conspicuous, as they were from fifty to sixty feet high. They were built of brick, and in good preservation. All other buildings were made of mud. For the rest of the way we passed over desert, occasionally passing a house on a small stream or spring in a hollow. There is a sort of half-dead air about this country; for every inhabited house, at least two in ruins are to be seen. In passing through villages, scarcely an inhabitant is met with, and in the fields no one seems to be working. If I had come from anywhere else but the Gobi, I should probably have found it extremely depressing.

The villages look very pretty at a distance, surrounded, as they are, with trees and green fields, forming a contrast to the neighbouring desert; but as they are approached they are seen to contain so many ruins and patches of ground formerly cultivated and now lying fallow, that the charm is lost. We halted at 11.30, at San-to-lin-tzu, a small village with four inns. As my boy said that fleas were very numerous in the rooms, I slept in the cart, where it was also a good deal cooler.

Day fine generally, with thunderstorm at noon. Thermometer—max., 96°; min., 66°.

July 10.—Left at 2.30 p.m., and passed over a stony plain gradually ascending towards the mountains. The slope was cut up by dry watercourses running down from the hills. At thirteen miles we passed a house surrounded with cultivation, forming a small oasis. There was a comparatively large plot of poppies, though one would have thought that in a desert like this all the land capable of cultivation would be needed for the production of necessaries. Shortly after, we passed twelve donkeys, laden with merchandise, going to Hami. We met little traffic on the road.

Halted at 10.30 p.m., at Lain-tung, a small settlement of inns, no cultivation. They had here some coal which was obtained from the Tian-shan. My boy told me coal could be obtained at Hami also, but I saw none myself. Distance ninety li.

Cloudy day. Thunderstorms on surrounding hills. Thermometer—max., 86°; min., 68°.

July 11.—We only halted at Lain-tung to feed the animals, and started again at 2.20 a.m. We gradually ascended the mountain slope in a transverse direction. The ground was a good deal cut up by dry watercourses, and was covered with stones, which delayed the carts.

Halted at 9 a.m. at I-wang-chuen, which consists of

one house and an inn in the midst of bare hills. There was no cultivation or pasturage. The inn was occupied by a military mandarin from Urumchi, who had with him a number of soldiers, so there was no room for our party. We drew up the cart a little beyond, and the boy cooked a meal, which I ate in the cart. These big carts are very comfortable. I have a mattress spread out on the top of all the baggage, so that I or the boy can lie down at any time. I sleep in the cart at night, and the boy occupies it during the marches.

July 11.—We started again at 2.55 p.m., passing through a hilly country, very bare, and covered, as usual, with gravel. I saw two *Ovis argali* horns, but they were of small size. Halted at 7.15 at Chê-ku-lu-chuen (fifty li)—a house and an inn in a gorge, which we had been descending for rather over a mile. Still no cultivation, and everything very brown and sterile. Had tea, and slept, as usual, in the cart. The boy would not sleep in the rooms of the inn, because the soldiers were to return here from the last stage, and he says they would turn him out and steal his things. They are a bad lot, apparently. They were civil enough to me, though. They mistook me for a Russian, but when I said I was English, they said, "Oh! you belong to the great English nation." Every one here speaks of the *great* English nation. Russian, French, and English, are the only European nations they seem to know. Dull day, but no rain; cool.

July 12.—Started at 4.40 a.m., passing down the gorge for four miles. The gorge was from fifty to one hundred yards broad, the hills being from one hundred to one hundred and fifty feet above it. The bottom was fine gravel, and the hills rocky and stony. After emerging from this, we still continued down the slope of gravel from the range, and nine miles further on crossed a plain covered with a light clay soil, bearing plenty of shrubs and trees, but no grass. The plain is surrounded on all sides by hills, and, if there were a more plentiful rainfall in this country, would form a lake, but there was no sign of water. One mile beyond, the road divided, the right-hand one going to Urumchi. We halted at 12.10 at Tuan-yen-kou (110 li), a house and inn situated at the foot of the range, which forms the western boundary of the plain. Water here particularly bad, and smelt horribly. Quite a good inn for these parts, as one room in three had a door to it—no windows yet, though, and during a thunderstorm the rain came through the roof as through a sieve. Started at 5.20, turning off in a south-westerly direction, and still passing over the plain for four miles, when we ascended the stony slope of the surrounding hills. It was a long trying pull of about nine miles, not steep, but continuous. We passed thirty donkeys, laden with grapes from the Turfan district, going to Hami. Donkeys are very plentiful in this country, and seem to be the only animals used for packs. The Turkis are very seldom seen on a pony; it is always a donkey they ride. At 10 p.m. we reached the end of the slope and entered the hills, descending very gradually down a gorge in a direction somewhat south of west. There were two or three houses at the entrance, but no inn. As usual, the hills were perfectly bare. Halted at 3.20 a.m. (13th) at Hsi-yang-chĕ. From 4.40 a.m. on the 12th to 3.20 a.m. on the 13th we have done 230 li, travelling seventeen hours twenty minutes, and resting five hours ten minutes. The two cart-mules went well throughout, the ponies not so well. These mules are certainly very good for cart work. Cloudy day. Thunderstorm in afternoon. Cool night.

July 13.—We started at 12.40 p.m., descending at first a narrow and precipitous gorge. The hills on either side rose in cliffs of six or seven hundred feet high. After two and a half miles, we left the hills and descended a barren, gravelly slope. At 10 p.m. we passed a deserted inn where the road divided, and the carter was uncertain which to take. We wandered about the plain for some hours, and then I ordered a halt till daylight. I did not feel at all comfortable, for we had no water with us, and the mules and ponies cannot go on, like camels, without it. As far as we could see while daylight lasted, the desert extended in all directions. When dawn broke, however, we saw trees in the distance, and the carter recognized his whereabouts. Our misfortunes were not yet quite over, for the cart stuck in a hole when we were close to the village, and we took nearly two hours getting it out. We finally reached Shi-ga-tai at 7.20 a.m. (14th). There is here a small fort built on a mound, occupied by a hundred Chinese soldiers. It has mud walls about twenty feet high, loopholed for musketry, but it is commanded at three hundred yards by a hill on the south. The village consists of some thirty houses, inhabited partly by Chinese and partly by Turkis. There is a little cultivation and some pasturage round the village. Day fine in the morning, thunderstorms falling in the neighbourhood in the afternoon.

July 14.—Started at 3.25 p.m., and crossed a desert with occasional oases every four or five miles. To the south are ranges of bare hills, some fifty to one hundred and fifty feet high, running parallel to the road. At two miles from Pi-chan the desert ended, and the country was covered with trees, cultivation, and small hamlets. The road was every here and there lined with rows of trees on either side. We lost the track again, and went wandering round the country till 1.30 a.m., when we arrived at the gate of the town, which we found shut. It was, however, opened for us, and we put up at a good inn— good only as inns go in Kashgaria. The smallest village in Manchuria would not call such a place an inn. There they put up cows in such places as these. Day very hot, thunderstorms as usual on the Tian-shan in the afternoon, and very slight rain fell down here at night.

July 15.—Pi-chan is surrounded by a wall about four hundred yards in length in each direction. It contains about two thousand inhabitants. In the only real street are a few shops, small, but clean, in which are sold ordinary articles of dress and consumption. Some are kept by Chinese, and some by Turkis. The Turkis here seem more well-to-do than at Hami; they are better dressed, and their houses are larger and cleaner. The women usually wear a long red gown and trousers. They tie a bright-coloured cloth round their head, but I have seen none of those big globe-shaped caps they wore at Hami. Started at 1.40 p.m., leaving Pi-chan by the north gate, and passing for two and a half miles through a very pretty, well-cultivated country, through which ran a charming little stream, its banks lined with graceful poplars and willows. Numerous little irrigation ducts were carried through the fields and straight across the road, rather to the hindrance of traffic; but now it is a positive pleasure to hear the cart splashing through water. There are a number of little hamlets dotted over the plain, and many mosques, all built of mud like everything else in the country. Many of them had piles of *Ovis argali* and ibex horns on the ledges of the roofs, but I saw no *Ovis argali* as fine as those which I obtained in the Gobi. At two and a half miles from Pi-chan the delightful piece of country came to an end abruptly, and we were on the same dreary old gravel desert again. From a piece of rising ground I obtained a good view of the country we had been passing through. It was extremely pretty. The plain, some six miles in length from east to west, and three or four from north to south, was covered over with trees, beneath the shade of which nestled the little Turki hamlets. About a mile to the south of Pi-chan was a range of sandhills like that which I saw in the Gobi, but of a darker colour and not so high. The afternoon was terribly hot on the gravelly desert, and, after passing over it for sixteen miles, we were glad enough to come upon another oasis. We halted at 8.15 at Liang-ming-chang (seventy li), a pretty village built on the steep bank of a little stream. There was a bustling landlord at the inn, who came out to meet us, and attended to us more in the Manchurian innkeeper style than in the usual listless way they have here.

I slept on the ground in the inn yard, as it was too hot even in the cart. There is one good point to be noted of this country—there are no mosquitoes or flies in number enough to trouble one. If there were, travelling in this heat would be almost unbearable. I should feel very much inclined to take myself off to the snowy Tian-shan Mountains which accompany us march by march, exhibiting their cool, refreshing peaks in the most tantalizing way to us perspiring mortals down below here.

July 16.—Started at 1.45 a.m., and entered the desert again at a mile from Liang-ming-chang. The road was very heavy on account of the sand. We passed several rows of holes dug in the ground. They were in long lines, the holes being about twenty yards apart, and from six to eight feet in circumference. The earth was piled up all round, and as the holes had been dug some time most of them had nearly filled up again. In some, however, the sides had been built up with wood, to form a well. It looked as if an army had pitched camp here, and had set to work to dig for water.

At seven miles from Liang-ming-chang we crossed some low hills and entered an extensive plain, well cultivated and covered with hamlets. This lasted for seven miles, and we then descended a narrow valley, the hills on either side being composed of clay, absolutely barren, and very steep and precipitous in places. A small stream ran at the bottom of the valley, but the banks were too steep to be cultivated. We passed a good many ruins of houses and mosques built up against the cliffs. They had evidently been destroyed by landslips.

Halted at 7.55 a.m. at Sang-ching-kou, an inn owned by a Turki. This was the first Turki inn I had visited. The *kang* was covered with a very handsome, though rather old, carpet.

Started again at two, leaving the gorge, and passing over the open desert again. The stream from the gorge flowed in a south direction, and its banks were lined with villages. About ten miles to the south was a range of hills running in an apparently east-by-west direction, and on the side of them was a strip of cultivated land running up as far as Turfan. At seven or eight miles from Lang-ching-kou the desert was covered with hundreds of wells, said to have been dug by Chinese soldiers. Line after line of them we passed, each line a couple of miles or so in length, with wells dug at intervals of twenty yards. These wells were not circular, but rectangular, about two and a half or three feet broad and seven or eight feet long. We could not see the bottom, but we halted at a house where one of these wells was in use, and this was one hundred and ten feet deep.

The origin of these wells I find it hard to explain. My boy told me that they had been dug by a Chinese army besieging Turfan. This army had not been able to obtain water otherwise, and had dug these wells. I am inclined to doubt the truth of this story, though. I would rather say they were what are known in Persia and Afghanistan as "karez," and intended to lead water obtainable below the surface of the ground along underneath it down the slope from one well to another, and so on till the level of the land to be irrigated is reached, and the water appears at the surface.

We stopped at 8.15 p.m. (sixty li) at a Turki house, as we should not be able to get into Turfan at night. The water from the well was delightfully cold, and the house clean and cool. Half the courtyard was covered over, and in this covered part was a low platform, on which sat the inmates of the house at table. I spread my mattress on the floor of the courtyard, and went off to sleep as fast as I could. It is a great advantage being able to sleep at night in the open air without any fear of mosquitoes. Weather hazy and very hot.

July 17.— Started at 3.15 a.m., still passing over desert for four miles, and then, after crossing a small stream, we travelled through tracts of deserted houses and burial-grounds, with here and there an inhabited house and some cultivation. To the left the country was covered with trees, hamlets, and cultivation. Some three miles from Turfan we passed a mosque with a curious tower, which looked as much like a very fat factory chimney as anything else. It was about eighty feet high, circular, and built of mud bricks, and it was ornamented by placing the bricks at different angles, forming patterns. It was built at the southern and eastern corner of the courtyard of the mosque. The gateway was of the ordinary Indian pattern.

As I rode past a house, an old Turki invited me in; but I could not delay the cart. We reached Turfan at 6 a.m., putting up at an inn just inside of the southern part of the Chinese town. As I passed through the street there was a murmur of "Oroos," "Oroos," and a small crowd of Turkis and Chinese collected in the inn yard to see me. My boy was told there was a Russian shop in the Turk city, so I went over there with a man to guide me. We dismounted at a shop, and I was received by a fine-looking man, who shook hands with me and spoke to me in Russian. I told him I was English. He then took me through a courtyard to another courtyard with a roof of matting. On the ground were spread some fine carpets, on which sat some fair-looking men in Turk dress. None of them looked quite like Russians. They spoke no language that I knew, and things were rather at a standstill, when I heard the word "Hindustani." I said at once, "Hindustani zaban bol sakta" ("I can speak Hindustani"), and they sent off for a man. When he appeared, I had a long talk with him. He was an Afghan merchant, he said, and the men of this house were Andijani merchants. He had travelled through a great part of India, and knew Bombay, Calcutta, Delhi, Lahore, and all the cities of the Punjab.

He asked me if Peking was as big a town as Calcutta. I said, "No, nothing like so big." He was struck at this, and told the Andijanis of it. He then asked if I had seen the Katai-Badshah (the Chinese emperor) at Ba-jing (Peking). I said, "No." He then asked me how many Englishmen there were at Peking, and if they were merchants. I said we had an Elchi there, like the Russians, and the French, and other European nations. Peking is so distant that these Central Asiatic merchants do not visit it, and the only accounts they probably have of it are from the Chinese, who exaggerate to any extent the greatness of the capital of China and its emperor. I asked the merchant about the trade of the place, and he said silk was the only thing produced. These Andijani merchants spin the silk from the cocoons, but the Chinese manufacture it. After a time some tea was brought us. I asked if it was Indian or Chinese. They said it was Chinese, but Indian was to be bought in the town.

The Andijanis were tall, handsome-looking men, dressed in long robes of cotton print, and wearing high black leather boots with high heels—exactly the same as the Cossacks wear, but the bottom part was not attached to the upper. It was a slipper which they kicked off before stepping on to the carpet, leaving the long boot still on, but with a soft, flexible foot.

After tea I again went to the Turk city to have a look at the shops. The chief—in fact, almost the only—articles sold here are cotton fabrics, principally chintz. Some of them were remarkably pretty, with patterns of flowers, and others handkerchiefs of many colours, arranged together in patterns very tastefully.

There was also a good deal of Andijani silk of various colours. The silk of this place was only white; I could find none coloured. I bought a yard, fifteen inches wide, for sixty tael cents (about three shillings). It is very coarse. The shops are open towards the street, but divided from it by a counter, behind which stands the shopman, surrounded on all sides by shelves, reaching from floor to roof, and containing rolls of cotton fabrics or silks. These shops are ten to twelve feet square, and are an improvement on the ordinary bazaar of an Indian town, but not so good as the Chinese shops.

While walking about looking at the shops, I saw a man with a different look to the Turks—more of the Hindustani appearance; so I addressed him in Hindustani, and to my delight he answered back. He said he was an Arab Hajji from Mecca. Some Turks, seeing us standing talking, very politely asked us over to a shop where there was a seat, so we had a long talk. The Hajji had travelled through India, Afghanistan, Persia, Egypt, Turkey, and Bokhara. I asked him where he was going next. He said wherever Fate led him. He was at Herat a year ago (1886), and, pointing his two forefingers at each other and bringing them together till they nearly touched, said that that was how the Russians and English were then. Then he let his forefingers pass each other, and, keeping them parallel, said that was how Russia and England were now. He then locked his two forefingers together, and said that was how England and the Amir of Afghanistan were. He said that this was a poor country—all jungle, no water, and no bread; whereas in India there was plenty of both. I asked him about the tribes of this part, and he said they were Turks (I could not get a definite name beside that). At Karashar there are Kalmaks, and also in the mountains. The Kalmaks are Buddhists. He asked if my boy was a Tungani, saying they were good men, but the other Chinese very bad. (He said this, of course, because the Tungans are Mussulmans.) His influence seemed to be very great. A large crowd of Turks collected round us, but by saying a few words he kept them clear of me, and they looked on silently. Now and then he addressed the crowd, and explained to them who the English were. I was glad of this, as he seemed to have a very good opinion of us. I heard him abusing the Chinese in the most open way, as there were several Chinamen there (Mohammedans, perhaps, though). A man like that might do a deal of good or a deal of harm, and I saw more clearly than before the great influence Mohammedanism has in these countries, and how dangerous this influence may be on occasions. The Mahdi was probably a man very like this Arab Hajji.

The owner of the shop in which we were gave me some tea, but I noticed the Arab took none. Whether he has caste, as in India, and won't drink with an infidel, I don't know. Both he and the Afghan came here from India *viâ* Peshawur, Kabul, and Bokhara. The Arab had been to Tashkent, and said it was as fine a town as Bombay. I felt quite brightened up by the conversations with these men. It was the first time for some months that I had been able to talk at all fluently with any one. Fancy an Englishman being so delighted to meet an Arab and an Afghan in Turkestan, and talking in Hindustani!

In the evening I saw two distinguished-looking men standing about in the courtyard of my inn, evidently wishing to see me, but not liking to intrude themselves on me as the Chinese do; so I went out to speak to them. They only spoke Turki, but I was able to make out that they were Kokhandees. Their country was Russian now, they said, and they called it "Ferghansky." I said I was Angrez (English), but they said at once, "Ingleesh." I got a few Turki words from them, and then they shook hands with me and went off.

I had read in some book that at Turfan it was so hot that

people lived in holes underground. I never quite believed it, but to-day I found it was a real fact. Here in the inn yard is a narrow flight of steps leading underground. I went down them, and found a room with a kang, and a Chinaman lying on it smoking opium. It was perfectly cool below there, and there was no musty smell, for the soil is extremely dry. The room was well ventilated by means of a hole leading up through the roof.

Turfan consists of two distinct towns, both walled—the Chinese and the Turk, the latter situated about a mile west of the former. The Turk town is the most populous, having probably twelve or fifteen thousand inhabitants, while the Chinese town has not more than five thousand at the outside.

The town is about eight hundred yards square. As usual, there are four gateways—N., S., E., and W. These are of solid brickwork, with massive wooden doors plated with iron. The gateway is covered by a semicircular bastion. The walls are in good repair. They are built of mud, and are about thirty-five feet high, twenty to thirty feet thick, and loopholed at the top. Outside the main wall is a level space fifteen yards wide, and then a musketry wall eight feet high, and immediately beyond it a ditch twelve feet deep and twenty feet wide. Over the gateways are drum towers. At the corners are small square towers, and between the corners and the gateways are small square bastions, two to each front.

There are few shops in the Chinese town, and those not good. Turfan is a "Ting" town. This town and its neighbourhood lies at an extremely low altitude. My barometer here read 29·48. My thermometer was broken, so that I cannot record the temperature, but it may be taken at between 90° and 100°—say 95°. Turfan must be between two and three hundred feet below the level of the sea.* It is very

---

* This depression was also noticed by Colonel Bell before my visit, and its existence has since been confirmed by Russian travellers.

remarkable that such a depression should occur so far inland in the heart of a continent.

July 18.—Started at 5.10 p.m., passing out of the Chinese town by the west gate and through the Turk town, after which we turned off south, passing over a plain with a good deal of cotton planted on it. Wheat has now nearly all been reaped. The poppy crop is also over. At five miles we rounded the end of a low spur running down from the Tian-shan, and passed over a level valley covered with scrub, but uncultivated. A tremendous wind was blowing, making our progress very slow, so we halted at 11 p.m., at a solitary inn, sixty li from Turfan.

July 19.—Started at 3 a.m., still crossing the plain, gradually approaching a line of cultivation to our left. Halted at 8.30 a.m., at Toksun. This is a small town, or rather two small towns, both walled, each about a quarter of a mile square, and half a mile apart. There is a small garrison here, probably four or five hundred men. The shops are small. Here and at Turfan grapes and melons are very plentiful. The Turfan grapes are very good, and nearly equal to those grown in English hothouses. They are large, very fleshy, and full of flavour. One kind is elongated, and some of them are one and a half to one and three-quarter inch long.

Started again at 3.40 p.m., in a southerly direction. The cultivation lasted for a mile, and then gave place to scrub, which three miles further ceased, and we ascended the bare gravelly slope of a range to the south. The gravel was mixed with sand, and loose, so the going was very heavy, and we got along slowly. Here, as at all the difficult pieces along the road, skeletons of horses were numerous, and we also passed two human skeletons. At sixteen miles from Toksun, we entered the hills, perfectly bare, as usual, and four miles further halted at an inn on a small stream.

Weather to-day cooler; very strong westerly wind.

July 20.—Started at 5.30 a.m., and had a very long hard

day's work, ascending the bed of a stream covered with loose shingle. We got the cart along by a succession of rushes—the carter on one side and the boy on the other, urging the animals for a short time, then stopping, then making another spurt, and so on. We should have thought nothing of this in Manchuria, but there the mules had less to pull. The stream, like others in these mountains, has a peculiar course. At the lower end of the gorge no stream was visible. As we ascended, a small trickle appeared, which gradually increased in size to a small stream, and then suddenly disappeared again beneath the gravel. We halted for a couple of hours where it was last visible, twelve miles from the inn, and fed the animals. In the afternoon we had the same hard pull up the gorge. On either hand were bare precipitous hills, eighteen hundred or two thousand feet high.

We halted at 6 p.m., at a spring of clear cold water at the base of a cliff. It came on to rain heavily later, but I was snug inside the cart, the boy slept underneath it, and the carter in a hollow of the cliff. One can make one's self very comfortable in the cart, with a mattress spread over the baggage and a waterproof sheet hung across the front.

Weather to-day cool; rain in the evening.

July 21.—We had now a very nasty piece to cross. A landslip had fallen right across the stream, which was blocked by huge boulders. We unloaded the cart, and put the baggage on the mules' backs and took it across to the other side. This they did in two or three trips, and then returned for the empty cart, which the two mules, two ponies, and two men managed with the greatest difficulty to get over the boulders. The cart was then reloaded, and we set off again, ploughing through the shingle, but not for long, for another landslip blocked the way, and the cart had to be unloaded again. We finally reached an inn, only one and a half mile from our camping-place of last night, in seven and a half hours. In the inn was a Su-chou merchant who had seen Colonel Bell at that place. The name of this inn was Wu-hau-pu-la.

Started again at 5.25 p.m. The shingle soon became firmer, and the hills less precipitous and more open. At nine miles from Wu-hau-pu-la we reached the summit of the range. The descent was easier. At sixty li we passed an inn, but continued through the night, emerging from the hills and descending the gravel slope to Kumesha, a hamlet of some twenty houses, and also barracks, in which a detachment of soldiers were stationed. Water obtained from a small spring and stream. Weather cool, and at night almost cold. Near the top of the pass I saw an ibex horn measuring thirty-two inches.

July 22.—Started at 3 p.m., crossing a plain between two parallel ranges of hills, the southern being from one to two miles, and the northern from ten to twelve miles distant. The plain was covered with scrub. At sixteen miles from Kumesha we entered the southern range by a gorge through which ran a stream, now dry. Going heavy. Halted at 9.35 at Yu-fu-kou, an inn and a small custom-house (sixty li).

Weather cool; wind northerly.

July 23.—Started at 4.30 a.m., ascending the bed of the stream for two and a half miles, the hills gradually opening out. The road then emerges on to a plain sloping very gradually toward the south, and bounded at a distance of about ten miles by a low range of hills. This plain is crossed in a direction west by south. At fifteen miles a small hut and well are passed. Halted at 2.30 at Ush-ta-le (Chinese pronunciation), Ushak-tae on Russian map, a village situated on the level at the foot of the sloping plain we had been descending. We had been told that this was a big place, but it does not boast more than fifty houses. Bread, however, was to be bought here, and eggs were thirteen for five tael cents (threepence) instead of only five, as at Kumesha. There is a small fortified barrack to the west of the village.

Started again at 8.15 p.m., passing over a plain covered with bushes and some trees. At two miles we crossed a small river, broad and shallow, running over a pebbly bed. This is the first stream of any size which I have crossed for nearly two thousand miles. At ten miles further we crossed another small river. These run down from the mountains four or five miles to the north, emptying themselves into a lake to the south. Twenty miles from Ush-ta-le we entered a country thickly covered with trees, like a park, with long coarse grass in tufts, and many small streams. The rainfall here must be considerably more than further east. The soil is sandy and apparently not worth cultivating, as we only passed one small hamlet, six and a half miles from Ching-shiu-kou, where we halted at 4.40 a.m. (distance ninety li).

This is a village situated on a stream some twenty yards broad and one and a half foot deep. One and a half mile from this we had crossed a stream, four feet deep, which nearly covered the mules and flooded the bottom of the cart.

Weather fine, and cool in evening.

July 24.—Started at 7.45 a.m., immediately outside the village passing a small fortified barrack with the eastern wall washed away, but the gap had been filled up with fascines. Rain began to fall as we started, and we had a wet march to Karashar, over a moorland covered with bushes and some trees, which looked like elm. At ten miles from Ching-shiu-kou we crossed a bog by a causeway. The country was almost uninhabited, though water was plentiful. It was not till within two miles of Karashar that we passed a small hamlet. We entered Karashar (ninety li from Ching-shiu-kou) at 2.30 p.m., by the eastern gate, passing out again at the southern, and putting up at an inn close by.

The town of Karashar, like all towns hereabouts, is surrounded by a mud wall, and the gateways are surmounted by the usual pagoda-shaped towers. There is a musketry wall running round outside the main wall, but it is now almost in ruins. Inside the wall are some yamens, but only a few houses. Outside, to the south, are a few shops and inns.

I had a conversation with some Tunganis who came to see me. They said the population of the place is almost entirely Tungani and Turks. In the mountains round are Kalmaks and Khirgiz. These Tunganis (they called themselves Tungani without my asking who they were) are not distinguishable in features from an ordinary Chinaman, but they seem cleaner and more respectable than the Chinese about here, who appear to be the scum of the central provinces of China proper.

July 25.—We had to make a half-halt to-day, to dry things which had been wetted in the river on Saturday night. I went for a stroll round the place. Outside of the walled city there are two streets running down to the river, which is rather more than half a mile from the walls; the northern street has most shops, but they are poor. Near the river were some encampments of Kalmaks. They are regular Mongols, living in yurts and dressed as other Mongols, and wearing pigtails, the round coloured caps with a tassel, and long coats. They are easily distinguishable from both Chinese and Turks. I questioned several people about the different races of this part of Turkestan, and was told that there were three different races—the Kitai (Chinese), Tungani, and Turks, and here at Karashar were a few Kalmaks. The Turks do not appear to be divided into tribes, but are called by the town they belong to. The Chinese call them Chan-teu (turban-wearers). One Turk, with whom I was trying to converse, took me off to a shop where there was a man who had been on a pilgrimage to Mecca, and had seen Lahore, Bombay, Suez, and Constantinople. He only spoke Persian, unfortunately. It is wonderful the distances these pilgrims travel. I could find no Hindustani-speaking men in Karashar.

I had told the innkeeper to look out for a good pony for

me, and two were brought up for inspection. I bought one for twenty taels (£5), a good weight-carrying cob, short back and legs, enormous quarters, but with much pleasanter paces than his looks would warrant. I thought he ought to carry me to India well.

We started at 4.10 p.m., and had to cross the river by ferry at the end of the town. The river was about one hundred and fifty yards wide, and three to four feet deep, running through a level country, which would be flooded out if the river rose another couple of feet. The boat, which just held our cart and my two ponies, was poled across by three Kalmaks. On the other side we found a party of Kalmaks, riding donkeys, waiting to be ferried over. They were escorting a Mongol lady, the wife of one of their chiefs, back to her husband; she had been captured in some raid, and was now returning. She was very strong and robust-looking, and had the whole party under her thumb, and was abusing them right and left, because she had just got a wetting in a branch of the river they had crossed. She bustled about, unsaddling her donkey and turning it off to graze, and ordered the rest about, here, there, and everywhere.

At a hundred yards after leaving the ferry we had to ford a branch of the river, some thirty yards broad, and deep enough in places to wet the inside of the cart again. After this we passed over a swamp, and three times our cart stuck. The first time we were three hours trying to get it out of the mud, and it was not till we had taken everything out of the cart, and engaged some Turks to help shove and pull, that we succeeded in doing so. We then got along all right for a couple of miles, when we stuck again, and a second time had to unload everything. We then got clear of the swamp, but stuck a third time in a deep rut! The animals were so exhausted, that it was impossible to get on that night, as it was one o'clock, and we went off to the house of one of the Turks who was helping us, leaving the boy in the cart. The

Turk showed us into a most comfortable room, made of mud only, but looking clean for all that. A kind of dado of chintz had been arranged round the walls, which brightened up the place. On the kang, piles of felts and bedding were rolled up. There were two fireplaces in the room, but no chimney, the smoke going out through a hole in the roof. All sorts of household utensils were hung round the walls, and some mutton and herbs were hanging from a rafter. Everything was clean and neatly arranged, and there was no smell. It was a far superior room to those which are inhabited by the same class of men in an Indian village. My host bustled about to get some bedding ready for me, and brought me some tea, after which I turned in sharp, as I was very tired.

July 26.—Early this morning the cart was got out of the rut. I gave twenty-five cents to each of the five men who had helped us, and presented my host with some tea, sugar, candles, and matches. He was delighted, and salaamed profusely; the old lady of the house bowed very gracefully to me, too, as the things were brought into the house. They insisted upon my having some tea, and the lady produced a tray with some tea, bread, and flowers. The Turk then told me that another Englishman had also put up at this house a short time ago. After leaving the house the road was good, leading over a sandy plain covered with little bushes. At three miles we passed a small village with the ruins of a barrack.

Halted at forty li from the Turk's house, at Sho-shok, which only consists of a Turki house and an inn, kept up by government, with no one to look after it, and it was almost in ruins. We dried our things here; my clothes-bag was full of water. At sunset the mosquitoes came in swarms; and though we lighted four fires to smoke them off, it had no effect. We were to start at 1 a.m., and I lay down between the fires, but could not get a wink of sleep—rather hard luck after having been up till one the night before.

July 27.—Started at 1.25 a.m., the carter distinguished himself again by getting the cart into a deep rut, although the Turk whom we had brought with us had pointed it out to him. He is the worst carter in Asia. The Turk then took the matter into his own hands, turning the carter out of the cart with ignominy. A good deal of knack is required in driving these teams. We have two mules and one pony abreast in front, and one pony in the shafts. The difficulty is to get them all to start together. Whipping is no good; the only way is by shouting. A good carter works himself up, and then gives a peculiar whoop, which sends all the mules into their collars. They are not good at it here, but in Manchuria, where the roads are so bad, they are first-rate, and will get a team of nine animals to work like one.

The road now passed through a country broken up into hillocks, and eleven miles from Sho-shok it entered a range of hills running in a north-and-south direction, and followed the bank of a river which cuts its way through the hills. Three and a half miles further a custom-house and the ruins of a fort are passed, which occupy the narrow space between the river on one side and precipitous hills on the other. The valley bottom varies in width from two hundred yards to a quarter of a mile. The river is rapid, and of some length. It is from thirty to forty yards broad, flowing over a pebbly bed. The roadway has been made along the base of the hills, large masses of stone and boulder having been cleared away for the purpose.

We passed the flourishing little village of Kholga two and a half miles from the custom-house, on the opposite bank of the river. Here there was a steep ascent of three hundred yards, to cross a projecting spur. The descent on the opposite side was easy. Another spur, less steep, was crossed a mile and a half further on, and then we descended gradually to Korlia. The view of Korlia from the hill was very pretty. The whole plain below, along the river-bank, was covered with trees and cultivated fields, amongst which could be seen the walls of Korlia. There was a greater extent of cultivated land here than in any other town we had passed. We reached Korlia at 9.25 a.m., and put up at an inn outside the south gate of the town. Korlia has two towns, the Chinese and the Turk. The Chinese is only some four hundred yards square, surrounded by a mud wall some thirty-five feet in height, and by a ditch. There are round bastions at the angles, but no bastion at the gateway. The entrance is on the south side only. One mile south is the Turk town, washed on its northern face by the river, which is crossed by a wooden bridge. The walls of the Turk town are in ruins. The town has one principal street running north and south, about seven hundred yards long. The shops are somewhat better than at Karashar, but not so good as at Turfan. The people here seem prosperous, and the country round is well cultivated. Wheat was just being reaped, maize was grown in large quantities, and rice was also cultivated.

We changed one of the cart-ponies here, and just before starting engaged a Turk to come with us to Kashgar. Starting again at 7.25 p.m., we took a northerly direction at first, till we reached the desert, along which we proceeded in a westerly direction, skirting the cultivated land. Halted at 11.10 p.m., at an inn where the cultivation ended (forty li).

July 28.—In the morning we found the Turk had disappeared. The carter, delighted to find somebody whom he thought he could lord it over, had abused and ordered him about, so that he had wisely taken his departure during the night.

Started at 4.45 a.m., crossing a desert covered with scrub. The cultivated land could be seen extending along the banks of the river in a south-westerly direction. At seventeen miles we passed the ruins of an inn, and, eight miles further, entered a country covered with trees, but with not much undergrowth. Halted at 2.40 p.m. at Charch, a small hamlet on the banks of a stream. There are ruined barracks here (140 li). Started again at 6 p.m., joining another cart, also going to Kuché. The country was like that which we passed over in the morning, well covered with trees. At twenty miles we passed a ruined house near some water. Halted at 3 a.m., at Yerum-kou (ninety li), a small village on a stream.

July 29.—We had an entire re-organization of the party here. The carter of the cart accompanying us agreed to come to India with me for six taels a month. He is young and strong, and understands the management of ponies, so I hope he will turn out useful.

The carter from Hami was turned off, and we took on a Chinaman, who was returning to Kashgar. My boy now told me that he had himself bought the cart and team at Hami for 125 taels (£25).

The boy has sold the cart and team to the new carter for eighty-two taels, promising him twenty taels if we get to Kashgar in twenty days more.

Started at 3.25 p.m., passing over a desert till the cultivated lands of Yang-sar are reached. These are of some extent, reaching about eight miles from north to south, and some five miles in width.

The village of Yang-sar is not large, but the whole country is dotted with houses. The stream which waters the fields is crossed by a good wooden bridge, and the road is lined with trees.

July 30.—Started at 4.15 p.m. The cultivation ended after two miles, and then the road became bad, and several very awkward pieces of bog had to be crossed before we reached Bu-yur. We arrived there at 12.10 p.m. (ninety li).

This is a somewhat larger oasis than Yang-sar, and the village of Bu-yur contains two streets of shops. There are also barracks here with about three hundred soldiers.

July 31.—Started at 2.30 p.m., passing through cultivated land for ten miles. Two small streams were crossed, their banks lined with fine pasture land. A desert was now crossed, and we halted at 11.30 p.m.

August 1.— Started at 6 a.m. The cultivation ended immediately, and we passed over a gravel desert, sandy in places; going heavy. We constantly saw oblongs of stones, with a big one at the head, facing towards Mecca. These are temporary praying-places in the desert.

Halted at 11.30 a.m. at an inn without a keeper, in a very small oasis, with only one other house.

Talking with a Turk, I found out that the people about here are chiefly Doolans, a branch of the Turk people. These extend up to Turfan, but not to Urumchi. I can at present see no difference between them and other Turks. My informant said that at Urumchi there were Turks, but not Doolans.

Started again at 1.45 p.m., passing over a desert. Halted at 7 p.m. One inn was full of soldiers returning to their homes. My boy, and, in fact, everybody, has a dread of soldiers, who have the reputation of stealing everything they can lay their hands on. When a crowd collects round my room or the cart, and he hears that there are soldiers among them, Liu-san shouts out to me in English, "Master! look out! Soldier man plenty steal!"

The oasis is some seven or eight miles in length from north to south, and from two to three miles in width, watered by streams running down from the mountains.

Weather fine and hot.

August 2.—Started at 2.10, crossing a desert again, watered however, at intervals by three streams running down the slope. At 8.30 we arrived at the Kuché oasis, and for three miles passed through a country covered with trees and houses. The road also was lined with trees, and a good many houses, before we reached the actual town. The number of trees is very noticeable, and on the roadside the houses are actually built on to the trees.

We drove into an inn yard, but found there was no room; and were told that a batch of soldiers were passing through, so all the inns had closed their doors. The gallant defenders of their country are not held in much esteem by their fellow-countrymen. After waiting for half an hour in the cart, the landlord made arrangements for a room for me.

A Turk who spoke Hindustani now appeared. He was a Hajji, and had spent ten years in India, horse-dealing. He was very friendly, and asked if he could be of any service. I said I wanted a Turk servant to go to India with me, and also wanted to buy a good pony. He went off, saying there were plenty of both, and soon the inn yard was full of ponies. He was a regular Indian horse-dealer, and I laughed when he began with the usual "Sahib, ham juth ne bolege" ("I will not tell a lie"), "d'am assi rupuiys" ("the price is eighty rupees"). I told him I never told lies either, and what I would give was twenty taels (he reckoned eighty rupees at thirty taels). All sorts of ponies appeared, and I rode between twenty and thirty up and down the main street, which was the only place handy for trying them. They were asking about three times the price usually given for ponies in these parts, so I only selected one, which I bought for twenty-five taels (£5). It was about the lowest-priced pony they brought, but they were going by a different standard to mine, for size and weight-carrying capacity is what they value. The Hajji was very keen upon my buying a two-year-old pony marked with black spots all over. I said it was too young. "Not at all," he said. "He will be three or four years old by the time you get to India." This after he had told me I could get there in two months! Two Afghans also, who had lived here for twenty years, visited me. I asked them if they were here in Yakoob Beg's time. They said, "Yes; that was a good time then." The Afghans spoke of the conduct of the Chinese as very *sabardasty* (oppressive), and said the Turks were like sheep in submitting to it. One of the Afghans had known Sir Douglas Forsyth, and had heard of his death.

The Turk Kotwal came to see me, to report to the Chinese who I was, and what I was doing. He was the most good-natured old gentleman, and took down my answer as if it were a most unnecessary business to satisfy Chinese curiosity. I said I was returning to India, where I lived. Kuchê town and district has, probably, sixty thousand inhabitants. The Hajji told me that numbers of people went up into the hills during the hot weather. The Chinese town is some seven hundred yards square, with a wall twenty-five feet high, with no bastions, and no protection to the gateways, but a ditch some twenty feet deep. The interior is filled with houses, and has a few bad shops. The houses of the Turk city run right up to the ditch. About eight hundred yards north of the Chinese city are barracks for five hundred men; I estimate the whole garrison at one thousand five hundred; they are armed with old Enfield rifles, with the Tower mark. There are remains of the walls of the old Turk city south-east of the Chinese, but the greater number of houses and all the shops are outside of this. The shops are small, like those in India, and nothing of native manufacture is sold, excepting sheepskins, which are very cheap. My boy bought two for his parents, seven taels each; he says in Peking they would cost twelve or fifteen taels. I also bought one. Silks and cotton goods come from Andijan, Russia, and China.

August 2.—Started at 7.30 p.m., passing through the Chinese city, and afterwards through a well-cultivated country for three miles, when the desert began again. We now gradually ascended towards a range of hills, up the bed of a stream. Going very heavy.

Halted at 3 a.m. at an inn, without anybody in charge, near a small spring. A Turk's house was close by.

August 3.—Started at 6.10 a.m., still ascending the gorge. The stream cuts through one range of hills, on the north side of which was a sea of broken hillocks leading up to a second range, the ascent of which, for a quarter of a mile, was very steep, and took an hour and a half. It is covered with pebbles. At the summit is a small house where water is sold. The descent is easy, but lasts all the way to Kizil, where we arrived at 3.10. All along the road, pillars, made by Yakoob Beg, were erected at intervals of ten li. We put up at a good inn on the left bank of the river which fertilizes the Kizil lands, but the main part of the village is on the opposite bank.

Weather cloudy; thunderstorms in the hills.

August 4.—Started at 5.10 a.m., and had to cross the river close to the inn. It was swollen by rain, and divided into four channels, two of which were up to a man's waist; three hundred yards broad, and flowing with a rapid current. We had two men to lead the cart over, as sometimes carts are swept away bodily in these freshets. The land was cultivated for a mile on the other side, and all along the banks of the river below the village as far as I could see.

At 8.50 we passed through the village of Sarám, which is surrounded by a wall about two hundred yards square, now in ruins. Outside the village were the remains of barracks, now unoccupied. From this place to Bai the country was cultivated for the greater part of the way, being level and watered by numerous streams running down from the mountains. The road was lined with trees the whole way, and the country looked extremely pretty with the snowy mountains in the background. Wheat, oats, and maize were the chief crops. Reaping was just beginning. A noticeable thing in this country is the absence of local carts. They are not used at all for farm purposes or for carrying country produce into town. Donkeys only were used for this, and one only sees a few travelling carts used for long journeys. Arrived at Bai at 4.50 p.m. (120 li). It is a poor place, built on the right bank of a small river. It contains, perhaps, three thousand inhabitants, but the districts round are very populous, the cultivated land extending eight or ten miles to the north, and five or six miles to the south. Three-quarters of a mile from the river-bank, and separated from the town, are two square fort-like looking places, which I was informed were mandarins' quarters, and not barracks. There is a large yamen just outside the west side of the town, which is not surrounded by a wall.

Weather fine during day, but a heavy thunderstorm came on at 7 p.m.

On August 7 we arrived at Aksu, the largest town we had yet seen. It had a garrison of two thousand soldiers, and a native population of about twenty thousand, beside the inhabitants of the surrounding district. There were large bazaars and several inns—some for travellers, others for merchants wishing to make a prolonged stay to sell goods. A man will bring goods from some distance, engage a room in one of these inns or *serais*, and remain there for some months, or even a year or two, till he has sold his goods. He will then buy up a new stock, and start off to another town. It is in these *serais* that one meets the typical travelling merchant of Central Asia; and often have I envied these men their free, independent, wandering life, interspersed with enough of hardships, of travel, and risks in strange countries to give it a relish. They are always interesting to talk to: intelligent, shrewd, full of information. Naturally they are well-disposed to Englishmen, on account of the encouragement we give to trade; but they are very cosmopolitan, and do not really belong to any country except that in which they are at the time living. And this habit of rubbing up against men of so many different countries gives them a quiet, even temperament and breadth of idea which makes them very charming company.

I engaged one of these men, a native of the Pathan state of Bajaur, to accompany me to Kashgar, by Ush Turfan, while my cart went by Maral-bashi—Rahmat-ula-Khan was his name. He was a good specimen of his class, and full of adventurous projects. His great ambition was to visit England, but as he wanted to do so by land and not by sea, which he was afraid of, he wished to know how he could work his way there; and said he had often thought of taking over some *white* camels, which another merchant had told him could be obtained on the borders of the desert. On my questioning him about these camels, he said he was not sure that they were actually white, but they were of a very light colour, and quite peculiar animals, which would make a sensation in the Zoo.* He asked me, however, whether, I had any better suggestions to make as to how he could make a journey to England pay. I told him that if he would search about among the old ruined cities of this country and those buried by the sand, he might find old ornaments and books for which large sums of money would be given him in England, and before he left me I wrote for him letters to the directors of the British Museum, and of the museums at Bombay and Calcutta.

Under the guidance of this man, I left Aksu on August 10. I rode one pony myself, and another was ridden by the Turki servant, and a third, carrying all the baggage we took with us, was led by him. In this way we could travel fast, and make long marches. Several of the merchants from India accompanied us for the first half of the march, and provided a lunch in a garden under the shade of fruit trees. Here it was very cool and pleasant, and the merchants very cheery and companionable. The country, for several miles beyond Aksu, was

* He had seen the "Zoo" at Calcutta.

well cultivated, and the road good. We crossed the Aksu river, divided into many branches, a mile wide in all, the water in the deep channels being waist-deep. Further on we passed the small village of Aral, and the next day arrived at Ush Turfan.

This is a picturesque little town at the foot of a rugged hill, with a fort on its summit. There is a good bazaar here, and I met in it an old man who had been one of Yakoob Beg's chief secretaries, but was now in very poor circumstances. He could only mumble away rather indistinctly, but when he saw me he uttered the word "Shaw," and I immediately asked the people to question him, and found out that he had had a great deal to do with my uncle, and had a great regard for him. I was getting now, in fact, into country where people were constantly met with who knew Shaw and the members of the Forsyth Mission, and the interest of the journey increased. In Central Asia changes of *personnel* are sharp and radical. One year Yakoob Beg is unknown; the next he rules a vast country, and is surrounded by courtiers and great officers of state. For a short time they remain in power, and then they are swept clean away, and Chinese rule in their place. Of the men who were all-powerful at the time of Sir Douglas Forsyth's Mission, and Shaw's last journey in the country, only eleven years before my visit, but very very few remained, and those in the poorest circumstances. But it was interesting to meet them, and get them to talk of better days, and the state and grandeur which they had known.

After leaving Ush Turfan, we passed through a country cultivated at first, but afterwards relapsing into the more or less barren condition which is characteristic of the district. The sides of the hills which bounded the valley we were ascending were not, however, so utterly barren as many we had passed. There was a good deal of scrub and small bushes on them, and, higher up, fine grassy slopes in places. At the end of

ROBERT SHAW AND HIS ATTENDANTS, BEFORE LEAVING FOR KASHGAR, 1874.

the march we reached a Kirghiz encampment of twenty-two tents. Here were the first Kirghiz I had met; but most of the men were with their flocks and herds, higher up on the mountain-sides, and it was only the very old and the very young that were left down below with what might be called the heavy camp equippage. Having no tent of my own, and there being no public inn, I was obliged to do as the people of the country do, and seek the hospitality of the inhabitants of the tents. This was, as usual, readily given. We rode up to a tent, and Rahmat-ula-Khan went in, said we were travelling to Kashgar, and asked for accommodation for the night. In this way I found myself quartered in a tent with four very old ladies, one of whom was a great-grandmother, and the youngest a grandmother. They were very hospitable old ladies, and we took a mutual interest in each other. The tent was similar in construction to the yurts of the Mongols, but these Kirghiz seemed much better off than any of the Mongols I had met, or than the Kirghiz we afterwards saw on the Pamirs. They were well clothed in long loose robes of stout cotton cloth — generally striped — of Russian manufacture. Round the tents were piles of clothes and bedding for the winter—good stout felts and warm quilts; and rows of boxes to contain the household goods and treasures. A small portion of the tent was always partitioned off, and there were kept all the supplies of milk, cream, and curds, which form the staple food of the Kirghiz. On the whole, the tents were very clean and comfortable, and by living *en famille* with these Kirghiz, I got to see a great deal more of their customs and habits than I otherwise should have done.

Meanwhile, while I was looking round the tent, my hostesses were examining all my kit, and showing great interest in it. I had to take off my boots and socks, and it so happened that my socks had holes. This immediately appealed to the feminine instinct; they were whisked away, and one of the old ladies proceeded carefully to mend them. Good old soul, it quite reminded one of more homelike times to be looked after in this way! After mending the socks, the lady said her prayers, and throughout the time I was with them one or other of the old ladies always appeared to be praying.

In the evening all the cows and sheep and goats—mostly those with young ones—which had been left in the encampment, were collected and milked, and one or two young kids brought into the tent to be better looked after. The milk was very rich in cream, and delicious to drink. But the Kirghiz drink whey mostly, and they have a method of rolling the nearly solidified curds into balls about the size of a man's fist, and drying these balls in the sun to keep for the winter or for a journey. Balls of curds like these are not very appetizing, but they are much consumed by the Kirghiz. All the bowls for collecting the milk are of wood, and by no means so cleanly kept as one would like to see; I doubt, in fact, if they are ever thoroughly cleaned. The milk of one day is poured out, and that of the next poured in, and so on for month after month. Still, the milk always seems fresh and good, and it is one of the luxuries which form the reward for travelling among the Kirghiz.

The proprietresses of the tent I was in had their dinner of curds and milk and a little bread, and then, as it grew dark, they said it was time to go to bed. They first said their prayers, then took down one of the piles of bedding (bedsteads were, of course, unknown), and insisted on making up a bed of quilts and felts for me; and then, having made up their own also, and pulled a felt over the hole in the roof in case it might rain during the night, took themselves to their beds, and we all slept comfortably till morning.

On the following day we continued up the valley, and every few miles passed a small encampment of Kirghiz. We were, in fact, regularly in the Kirghiz preserves. The nomads are not cultivators, as a rule, but we passed a few patches of cultivation, and what was very remarkable was that this cultivation was very often—generally indeed in this valley—of poppies. On inquiry, I found that, though the Kirghiz do not smoke opium themselves, they find poppies a most paying crop to grow, and can sell the produce much more profitably than that of any other crop.

On August 14, after passing through a camping-ground called Sontash, we put up for the night at another named Ak-chak, and on the following day crossed the Kara-kara Pass, entered a rather bare plain sloping westward, and about fifteen miles beyond the first pass crossed a second. We were now in what is known as the Syrt country. There was no particular road, but the tracks of animals leading in many directions. We had brought a Kirghiz with us to show us the way, but he now refused to do so, and eventually left us stranded in the midst of a series of bare, low hills and sterile plains, without apparently any water, or any inhabitants, or any special road. We knew, too, that what people we should meet had not a good reputation, and were said to rob and murder travellers occasionally, and matters looked unpleasant. We pushed on, however, in the general direction of Kashgar, and towards evening, after a very hard march, reached an encampment of six tents. The owner of the one we applied to was very surly, but eventually agreed to give us accommodation for the night. As we entered the tent, I was startled on seeing a huge, fierce-looking eagle tied by the leg just at the door. From all appearances, it would require very little provocation to cause it to fly at one, and I was relieved when I found myself safely past it. It was one of the eagles which the people of the part keep for hawking purposes, and with these they secure even small deer. I never saw them at this sport, but I recollect some years afterwards, on the Pamirs, seeing a Kirghiz catch an eagle for this purpose by *riding* it down. When I first saw the man starting off to gallop down an eagle, I thought he must be mad. We had seen two eagles on the ground in the distance, and as soon as the Kirghiz caught sight of them he set off wildly after them. They, of course, rose on seeing him, but he went careering down the valley after one of them till gradually the bird sank down to the ground. It was, in fact, gorged with the flesh of the carcase it had been feeding on, and could no longer fly. The Kirghiz dismounted, seized hold of the bird, bound his waist-cloth round and round the body and wings till he had made it up into a neat parcel, and then tucked it under his arm, mounted, and rode back to me. He said that, if it turned out to be a good one for hawking, he might get two hundred rupees for it. I questioned the owner of the eagle in the tent in which we were now staying about the training of these eagles, but he was too surly to give me any satisfactory answers, and it was with no very grateful feelings towards him that we left his camp on the following morning.

We travelled hard all day, and, at the end of a march of forty-six miles, over a country mostly composed of bare hills and gravel plains, but with occasional clumps of trees in the hollows, we reached a wide plain of light clay, in the middle of which we found a very large encampment of fully a hundred tents. But the inhabitants were far from friendly, and it was only after considerable difficulty that a man was found who was willing to put us up. Rahmat-ula-Khan was very tactful and persuasive, but he told me that night that the people were very badly disposed towards us, and advised me to be watchful.

Next morning matters were worse. As I mounted to ride away, crowds of these rough Kirghiz collected round me, gesticulating wildly. I asked Rahmat-ula-Khan what was the matter, and he said that they had determined not to let me through their country. They argued that no European had been through before (though this was not true, as a party of British officers from Sir Douglas Forsyth's Mission came into their country as far as the Below-ti Pass), and that they did not see any reason why I should be allowed to. Some of the more excited were for resorting to violent measures, but Rahmat-ula-Khan, who all the time was keeping very quiet and even smiling, talked and reasoned with them, while I sat on my pony and looked on, well knowing that the Pathan could arrange matters best by himself.

It was curious to watch the gradual effect of his arguments, and the cool way in which he proceeded. He first of all drew them out, and allowed them to expend all the spare energy for vociferation they possessed, and then asked them what advantage was to be gained by stopping me. He said I had come direct from Peking, and had a passport from the Emperor of China, which I could show them; and that, having that passport, I was known, and my whereabouts was known, so that if anything happened to me they would have Chinese soldiers swarming over their country, and every sort of harm done them. He then went on to say that as far as he was concerned it was a matter of indifference whether they let me through or not; but, looking at the question from an outside point of view, it certainly seemed to him wiser on their part to let me go quietly on to the next place, and so end the matter. If they did this, nothing more would be heard of me; whereas, if they did anything to me, a good deal more might come of it. The upshot of the affair was that they allowed themselves to be persuaded, and it was agreed that I should be permitted to proceed on my way. Rahmat-ula-Khan had successfully extracted me from what might have been a very awkward situation.

He was one of the best men for this kind of work I could have found, for he was always well-spoken with the people, and cool in difficulties. He was a good companion, too, and on the long marches and after them, in the tent, he used to tell me of his travels, in the course of which he had been in Egypt, and was in Constantinople at the time of the Russian war. What struck him most about the Russians was that their soldiers were "pukka," that is, hardy. They were not so well treated as ours in the way of food and clothing, but they were "pukka," he kept on repeating, and ready to go through any amount of hardships. The trait he did not like in the Russians was their passion for passports; they were always at him for his passport, so that there was always a certain amount of difficulty or obstruction in moving about, and this interfered with his constitutional habit of roving. He was a strict Mohammedan, and seemed to me to be always praying, though he assured me he only did so the regulation five times a day. As to us, he thought we had no religion. He had observed us going to church on Sundays, but that was only once a week, and he did not know what we did for the remainder of the seven days. I knew that this man could be relied on, and so left this dispute with the Kirghiz entirely in his hands; and when he had settled it, we set out from the encampment.

This was the largest settlement I had met with, and the Kirghiz besides keeping flocks and herds, also cultivated a good deal of land. I noticed some houses scattered about the plain, and asked who lived in them, but was told that they were merely storehouses. The Kirghiz said that houses were good enough to put supplies of grain in, but they would not live in them for fear of their falling down.

From this place we determined to march on as hard as we could till we got out of the country inhabited by Kirghiz, and down into the plains again, where the people are all Turkis. This we succeeded in doing the same day. We followed down a stream, and then, after passing a small

Chinese post, emerged on to the great central plain of Turkestan again near Artysh. From here I saw one of those sights which almost strike one dumb at first—a line of snowy peaks apparently suspended in mid-air. They were the Pamir Mountains, but they were so distant, and the lower atmosphere was so laden with dust, that their base was hidden, and only their snowy summits were visible. One of these was over twenty-five thousand feet high, and another twenty-two thousand, while the spot where I stood was only four thousand; so their height appeared enormous and greater still on account of this wonderful appearance of being separated from earth.

Here, indeed, was a landmark of progress. More than a thousand miles back I had first sighted the end of the Tianshan Mountains from the desert. I had surmounted their terminal spurs, and then travelled week after week along their base, their summits constantly appearing away on my right hand. Now at last arose in front of me the barrier which was to mark the point where I should turn off left and south to India. It was a worthy termination of that vast plain, for the greater part desert, which stretches away from the borders of Manchuria to the buttress range of the Pamirs.

That evening we reached Artysh. Everything here looked thriving and prosperous. The fruit season was at its height, and all along the road, at any little garden, the most delicious grapes and melons could be obtained. Nor was there now any difficulty with the people, and they were always ready to allow us to rest for a time in their gardens or put us up for the night. I noticed a very large canal, which struck me as being an unusually fine work for the people of the country to undertake, and was informed that it had been made by Yakoob Beg. His intention had been to water a large desert tract beyond, but he had not lived to complete his task, and only a comparatively small piece of country is now irrigated by it. But it is a standing mark of his large ideas for the improvement of the country, and the people spoke regretfully of the indifference the Chinese showed towards the project.

On the following day we should reach Kashgar, and the second great stage of the journey would be completed. Half way from Artysh we passed through one of the most remarkable defiles I have seen. It lay through a low range of hills a few hundred feet high, and was up the course of a stream which had cut a passage in the rock so sheer and narrow that there was not room for much more than a laden mule to pass through, and the cleft was but little wider at the top to what it was at the bottom.

From this we emerged on to the Kashgar plain, passed through a populous, well-cultivated district covered with trees and fruit gardens, and at length entered the town of Kashgar, the distance to which, when I was starting from Peking, had seemed so vast. Here I was at last, and the culminating point of my journey had been reached. For the rest of the way I should be, so to speak, on my return. Kashgar was well known, too, from the Indian side, and there was a Russian consul stationed there. So when I reached the place I appeared to have arrived again on the fringes of civilization.

Passing through the native town, we put up at an inn on the southern side. I sent my card and passport to the yamen, and very shortly afterwards the Afghan Aksakal and a number of Indian traders came to see me. These Aksakals are men selected by the Chinese from among the traders of each country as their representative. They are responsible for reporting any new arrivals, and all dealings with their countrymen are carried on by the Chinese through them. They correspond to a certain extent to consuls, and perform some of the functions of a consul, but they are appointed and removed at the pleasure of the Chinese. This Afghan Aksakal, though he was afterwards suspected of having sheltered the murderer of Mr. Dalgleish (to whom I will refer presently), and had to leave

Kashgar, made himself very useful to me, and greatly impressed me. He struck me as a born soldier: strong-willed, capable, and made to command. He and many of the traders of the place—Afghans, Peshawuris, Badakhshis, and others—were with me nearly the whole day long during my few days' stay in Kashgar. Tea and fruit were always ready, and they used to sit round and talk. The Afghan's conversation was mostly of fighting, and of rifles and revolvers. Every kind of firearm he seemed to know, and to have his own opinion about it as to its efficiency. The Russian Berdan rifle he seemed to prefer to our Martini, and he thought the Americans made better revolvers than we did. At the time the Chinese re-took Kashgar he was in the town, and said there was practically no fighting. Yakoob Beg had died, or been poisoned, away westward some weeks before, and he being dead, there was no one to lead the defence, and the people of the country were absolutely apathetic. What soldiers there were, when they heard the Chinese were close to the town, hastily threw aside their uniforms or disguises as soldiers, and, assuming the dress of cultivators, walked about the fields in a lamb-like and innocent manner. The Chinese entered the town, and everything went on as if nothing had happened—the shopkeeper sold his wares, and the countryman ploughed his fields, totally indifferent as to who was or who was not in power in Kashgar. Only the ruling classes were affected, and most of them had fled.

The Afghan merchants would often talk, too, of our last war with them. Some of them had fought against us. They asked me one day where "Ropert" was. I did not quite understand at first who or what they meant. But they explained that he (it was a person apparently) was a first-rate man to fight, and then it struck me that they meant General Roberts. They had a great admiration for him. One of them said that he had set out from Kandahar to Kabul, but on the way had "met" General Roberts, and had returned. I was told afterwards that he had been in three fights with the British, but here, outside his own country, he was friendly enough with an Englishman, and he said he admired us for being able to fight quite as well as Afghans! They have a rather overpowering pride at times, these Afghans; but, on the whole, one likes them for their manliness. They are *men*, at any rate, and they are very good fellows to meet and talk with as one could do in a Kashgar *serai*. It was noticeable, too, that they never lost their respect either for themselves or for the Englishman they were talking with, so that we could converse away perfectly freely and openly. Altogether I much enjoyed my talk with them.

I was rather out of sorts the day after my arrival, but on the second I went to call on the Russian consul. The Afghan Aksakal had an idea that Russians and Englishmen were rather like cats and dogs in their relation towards each other, and that they could not meet without fighting. So, just as I was mounting my pony to go off, he caught me by the arm and whispered confidentially to me, "Now, sahib, do your best to be polite, and don't go fighting with that Russian." I found M. Petrovsky, the Russian consul, living in a native house, which, by improvements, he had made very comfortable. He and his secretary, M. Lutsch, received me very cordially, and sent for a missionary, M. Hendriks, who lived close by, to come and see me and hear the account of my journey from Peking. The talk turned on India, and I was astonished to find how well acquainted M. Petrovsky was with that country. He showed me with pride many volumes by the best English writers on Indian subjects, and the most recent parliamentary Blue Books on the country. The annual parliamentary report on the "Material and Moral Progress of India" was one which he took in regularly, and admired very much. He had known the present Amir of Afghanistan, Abdul Rahman, at the time he was a refugee in Samarcand, and he knew the names and a good deal of the personal history of most of the leading men in Kashmir. On the Central Asian question he spoke very freely, and said that we English always suspected the Russians of designs upon India, but that in reality nothing was further from their minds.

But comprehensive as was M. Petrovsky's knowledge of India and Central Asian affairs, I am not sure that they were what chiefly attracted him; and I am inclined to think that his heart really lay in scientific pursuits. In his library were large numbers of books of science, and his room was full of instruments of various descriptions—an astronomical telescope, barometers, thermometers of all kinds, an apparatus for measuring the movements of earthquakes, and various other instruments. He was evidently a man of considerable attainments. The consulate had been established in Kashgar about seven years, and both M. Petrovsky and M. Lutsch had been there from the beginning. They both understood English and read it, but had had little practice in speaking it. The Chinese they did not speak of at all favourably. According to them, they were lazy and corrupt, and administered the country very badly.

M. Hendriks had been in Kashgar for two or three years, and had previously belonged to a mission establishment on the borders of Mongolia. He was a man of varied accomplishments, who had travelled much, and who spoke or read most languages from Russian to Tibetan. So far he had had little success in actually converting the people of Kashgar, who are very apathetic, and little inclined to think much about religion of any sort, much less to take the trouble of changing that in which they were brought up. But M. Hendriks was a good doctor as well as a missionary, and often spent his time in visiting and prescribing for the sick, in this way doing much practical good.

When I returned to the *serai* from my visit to the consul,

the Afghan Aksakal eyed me closely, to see if there were any signs of a scrimmage with the Russian, and when I told him that M. Petrovsky was coming on the following morning to return my visit, he seemed relieved. I said I should want the room I was occupying made respectable to receive him in, and he immediately darted off in his usual impetuous manner, saying he would arrange everything. Shortly afterwards good carpets, chairs, a table, teapot, cups, saucers, and plates, came pouring in, and the room was in a few moments transformed into a civilized abode.

On the following morning the consul, with an escort of sixteen mounted Cossacks and the Russian flag, rode into the *serai*. We had another long conversation together, and it was a great pleasure to talk again with a European, after so many months of travel. M. Petrovsky is an especially interesting man to talk with, and I was sorry I could not stay longer in Kashgar to see more of him.

But, Liu-san having arrived with the cart, I had to start off again for Yarkand. Liu-san had fulfilled his contract, and landed everything in Kashgar exactly in the time stipulated—forty days from Hami—a good performance, with which I was very much pleased. Between Kashgar and Yarkand there was nothing of special interest that had not been noted by previous travellers. We had made the turn southwards, and now the Pamir Mountains, instead of being straight in front of us, were passed by on our right hand.

On August 29 we reached Yarkand, and were met outside by the Kashmir Aksakal and a large number of Indian traders, who had heard that an English officer was coming to Yarkand, and had come out to meet me. An Englishman always gets a warm welcome from natives of India in foreign countries. I have been told that it is all because of self-interest, and that they merely do it because they hope to get something out of him. Possibly this may be so, but I prefer to think that there

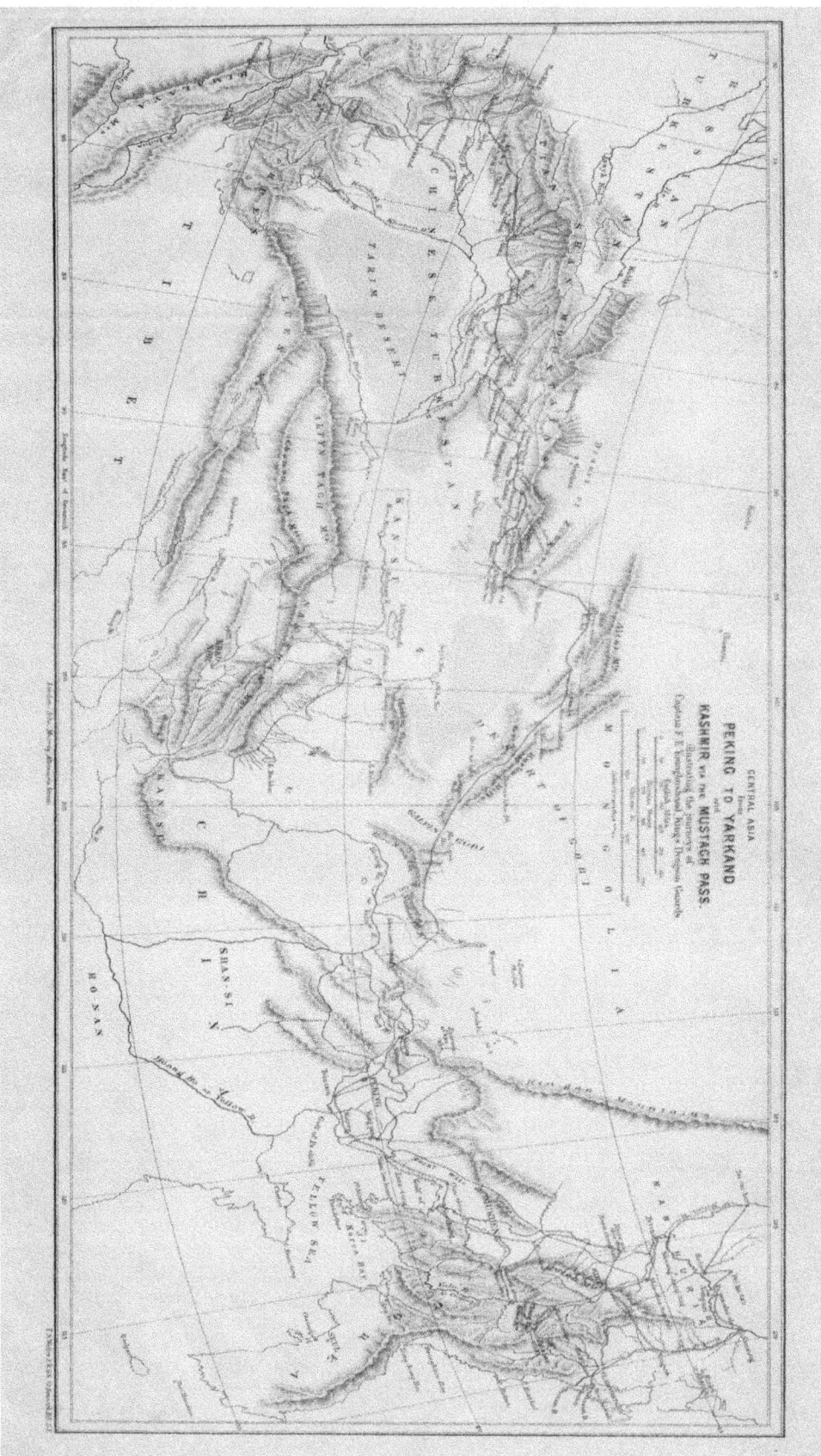

is also some tinge of warmth of heart in it, and a feeling of kinship with their rulers which attracts them in a strange land to an Englishman. At any rate, that was the impression produced upon me by my reception in Yarkand, and I would rather retain that than make way for the colder reasoning which has been suggested to me.

In the best Chinese inn in the place the chief room had been made ready for me by the Kashmir Aksakal. Carpets, chairs, and tables from his own house had been brought in, and large plates and baskets piled with fruit—presents from the merchants—came pouring in. Everything was done to make me comfortable, and the feeling that I was nearing my destination increased.

CHAPTER VII.

INTO THE HEART OF THE HIMALAYAS.

YARKAND was the last town of Chinese Turkestan I visited, and now that I had traversed the entire length of the country, a brief general description of it may be interesting. The chief characteristic of its physical features is undoubtedly the amount of desert comprised in it. The whole country is, in fact, nothing but a desert, with patches of cultivation along the streams which flow down from the mountains, showing out sharp and distinct like green splotches on a sepia picture. On three sides this desert is shut in by ranges of snowy mountains, very like the letter U, and on the fourth side it stretches away uninterruptedly for nearly two thousand miles. The mountain slopes are as bare as the plains, and were it not for the oases, no more inhospitable country could be imagined. But these oases are what save it. Once out of the surrounding desert, the traveller finds himself amidst the most inviting surroundings—cool shady lanes with watercourses running in every direction, alongside the road, across it, and under it, giving life to everything where before all was dead and bare and burnt. On either hand, as far as can be seen, lie field after field of ripening crops, only broken by the fruit gardens and shady little hamlets. Everything seems in plenty. Fruit is brought before you in huge trayfuls, and wheat is cheaper than even in India.

In this way it is a land of extremes. On one side nothing

AN OASIS IN CHINESE TURKESTAN.

—not the possibility of anything; on the other—plenty. And the climate has as great extremes as the physical appearance. The summer is scorchingly hot anywhere outside the small portion that is cultivated and shaded with trees; and in the winter the thermometer falls to zero Fahrenheit. This is the natural result of the position of the country in the very heart of the greatest continent, where none of the tempering effects of the sea could possibly reach it.

The people, however, do not share this characteristic of running to extremes. They are the essence of imperturbable mediocrity. They live in a land where—in the places in which anything at all can be grown—the necessaries of life can be produced easily and plentifully. Their mountain barriers shield them from severe outside competition, and they lead a careless, easy, apathetic existence. Nothing disturbs them. Revolutions have occurred, but they have mostly been carried out by foreigners. One set of rulers has suddenly replaced another set, but the rulers in both instances have nearly all been foreigners. Yakoob Beg was a foreigner, and most of the officials under him were foreigners, so that even when their hereditary rulers—the Chinese—were driven out for a time, the people of Chinese Turkestan did not rule themselves. On the contrary, in all these changes, they appear to have looked on with indifference. Such a people are, as might naturally be inferred, not a fighting race. They are a race of cultivators and small shopkeepers, and nothing more, and nothing would make them anything more. It is their destiny, shut away here from the rest of the world, to lead a dull, spiritless, but easy and perhaps happy life, which they allow nothing to disturb.

How different all this is to what we had found in Manchuria! There we had the keen, industrious Chinaman, working his very hardest—working away from morning to night, not to live merely, but to get the utmost he could out of the land, accumulating his wealth, seeking your custom, doing all he could to improve his position. The ruins, the dilapidated towns of Turkestan, were practically unknown there, and the large concentrated villages, instead of farmhouses scattered, as in Turkestan, indifferently over the country or situated among the fields of the owner, spoke of a people among whom the sterner habits of brigandage were unknown. Of the two races, the Chinese were evidently born to have the upper hand; but whether they therefore enjoy life so thoroughly as the easy-going Turki is a question open to doubt.

Yarkand, as I have said, was the last town in Turkestan I should pass through, and here I had to make preparations for the journey across the Himalayas. On entering the town I received a letter from Colonel Bell, written on the Karakoram Pass, saying he had just heard of my being in Chinese Turkestan, and telling me, instead of following him along the well-known and extremely barren and uninteresting route by Leh to India, to try the unexplored but direct road by the Mustagh Pass on Baltistan and Kashmir. This was a suggestion which delighted me. It was something quite new, and promised to be difficult enough to be really worth doing. I therefore set to with my preparations for it with a will.

The first thing, of course, was to get guides. Fortunately, there are a large number of Baltis—about two thousand—settled in the Yarkand district, and the Kashmir Aksakal said he would easily be able to obtain men for me. Then ponies had to be collected. Here, too, there was no difficulty, for Yarkand abounds in ponies. I used to examine thirty or forty a day. Sheepskin coats for the men, supplies for the road, shoes for the ponies, etc., were also things which could all be easily procured. So, having set one or two of the merchants to work at these preparations, I took a look round Yarkand.

The first place I visited was poor Dalgleish's house. For

ten or twelve years he had been settled in Yarkand as a trader —a true pioneer of commerce—and for the last two he had been the companion of Mr. Carey, of the India Civil Service, in one of the most adventurous and daring journeys that has ever been made in Central Asia—a journey right round Chinese Turkestan and into the very heart of Tibet. He was now in India, preparing to return to Yarkand, but he was fated never to reach that place again. On his way there, near the summit of the Karakoram Pass, he was treacherously murdered by an Afghan, and so ended the career of one who had done much for our good name in this distant land. Every one who mentioned his name spoke of him with kindliness and respect. It was hard to drive a bargain with him, the traders said, as it is with every other Scotchman, but they appreciated this sign of business capacity, and they liked his openness and fairness and truthfulness. Whenever he could, he was ready to help them; he regularly threw in his lot with them, and lived amongst them in every way as one of themselves. In this manner he secured their affection to an extraordinary degree—to such an extent, in fact, that the Russian consul at Kashgar afterwards told me that when one of his servants, after his murder, came to him, the man could not restrain himself from crying, evidently from unaffected grief; and M. Petrovsky said he could never have believed that an Asiatic could become so devoted to a European. These are the men, quite unremarkable though they appear when met with in ordinary life, who are the true missionaries of all that is best in our civilization. Their real greatness is only apparent when they are separated from us by the distance of death—like a picture, coarse and rough when viewed too closely, but instinct with depth of feeling when viewed from a distance. It is they who, going ahead, pave the way for others to follow; and every Englishman and every European who visits Yarkand territory after Dalgleish, must owe a debt of gratitude to the first impression of good feeling which he established for us there.

And, relation of mine though he be, and biassed as I may be thought towards him, I do not think that in this place I ought to omit a mention of my uncle, Robert Shaw, the first of all Englishmen, together with Hayward, to visit Yarkand, and the officer selected by the Government of India, in Yakoob Beg's time, as Political Agent to that prince. Schlagentweit, the only European who had ventured into Chinese Turkestan from India before Shaw and Hayward, had been murdered. Nothing was known of the country. It was hidden in mystery far away beyond the Himalayas. Alone, in the capacity of a merchant, he set out with a caravan to penetrate into the weird unknown. On the confines of the country he was overtaken by Hayward—an explorer as bold as himself, who was afterwards murdered in Yasin, a valley of the Hindu Kush. Together they were escorted on to Yarkand—together, but separated, for they were always kept apart, and communication between them was forbidden. After many trials and dangers, these two returned safely to India, with a favourable report of the country. A year or two afterwards the Government of India sent there an imposing mission under Sir Douglas Forsyth, and subsequently Shaw again visited the country as Political Agent. He stayed there then for more than a year; he composed a valuable grammar and vocabulary of the language, and also a history of the country, which is now with his relatives, in manuscript. During this time he instinctively attached himself to the people, and to illustrate the lasting effect of the devotion which he evoked, I will give one story. Two years ago the servant of an English officer was travelling alone on the borders of this country, and unexpectedly found himself in a peculiarly awkward position, which placed him absolutely in the hands of a native official. This man could have ruined the servant, but, knowing he was in the employ of an Englishman, he said, "I too was once an Englishman's servant; I was in the employment of Shaw Sahib, and out of gratitude to him I will now let you off."

The house where Shaw had lived chiefly, I was told, had all been pulled down by the Chinese, and official yamens built in its place. Dalgleish's residence was a comfortable little native house in the old city, where he used to sell his goods himself. Here the usual trays of fruit were brought me, and after spending the morning there talking to the numerous visitors, I returned to the inn and prepared for a visit I was to make to the Chinese governor of Yarkand in the afternoon. Hitherto, since leaving Peking, I had purposely kept from visiting the Chinese officials, partly because I had no proper interpreter, and partly because I was travelling in such a quiet way that the official probably would not care to return my visit in a wretched traveller's inn. Chinese officials surround themselves with a good deal of state when they appear in public, and it seems to go as much against the grain with them to visit a stray foreigner in a traveller's *serai*, as it would to the mayor of an English town if he were expected to get into his full livery and go with all civic ceremony to call upon a wandering Chinaman putting up at the local Blue Posts. As a rule, therefore, I merely sent my passport and my card up to the chief official, said I had just arrived, and would leave the next day, or whenever it was, and that I regretted I should not be able to do myself the pleasure of calling on him. But this governor of Yarkand showed particular civility, and sent me several friendly messages, so I called upon him on the afternoon after my arrival.

He received me with the usual politeness of a Chinese official, but with more cordiality. His residence here in Yarkand, at the very extremity of the Chinese Empire, was of precisely the same pattern and character as those in Peking itself, and the governor's dress was exactly similar to that of any official in the heart of China. In whatever part of the Chinese Empire you visit an official, you will always find both his residence and his official dress precisely the same: the loose blue silk jacket and petticoat, and either the mushroom hat in summer, or the pork-pie hat in winter. No change or variation, whether the office is civil or military. Difference in rank is shown only by a slightly increased amount of gold for the higher grades on the square plate of embroidery in the centre of the jacket, and by the colour of the button on the top of the hat.

The Governor of Yarkand received me in one of his private rooms, and we had a long conversation together. He had never been to Peking, and asked many questions about it, and about the road by which I had come, which he said no Chinese officials ever thought of using. An hour after I had reached the inn again, he came to make a return call upon me, and in every way showed a friendly feeling. This Amban was one of the best governors Yarkand has had, and, contrary to the usual custom of the Chinese officials, he had taken considerable pains to construct canals for the extension of cultivation, and to build new bazaars in the city.

Yarkand is the largest town I had seen in Turkestan. There are, as everywhere in this country, two towns, the native and the Chinese, but at Yarkand these are connected by a bazaar a few hundred yards in length. The latter is almost entirely new, but the native town is old and dilapidated. The houses are built of mud, as a rule, and there are no very striking buildings to arrest one's interest. All the streets have that dusty, dirty, uncared-for appearance so characteristic of Central Asian towns, and outside the bazaars there is little life. Yarkand, however, is the centre of a considerable trade, and in the autumn large caravans start for and arrive from India at frequent intervals, and the bazaars are then crowded.

A large number of the merchants engaged in this trade

gave me one day a sumptuous feast in a fruit garden a short distance outside Yarkand. Few people know the way to enjoy life and make themselves comfortable better than these merchants. We first of all sat about under the shade of the trees, while huge bunches of grapes and delicious melons and peaches were freshly plucked and brought to us to eat. Then dinner was announced, and after water for washing the hands had been passed round, we set to at dish after dish of "pillaos" and stews, all beautifully cooked, and we ended up with a pudding made of whipped egg and sugar and some other ingredients, which it would be hard to beat anywhere. All the time the merchants were chaffing away amongst themselves, and were as "gay" and talkative as Frenchmen. You could scarcely wish for better company or more genial hosts. On the way home we had races, each merchant trying to make out that his own horse was better than the others. These men are a curious mixture of Eastern gravity and politeness, and boyish spirits and fun. They will come to call on you, and talk away with the greatest solemnity and deference. You meet them next day out for a burst of enjoyment, and every sign of gravity is thrown away, and they are as free and natural and full of life as children.

With the aid of a committee of some of these, my preparations for the attack of the Mustagh Pass progressed most favourably. The services of a first-rate guide were secured; his name was Wali, and he was a native of Askole, the nearest village on the Baltistan side of the pass. He had come to Yarkand by the route many years before, but undertook to say he had not forgotten it, and could guide me by it all right. Beside him, three other Baltis were enlisted to carry loads, if it should be found impossible to take ponies over the pass. Thirteen ponies were bought, and four Ladakis engaged to look after them. Among these Ladakis was a man named Mohamed Esa (formerly Drogpa), who had accompanied Messrs.

Carey and Dalgleish to Tibet, and whom Colonel Bell had sent back to me to help me through. He was placed in charge of the caravan, and made responsible for its efficiency. Three complete sets of shoes for each pony were taken, and new pack-saddles and blankets. All the men were thoroughly well equipped with heavy sheepskin coats, fur caps, and new foot-gear. Orders were sent on to Kugiar, the last principal village on the Yarkand side, to have three weeks' supplies for men and ponies ready there, and these supplies for the men included rice, *ghi* (clarified butter), tea, sugar, and some sheep to drive along with us, so that the men should be fit and work willingly; for, after all, the success of the enterprise would depend upon them, not upon me. All I could do was to see that nothing which foresight could provide for should be left undone before the start was made. Lastly, we took some good strong ropes and a pickaxe or two, to help us over the ice and bad ground.

All these preparations having been completed, we left Yarkand on September 8. The next day we reached the thriving little town of Kargalik. It was market day, and all the roads were crowded with country people coming in to sell their produce, and buy any necessaries for the week. I have not mentioned these market days before, but they are a regular institution in Turkestan. Each town and village fixes a day in the week for its market day, and on that day the bazaars are crowded with people, and it is then that the country people do all their business. In small places the bazaar is absolutely empty all the rest of the week; the shops are there, but their doors are shut. Then on the market day everything bursts into life, and hundreds of men and women from the country round, all dressed in their best, come swarming in.

We put up that day in a delightful fruit garden, and my bed was made in a bower of vines, where the grapes hung in enormous clusters, ready to drop into my mouth. Two days later we reached Kugiar, an extensive village, where all supplies were gathered, in preparation for our plunge into the mountains. We were now among the outlying spurs of the great barrier which divides the plains of India from those of Turkestan. Of this barrier the nearest range is called the Kuen-lun, the centre the Mustagh or Karakoram, and the furthest the Himalayas.

On leaving Kugiar we headed directly into these mountains, and were fairly launched on our voyage of exploration, though the first three marches had been traversed by members of the Forsyth Mission. We crossed an easy pass named the Tupa Dawan, and then ascended a valley in which were a few huts and some felt tents belonging to a race called Pakhpu, whom Dr. Bellew, the skilled ethnologist who accompanied the Forsyth Mission, considered to be of a pure Aryan stock. They were very fair, and their features fine and regular.

Leaving this valley, I crossed the Chiraghsaldi Pass, over the main ridge of the Kuen-lun Mountains. The only aneroid I had was unfortunately not made to register up to such heights as the pass, but I computed its height at about sixteen thousand feet. We were now getting into the heart of our work, and as I looked out from the summit of that pass on to the labyrinth of pathless mountains, rising into tier after tier of snowy peaks, I felt that there was some real stern work before us, and that each one of our little party would have to brace himself up to do his very best if we wished to accomplish the task that had been set us. There were now no paths and no inhabitants. We were alone among the mountains, and it was not only the difficulties which they might present that we had to contend against; we also had to be ever-watchful against an attack from the Kanjuti robbers, who had for many years infested these parts, issuing from their strongholds in Hunza, and raiding on caravans trading between Yarkand and Leh by the Karakoram route, and even levying blackmail from villages in the Kugiar district. Three of the men I had with me had actually been captured by these robbers and afterwards sold into slavery. It was necessary to take every precaution, and as it is their habit to attack at night, and cut the ropes of the tent and let it down on the top of you, if you are unwary enough to use one, we had to live in the open, even on the glaciers, and, however cold it might be, sheltering ourselves behind any friendly rock we could find, and after dark always altering the position we had ostentatiously assumed during daylight, so that if any Kanjutis happened to have been watching us then, we might, under the shelter of the night, stand less risk of them finding us.

Descending from the Chiraghsaldi Pass, we followed down the pebbly bed of a stream. But soon the stream disappeared under the stones, nor could we find grass or bushes for fuel. Darkness came on, and with it a snowstorm; but still we plodded on, as under these circumstances there was no possibility of encamping. Stumbling along over the heavy boulders, we at last came across some bushes, and a little further on the stream appeared again; grass was found on its edges, and we encamped for the night.

On the following day we reached the Yarkand River at Chiraghsaldi camping-ground—the furthest point reached by Hayward on his march down the river nearly twenty years before. The river was at this time of the year fordable, and ran over a level pebbly bed, the width of the valley at the bottom being three or four hundred yards. All along the bottom were patches of jungle, and here and there stretches of grass; but the mountain-sides were quite bare.

Proceeding down the Yarkand River, we reached, the next day, the ruins of half a dozen huts and a smelting furnace, on a plain called Karash-tarim. There were also signs of furrows, as of land formerly cultivated, and it is well known that up to a comparatively recent period, certainly within eighty years ago, this valley of the Yarkand River was inhabited,

IN THE HIMALAYAS.

and spots like this, which included about a hundred and fifty acres of arable land, were cultivated. The district is known as Raskam, which, I was told, is a corruption of Rást-kán (a true mine), a name which was probably given it on account of the existence of mineral deposits there. Both on this journey and another which I made down this valley in 1889, I found the remains of old smelting furnaces in several places, and was informed that copper was the mineral extracted. In the Bazardarra valley, on the right bank of the Yarkand River, there are said to be traces of gold. The Kanjuti raids were the cause of the country becoming depopulated, and now that these have been effectually stopped by the British Government, we may expect to see Raskam, in future years, again spring into life.

One march below Karash-tarim the valley narrowed considerably, and high cliffs constantly approached the river, making it necessary for us to cross and recross it frequently. At length it became confined in a gorge, called the Khoja Mohamed gorge, and was here shut in between cliffs of enormous height and nearly perpendicular. Through this gorge the river rushed with great force, and, as it was quite unfordable, we were brought to a standstill. We unloaded the ponies, and every man of us set to work to make a road round the base of the cliff by throwing rocks and boulders into the river, and so building up a way. By the next morning we had succeeded in making a narrow pathway round the cliff. The loads were first carried over this; then the ponies were carefully led along, till at last the whole party was safely conveyed to the other side of this formidable obstacle.

A short distance below this, on the left bank of the Yarkand River, we struck a tributary named the Surakwat, up which led the route to the Mustagh Pass, so we here left the valley of the Yarkand River. For a few hundred yards above the junction the Surakwat flows through a very narrow gorge, which the stream fills up completely, and through this gorge the guide now led us, though I found, in 1889, that a much better road led over the top. The boulders over which the torrent dashed were covered with ice, and it was cruel work taking the ponies up. They were constantly slipping and falling back, cutting their hocks and knees to pieces. But we got them through without accident, and emerged on to a wide plain, evidently the bed of a lake, which must have been formed by the rocky obstacle we had passed through before the stream had cut its way down to its present level and thus afforded an outlet to the dammed-up waters.

This plain, which was covered with jungle of dwarf birch and willow or poplar, extended for about two miles. At a couple of miles from the gorge, and again at about nine miles, considerable streams flow in on the right bank of the Surakwat, and, at a mile from the last, two more narrow gorges were passed through; though here again, on my journey up here in 1889, we succeeded in making a road round to circumvent them. It was altogether a bad day's march for both men and ponies, but at last, toward evening, we found the valley opening to a wide plain, with plenty of scrub on it, and here we encamped. Before us rose a great wall of snowy mountains, with not the very smallest sign of a pass, though the guide said we should have to cross them on the following day. I felt some misgivings on looking at this barrier which now stopped our way, for the guide frankly confessed that he had forgotten the way across, and of course there was no sign of a path to guide us. He said, however, that possibly, as we got nearer, he might remember which turning we should have to take, and with that amount of consolation we had to settle down for the night.

We now had our first taste of real cold. We were about fifteen thousand feet above the sea-level, and as soon as the sun set one could almost *see* the cold stealing over the mountains—a cold grey creeps over them, the running streams become coated with ice, and as soon as we had had our dinner—we always dined together, to save trouble and time in cooking—and darkness had fairly fallen, we took up our beddings from the places where we had ostentatiously laid them out to mislead any prowling Kanjutis, and hurried off to deposit them behind any rock which would shelter us from the icy wind which blew down from the mountains. It is a curious fact, but when real difficulties seem to be closing around, one's spirits rise. As long as you have health—that is the main point to look after, but it is easily attained in mountain travel—and provided that you take plenty of food, difficulties seem only to make you more and more cheery. Instead of depressing you, they only serve to brace up all your faculties to their highest pitch; and though, as I lay down that night, I felt that for the next two or three weeks we should have harder and harder work before us, I recollect that evening as one of those in all my life in which I have felt in the keenest spirits.

At the first dawn of day on the following morning we were astir. The small stream was frozen solid, and the air bitingly cold; so we hurried about loading up, had a good breakfast, and, as the sun rose, started off straight at the mountain wall —a regular battlement of rocky peaks covered with snow, where it was possible, but for the most part too steep for snow to lie. After travelling for three or four miles, a valley suddenly opened up to the left. The guide immediately remembered it, and said that up it was an easy pass which would completely outflank the mountain barrier. The going was good. I left the ponies, and in my eagerness hurried on rapidly in front of them, straining to see the top of the pass, and the "other side"—that will-o'-the-wisp which ever attracts explorers and never satisfies them, for there is ever another side beyond. The height was beginning to tell, and the pass seemed to recede the nearer I approached it. One rise after another I surmounted, thinking it would prove the summit, but there was always another beyond. The valley was wide and open, and the going perfectly easy, leading sometimes over round boulders, but more often loose soil. At length I reached a small lake, about a quarter of a mile in length, and a small rise above it at the further end was the summit of the pass. I rushed up it, and there before me lay the "other side," and surely no view which man has ever seen can excel that. To describe the scene in words would be impossible. There are no words with which to do so, and to attempt it with those that are at our disposal would but stain its simple grandeur and magnificence.

Before me rose tier after tier of stately mountains, among the highest in the world—peaks of untainted snow, whose summits reached to heights of twenty-five thousand, twenty-six thousand, and, in one supreme case, twenty-eight thousand feet above sea-level. There was this wonderful array of mountain majesty set out before me across a deep rock-bound valley, and away in the distance, filling up the head of this, could be seen a vast glacier, the outpourings of the mountain masses which give it birth. It was a scene which, as I viewed it, and realized that this seemingly impregnable array must be pierced and overcome, seemed to put the iron into my soul and stiffen all my energies for the task before me.

Buried in the stirring feelings to which such a scene gives rise, I sat there for more than an hour, till the caravan arrived, and then we slowly descended from the pass into the valley bottom at our feet. The way was rough and steep, but we reached the banks of the river without any serious difficulty. Here, however, we were brought to a standstill, for there was a sheer cliff of a couple of hundred feet or so in height running far away on either hand along the river's edge. This at first seemed a serious obstacle, but I had noticed on the way down some tracks of kyang (wild asses), and as there was no water above, I knew that these animals must get down to the river to drink some way or other, and that where they could go we could go also. I therefore went back to these tracks, carefully followed them up, and was relieved to find they led down a practicable "shoot" in the cliff. It was very steep and rocky, but by unloading the ponies, and putting one man on to lead each in front and two others to hold on to the tail behind, we managed to let the ponies down one by one, and after a good deal of labour found ourselves, bag and baggage, on the edge of a river, which in some ways might be considered the main branch of the Yarkand River.

This tributary, which the Baltis with me called the Shaksgam, but which the Kirghiz seems to know as the Oprang, was previously unknown. It rises among the glaciers of the main watershed. Two years later I followed it down to its junction with the other branch of the Yarkand River.

Another geographical point of some importance I had now discovered was, that between the Kuen-lun Range and the main watershed which divides the rivers of Turkestan from those flowing to India, and which is sometimes called the Mustagh Range and sometimes the Karakoram, there lies a subsidiary range, over which leads the Aghil Pass, which I had just crossed. Hayward and the members of the Forsyth Mission, when mapping the course of the Yarkand River, had made the tributaries on the southern side run directly down from this Mustagh or Karakoram Range; but this was an error. The tributaries which they met with flow from the intermediate range, and that and the Oprang River lie in between this northern branch of the Yarkand River, which they explored, and the Mustagh Mountains.

A word now as to the proper name for the great watershed between Turkestan and India. Why call it the Karakoram? Karakoram means "black gravel," and no more inappropriate name could be imagined for a range of the highest snowy peaks in the world. The name Karakoram was apparently applied to it because a pass to the eastward, where there is black gravel, or something like it, is so called. But there is also a pass called Mustagh across the range. Mustagh means "ice-mountain," and surely that is a far more appropriate name for this stately range of icy peaks, which form the watershed of Asia.

To return to the narrative. We had now reached the waters of the Oprang River. This we followed down for a mile or two to a patch of jungle called Shaksgam. The valley bottom was here of loose pebbles, and from a quarter to half a mile broad. The river flowed over it in several branches, and was generally fordable. On either bank the mountains rose very steeply out of the valley, and were quite barren, except for a small growth of the hardy wormwood. There were no trees, and shrubs or bushes were only to be found in small patches along the river-bed.

Next day we continued down the valley of the Oprang (Shaksgam) River, till we came to another, which my Baltis called the Sarpo Laggo, flowing down from the main range and joining it on the left bank. This we ascended till we reached a patch of jungle called Suget Jangal. Just before arriving there I chanced to look up rather suddenly, and a sight met my eyes which fairly staggered me. We had just turned a corner which brought into view, on the left hand, a peak of appalling height, which could be none other than K.2, 28,278 feet in height, second only to Mount Everest. Viewed from this direction, it appeared to rise in an almost perfect cone, but to an inconceivable height. We were quite close under it —perhaps not a dozen miles from its summit—and here on the northern side, where it is literally clothed in glacier, there must have been from fourteen to sixteen thousand feet of solid ice. It was one of those sights which impress a man for ever, and produce a permanent effect upon the mind—a lasting sense of the greatness and grandeur of Nature's works—which he can never lose or forget.

For some time I stood apart, absorbed in the contemplation of this wonderful sight, and then we marched on past Suget Jangal till we reached the foot of the great glacier which flows down from the Mustagh Pass. Here we bivouacked. The tussle with these mountain giants was now to reach its climax, and our subsequent adventures I will describe in a separate chapter.

CHAPTER VIII.

THE MUSTAGH PASS.

> "The palaces of nature, whose vast walls
> Have pinnacled in clouds their snowy scalps,
> And throned eternity in icy halls
> Of cold sublimity, where forms and falls
> The avalanche—the thunderbolt of snow!
> All that expands the spirit, yet appals,
> Gather around those summits, as to show
> How earth may reach to heaven, yet leave vain man below."

THE description of the crossing of the Mustagh Pass I will begin by quoting from the account which I gave in a letter written to my father from the other side on my arrival in Kashmir territory.

"On ascending towards the Mustagh Pass my real difficulties began. Since my guides had crossed, an immense glacier had advanced, completely blocking up the valley with ice and immense boulders. For three days I dragged my ponies up this. Twice I gave it up, and ordered the ponies to go round by Ladak, while I went on with a few men, and twice I resumed the struggle, till I got them on to the smooth snow in the higher part of the mountain. It was terribly hard work. From daybreak till after dark I was on my legs, first exploring ahead, then returning and bringing on the party; and at the great elevation we were at, one gets very much exhausted. At night I lay on the ground in the open, warmly wrapped up in a sheepskin bag.

"On the third day of the ascent proper, I sent two men on

ahead to report on the pass. They returned at night to say that the pass which used to be practicable for ponies was now quite impassable, owing to ice having collected, and that the only thing now was to go by the other pass (there are two separate passes, the real Mustagh Pass and the one ten miles to the west of it, which had once been practicable for ponies), and bring back a number of men from the upper valleys of the Skardu district to make a road for the ponies.

"The pass is over the main axis of the Himalayas, and divides the Chinese dominions from the British dependencies. It is also on the watershed between the rivers which flow into the Indian Ocean and those which flow towards Turkestan. So one might expect something of a pass, and it is, in fact, one of the highest and most difficult in the Himalayas.

"The ascent was easy enough, leading over smooth snow, but we went very slowly on account of the difficulty of breathing. On reaching the summit we looked about for a way down, but there was nothing but a sheer precipice, and blocks of ice broken and tumbled about in such a way as to be quite impracticable.

"I freely confess that I myself could never have attempted the descent, and that I—an Englishman—was afraid to go first. Luckily my guides were better plucked than myself, and, tying a rope round the leading man's waist, the rest of us hung on while he hewed steps across the ice-slope which led down to the precipice.

"Step by step we advanced across it, all the time facing the precipice, and knowing that if we slipped (and the ice was very slippery) we should roll down the icy slope and over the precipice into eternity. Halfway across, my Ladaki servant, whom Colonel Bell had sent back to me as a man thoroughly acquainted with Himalayan travel, turned back saying he was trembling all over and could not face the precipice. It rather upset me seeing a born hill-man so affected; but I pretended not to care a bit, and laughed it off, *pour encourager les autres*, as the thing had to be done.

"After a time, and a very nasty time it was, we reached *terra firma* in the shape of a large projecting ledge of rock, and from there began the descent of the precipice. The icy slope was a perfect joke to this. We let ourselves down very gradually from any little ledge or projecting piece of rock. On getting halfway down, I heard my Ladaki servant appealing to me from above. He had mustered up courage to cross the icy slope, and had descended the precipice for a few steps, and was now squatting on a rock salaaming profusely to me with both hands, and saying he dare not move another step, and that he would go back and take my ponies round by Ladak. So I sent him back.

"For six hours we descended the precipice, partly rock and partly icy slope, and when I reached the bottom and looked back, it seemed utterly impossible that any man could have come down such a place.

"For several hours after we trudged on in the moonlight over the snow, with crevasses every fifty yards or so. Often we fell in, but had no accident; and at last, late at night, we reached a dry spot, and I spread out my rugs behind a rock while one of my men made a small fire of some dry grass and a couple of alpenstocks broken up to cook tea by. After eating some biscuits with the tea, I rolled myself up in my sheepskin and slept as soundly as ever I did."

This rough description needs some amplification and explanation, but I give it as it stands, because it was written only a few days after I had crossed the pass, and with the memories of it fresh on me. When we ascended the valley of the Sarpo Laggo stream towards the Mustagh Pass, we came to a point where the valley was blocked by what appeared to be enormous heaps of broken stones and fragments of rock. These heaps were between two and three hundred feet in height, and stretched completely across the valley. I was on ahead by myself, and when I saw these mounds of *débris*, I thought we might have trouble in taking ponies over such rough obstacles; but I was altogether taken aback when, on coming up to the heaps, I found that they were masses of solid ice, merely covered over on the surface with a thin layer of this rocky *débris*, which served to conceal the surface of the ice immediately beneath. And my dismay can be imagined when, on ascending one of the highest of the mounds, I found that they were but the end of a series which extended without interruption for many miles up the valley to the snows at the foot of the pass. We were, in fact, at the extremity of an immense glacier. This was the first time I had actually been on a glacier, and I had never realized till now how huge and continuous a mass of ice it is. Here and there, breaking through the mounds of stone, I had seen cliffs of what I thought was black rock, but on coming close up to these I found them to be of solid dark green ice. I discovered caverns, too, with transparent walls of clear, clean ice, and enormous icicles hanging like fringes from the roof. It was an astonishing and wonderful sight; but I was destined to see yet more marvellous scenes than this in the icy region upon which I was now entering.

To take a caravan of ponies up a glacier like this seemed to me an utter impossibility. The guides thought so too, and I decided upon sending the ponies round by the Karakoram Pass to Leh, and going on myself over the Mustagh Pass with a couple of men. This would have been a risky proceeding, for if we did not find our way over the pass we should have scarcely enough provisions with us to last us till we could return to an inhabited place again. Supplies altogether were running short, and the longer we took in reaching the pass, the harder we should fare if we did not succeed in getting over it. But while I was deciding upon sending the ponies back, the caravan men were gallantly leading them up the glacier. I rejoined the men, and we all helped the ponies along as well as we could; hauling at them in front, pushing behind, and sometimes unloading and carrying the loads up the stone-covered mounds of ice ourselves. But it was terribly hard and trying work for the animals. They could get no proper foothold, and as they kept climbing up the sides of a mound they would scratch away the thin layer of stones on the surface, and then, coming on to the pure ice immediately below, would slip and fall and cut their knees and hocks about in a way which distressed me much. I did not see how this sort of thing could last. We had only advanced a few hundred yards, and there were from fifteen to twenty miles of glacier ahead. I therefore halted the ponies for the day, and went on with a couple of men to reconnoitre. We fortunately found, in between the glacier and the mountain-side, a narrow stretch of less impracticable ground, along which it would be possible to take the ponies. This we marked out, and returned to our bivouac after dark.

That night we passed, as usual, in the open, thoroughly exhausted after the hard day's work, for at the high altitudes we had now reached the rarefaction of the air makes one tired very quickly, and the constant tumbling about on the slippery glacier in helping the ponies over it added to one's troubles.

At daybreak on the following morning we started again, leading the ponies up the route we had marked out; but a mile from the point where our previous exploration had ended we were confronted by another great glacier flowing down from the left. We now had a glacier on one side of us, mountains on the other, and a second glacier right across our front. At this time my last remaining pair of boots were completely worn out, and my feet so sore from the bruises they received on the glacier I could scarcely bear to put

CAMP ON THE GLACIER, MUSTAGH PASS.

them to the ground. So I stayed behind with the ponies, while two men went on to find a way through the obstacles before us. The men returned after a time, and said they could find no possible way for the ponies; but they begged me to have a look myself, saying that perhaps by my good fortune I might be able to find one.

I accordingly, with a couple of men, retraced my steps down the edge of the main glacier for some little distance, till we came to a point where it was possible to get ponies on to the glacier and take them into the middle of it. We then ascended a prominent spot on the glacier, from which we could obtain a good view all round. We were in a sea of ice. There was now little of the rocky moraine stuff with which the ice of the glacier had been covered in its lower part, and we looked out on a vast river of pure white ice, broken up into myriads of sharp needle-like points. Snowy mountains rose above us on either hand, and down their sides rolled the lesser glaciers, like clotted cream pouring over the lip of a cream-jug; and rising forbiddingly before us was the cold icy range we should have to cross.

This was scarcely the country through which to take a caravan of ponies, but I made out a line of moraine extending right up the main glacier. We got on to this, and, following it up for some distance, found, to our great relief, that it would be quite possible to bring ponies up it on to the smooth snow of the *névé* at the head of the glacier. Having ascertained this beyond a doubt, we returned late in the afternoon towards the spot where we had left our ponies. Darkness overtook us before we reached it. We wandered about on the glacier for some time, and nearly lost our way; but at last, quite worn out, reached our little caravan once more.

That night we held a council of war as to which of the two Mustagh Passes we should attack. There are two passes, known as the Mustagh, which cross the range. One, to the east, that is to our left as we were ascending the glacier, is known as the Old Mustagh Pass, and was in use in former days, till the advance of ice upon it made it so difficult that a new one was sought for, and what is known as the New Mustagh Pass, some ten miles further west along the range, had been discovered. It was over this latter pass that the guides hoped to conduct our party. They said that even ponies had been taken across it by means of ropes and by making rough bridges across the crevasses. No European had crossed either of them, but Colonel Godwin-Austen, in 1862, reached the southern foot of the new pass in the course of his survey of Baltistan. The New Mustagh Pass seemed the most promising of the two, and I therefore decided upon sending two men on the following morning to reconnoitre it and report upon its practicability.

At the first streak of daylight the reconnoitrers set out, and the remainder of us afterwards followed with the ponies along the route which we had explored on the previous day. We took the ponies up the glacier without any serious difficulty, and in the evening halted close up to the head of the glacier. At dusk the two men who had been sent out to reconnoitre the new pass returned, to say that the ice had so accumulated on it that it would be now quite impossible to take ponies over, and that it would be difficult even for men to cross it. The plan which they now suggested was to leave the ponies behind, and cross the range by the Old Mustagh Pass, push on to Askoli, the first village on the south side of the range, and from there send back men with supplies for the ponies and the men with them sufficient to enable the caravan to reach Shahidula, on the usual trade route between Yarkand and Kashmir. This was evidently all we could do. We could not take the ponies any further, and we could not send them back as they were, for we had nearly run out of supplies, and Shahidula, the nearest point at which fresh supplies could be obtained, was one hundred and eighty miles distant. All now depended upon our being able to cross the pass. If we were not able to, we should have to march this one hundred and eighty miles back through the mountains with only three or four days' supplies to support us. We might certainly have eaten the ponies, so would not actually have starved; but we should have had a hard struggle for it, and there would still have been the range to cross at another point.

Matters were therefore approaching a very critical stage, and that was an anxious night for me. I often recall it, and think of our little bivouac in the snow at the foot of the range we had to overcome. The sun sank behind the icy mountains, the bright glow disappeared from them, and they became steely hard while the grey cold of night settled shimmering down upon them. All around was pure white snow and ice, breathing out cold upon us. The little pools and streamlets of water which the heat of the sun had poured off the glacier during the day were now gripped by the frost, which seemed to creep around ourselves too, and huddle us up together. We had no tent to shelter us from the biting streams of air flowing down from the mountain summits, and we had not sufficient fuel to light a fire round which we might lie. We had, indeed, barely enough brushwood to keep up a fire for cooking; but my Chinese servant cooked a simple meal of rice and mutton for us all. We gathered round the fire to eat it hot out of the bowl, and then rolled ourselves up in our sheepskins and went to sleep, with the stars twinkling brightly above, and the frost gripping closer and closer upon us.

Next morning, while it was yet dark, Wali, the guide, awoke us. We each had a drink of tea and some bread, and then we started off to attack the pass. The ponies, with nearly all the baggage, were left behind under the charge of Liu-san, the Chinaman, and some of the older men. All we took with us was a roll of bedding for myself, a sheepskin coat for each man, some native biscuits, tea and a large teakettle, and a bottle of brandy. The ascent to the pass was easy but trying, for we were now not far from nineteen thousand feet above sea-level, and at that height, walking uphill through deep snow, one quickly becomes exhausted. We could only take a dozen or twenty steps at a time, and we would then bend over on our sticks and pant as if we had been running hard uphill. We were tantalized, too, by the apparent nearness of the pass. Everything here was on a gigantic scale, and what seemed to be not more than an hour's walk from the camp was in fact a six hours' climb. It was nearly midday when we reached the top of the pass, and what we saw there I have already related in the letter quoted above. There was nothing but a sheer precipice, and those first few moments on the summit of the Mustagh Pass were full of intense anxiety to me. If we could but get over, the crowning success of my expedition would be gained. But the thing seemed to me simply an impossibility. I had had no experience of Alpine climbing, and I had no ice-axes or other mountaineering appliances with me. I had not even any proper boots. All I had for foot-gear were some native boots of soft leather, without nails and without heels—mere leather stockings, in fact—which gave no sort of grip upon an icy surface. How, then, I should ever be able to get down the icy slopes and rocky precipices I now saw before me I could not think; and if it had rested with me alone, the probability is we never should have got over the pass at all.

What, however, saved our party was my holding my tongue. I kept quite silent as I looked over the pass, and waited to hear what the men had to say about it. They meanwhile were looking at me, and, imagining that an Englishman never went back from an enterprise he had once started on, took it as a matter of course that, as I gave no order to go back, I meant to go on. So they set about their preparations for

CROSSING AN ICE-SLOPE ON THE MUSTAGH PASS.

the descent. We had brought an ordinary pickaxe with us, and Wali went on ahead with this, while the rest of us followed one by one behind him, each hanging on to a rope tied round Wali's waist to support him in case he slipped while hewing steps across the ice-slope. This slope was of hard ice, very steep, and, thirty yards or so below the line we took, ended in an ice-fall, which again terminated far beneath in the head of a glacier at the foot of the pass. Wali with his pickaxe hewed a way step by step across the ice-slope, so as to reach the rocky cliff by which we should have to descend on to the glacier below. We slowly edged across the slope after him, but it was hard to keep cool and steady. From where we stood we could see nothing over the end of the slope but the glacier many hundreds of feet below us. Some of the men were so little nervous that they kicked the fragments of ice hewed out by Wali down the slope, and laughed as they saw them hop down it and with one last bound disappear altogether. But an almost sickening feeling came on me as I watched this, for we were standing on a slope as steep as the roof of a house. We had no ice-axes with which to anchor ourselves or give us support; and though I tied handkerchiefs, and the men bits of leather and cloth, round the insteps of our smooth native boots, to give us a little grip on the slippery ice, I could not help feeling that if any one of us had lost his foothold, the rest of us would never have been able to hold him up with the rope, and that in all likelihood the whole party would have been carried away and plunged into the abyss below. Outwardly I kept as cool and cheerful as I could, but inwardly I shuddered at each fresh step I took. The sun was now pouring down on to the ice, and just melted the surface of the steps after they were hewn, so that by the time those of us who were a few paces behind Wali reached a step, the ice was just covered over with water, and this made it still more slippery for our soft leather boots, which had now become almost slimy on the surface. It was under these circumstances that my Ladaki servant Drogpa gave in. He was shaking all over in an exaggerated shiver, and so unsteady, I thought he would slip at any moment, and perhaps carry us all with him. We were but at the beginning of our trials. We had not even begun the actual descent yet, but were merely crossing to a point from which we should make it. It was dangerous to have such a man with us, so I told him he might return to the ponies and go round with them.

At last we reached the far side of the slope, and found ourselves on a projecting piece of rock protruding through the ice. Here we could rest, but only with the prospect of still further difficulties before us. We were at the head of the rocky precipice, the face of which we should have to descend to reach the ice-slopes which extended to the glacier at the foot of the pass. At such heights as those which we had now reached, where the snow and ice lie sometimes hundreds of feet thick, it is only where it is very steep that the bare rock shows through. The cliff we had now to descend was an almost sheer precipice: its only saving feature was that it was rough and rugged, and so afforded some little hold for our hands and feet. Yet even then we seldom got a hold for the whole hand or whole foot. All we generally found was a little ledge, upon which we could grip with the tips of the fingers or side of the foot. The men were most good to me, whenever possible guiding my foot into some secure hold, and often supporting it there with their hands; but at times it was all I could do to summon sufficient courage to let myself down on to the veriest little crevices which had to support me. There was a constant dread, too, that fragments of these ledges might give way with the weight upon them; for the rock was very crumbly, as it generally is when exposed to severe frosts, and once I heard a shout from above, as a huge piece of rock which had been detached came crashing past me, and as nearly as possible hit two of the men who had already got halfway down.

We reached the bottom of the cliff without accident, and then found ourselves at the head of a long ice-slope extending down to the glacier below. Protruding through the ice were three pieces of rock, which would serve us as successive halting-places, and we determined upon taking a line which led by them. We had brought with us every scrap of rope that could be spared from the ponies' gear, and we tied these and all the men's turbans and waist-clothes together into one long rope, by which we let a man down the ice-slope on to the first projecting rock. As he went down he cut steps, and when he had reached the rock we tied the upper end of the rope firmly on to a rock above, and then one by one we came down the slope, hanging on to the rope and making use of the steps which had been cut. This was, therefore, a comparatively easy part of the descent; but one man was as nearly as possible lost. He slipped, fell over on his back, and came sliding down the slope at a frightful pace. Luckily, however, he still managed to keep hold of the rope with one hand, and so kept himself from dashing over the ice-fall at the side of the slope; but when he reached the rock his hand was almost bared of skin, and he was shivering with fright. Wali, however, gave him a sound rating for being so careless, and on the next stage made him do all the hardest part of the work.

The other men got down the slope without mishap, and then came the last man. He, of course, could not have the benefit of a rope to hang on by, for he would have to untie it from the rock and bring it with him. Wali had selected for this, the most dangerous piece of work in the whole descent, the man who had especially troubled me by knocking pieces of ice over the precipice when we were on the ice-slope at the head of the pass. He was one of the slaves I had released at Yarkand; an incessant grumbler, and very rough, but, next to Wali, the best man I had for any really hard work. He tied the end of the rope round his waist, and then slowly and carefully came down the steps which had been hewn in the slope. We at the end of the rope pulled it in at every step he took, so that if he slipped, though he might fall past us, we should be able to haul in the rope fast, and so perhaps save him from the ice-fall. He reached our rock of refuge in safety, and we then in the same manner descended two more stages of the ice-slope, and finally reached a part where the slope was less steep, and we could proceed without cutting steps the whole way.

At last, just as the sun set, we reached the glacier at the foot of the pass. We were in safety once more. The tension was over, and the last and greatest obstacle in my journey had been surmounted. Those moments when I stood at the foot of the pass are long to be remembered by me—moments of intense relief, and of deep gratitude for the success that had been granted. Such feelings as mine were now cannot be described in words, but they are known to every one who has had his heart set on one great object and has accomplished it. I took one last look at the pass, never before or since seen by a European, and then we started away down the glacier to find some bare spot on which to lay our rugs and rest.

The sun had now set, but, fortunately for us, there was an abundance of light, and the night was marvellously beautiful, so that, tired as I was, I could not but be impressed by it. The moon was nearly full, the sky without a cloud, and in the amphitheatre of snowy mountains and among the icy seracs of the glacier, not one speck of anything but the purest white was visible. The air at these altitudes, away from dust and with no misty vapour in it, was absolutely clear, and the soft silvery rays of the moon struck down upon the glistening mountains in unsullied radiance. The whole effect was of some enchanting fairy scene; and the sternness of the mountains was slowly softened down till lost, and their beauty in its purest form alone remained.

With our senses enervated by such a scene as this, and overcome with delight as we were at having successfully crossed the pass, we pushed on down the glacier in a dreamy, careless way, perfectly regardless of the dangers which lay hidden around us. Under ordinary circumstances we should have proceeded cautiously down a glacier which, beautiful though it was, had its full share of crevasses; and it was only when I turned round and found one man missing, that I realized how negligent we had been. We retraced our steps, and found the poor fellow had dropped down a crevasse, the mouth of which had been covered with a thin coating of ice and snow, which had given way under his weight, so that he had dropped through. Very fortunately, the crevasse was not wide, and after falling about fifteen feet, he had been wedged in between the two sides by the load of my bedding which he was carrying; so by letting a rope down we were able to extricate him in safety. This taught us a lesson, and for the rest of the way we went along roped together, as we ought to have been from the first, and tested each step as we advanced.

I now kept in rear, and the man with my bedding was in front of me. As we were closed up during a temporary halt, I detected a strong smell of brandy coming from the bundle of bedding. A distracting thought occurred to me. I tore open the bundle, and there was my last bottle of brandy broken! Lady Walsham, on my leaving Peking, had insisted upon giving me at least two bottles of brandy for the journey. I had drunk one in the Gobi Desert, and I had made up my mind to keep the other till the day I had crossed the Mustagh Pass, but here it was broken, and the brandy wasted, just when both the men and myself were really needing something to pull us together. The bundle of bedding had been thrown over the pass to save carrying it down, and though the bottle had been wrapped up in my sheepskin sleeping-bag, it had been smashed to pieces.

About eleven o'clock we at last reached a piece of ground on the mountain-side free from snow, and here we halted for the night. There was no wood, and only a few roots of weeds about with which to light a fire, so we had to break up a couple of our alpenstocks to make a small fire, by which we managed to boil sufficient water to make a few cups of tea. We had some biscuit with that, and then I got into my sheepskin bag, and the men wrapped themselves up in their sheepskin coats, and we lay down and slept as if nothing could ever wake us again. The work and anxiety on the last few days had been very great, and on this day we had been on the move for eighteen hours continuously. Now the worst was over, and we slept proportionately to the work we had been doing.

But at daybreak the next morning we were on our legs again. We had still a long way to go before we could reach Askoli, the nearest village, and our men remaining behind on the pass were waiting for supplies. We had to start without anything to warm us, for we could find no materials for a fire; but at about ten o'clock, at a point near where our glacier joined the great Baltoro glacier, we found an old hut, built at the time when this route was in use, and from the fragments of wood about we made up our first good fire, and had a fairly substantial meal. But we could not indulge ourselves at all freely, for we were very short of provisions. We had left with the men on the pass all but just sufficient to carry us through to Askoli, and a few mouthfuls of meat, with some biscuit and some tea, were all we could allow ourselves. Having eaten this and rested for an hour, we again pushed on, and struck the Baltoro glacier nearly opposite the great Masher Brum peak, which stands up over twenty-five thousand feet high just across the glacier. Then, turning to our left in the opposite direction to Askoli, we could see far away up this, the largest mountain glacier in the world, other peaks of even greater height, rising like snowy spires in the distance. There are four peaks over twenty-six thousand feet at the head of the Baltoro glacier, and away to our left, though hidden from us, was the peak K.2. Five years afterwards, Sir William Conway's party explored the entire length of the glacier, and ascended a peak twenty-three thousand feet in height at its head; but, fascinating though it would have been to have wandered among these mountain giants, in a region unsurpassed for sublimity and grandeur by any in the world, I could only now think of reaching an inhabited spot again as rapidly as possible.

We turned to the right, then down the glacier, keeping along the moraine close to the mountain-side. This and the two following were days of agony to me, for my native boots were now in places worn through till the bare skin of my foot was exposed, and I had to hobble along on my toes or my heels to keep the worn-out part by the balls of my feet from the sharp stones and rocky *débris* of the glacier. On account of this tenderness of my feet, I was always slipping, too, falling and bruising my elbows, or cutting my hands on the rough stones in trying to save myself.

All that day we plodded wearily along down the glacier, till at sunset we came upon a little clump of fir trees on the mountain-side. Here we were able to make up as big a fire as we wished, and if we could only have had more to eat, would have been perfectly happy; but there was now no meat left, and tea and biscuit was all we had to eat. Next day we reached the end of the glacier, and here I had an unpleasant little accident. A strong gushing stream was flowing out of the glacier, and this we had to cross. It was more than waist-deep, and filled with blocks of ice from the glacier. I had no change of clothes, and when good old Shukar Ali—a faithful attendant, who afterwards accompanied me on two other journeys—volunteered to carry me over on his back, I could not resist the temptation of what I thought would be a dry passage. But halfway over Shukar Ali slipped; in struggling to save himself he kept pushing me under water, till I was nearly drowned, and when I reached the opposite side of the stream I was numbed through with cold. We halted for an hour while I got into my sleeping-bag, and my clothes were spread out in the sun to dry, and then we pushed on again down a narrow rock-bound valley. At night we slept in a cave, and next day made our last march into Askoli. Never did I think we were going to reach that spot. By midday we saw its green trees and fields in the distance; but I could only get along slowly, as the way was very rough and stony. At last, however, at four o'clock, we did reach it. We sent for the headman, and told him to bring us some food. A bed was brought me to lie on, and then, with a stewed fowl and some rice to eat, fresh life and energy came into me.

But that was a dirty little village! The trees and the fields looked fresh and green, but the houses and the inhabitants were repulsively dirty; and the latter by no means well disposed. These mountain people are dreadfully nervous about strangers. They had thought the way into their country from the north was entirely closed, and they did not at all welcome this proof that it was not. Wali, the guide, was himself a native of this village, which he had left some thirty years before. Another of my men also belonged to it. But they said they feared these people would do some injury to them for having shown me the way, and they kept by me constantly, and left the village with me, subsequently returning to Yarkand by Leh and the Karakoram Pass, instead of directly by the Mustagh Pass, as they might have done.

Immediately after we had had something to eat, we set about preparing to send back supplies to the men and ponies on the pass. With great difficulty we induced the people to do this; and on the following day a party was started off back towards the Mustagh Pass. They took with them ropes and poles, and though three men were badly injured in doing so, they succeeded in crossing the pass and giving my men the needful supplies.

I would now willingly have had a rest, but, though I could not start on the day following our arrival, for I was seriously unwell from having, in the excess of my hunger, eaten too much of the messy greasy dishes the inhabitants had provided for me, on the day after I set out to try the other Mustagh Pass—what is called the New Mustagh Pass. It was depressing, just as I had reached the first village on the Indian side, to have to turn my back on India; but I did not like to leave this pass untried, and with Wali and a party of men from Askoli we set out on the second day after our arrival to explore it.

These men of Askoli were in dread of the mountains, and on the first evening, at the foot of a mountain whose summit was supposed to be the abode of a guardian deity, they, although Mohammedans, sacrificed a bullock to this deity, and prayed and salaamed to it. As they subsequently ate the bullock, and as I paid for it, this little ceremony was doubtless very helpful to them. At any rate, they were much more cheerful after it, and as I now had some new foot-gear, we were able to push along rapidly up the Punmah glacier. But on the third day from Askoli, opposite a camping-ground called Skinmang, we were brought to a standstill. At this point the glacier flowing down from the New Mustagh Pass joins the Punmah glacier, and we were completely "cornered" between the two glaciers. To reach the pass we should have had to cross the glacier flowing down from it; but this we found it impossible to do, for just at this point there had evidently been an immense ice-slip on to the glacier, and gigantic blocks of ice were tumbled about one on the top of the other in a way which made it perfectly impossible to get any footing at all on the glacier. So we turned round and faced for Askoli once more.

I think now of that wonderful glacier region, and the amphitheatre of snowy peaks at the head of the Punmah glacier, and recall all the marvellous beauties of a scene such as can only be witnessed in a few rarely visited spots on the face of the earth, but at the time my thoughts were almost entirely directed towards India. I was wearied out by my struggle with the mountains, and longed to be free of them and at rest once more.

On the day after our return to Askoli, the men who had been sent by the Old Mustagh Pass to the party with the ponies arrived back also. They had handed over the supplies to them, and Liu-san, Drogpa, and the rest had started off to take the ponies round by the Karakoram Pass to Leh. Having satisfied myself about this, I set out by double marches for Kashmir and the Punjab. Just beyond Askoli we had to cross one of those rope bridges so common in the Himalayas. A rope bridge is made of three thick ropes of plaited birch-twigs. In crossing, you tread on one and support yourself by the other two, one on each side. This particular bridge led across a narrow rocky chasm, at the bottom of which the river from the Baltoro rushed foaming along. It was certainly a disagreeable place to have to cross, but I was astonished to find that Wali, the man who had crossed the Mustagh Pass without the slightest sign of nervousness, and certainly without any hesitation, absolutely refused at first to cross this bridge. To me it seemed such a paltry thing, after what we had so recently gone through, and with two ropes to hang on by there seemed no danger at all; but Wali shivered and shook, and could only be induced to come over when he had two men to support him. This is one of the most remarkable instances I have met with of a man, who had no fear when faced by one form of danger, being totally taken aback when faced by another.

ROPE BRIDGE, NEAR ASKOLI.

We then followed down the valley of the Braldo River till it joined the open Shigar valley, and here at last I was able to mount a pony again, and, instead of plodding wearily along, to travel in comfort and enjoy the wonderful scenery around me. How great a difference one's mere animal feelings make in the ability to appreciate the beauties of nature! Worn and tired out, it was only something unusually striking that had produced any impression upon me, and I would pass by peaks of marvellous grandeur with only a weary upward glance at them, and sometimes even a longing that they had never existed to bar my way and keep me from my journey's end. But now, seated on the back of a pony—miserable little animal though it was—I had no longer that load of weariness weighing upon me, and could quietly drink in all the pleasure which looking on that glorious mountain scenery gives.

The Shigar valley is from two to three miles broad; its bottom is covered over with village lands, where apricot trees are grown in hundreds, and these apricot trees now, in the autumn season, were clothed in foliage of every lovely tint of red and purple and yellow. This mass of bright warm foliage filled the valley bottom, then above it rose the bare rugged mountain-sides, and crowning these the everlasting snows. The sun shone out in an unclouded, deep-blue sky; the icy blasts of the Mustagh were left behind for good and all; and we were in an ideal climate, with no extremes of either heat or cold to try us. The grave, anxious look on the men's faces passed away; they now stepped cheerily along by my side, chaffing over all the difficulties they had gone through, and, at each village we came to, taking a fill of dried apricots and grapes and walnuts, so plentiful in this fruitful valley.

The country we were now in was Baltistan, the inhabitants of which—called Baltis—are a patient, docile, good-natured race, whom one hardly respects, but whom one cannot help liking in a compassionate, pitying way. The poor Balti belongs to one of those races which has gone under in the struggle of nations. In their better days the Baltis are said to have been able to fight well; but their fighting-days are past. They could not resist the Dogra invasion; and now they are ruled by a foreign race, and because they were such good carriers, and because the roads through their own and the adjoining countries were so bad, it fell out that they were employed more and more for carrying purposes, till the patient, long-suffering Balti coolie became a well-known feature in the valleys of this frontier. There is little that is strong or masculine about the Balti to cause one to admire him, but yet one likes him for his very patience and the ease with which he can be pleased. And among these Baltis I have employed have been some for whom I have borne respect for their intense devotion to what they believed to be their duty. I now was on the eve of parting with those five who brought me over the Mustagh Pass, and for Wali, their headman, I entertain a regard such as I do for few other men. I picture him now as he was first brought before me at the inn at Yarkand—a short, thick-set man, with an iron-grey beard, a prominent, rather hooked nose, and an expression of determination and proud indifference to danger about his chin and underlip. Asked if he were willing to conduct me over the Mustagh Pass, he replied that he did not want to go, but if he were really required he would undertake to guide me; the only condition he would make would be that I should not look at a map. He had heard Englishmen were rather inclined to guide themselves and trust the map rather than the man with them; if I was going to do that, I might, but he would not go with me. On the other hand, if I would trust him, he would take me safely over. On this understanding I engaged him. No one could have more loyally carried out his compact, and but for him we should never have been able to cross the Mustagh Pass. He went to work in a steady, self-reliant way which gave every one confidence, and all the men looked up to him and obeyed him implicitly. The more I see of men like him, the more convinced I am, that weak in many respects though such men as these Baltis are, yet if once they are given responsibility, shown trust, and left to work out their own salvation, they develop many latent qualities which probably neither they nor anybody else believed to be in them. Old Wali went back to Yarkand by Leh, and three years later, when I again visited Yarkand, he came to see me, looking precisely the same, and dressed, I believe, in the very same clothes as when we had parted, and it was a real pleasure to see again a man who done me such loyal service.

Another of the Baltis who had done excellent work was the slave whose release I had purchased at Yarkand. He was a wild-looking character, but the hardest-working man I have known. Now that he had regained his freedom, was being liberally paid, and was on his way home, he did not mind how much work he did, and all through the march from Yarkand he behaved splendidly. We passed by his native village one day as we were marching through Baltistan, and left him there. But on the following day he caught us up again, carrying an immense load of fruit and provision for a big dinner for the men. He had brought all this twelve miles, and he came and kissed my hands and feet, and said he could not allow us to go away without showing how grateful he felt. These Baltis are a warm-hearted people when once their deeper feelings can be reached, and when their hearts have not been crushed out of them by that fatal load-carrying, and I parted from my faithful followers with sincere regret.

A march or two after passing Skardu, the chief place in Baltistan, I met the first European on the south side of the Himalayas. He was not an Englishman, but a Frenchman, M. Dauvergne; and in his tent I had the first good meal and talk in English I had had for many a month. A few marches further on I met another European. This one at any rate, I thought, *must* be an Englishman, and I walked up to him with all the eagerness a traveller has to meet a countryman of his own after not seeing one for nearly seven months. But this time it turned out the stranger was a Russian! He announced himself as M. Nicolas Notovitch, an adventurer who had, I subsequently found, made a not very favourable reputation in India. I asked M. Notovitch where he had come from, and he replied that he had come from Kashmir. He then asked me where I had come from. I said from Peking. It much amused me, therefore, when on leaving he said, in a theatrical way, "We part here, the pioneers of the East!"

This same M. Notovitch has recently published what he calls a new "Life of Christ," which he professes to have found in a monastery in Ladak, after he had parted with me. No one, however, who knows M. Notovitch's reputation, or who has the slightest knowledge of the subject, will give any reliance whatever to this pretentious volume.

On the day after leaving M. Notovitch I crossed my last pass, the Zoji-la, eleven thousand four hundred feet high. It was perfectly easy, and then on descending the southern side we found all the mountain-sides covered with forest. The change from the bare hillsides on the north was very striking and very pleasant. Hitherto, from far away at their rise from the Yarkand plains, the mountains had been barren and destitute of any trace of forest. Occasionally in some favoured sheltered spot a dwarfed tree or two might be seen, but as a whole it was only in the valley bottoms and on cultivated lands that any trees were met with. Now of a sudden all was changed. We had reached the southern-facing slopes of the outward ridge of the Himalayas, and upon these slopes all the rains of the monsoon are expended, while none is left to reach the parched hill slopes beyond. Consequent upon this, the mountains on the one side of the water are densely packed with forest, and on the other are bare sun-baked rocks only.

We passed rapidly down the beautifully wooded Sind valley, with its meadows and pine forests, its rushing torrents and snow-clad mountain summits, and at last reached the open valley of Kashmir itself. Some seven or eight miles' march through this brought us to Srinagar, that most picturesquely situated but dirtiest of all towns, and then for the first time I realized how very dirty I myself was, and how rough I had become. Dressed in a Yarkand sheepskin coat and long Yarkand boots, and with a round Tam-o'-shanter cap as the only European article of dress about me, and with a rough beard, and my face burnt by exposure in the desert and cut and reddened by the cold on the glaciers, I was addressed by the people of the place as a Yarkandi. My first care, therefore, was to go off to one of the native shops which provide all necessaries for Europeans, and purchase a knickerbocker suit, such as officers wear out shooting in Kashmir, and a clean shirt, and to have my hair cut, my beard shaved off, and to get a good wash. When I had expended nearly two hours upon these preparations for my plunge into civilization, I went to see Captain Ramsay, the political agent on duty at Srinagar at the time. It was very trying, therefore, when Captain Ramsay, almost immediately after shaking hands, said, "Wouldn't you like to have a wash?" This was the first of the many shocks I had on returning to civilization.

But there were some pleasant surprises as well as a disagreeable shock like this, and I remember the satisfaction I felt at receiving a telegram at Srinagar, conveying to me the congratulations of Sir Frederick Roberts upon my having successfully accomplished the journey, and a very kind letter from General Chapman, then Quartermaster-General in India, who had himself been to Yarkand and Kashgar, and, knowing how welcome they are to travellers, had thoughtfully sent a box of cigars to await my arrival.

Only one day was given up for rest in Srinagar, and then I started on the last stage of my journey, that to Rawal Pindi; for I was anxious to accomplish my task in precisely the seven months which I had said at Peking would be the time necessary for it. So I pushed on, and now at the end of a very long journey I was feeling "fitter" than when I started, and able to cover the distance rapidly. After arriving at seven o'clock on the evening of November 2, I had my dinner, lay down for an hour or two, and then at twelve o'clock at night started again walking the first march of twelve miles; then getting into an "ekka," or native cart, which conveyed me for three marches down the newly constructed cart-road. At the end of these three marches I rode another ten miles uphill towards Murree, and arrived at a dak bungalow at sunset. Here I rested, and at three o'clock in the morning started again, marching the ten miles into Murree on foot. From there I took a tonga, and drove rapidly down the hill the last thirty-nine miles into Rawal Pindi. The change was wonderful. I had thought riding a miserable little native pony luxury in comparison with the weary marching on foot. Then the trundling along at a jog-trot in a native cart on the Kashmir road had seemed the very essence of all that was comfortable in travelling. But now I was in a conveyance with a pair of ponies galloping down the hill, and with what seemed perfect rest to me I was covering every hour three or four times the distance I had been able to accomplish on foot, and, still better, I was freeing myself from the nightmare of the mountains, and, in place of the continual barrier after barrier of mountain ranges blocking the way and shutting me in, there was stretched out before me the wide plains of the Punjab. From the plains of Turkestan on the one side, I had made my way through the labyrinth of mountains, over one range after another, past each succeeding obstacle, till I had now reached the plains on the southern side. My whole long journey from Peking was at an end. My utmost hopes had been fulfilled, and I had reached that destination which, as I rode out of the gates of Peking, had seemed so remote and inaccessible.

On April 4 I left Peking, and on November 4 I drove up to the messhouse of my regiment at Rawal Pindi. Two days later I reached Simla, and saw Colonel Bell, from whom I had parted at Peking, and who, travelling more rapidly than me, had reached India a month before. To him, therefore, belongs the honour of being the first European to reach India from China by land. Poor Liu-san, the Chinese servant, arrived six weeks later with the ponies, which we had been obliged to send back from the Mustagh Pass round by the Karakoram and Leh. He was suffering badly from pleurisy, brought on by exposure; but when he was sufficiently recovered he was sent back to China by sea, and he afterwards accompanied the persevering American traveller, Mr. Rockhill, to Tibet. He was a Chinaman, and therefore not a perfect animal, but he understood his business thoroughly, and he did it. So for a journey across the entire breadth of the Chinese Empire I could scarcely have found a better man. As long as he felt that he was "running" me, and that it was his business to convey me, like a bundle of goods, from one side of China to the other, he worked untiringly. And the success of the journey is in no small degree due to this single servant, who had not feared to accompany me throughout.

CHAPTER IX.

THE KANJUTI RAIDS.

> "Are not the mountains, waves, and skies a part
> Of me and of my soul, as I of them?
> Is not the love of these deep in my heart
> With a pure passion? should I not contemn
> All objects, if compared with these? and stem
> A tide of suffering, rather than forego
> Such feelings for the hard and worldly phlegm
> Of those whose eyes are only turn'd below,
> Gazing upon the ground, with thoughts which dare not glow?"
>
> BYRON.

IN the spring of 1889, the exploring fever came strong on me again, and, seeking the advice of Mr. Ney Elias, a journey across Tibet, by much the same route as that afterwards so successfully explored by Captain Bower, was suggested to me. I had begun to think over details for this and plan out the journey, when my hopes were utterly shattered by the stern refusal of my commanding officer to allow me to go, and I was left in despair to wile away the dreary hot-weather months in an Indian cantonment, spending hour after hour in looking out for microscopic atoms of dust on my men's uniforms or saddling, and in watching horses being groomed and fed and watered. But just when I was most despairing, a ray of hope came. A telegram was put in my hands, and this proved to be from the Foreign Office at Simla, asking me to undertake an exploration on the northern frontier of Kashmir. Here was the very chance I had been longing for. I went straight up to Simla to see the foreign secretary, Sir Mortimer Durand, and received instructions regarding my mission.

In describing my journey from Yarkand to Kashmir in the last two chapters, I have referred to a tribe of raiders who inhabit the little state of Hunza (or Kanjut, as it is always called on the Yarkand side), which is situated to the north of Kashmir. Deep-set among the mountains, accessible only by lofty snowy passes or through narrow impracticable defiles, the little state had bred and harboured a race of men who, issuing from the mountain fastnesses, had raided incessantly upon all the countries round. The traders on the road from Yarkand to India continually suffered from these wild freebooters; the peace-loving inhabitants of the Yarkand valleys were ever subject to their attacks, and compelled to hand them over black-mail; the nomadic Kirghiz, scattered defenceless in their tents over the open valleys of the Pamirs, had to pay their "tribute," or suffer the consequences of refusal; the Kashmir troops at Gilgit dreaded their attacks; and even the poor Baltis in distant and inaccessible Askoli shuddered at the thought of them. No one could get at these wild Hunza raiders, secure as they were in their impenetrable valleys, but they could strike at every one round them.

In the autumn of 1888—the year after I had crossed the Mustagh Pass—these robbers had made an unusually daring attack upon a large caravan, and had carried off a number of Kirghiz from Shahidula, on the Yarkand road. The Kirghiz had applied to the Chinese for protection against such raids, but had been refused it, and they thereupon, in the spring of 1889, made a similar petition to the British authorities. It was to inquire into and report upon the circumstances of this raid, and to examine all the country between the trade route and Hunza, with a view to stopping such raids for the future, that I was now to be sent by the Government of India. I was to take a small guard of six Gurkhas with me, and a native surveyor, and the Kirghiz who had brought the petition in to Leh was to await my arrival there, and accompany me to

Shahidula. Sir Mortimer Durand kept continually begging me to ask for anything which could possibly assist me, and showed a sympathy in the enterprise which encouraged me in carrying it out. On the night before I started, he said, "It is very easy for me, sitting comfortably in my drawing-room here, to ask you to go and do a thing of this sort; but you must not imagine that I do not fully realize all the hardships and difficulties you will encounter; so ask me for anything you like that can possibly help you along."

The hardships and difficulties, I think, he more than realized, for my experience is that they appear far worse in a drawing-room than anywhere else; but I was made to feel, at any rate, that I had his sympathy, and that was ample encouragement for me to do the utmost to justify the confidence that had been reposed in me. My preparations did not take long, for we were now in July, and it is only in the summer and autumn months that it is possible to travel in the mountains which had now to be explored, and arrangements had accordingly to be made as rapidly as possible. On July 5 I left Simla, spent a few days at Rawal Pindi collecting camp equipage, stores, etc., and then, on July 11, went to Abbottabad to inspect the six men of the 5th Gurkhas who had been selected to go with me. I was taken down to the orderly-room of the regiment, and there saw the six men drawn up, each with a little heap of clothing and equipment beside him, and with a crowd of envious Gurkhas gazing at them, while they themselves were looking preternaturally solemn, though it was evident that on the smallest provocation they would go off into a broad hearty chuckle. Each of them was receiving a free issue of special warm clothing, a waterproof sheet, a great-coat, etc.; they were to have extra pay while away, and they were to lead, for the next few months, a free wild life, with the chance of a fight, perhaps, before they got back again; so no wonder they were pleased with themselves and envied by their comrades. Having found that everything had been satisfactorily arranged, and that they themselves and all their equipment were, as far as could be seen, in proper working trim, I packed them off in ekkas to Kashmir, and they drove away from the regimental lines with broad grins on their jolly round faces, hugely delighted with themselves.

Meanwhile, I had to go round by Murree to pick up my own kit. I had been travelling in the train and in the tonga by road to Abbottabad all the night, and now, before evening, I had a forty-mile ride into Murree. But it was a delightful trip amid the most lovely scenery, as the road passed along near the crest of a pine-clad ridge, with long vistas over the plains of the Punjab on the one side, and here and there on the other side glimpses through the beautiful deodars of the snowy ranges of Kashmir, and once of the distant Nanga Parbat —the Naked Mountain—standing out over twenty-six thousand feet above sea-level, a true monarch of the mountains.

One day I spent in Murree, and then finally started on my journey, catching up my little Gurkhas on the following day at the then terminus of the cart-road, five marches from Murree. It was necessary to push my party along as rapidly as possible, so I mounted the Gurkhas on ponies and made them do double marches. A Gurkha is not at home on the back of a pony. He is made for climbing hills, and not for riding. And these little men were not at all happy at first, but they, at any rate, found it better than walking twenty-five miles a day in the hothouse atmosphere of the Jhelum valley in July.

While they marched up this valley and then crossed the Wular Lake in boats to the entrance of the Sind valley, down which I had come two years before on my way from Peking, I went to see the British Resident, Colonel Parry Nisbet, from whom, on this as on many another occasion, I received not only that help which I might expect officially, but also that thoughtful consideration which was more like what a father gives his son than what an official gives his subordinate. Then I once more rejoined my escort, and Shahzad Mir, a sowar of the 11th Bengal Lancers, who was to accompany me as orderly and surveyor, when surveying was to be done, having also now caught us up, our party was complete. And no one could have wished for a better little party—the six sturdy little Gurkhas, grim and stern when any business had to be done, but round the camp fire and off duty cheery and jolly, for ever chaffing one another and roaring with laughter; and Shahzad Mir, a different man altogether, but equally good, not jovial like a Gurkha, but a Pathan, grave and serious, and with his mind thoroughly set on the business in hand and determined to do it well. I used to talk to the men on the march, and tell them that I had been through the mountains before and knew that there was a rough time before us. The jolly Gurkhas laughed and said, "All right, sahib, we don't mind." If they were to have a rough time, they would get through it somehow or other when the time came; in the meanwhile they meant to enjoy themselves thoroughly. The Pathan knit his brows and prepared himself there and then for the struggle if there was to be one, and told me that he only wanted a chance of making a name for himself, and if he could do well on this occasion perhaps I should be able to get him promotion. My story will show how faithfully these men served me, and I was delighted with my first real experience of the native troops of India.

Crossing the Zoji-la, the last of the passes on my way from Peking, we left behind us all the wooded beauties of Kashmir, its shady pine forest and bright flowery meadows, and entered that desolate region of barren mountains and unshaded valleys, where the sun beat down upon the unprotected rocks and produced a degree of heat which would never have been expected at altitudes of nine thousand feet and over, and which made still more trying the cold blasts which, when

IN THE SIND VALLEY.

the sun had set, came down from the snow above. We were entering Ladak, an offshoot of Tibet, and the only redeeming feature in the country was the picturesqueness of its monasteries, perched high upon every prominent rock. As regards its natural scenery, it would be difficult to find any more dreary-looking country than Ladak. Its mountains, though lofty, are not grand or rugged, but resemble a monotonous succession of gigantic cinder-heaps. But the Buddhist monasteries, the fluttering prayer-flags, the chortens, and the many other signs of a religion almost totally unrepresented in India, gave the country a charm which just relieved it from utter condemnation. These signs of Buddhist life have many times before been described, so I need only refer here to the long rows of what appeared to be immense graves, overlaid with hundreds of slabs, each engraved with the formula, "Om mane padme hum" ("Oh! the jewel of the lotus"), the talismanic prayer which the devotees of this religion believe will produce more and more beneficent results the oftener it is repeated; the many-coloured flags fluttering in the breeze inscribed with the same magic formula, and breathing with each new flutter one fresh prayer to heaven; the dirty, yellow-clad monks, with their shaven heads, their string of beads round their necks, and their prayer-wheels reeling off a prayer with each successive revolution. All these are well-known characteristics of Buddhist life, and require only a passing reference here. I admired their picturesqueness and wondered at the quaintness of such superstitions, but had no time to study in detail the particular phase the Buddhist religion has taken in this far-away corner of Tibet.

We travelled rapidly through the country, and on July 31 reached its principal place, Leh. In twenty days our party had travelled just over four hundred miles, and crossed one pass of eleven thousand and three of thirteen thousand feet—all, however, very easy. On entering Leh I was met by old Shukar Ali, the only Ladaki who had come across the Mustagh

Pass. Hearing of my return to these parts, he had come to offer his services, and I gladly accepted them, for a more willing, cheery servant I never had. From pony-man he was now promoted to cook. He had no experience of cooking, and these rough hill-men are not the persons one would ordinarily choose for cooks; but, knowing the hardships my men would have to go through, I was determined not to have a man from the plains of India, who might become ill or give in just when his services were most needed. Only men accustomed to "roughing" it could come with me now, and no one could stand hard work better than Shukar Ali. So, although I could not look forward to any very *recherché* dinners while he was at the head of the cooking department, I knew that I should always be sure of a dinner of some sort, and with Shukar Ali as one of the party there would always be a volunteer for hard work when anything specially trying had to be done.

At Leh I was the guest of Captain Ramsay, the British Joint Commissioner, and the same officer whom I mentioned as being Political Agent at Srinagar when I arrived there from Peking.* He had been asked to have ponies ready for me, and to have other necessary arrangements made for my onward journey, and he had done everything so thoroughly that I had little else to do but take over charge. A matter which gave us, however, considerable anxiety was in regard to an additional escort of twenty-five Kashmir Sepoys, who were to be taken on as far as Shahidula. The garrison of Leh was paraded, but it only numbered seventy-nine all told, and was composed of miserable, decrepit old men, thin and half-starved, who looked at me imploringly as I went down the ranks—each one seeming to beseech me not to take him with me, while a look of horror came over each one that I selected. It is impossible to conceive a greater difference than there was between the look and the spirit of the Gurkhas

* Page 211.

of the regular Indian Army I had seen at Abbottabad and these woe-begone troops of the Kashmir army. The one, well looked after, well paid, well equipped, and well fed, were ready to go anywhere, and looked upon a few months' hard work as a welcome change from the monotony of barrack life; the other, poorly fed, badly equipped, and under-paid, dreaded hard work, because they knew they were not physically fit to undergo it, and because they could feel no assurance that sacrifices on their part would be recognized or rewarded. This was the state of the Kashmir army in 1889. How different it is now that it has been re-organized under the supervision of British officers is shown by their deeds in Hunza and Chitral.

With great difficulty, then, Captain Ramsay and I selected seventeen men who, with a proper equipment of additional warm clothing and with extra rations, we thought might just be able to pull through the work required of them. They seemed to shrink together as they were told they would have to march two hundred and forty miles and cross four high passes to reach Shahidula; but they really came of a soldier race—the Dogras—and as soon as they saw that they were to be properly cared for, they plucked up courage, and they afterwards did what was required of them well and without ever giving me the slightest trouble.

Besides Kashmir soldiers, I made at Leh an addition to my party of two Baltis, with a portable raft of goatskins for crossing unfordable rivers. These goatskin rafts are much used in Baltistan. From sixteen to twenty or more goatskins are inflated and lashed to a framework of wood, which can then be punted or paddled across the river. In the rafts ordinarily in use the framework is a fixture, but in the one which we were to take, the poles for it were of course taken separately and the skins carried flat.

Captain Ramsay and I, while these preparations were going on, discussed a plan of operations. Musa, the Kirghiz who had brought the petition to the British authorities, was still in Leh. From him we learnt the details of the Kanjuti raid in the previous year, and gained some information regarding the road which the raiders had followed from Hunza. This was one of the roads which I wished to explore, and, as it lay through a totally unknown country, it was necessary to acquire all possible information about it before going there. My chief anxiety was regarding transport. In a country which was a labyrinth of mountains without any roads, coolies would obviously be the best transport to employ. Men could go where a four-footed animal could not; and, if I employed coolies, I could follow a route which would be out of the question if I employed ponies or mules. But there was one fatal objection to the employment of coolies, and that was that if the men had to carry provisions for themselves for any length of time, they would not be able to carry any load besides. We should be several weeks away from any inhabited spot—in fact, we were afterwards travelling for fifty-seven days without seeing a single inhabitant—and as each man requires about two pounds of food each day, and cannot carry a greater load than sixty pounds over these rough mountains, it is obvious that if he had to travel thirty days away from the base of supplies, he would only be able to carry sufficient food for himself and nothing for anybody else, and that if he had to march any longer than thirty days he would starve. So coolies, though the best means of transport for crossing bad places, could not be employed.

The same objection, in a modified form, applied to the use of ponies. Ponies eat four pounds a day, and carry one hundred and sixty pounds. They could, therefore, go a little further than coolies; but even ponies, if the expedition were a month away from the base, would only be able to carry forty pounds of baggage each in addition to grain supplies for themselves. For anything over a month they would be useless. I then thought of employing donkeys. These animals are supposed to be able to pick up a living anywhere, and a handful or two of grain a day for each would probably be sufficient, but a very grave objection to using them was their small size. We should constantly be crossing rivers, and little donkeys would be swept away at once.

I was planning out a system of depôts and combined employment of ponies, donkeys, and men, when Musa, the Kirghiz, relieved my mind by suggesting camels. He said a certain number could be procured at Shahidula, and that they could be taken along a great part of the route to Hunza. This at once solved the difficulty, for camels can pick up a certain amount of grazing along the mountain-sides, so that they only need—or, at any rate, are only given—two pounds of grain a day, while they carry loads of from two hundred and fifty to three hundred pounds. Their size, too, would be of great advantage in crossing deep rivers. I had already employed camels on my way from Yarkand to the Mustagh Pass in 1887, and had seen then how well these hill camels can work over really difficult ground, so I at once sent off a messenger to Shahidula to have as many as possible collected for me. They would not be able to go the whole way, but they could work along the valley bottoms and easier passes; then we would have a few ponies to carry us over the more difficult passes, and two or three men for the worst of all.

The transport question having been decided, the next matter which had to be attended to was supplies. Though I have spoken of Shahidula as a base, it was not a base in the ordinary acceptance of the term. It lies over twelve thousand feet above the sea; nothing whatever is grown there; and there is not a single permanently inhabited house in the place. There was an old fort there, but Shahidula was really only the head-quarters of nomadic Kirghiz, and a convenient halting-place for caravans; and all supplies of grain had to be brought from the villages of Turkestan, six days' march across a pass seventeen thousand feet high. This was the only "base" for the exploration of a mountainous region where for two months we should not meet with inhabitants. There were not at this time sufficient supplies for our party in Shahidula, and the question was how to get them there. If I sent into the villages of Turkestan for them, the Chinese might object to this, for these villages were under Chinese authority, and the Chinese have been known to be obstructive. On the other hand, to carry up supplies from Leh would have been a serious undertaking. The furthest village in the Ladak district is one hundred and eighty miles from Shahidula, and separated from it by three passes averaging over eighteen thousand feet in height. As, therefore, the Chinese had been very civil to me on my former journey, I trusted to their being so again, and sent on a man to procure supplies from the Turkestan villages to bring to Shahidula.

All these preparations having been made, I said good-bye to Captain Ramsay, and on August 8 again set out. Directly behind Leh a high pass, the Khardung, seventeen thousand six hundred feet above the sea, has to be crossed, and as the ascent to it from Leh is very abrupt, I experienced a bout of mountain sickness, which depressed me greatly for the time. When the ascent to high altitudes is gradual, one becomes accustomed to the changed condition of the atmosphere; but when the ascent to such a height as seventeen thousand feet is abrupt (as in this case) most men seem to feel the change, and a racking headache and feeling of sickness and depression soon lets the traveller know that mountain sickness has come over him. On this occasion I became terribly depressed. I thought that if I was so bad as this at the very start, how should I fare when there were three still higher passes to cross before even Shahidula, the starting-point of my real journey, could be reached, and when there were ten others besides to cross before I should find myself in Kashmir again? Fortunately, however, mountain sickness wears off as one becomes accustomed to high altitudes, and I was never troubled with it again.

The journey to Shahidula it is unnecessary to describe in detail, for it is now well known. We ascended the picturesque Nubra valley, with its orchards of apricot trees and Buddhist monuments, and then crossed the Saser Pass, seventeen thousand eight hundred feet—a pass which, on account of the glacier at its summit, is often very dangerous, but which at this season presented no difficulty whatever. The mountains about here and at the head of the Nubra are very grand and bold, and rise to peaks of twenty-three thousand and twenty-four thousand feet in height, with fine glaciers rolling down their sides; but beyond the Saser Pass we entered the most utterly desolate country that exists on the face of the globe. The Depsang Plains are more than seventeen thousand feet above sea-level, and are of gravel, as bare as a gravel-walk to a suburban villa. Away behind us the snowy peaks of Saser and Nubra appeared above the horizon like the sails of some huge ships; but before us was nothing but gravel plains and great gravel mounds, terribly desolate and depressing. Across these plains blew blinding squalls of snow, and at night, though it was now the middle of summer, there were several degrees of frost. Crossing the Depsang Plains, we ascended a shallow valley covered with the skeletons of ponies, which every traveller who passes through it instinctively names the Valley of the Shadow of Death, to the Karakoram Pass, eighteen thousand eight hundred and fifty feet. It might have been supposed that at such height the snow would have been lying thick; but there was not a speck of snow either on it or on the mountain summits by it, which are well over nineteen thousand feet in height. Karakoram (Black Gravel) is, as I noted above, the very name for this pass and range; but it is strange that these mountains, at so great an altitude above sea-level, and forming, as they do, the watershed between India and Turkestan, should have no signs of snow upon them. The only reason I can think of to account for it is that behind this range and between it and the ocean, from which the rain comes, are other far more lofty mountains which intercept the greater part of the moisture; and as there are no deep trough-like valleys in which the little snow that does fall would collect and be preserved in the form of glaciers, but only wide shallow valleys where the snow would lie where it fell in a thin coating over the surface of the mountain, and soon melt under the rays of the sun, it happens that these mountains, whose summits are as high as Snowdon placed on the top of Mont Blanc, are in the summer months as free from snow as our little hills in England.

Descending the northern side of the Karakoram Pass, we passed the spot where poor Dalgleish had been murdered by an Afghan in the previous year, and saw the memorial tablet which had just been placed there by Mr. Dauvergne, Major Cumberland, and Captain Bower. No more dreary spot could be imagined; and here, on the dividing-line between India and Central Asia, in the very core of these lofty mountain ranges, hundreds of miles away from his nearest fellow-countrymen, had fallen the one solitary Englishman who had tried to make his home in Central Asia. It was sad to think of such a life being so sacrificed; and that after he had succeeded, as he had done, in gaining the affections and good-will of the people of the country in which he had settled, he should have been treacherously murdered in a fit of fanaticism or temper by one who was a stranger like himself.

From the Karakoram Pass we traversed a region only less desolate than that we had passed over on the southern side, and then, after crossing the Suget Pass, seventeen thousand six hundred feet high, we descended rapidly to Shahidula, which we reached on August 21, having in the last six days travelled one hundred and seventy miles of country in which no supplies, very little grass, and only roots for fuel could be obtained, and in those six days crossed, besides a minor pass of fifteen thousand feet, three others averaging seventeen thousand six hundred feet above sea-level. In just six weeks from the time of leaving the cantonment of Abbottabab my party was six hundred and forty miles in the heart of the mountains.

At Shahidula we were met by a deputation of Kirghiz, headed by Turdi Kol, the chief man, a quiet, careworn old gentleman, who, as he was himself present at the time of the raid, could give me a full and accurate account of it. What had happened was this. In the autumn of the previous year, a party of eighty-seven men of Hunza (Kanjutis), armed some with matchlocks, some with swords, and some with picks only, had come from the Shimshal Pass, one hundred and ninety miles distant, and had suddenly appeared near Shahidula. They had attacked a caravan and carried off a quantity of goods, and had captured, to take away as slaves, some stray Kirghiz, whom they had found about the valley tending their flocks and herds. They took some of these men, and on pain of death made them show where Turdi Kol, their chief, was living, and compelled them to go up to the tent and call to him to come out, while the Kanjutis lay hidden, ready to capture him directly he appeared. But Turdi Kol told me he suspected something from the manner in which he was called, and from the fact that his men did not usually stand outside and call him, but came in and asked him. So he took care to lay hold of his rifle, an English one, and, pushing aside the door of the tent, caught sight of the Kanjutis. He fired at them and they ran away; but they took with them twenty-one Kirghiz, men and women, and these were only subsequently released on the payment of eighty rupees for each.

Turdi Kol and all the Kirghiz implored me, as the representative of the British Government, to make some arrangements for stopping these cruel raids. They said the Chinese would do nothing for them, and their only hope now was in the British. I was able to tell them that the Government of India was sending Captain (now Colonel) Durand to Hunza to see the chief of that country, and, amongst other things, to try to come to some understanding with him in regard to this raiding, and that for the protection of the trade route during the present year I was going to leave some Kashmir sepoys at Shahidula. But I also desired to explore the route from Shahidula by which the raids were committed, and I would ask, therefore, that guides should be furnished me to enable me to effect this. Turdi Kol himself at once volunteered to accompany me, and as he had been to Hunza before, and knew the road, his assistance was likely to prove most valuable.

These Khirghiz were not an attractive set of men. They were timid, irresolute, and shifty. It is true that their mode of life renders them rather liable to attack, for they live by their flocks and herds, and have to scatter themselves over the valleys wherever pasture for their animals can be found. They are, therefore, necessarily exposed to attacks from a compact body of raiders. But, on the other hand, these raiders had to come nearly two hundred miles through a difficult mountainous country; and the Kirghiz, if they were worth anything at all, ought to have been able, in the defiles and passes of their country, to give the Kanjutis some sort of punishment, or to effect some little retaliation that might at any rate have checked the audacity of the raiders. But except Turdi Kol, who really had some pluck and nerve, they were a flabby lot, who, like parasites, preferred to hang on to some greater power and get protection from it rather than make any attempt at defence themselves. There were at the time of my visit about forty families in Shahidula and its neighbourhood, living, like all Kirghiz, in the round felt-covered tents, called *akois*. They were well dressed in long loose robes and turbans, or round fur caps. They appeared to be in more flourishing circumstances than the inhabitants of Ladak, and they make considerable profits from hiring out their camels, yaks, and ponies, and selling their sheep and goats to the traders passing through Shahidula on the caravan route from Yarkand to Leh. About twenty or thirty of them possessed matchlocks of a primitive pattern; the remainder were unarmed. All of them were in the most abject terror of the Kanjutis, and assured me that the first man who entered Hunza territory would be killed without a doubt. They proclaimed this loudly in a large gathering which I had called together, and when they said it I turned round and said in chaff to the naik (corporal) of the Gurkhas, "All right, you shall go first." The little man was quite delighted, and beamed with satisfaction at the prospect. Little touches like this show up in a flash the various characteristics of different races. Asiatics interpret these signs even more quickly than Europeans, and the six little Gurkhas produced by this and similar actions a marked impression upon the people wherever they went. The Kirghiz soon discovered the difference between the Gurkhas and themselves, and the feeling of terror and despondency which had hung over them when we first arrived soon gave place to one of confidence and security.

CHAPTER X.

AMONG THE GLACIERS.

"To reside
In thrilling regions of thick-ribbed ice."
MEASURE FOR MEASURE.

THERE was no need to hurry my departure from Shahidula, for it was necessary to wait till the Yarkand River, down the valley of which we should have to march for several days, should have fallen, as the summer floods from the melting of the snows decreased. The region which was now to be explored was entirely uninhabited, and without roads, tracks, bridges, or any of the usual means of communication. I had had a sample of it on my journey across the Mustagh Pass, and I knew that we should have to work along the beds of rivers and bottoms of deep, precipitous-sided valleys, and clamber over ranges by any sort of opening which could be dignified by the name of a pass. The first sixty-five miles had been explored by Hayward, and I had myself, in 1887, traversed another ninety miles, but otherwise the region from Shahidula to the Tagh-dum-bash Pamir and Hunza was perfectly unknown; and how the rivers and ranges ran, and where this Shimshal Pass was situated by which the Kanjuti raiders issued from Hunza, were all matters for conjecture.

There were two things which I desired especially to do. I wished to discover this Shimshal Pass, and see how the raiders came, and I wished on my way there to satisfy my curiosity as to the existence of a mysterious pass called the Saltoro Pass, which my old guide Wali had pointed out to me in the distance on our way to the Mustagh. I felt sure that this could only be a second Mustagh Pass; but still, such as it was, I wanted to see it. And after I had had a look at both these passes, it was my intention to make my way up on the edge of the Pamir plateau, and afterwards work my way homeward by one or other of the passes leading from these down through Hunza to Gilgit. Captain Durand, in the meanwhile, during the visit he had already planned to make to Hunza, was to arrange with the ruler of that country for my safe conduct through it.

The supplies which had been sent for from Turkestan arrived by the end of August. The Chinese had raised no objection to their being forwarded, and indeed had sent me a polite message in return for the one I had sent them. We had now for consumption on the journey 3200 lbs. of grain for the ponies, 1440 lbs. of flour for the men, 160 lbs. of rice, 48 lbs. of ghi (clarified butter), besides a miscellaneous supply of tea, sugar, etc., and a flock of seven sheep and six goats. We took also some tools for road-making, and of course a full supply of shoes and nails for the ponies.

For the carriage of this and of the men's baggage I had eighteen ponies and thirteen camels; but as these supplies were only sufficient for about a month and a half, I had to arrange for sending back the camels to fetch a further instalment, which was to be brought from the Turkestan villages and meet me at a certain junction of rivers (I could only hope that the two particular rivers did join, for of that point I had no certain information) at the conclusion of my exploration of the Shimshal and Saltoro passes. This exploration would of course take some time, and meanwhile the camels would be able to make their journey to Shahidula and back. I knew we were running a risk in starting without our supplies complete, but the exploration of such a region could not be accomplished without running risks of some sort. Camels in sufficient numbers could not be obtained, and it was therefore necessary to make the most of those that were available, and trust to the second instalment of supplies reaching us as arranged for.

The ponies and their equipment having been thoroughly looked to, the pack-saddles repaired, and the loads properly made up, we left Shahidula on September 3, leaving behind the seventeen Kashmir sepoys, who were to stay for a month at Shahidula to protect the trade route, and then return to Leh. The party now consisted of six Gurkhas (guard); one orderly surveyor; one interpreter (an Argoon of Leh); one cook (a Ladaki); two Balti raft-men; five Kirghiz. Total, sixteen men, with nineteen ponies (including one riding-pony for myself) and thirteen camels. The Kirghiz all rode ponies in addition.

We struck off westward from Shahidula, following the route which Hayward had taken on his exploration of the upper course of the Yarkand River. We followed the valley of a river on which were several patches of fine grazing, and till the previous year had been well inhabited, but was now deserted on account of Kanjuti raids. This valley is known by the name of Khal Chuskun. Chuskun in Turki means "resting-place," and Khal is the name of a holy man from Bokhara who is said to have rested here many years ago. The mountains bounding the north of this valley are very bold and rugged, with fine upstanding peaks and glaciers; but the range to the south, which Hayward calls the Aktagh Range, was somewhat tame in character, with round mild summits and no glaciers. The Sokh-bulak is an easy pass, and from its summit to the east could be seen the snowy range of the eastern Kuenlun Mountains, while to the west appeared a rocky mass of mountains culminating in three fine snowy peaks which

Hayward mistook as belonging to the main Mustagh Range, but which, in fact, in no way approach to the height and magnificence of these mountains, and really belong to the Aghil Range, which is separated from the Mustagh Mountains by the valley of the Oprang River.

The wind was blowing with such violence on the summit of the pass that I found it impossible, after trying for three-quarters of an hour, to obtain the height by boiling-point of the thermometer. It has, however, been fixed by Hayward at seventeen thousand and ninety-two feet. Descending from the pass through a narrow rocky gorge, towards evening we reached the valley of the Yarkand River, and halted at an open strip of jungle known as Kirghiz Jangal. The valley is here a mile or more broad; the bottom is mostly covered with pebbles, with the stream running in many channels over it. The mountain-sides are steep, rocky precipices, and no grass or wood is seen, except at a few spots along the bed of the river.

On September 5 we made a short march of eleven miles to Kulanuldi, a camping-ground called by this name on account of a kulan, or wild ass, having once been found dead there. The weather at this time was delightful, very clear and bright, neither too hot nor too cold—just perfection for travelling. The route, too, was easy and level, leading down the broad pebbly bed of the Yarkand River. The snowy peaks of the Kuenlun Mountains rose up to a height of twenty-one thousand feet to the north, but the real summit of the Aghil Range to the south could only be seen occasionally in peeps up narrow ravines. Far down the valley of the Yarkand River to the westward could be seen a very prominent knot of peaks, the height of which was approximately fixed by Hayward at twenty-three thousand feet.

On the following day we made an early start in order to make up for our short march the day before, and advanced twenty-six miles, passing on the way the camping-grounds of Chiraghsaldi, where the route from Yarkand, which I followed in 1887, joins in, and which is the furthest point reached by Hayward. From this point the valley narrowed considerably, and as the stream runs at places between enormously high cliffs, it is necessary to be constantly crossing and recrossing the river, which gets deeper and deeper as streams from either side add to its volume, till at last it becomes too deep to be forded by laden ponies, and we were brought to a standstill at the same gorge where I was delayed two years ago. The river at this point was up to the ponies' backs, and flowing with a strong rapid current over a rocky bottom, so that it was out of the question to take our baggage over on ponies; and we had to halt for the night (September 7) and wait till the morning, when the river is less deep than during the afternoon, as its volume is then increased owing to the sun melting the snows.

On this march we passed some ruins on a grassy plain called Karash-tarim (*i.e.* the cultivated lands of Karash, a man who is said to have lived here some eighty years ago). There were remains of half a dozen huts and some smelting furnaces, and there were also signs of furrows where land had been cultivated. This strip of grass and jungle was over half a mile long and six hundred yards broad, and doubtless in former times was a flourishing spot. There were evident signs, too, of the existence of minerals, copper and iron, and possibly even gold in small quantities may be found, for quartz and pieces of iron ore were abundant; while there are many traditions of the presence of minerals in these mountains, and the name of the country, Raskam, a corruption of Rastkan (a real mine), clearly shows that minerals may be expected.

Lower down we passed a considerable stream called the Bazar Darra, up which a route leads to Pakhpulu. The size of the stream, twenty-five yards broad by one and a half foot deep, shows that the main range of the Kuenlun Mountains must recede considerably from here. I was informed by Turdi Kol that, after ascending the Bazar Darra River, and crossing a pass (the Kokalang), you do not enter the basin of the Tisnaf River, as you would in the case of the Yangi and Chiraghsaldi passes further east, but you descend into the valley of a river called the Kulanargu, which joins the Yarkand River in its lower course somewhere near Pil; and you have to cross another pass, the Takhta-kuran, before you enter the valley of the Tisnaf River; so that it is evident that a little to the west of the Chiraghsaldi Pass the Kuenlun Range must split up, the two branches being separated by the Kulanargu River. The lower part of this river is called Chukshu, and is inhabited by Turkis, who are under Chinese jurisdiction, though they, like the Kirghiz, were refused protection from Kanjuti raids, and were told by the Chinese authorities that they lived outside the frontier passes, and must therefore expect no assistance.

The great height of these mountains was deeply impressed upon me on this day's march. Tired of marching monotonously along the bottom of the valley, cooped in by the mountains all round, I determined to climb a projecting hill, from which it seemed a view might be obtained of the higher portions of the ranges which were shutting us in. For some hours I toiled up a shingle slope, at each step sliding back, in the moving stone shoot, almost as much as I ascended, and when at last I reached the summit of the hill, I found it but the extremity of a spur which stretched back higher and higher to the range behind. My caravan below looked like specks in the valley bottom, but the snowy peaks above were still as distant as ever. I saw little more of the great main ranges than could be seen from the valley bottom, and, beginning to realize something of what these mountain heights truly are, I descended the opposite side of the hill and rejoined my party just as they were brought to a standstill in the gorge I have mentioned above. The river was dashing along at a furious rate over huge rocks and boulders, and was quite impassable for the ponies, so we were compelled to halt for the night; and the next morning, selecting a place where the river-bottom was least rugged, we crossed the river on camels, halting a few miles on the other side of the gorge at a pleasant little camping-ground called Karul, at the junction of the Surakwat stream. Here there was plenty of thick green grass and shrubs quite twenty feet high; so we remained the following day also, that the ponies might have a good feed of grass such as they were not likely to see for a long time to come.

Turdi Kol took me a few miles lower down the river and showed me two other equally good camping-grounds, and he says that there is considerably more pasture in the lower part of this valley than in that of the Karakash River, where Shahidula is situated, and that in the old days the valley was populated and cultivated, and merchants went to and fro by the Mustagh Pass to Baltistan. Kanjuti raids, however, put a stop to this, and a story is told of a great raid which took place at this gorge. The Kanjutis lay hid on the cliffs overhanging the river, and as a man called Khoja Mohammed was passing through with his family and a large party, they fired down on them, and afterwards attacked them with the sword, killing all the men, and taking the women and children captive. Since that time this gorge has always been known by the name of Khoja Mohammed.

We now had to leave the valley of the Yarkand River and cross the Aghil Range into the valley of the Oprang River. I took the camels on, one day's march further, to the foot of the Aghil Pass, and then sent them back to Shahidula to bring on the second instalment of supplies, which I had arranged that Turdi Kol should bring to meet me at Chong Jangal, near the junction of the Oprang with the Yarkand River, after the exploration of the Saltoro and Shimshal Passes. The ascent of the Surakwat stream towards the Aghil Pass is in parts very difficult, as the valley narrows to a gorge, and at two places we had to spend some hours in building up a staircase to enable the ponies to get round steep rocky cliffs. The numerous boulders, too, with which the valley bottom is strewn, made it very trying work for the ponies; but we eventually emerged on to a small plain, at the further end of which the main summits of the Aghil Range rise up like a wall in front of one rugged and uncompromising. Here we passed the same rock behind which, in 1887, I had spent the night lying in the open, as I had always been obliged to do during my passage of these mountains, for fear of attack from Kanjutis, should I make my presence known by setting up a tent. Retracing my former footsteps on September 11, we crossed the remarkable depression in the range which is known as the Aghil Pass.

So far we had been travelling over known ground, though I was the only European who had been over this pass before; but now there was some new exploration to be done. I have before described the wonderful view that is to be obtained from the summit of the Aghil Pass—snowy peaks, the grim wall of mountains, and the glaciers, like some huge dragons, creeping down the valley bottoms. Away to the eastward, up a glacier which stretched across the valley of the Oprang River at our feet, Wali the guide had told me there was a way to Baltistan by a pass called the Saltoro. No one, apparently, had crossed this pass for many years, and it was more than likely that it would prove just as difficult as the Mustagh Pass had been; but before going on to the Shimshal I thought I might well employ a week or ten days in seeing what it was really like. We descended to the valley of the Oprang River, and camped at a spot where some little grass could be obtained, and here I left my Gurkha escort with the heavy baggage and went on with Shahzad Mir, my orderly, Shukar Ali, and a Balti. We took five ponies and ten days' supplies, including fuel, and

I took a pony to ride myself whenever it was possible to do so.

On September 12 we made our start. The first march was easy enough, leading up the broad pebbly bed of the Oprang River. Up one of the gorges to the south we caught a magnificent view of the great peak K.2, twenty-eight thousand two hundred and seventy-eight feet high, and we halted for the night at a spot from which a view both of K.2 and of the Gusherbrum peaks, four of which are over twenty-six thousand feet, were visible. On the following day our difficulties really began. The first was the great glacier which we had seen from the Aghil Pass; it protruded right across the valley of the Oprang River, nearly touching the cliffs on the right bank; but fortunately the river had kept a way for itself, by continually washing away the ice at the end of the glacier, and so by taking our ponies through the water, which was filled with blocks of ice, we were able to get round the end of the glacier, a great wall of ice of one hundred and fifty to two hundred feet high. This glacier runs down from the Gusherbrum Mountains, and is about one and a half mile broad at the end; the central portion is a mass of pure ice-peaks, and the view looking up it is very fine, with the sea of ice beneath, and the Gusherbrum in the distance towering up to a height of over twenty-six thousand feet.

The passage round the end of the glacier was not unattended with danger, for the stream was swift and strong; and on my own pony I had to reconnoitre very carefully for points where it was shallow enough to cross, while there was also some fear of fragments from the great ice-wall falling down on the top of us when we were passing along close under the cliffs of ice which formed the end of the glacier. After getting round this obstacle, we entered a gravel plain some three-quarters of a mile broad, and were then encountered by another glacier running across the valley of the Oprang River. This proved to be the glacier we should have to ascend in order to reach the Saltoro Pass, while the Oprang River could be seen to flow down from another glacier to the south; and still another appeared in view, coming in a south-east direction, and rising apparently not very far from the Karakoram Pass. We were therefore now in an ice-bound region, with glaciers in front of us, glaciers behind us, and glaciers all round us. Heavy snow-clouds, too, were unfortunately collecting to increase our difficulties, and I felt that we should have a hard task to reach the pass.

On first looking at one of these glaciers, it would appear impossible to take the ponies up them; but the sides are always covered with moraine, and my experience in the exploration of the Mustagh Pass in 1887 showed that, by carefully reconnoitring ahead, it was generally possible to take the ponies for a considerable distance, at least, up such glaciers. We, therefore, now ascended the left side of the glacier, and halted for the night at a point from which a full view of the pass at the upper end of the glacier was obtained. The pass, indeed, seemed quite close, but distances in the clear atmosphere of these high mountains are very deceptive; and though my orderly, inexperienced in mountaineering, on first seeing the pass, was delighted to think that we should reach its summit on the following day, we did not actually approach it for three days yet to come, and our adventures on the way may perhaps be best described by extracts from my journal written day by day on the spot.

September 14.—A very hard, trying, and unsatisfactory day. I started off this morning full of zeal, ready to go anywhere and do anything, but finished up utterly tired out and careless of what might happen. These glaciers are terribly hard going, and after working the whole day we are only as far as where I originally hoped to be last evening, and the pass is as far off as ever. I started off early this morning before the camp was struck, and climbed the mountain range on the left bank of the valley to a gap, from which I hoped to get a view of what might be on the other side. But after a stiff climb of nearly two thousand feet, I was only rewarded by seeing the great glacier which flows down from the Gusherbrum and another ridge on the opposite side. Snow was falling, and the view which I had expected to get was hidden by the clouds.

These snow-clouds are remarkable for their soft, fleece-like intangibility. They are formed of very fine powder-like snow, and they softly obliterate a mountain peak while the change is scarcely perceptible. I have seen a peak standing out sharp and distinct before me, and then watched it slowly fade from sight, its outline become first hazy, then more and more difficult to distinguish, till all was of a dull grey hue like the sky around. One of these snow-clouds had settled down upon it, the powdery snow first falling lightly, then heavier and heavier, till the mountain was completely blotted out.

There was, therefore, nothing to be seen from the spur which I had ascended, and I rejoined my party. We then started off to tackle the glacier, and at first the way was good enough—that is, we could get along at the rate of one and a half mile an hour—and, as things seemed fairly smooth for some way ahead, I went off to make a small exploration of a glacier coming down from the westward. But after tumbling about on it for some time, and getting two nasty falls, I was brought up by a steep ice-fall. I tried to climb the mountainside, and had got up it for about two hundred feet, clinging to projecting rocks, but when these failed me, I had to give up the attempt, as it was too dangerous to cross the fall by myself without the aid of ropes. So I was again unsuccessful, and, making my way back to my party, found them halted in front of a great mass of accumulated ice fallen from the seracs, or ice-pinnacles, above. It was a wonderful sight to look at the great walls and blocks of pure ice, white on the surface, and a beautiful transparent green where it was broken. But it was a hard thing to encounter on the way. We formed a plan of carrying the loads over the *débris* of ice, and swimming the ponies across a strip of water; but on exploring ahead we found it even worse, and there was nothing for it but to go back some distance and try another way. This we did, but were yet again brought to a standstill by some crevasses, and here we halted for the day.

September 15.—We went back again, and at last found a way which led us straight up the centre of the glacier. We got along famously, and are now encamped at the head of the glacier, close under the pass, which we will attempt to-morrow. It looks rather like a repetition of the Mustagh, rising like a wall for about two thousand feet, and nothing but snow and ice. It may, however, turn out easier upon closer acquaintance.

September 16.—To-day we made an unsuccessful attempt to cross the Saltoro Pass. I had given orders to be called at 2 a.m., and after having some chota hazri, and making all necessary preparations, we started at 3.30 a.m. It was snowing hard and freezing hard, while dense clouds overhead hid the moon, so that we had barely sufficient light to find our way. Yesterday afternoon Shukar Ali and I had reconnoitred ahead, and determined the general line of advance and the best point at which to attack the pass, and we now proceeded steadily up the *névé* at the head of the glacier. At first crevasses were frequent, some visible—great staring rents in the ice fifty or sixty feet deep—others invisible, being covered with snow; these last were the dangerous ones, for the snow would suddenly give way under you, and your legs would go down a deep, dark hole. But, though this frequently happened, we had no accidents, and the higher we climbed the less frequent became the crevasses, though the snow became softer, and it was heavy work trudging along and sinking knee-deep at every step.

Day now began to dawn, but the heavy snowstorm did not cease, and we could only see the lower parts of the mountains, while their summits were hidden in the clouds. We were making towards a ravine, up which we conjectured could be the only possible way to the top of the pass, and were rounding an icy slope forming one side of the ravine, when suddenly we heard a report like thunder, and then a rushing sound. We knew at once that it was an avalanche; it was coming from straight above us, and I felt in that moment greater fear than I ever yet have done, for we could see nothing, but only heard this tremendous rushing sound coming straight down upon us. One of the men called out to run, but we could not, for we were on an ice-slope, up which we were hewing our way with an axe. The sound came nearer and nearer, then came a cloud of snow-dust, and the avalanche rushed past us in the ravine by our side. Had it happened a quarter of an hour later, or had we started a quarter of an hour earlier, we should have been in the ravine and buried by the avalanche.

We now continued the ascent of the ice-slope, hoping we might find a road by that way; but we were brought up by a great rent in the ice, a yawning chasm with perpendicular walls of solid ice. This effectually put an end to our attempt to cross the pass, for I dared not descend into the ravine, through fear of avalanches. We therefore were obliged to return and give up all hopes of reaching the top of the Saltoro Pass. On our way back we saw another avalanche rush down the mountain-side, and over the very path we had made in ascending, covering up our actual footsteps left in the snow. Seeing, therefore, how dangerous it was to remain where we were, we hastened on, and very thankful I was when we again reached the open glacier, and were out of the reach of avalanches. Snow continued to fall heavily, and we heard the roar of avalanches on the mountains all around us. Shukar Ali said that if the sky were to clear, and we could wait a week for the snow to settle, we might find a way over the pass. But in any case it would have been a piece of difficult mountaineering, and I could not afford to wait a week in a place where neither fuel nor grass could be obtained, and where everything was buried in snow and ice. So I determined upon returning to my camp on the Oprang River, and gave up any further attempts at crossing the pass. We accordingly hastened back to our camp at the head of the glacier, packed up, and marched round the glacier, the snowstorm still continuing.

September 17.—A heavy snowstorm during the night, and our camp in the middle of the glacier looked very cheerless this morning. Ponies, tents, baggage, and everything, were covered with snow, and snow was still falling heavily when we struck camp and continued our march down the glacier. We were able to make a double march, as we had the track marked out, and the bad places improved by our march up; and now we are once again on *terra firma*, and camped where we can get grass for the ponies, and a certain amount of fuel, and nice smooth sand to lie upon at night, instead of the thin layer of sharp stones which separates us from two or three hundred feet of solid glacier ice.

The length of this glacier is eighteen miles, and its average breadth is half a mile; it is fed by three smaller glaciers on the west and one on the east. At its upper part, immediately under the pass, it is a smooth undulating snowfield about a mile and a half in width. Lower down the *névé* is split up into crevasses which increase in size the further down we get. Then the surface gradually breaks into a mass of ice-domes, which lower down become sharp needles of pure white ice. On each side lateral gravel moraines appear, and other glaciers join, each with its centre of white ice-pinnacles and its lateral moraines, and preserving each its own distinct course down the valley until some three miles from its termination, when the icy peaks are all melted down and the glacier presents the appearance of a billowy mass of moraine, and would look like a vast collection of gravel heaps, were it not that you see, here and there, a cave or a cliff of ice, showing that the gravel forms really only a very thin coating on the surface, and that beneath is all pure solid ice. This ice is of an opaque white, and not so green and transparent as other glaciers I have seen, and the snow at the head of the glacier was different to any I had seen before, for beneath the surface, or when it was formed into lumps, it was of the most lovely pale transparent blue. Yesterday I forgot to mention, too, that every flake of snow that fell in the storm was a perfect hexagonal star, most beautiful and delicate in form. The mountains on either side of the valley, especially on the eastern side, are extremely rugged and precipitous, affording little or no resting-place for the snow, which drains off immediately into the glacier below. The western range, the main Mustagh Range, was enveloped in clouds nearly the whole time, and I only occasionally caught a glimpse of some peaks of stupendous height, one of them, the Gusherbrum, over twenty-six thousand feet, and others twenty-four thousand feet. The snowfall on these mountains must be very considerable, and it seems that this knot of lofty mountains attracts the great mass of the snow-clouds, and gets the share which ought to fall on the Karakoram, while these latter, being of less height, attract the clouds to a less degree, and are in consequence almost bare of snow.

Another heavy snowstorm fell during the night, and on the following morning, September 18, I rode into the camp where the Gurkha escort and heavy baggage had been left, and thence sent back some men and fresh ponies to assist the other wretched ponies, who were in a bad way, for they had had no grass for four days, and at these high altitudes it is not wise to give them more than four pounds of grain a day, for if more than that is given, they seem to lose their breath easily; and my own pony, a few marches further on, died from this very cause.

During the exploration of the Saltoro Pass I had lived in a small tent d'abri, not large enough to stand upright in; and the return to my larger tent with a table and chair was like a return to real civilization. My mind was now set at rest regarding the Saltoro Pass. I should like to have reached its summit, if the fates had been propitious, but I had seen enough to satisfy most people that there was no high-road to India by that way, and I now turned to the exploration of the Shimshal Pass into Hunza.

On September 21 the whole party started down the valley of the Oprang River, and then up the Sarpo Laggo stream to Suget Jangal, one of my camping-grounds on the way to the Mustagh Pass. Near here I again had a sight of that glorious peak K.2. The sun was just setting, and long after the other mountains round had become cold and grey, the warm red hues of sunset were still clinging to this loftiest tower of the Mustagh Mountains. From the spur which I had ascended I could see also the length of the glacier leading up to the Mustagh Pass, and the snowy barrier over which it leads. When two years before I had painfully struggled up, I had thought I should never set eyes on it again, but here once more it lay before me, and I pictured to myself each little incident in that hard tussle with the mountains.

Descending the spur, I found the caravan was still far behind. Darkness had come on, and Suget Jangal, the only spot in the valley where grass and firewood could be obtained, was still some miles distant. The caravan did not know where I was, and I did not know where the caravan was, except that it was not above me in the valley, and must therefore be below. So I employed a means of signalling which was of the greatest service to me on this occasion. This was a piece of magnesium wire which I lighted, and so at once attracted the attention of my men far away down the valley, and as they came near enough they answered with the whistles which had been served out to each man of the escort. Shortly after ten o'clock at night, after a rough scramble over the rocky boulders which strewed the valley bottom, we reached our camping-ground at Suget Jangal.

From about a mile above this a large glacier could be seen flowing from the westward down a wide valley, at the head of which I thought might be the Shimshal Pass. My Kirghiz guide assured me that the Shimshal Pass did not lie there. But guides are not infallible. On our maps the Shimshal Pass was marked very nearly where the head of the glacier would be; and though I knew this was only from conjecture, for no European had yet been anywhere near the Shimshal Pass, I thought I would just have a look, and if I was wrong, as I indeed proved to be, I could come back and meekly follow this Kirghiz guide wherever he chose to take me.

I therefore left the heavy baggage under the charge of one Gurkha and a Balti coolie, and set out for the exploration of the glacier, with twelve ponies carrying supplies and fuel for twelve days for my party and escort. On September 23 we left Suget Jangal, and by midday were again on a glacier.

We had rather a rough march up the glacier that day, but not so bad as on the way to the Saltoro Pass. The way to attack these glaciers is evidently this: first to keep along the side of the glacier, on the lateral moraine, close to the mountain-side; you here get some very fair going, though also, at times, some nasty pieces, where great, rough, sharp boulders are heaped one on the other, as at the mouth of a quarry. Presently the glacier closes in on the mountain-side, and you have then to take a favourable opportunity of plunging into the centre of the glacier, and ascending the part of it which is best covered with gravel moraine. Some very careful steering is here necessary to keep clear of the crevasses; and the ponies, and men too, often have a hard time of it, trying to keep their legs in ascending slopes where the gravel barely covers the ice. We took our plunge into the middle of this glacier at midday. Snow was falling, and at 4.30 p.m. the clouds became so heavy, and it was altogether so threatening, that I thought it best to halt. Of course, no grass or fuel was obtainable; but we had brought two pony-loads of wood with us, so were quite happy, though this was not a particularly cheerful-looking spot, with the snow falling hard, the great white ice-pinnacles of the glaciers rising all round, the mountains hidden by the heavy snow-clouds, and no place to encamp on but a very stony hollow.

The Gurkha havildar was in great form. He had a joke about getting hold of some "narm pattar," soft stones, to lie on, which kept him and all the Gurkhas in roars of laughter. I asked him where he had got the joke from, and he said some sahib had made it at Kabul in the Afghan war.

On the following morning we set out in a heavy snowstorm —so heavy that even the bases of the mountains on each side of the glacier were at times not visible, and the summits were not seen till midday, and then only in glimpses. Immediately on leaving camp we were confronted by a series of very bad crevasses, running right across our path. Things looked hopeless at one time, and it was like finding a way through a maze. The naik and I went on ahead, and by going from one end of each crevasse to the other, we managed in every case to find a way across, though to advance a hundred yards we often had to go at least six times that distance, and once we completely lost our front in the maze and the snowstorm, and were wandering off up a side glacier, till I recognized that we were in the wrong direction by a hillside appearing through the mist.

We finally got clear of the bad crevasses, and then had a fairly clear run for a couple of miles, and were beginning to congratulate ourselves that we had got over the worst of the glacier, when we came upon another series of crevasses of the most desperate description—the ice, in fact, was so split up that, though the whole party explored in all directions, we could find no possible way of getting the ponies along. I therefore decided upon encamping, and going on the morrow with a few men lightly loaded to the pass. I had some tiffin—rather an important point on these occasions when the time of the real tussle has arrived, and you are feeling rather down with things in general—and then started off to explore a route for the men to follow; but although I went in and out everywhere along the whole front, I found it impossible to get ahead. I then returned to camp, had a cup of good hot tea, and set out again backwards; but it was no go. We were in a regular *cul de sac;* ahead were impassable crevasses, and on each side were the main lines of the glacier pinnacles of pure ice, still more impracticable than the crevasses.

On September 16 we started back down the glacier, snow still falling heavily. The Gurkha naik, Shahzad Mir, and myself kept looking everywhere for some way of getting off the glacier on to the mountain-side, where it was evident we should find a passable road. Once or twice we got right up to the edge of the glacier, but just a few crevasses and broken crags of ice always prevented us from actually reaching *terra firma*. I was on the point of giving up, when I saw what seemed to be a practicable route. The others stayed behind, saying it was impossible; but I went on and on, and at last reached the edge of the glacier, and only a pond, heaped up with blocks of ice and frozen over, separated me from the mountain-side. The ice was very treacherous, but, by feeling about with my alpenstock, I got across safely; and then, going along the mountain-side for some distance, found a very promising route, which I followed up for some little distance.

On returning to the lake I found the naik and Shahzad Mir had followed me, the former having got across all right, but Shahzad Mir had gone through the ice up to his waist. The water was far out of his depth, and he had only saved himself by clinging on to a large block of ice close by. On returning across the lake I also went through twice, but as I thought the ice would be stronger by the next morning, I hurried after the rest of the party, whom I had ordered to stop at a certain point, and then brought back my own kit, some supplies, grain for the ponies, and a pony-load of wood to a spot as near to the lake as ponies could go, while I sent the Gurkhas back to Suget Jangal.

My intention was to try and reach the supposed pass with three men carrying loads. I at first meant to go without a tent, but as it was still snowing hard, and a bitter wind blowing, while in the night the thermometer had fallen to six degrees, and at the head of the glacier would probably be below zero, I decided upon taking the small servants' tent which I was using on this detached expedition. We carried the poles as alpenstocks, leaving the pegs behind, as we could use stones instead, so that the whole weight of the tent was not more than twenty pounds; and all four could sleep in it at night. The weather was anything but cheering, and the snow very trying, especially for the men, who had to do the cooking in the open. I, fortunately, brought only hill-men well accustomed to this work. I knew well what it would be, and would on no account bring a plain-servant or even a Kashmiri with me. The packs arrived covered thick with snow, and neither my men nor myself had a single dry pair of boots; nor could we dry our clothes, for we could only afford a very small fire, which was not sufficient to dry anything faster than the falling snow wetted it again. The floor of my tent was snow, under that a few inches of gravel, and then two or three hundred feet of ice. However, a good comfortable sheepskin coat helps one to defy a lot of discomfort. Each of the men had also a good sheepskin coat, with which I provided them at Shahidula, so we were pretty cheery in spite of the snow and cold.

September 27 was a fine sunny morning. We started off,

three men (Shukar Ali, Ramzan, and Abdula) carrying loads, and I had prepared a light load for myself, but the men would not hear of my doing so, and insisted upon carrying it. I could not have had better or more willing men; no amount of hard work ever stopped them. We got down to the lake all right, and there we were suddenly brought up. The lake is fed from the melting of the glacier, but, as the sun had not appeared for the last few days, the water had diminished several feet, while the layer of ice remained at the top. This layer had now fallen here and there, and though on the previous day it was treacherous enough, now it was quite impracticable, especially for men with loads. I ventured a few yards on to the ice, but, seeing it falling through all round me with sharp reports, I hurried back, and we had then to give up all hopes of reaching the pass. With time and with a proper Alpine equipment we might doubtless have found a way up the glacier and perhaps over the depression in the range at its head, which we had supposed to be a pass, but we had gone far enough to see that this was not the real Shimshal Pass, for which we were searching; so, as we could not afford to spend any more time on these ineffectual struggles with the glacier, we returned to our late camping-ground, loaded up the ponies, and started off back to Suget Jangal.

But though I had not found the pass I was seeking, I could never regret spending those six days on the glacier in the heart of the mountains. The glacier itself was marvellously beautiful, and the mountains from which it flowed, and which towered above it, formed the main range of the Himalayas. With the sides of the valley hidden by the clouds, one could believe one's self to be in the midst of the Arctic region. The centre of the glacier was a mass of pinnacles of opaque white ice, of every fantastic form and shape. Then among these were beautiful caverns of ice with walls of transparent green, long icicles hanging from the roof, and the entrance screened by fringes of these same dainty pendants. When I can free my mind from the overpowering sense of grandeur which the mountains produce, and from the thoughts of the stern, hard work we had to go through in those parts, I think of the beauty of that glacier scenery, the delicate transparency of the walls of ice, the exquisite tinting of the blues and greens upon it, the fairy caverns, the deep crevasses, and the pinnacles of ice, as forming a spectacle unsurpassed in its purity of loveliness. Other scenes are beautiful, and yet others are impressive by their grandeur. The verdure-covered hills and vales of England; the clear, placid lakes of Switzerland; and rivers with their verges fringed with foliage, are beautiful; and the frowning precipices and bold, rugged peaks seen in any mountain country are grand. But it is high up among the loftiest mountain summits, where all is shrouded in unsullied whiteness, where nothing polished dares pollute, that the very essence of sublimity must be sought for. It is there indeed that the grand and beautiful unite to form the sublime.

I called the glacier the Crevasse Glacier, on account of the great number and size of the crevasses, which were wider, deeper, and far more frequent than I have seen on any other glacier, and this I attribute to the bends. The widest branch comes from the south and makes a bend almost at right angles at the furthest point we reached, and is here joined by a longer but narrower branch from the pass. The length is about twenty-four miles, and the breadth from a thousand to twelve hundred yards. It ends at an elevation of thirteen thousand feet above sea-level, at a projecting spur of black rock, which is opposite to a stream issuing from a small glacier running down from the second peak on the southern side. Its lower extremity, for more than two miles, is entirely covered with moraine, but higher up it presents the magnificent spectacle of a sea of pure white peaks of ice, with numerous similar glaciers of smaller size running down to it from the lofty snowy mountains on the southern side. On the north only one glacier of any size joins in, and it is evident that the southern range gets far the greater portion of the snowfall, although the mountains on the north are in some cases very little inferior in height. The Crevasse Glacier seemed to me to be retiring; at any rate I should certainly say it was not advancing, for the moraine was deposited some few hundred yards in advance of the ice of the glacier, and there were marks of glacial action on the mountain-sides far above the present level of the glacier. The small glaciers—those resembling clotted cream—on the mountain slopes were certainly retiring. The glacier was very much lower in the centre than at the sides, and at the sides were the remains of successive beds of conglomerate, compact and hard, and level at the top, of a different character altogether to glacial moraine, so that it appeared as if there had formerly been a thick bed of conglomerate filling up the valley, and that it had now been swept out by the glacier. This, however, is only in the lower half, where the mountain slopes are comparatively gentle and formed of shingle; higher up, the sides are precipitous, and there are no signs of the conglomerate formation. The fall of the glacier as far as we went was two thousand two hundred and eighty feet in twenty-four thousand four hundred yards, or about one in thirty-two. Its general direction is N.N.W.

It was a glorious morning as we descended the glacier—clear and bright, as it can be only at these great mountain heights. I set off at a good pace ahead of the men and ponies, so as to get back to the luxury of my larger tent, table, chairs, books, and papers as quickly as possible. As I approached the Suget Jangal camp, the men, when they saw me alone, came rushing out, thinking something desperate must have happened. I told them that all the matter was that I wanted some lunch and a change of lower garments, for I had had to ford the glacier stream, which, being of melted ice, was so cold that it took the breath completely out of my body as I waded through the water. It was glorious getting into some clean dry clothing, then into a comfortable ulster, and then, after a good tiffin, sitting in a chair and having a quiet read. My appearance, though, was not becoming, for my eyes were bloodshot and inflamed from partial snow-blindness, and my nose, ears, and lips blistered from the bitter wind, while my hands were cut and scratched from frequent falls on the slippery glacier, and my knuckles cracked from the cold. But I and all my party were very fit and well—far better, I think, than when we left India.

CHAPTER XI.

A KANJUTI STRONGHOLD.

ON September 30, after a day's rest at Suget Jangal, we resumed our journey down the valley of the Oprang River, and halted that night at a fine patch of grass about a quarter of a mile long, to see which was a welcome relief after the never-ending snow and rocks usually met with. Our next day's march was a very disagreeable one, as a bitter wind, which brought with it clouds of gritty dust, was blowing straight in our faces up the valley. My pony to-day, although he had been left at Suget Jangal while I was exploring the glacier, and although he was a hardy Yarkandi, had now become so weak that three men could not drag him along, and at last he sank down by the way, and as we could not get him up again, I had to shoot him.

We made another march down the valley of the Oprang River, and a very trying one it proved, for we had to cross the river eleven times, and, as it had now become more than waist-deep, and very rapid, running over a bottom covered with boulders, it was at times dangerous work. As I rode the only pony without a load, I used to do the reconnoitring for fords. But even when a place fairly passable had been found, it was hard to keep the ponies straight to it; they would drift away with the current into deep places, and the packs got horribly wet. The crossings were most exciting work, everybody shouting with all his might at the ponies, and throwing stones at them to keep them straight. In spite of it all, we would see the ponies, with our clothes or bedding, fall into a pool with the water nearly over their backs. Most of the men got on the top of the packs, but some waded through the water, and they had a rough time of it.

We passed the Shimshal River, up which lies the route to Hunza we were seeking for, but we were rather short of grain for the ponies, on account of their having had more than their usual share on the glaciers, where they could get no grass, and, as I calculated from observations for latitude that we could not be far from Chong Jangal, where I hoped to find Turdi Kol with a fresh relay of supplies, I thought it best to go there first.

Chong Jangal was the point on the Yarkand River where it was believed the Oprang River joined it. As I have already said, we could not carry all the necessary supplies with us, but had to carry them in two instalments. We had reached the end of our first instalment, and had to look out for the second. There was no map of this region, and I could find no man with any full or accurate knowledge of it, or any information at all about what lay between the Shimshal Pass and the Yarkand River. All I could do was to tell Turdi Kol to go along the Yarkand River with the second instalment to this place, Chong Jangal, where he said a large river joined in from the north. This he thought must be the Oprang River, whose upper waters I should be exploring. The supplies would therefore be at Chong Jangal; but whether the river which joined in there really was the Oprang River, and whether, even if it was, my party would be able to get along it, nobody knew. The river might have flowed far away from Chong Jangal. It might never join the Yarkand River at all, or it might flow through gorges along which it would be impossible to take our ponies. Of all this we had to take our chance. But Turdi Kol had been down the Yarkand River before, and before leaving it at Surakwat I had got him to tell me about how many miles lower down Chong Jangal was, and the general direction in which it lay, and, marking that point approximately on the map, I had worked out my own survey down the Oprang River and calculated that we must be now nearing the meeting-place, so our next few marches were full of interest and excitement, and each turn we took I expected to see some signs of the Yarkand River.

On October 3, then, we continued our march down the Oprang River; but just when it ought to have struck Chong Jangal it turned round and went back again, upsetting all my calculations, and after a very hard and trying day we were still far from Chong Jangal, although at about noon I thought we had really reached there. I saw ahead one valley running in a direction east to west, and another in a northerly direction, and at the junction a patch of good jungle and grass. This exactly answered to Turdi Kol's description of the position of Chong Jangal, and it was a great blow when I found, instead of the Yarkand River flowing down the valley ahead in a westerly direction, it was still this Oprang River which flowed down it in an easterly direction, having deliberately turned round and gone backwards. It was very trying, because it has to be crossed and recrossed so many times, and each crossing becomes more difficult, and even dangerous. Three times that day, in reconnoitring for a ford, my pony was as nearly as possible washed off his legs, and the water came over the seat of the saddle, leaving only the pony's head and the upper part of my body out of the water, while I was expecting every minute to have to swim for it. The water, too, was fearfully cold, for there was not a drop of water in this river that did not come from the glaciers. And to add to our troubles, a nasty wind, with clouds of gritty sand, was blowing down the valley the whole day long. Altogether it was one of the most trying days I have experienced on a journey, though I ought not to complain so much as the unfortunate men, who had to wade through the icy water.

The Gurkhas managed to clamber along the hillsides like goats, but, unfortunately, at the end of the day they were at the other side of the river to our camp. We had halted because we had not been able to find a ford; for the water had risen, as it always does in the afternoon, on account of the melting of the glaciers during the day. I was very anxious as to how I should get them across, and was just mounting a pony to try the stream, when the first two Gurkhas appeared on the other side, and, without cogitating about it for half an hour, as I had done, promptly proceeded to wade through the water in the most happy-go-lucky way. I shouted to them to stop till I had tried the depth, but on account of the roar of the water they did not hear. How they got through I don't know, for the water came nearly up to their armpits; it was icy cold, the current very strong, and the bottom covered with boulders, and I know from our experiences in Manchuria what that means. However, they got across all right, and landed with a broad grin on their faces, as if crossing rivers was the greatest possible joke. I then rode across, leading another pony with me. I took up one Gurkha behind me from the other side, and mounted the remaining two on the second pony, which I brought across. We then started back. Once or twice my pony gave some ugly lurches, and I thought we were gone; but we got across all right, and I gave the Gurkhas a drop of whisky all round to cheer their stout little hearts.

We arrived at Chong Jangal at last, but found no Turdi Kol, no supplies, and no letters. I thought we were never going to arrive there. We rounded spur after spur, and at each I expected to see the Yarkand River, and Chong Jangal on the other side. In the afternoon, after rounding a great bend of the Oprang River, we entered a wide pebbly plain, and in the distance could see an extensive jungle. I thought it might be Chong Jangal, but could see no signs of the Yarkand River. After riding a mile or two, however, I crossed a considerable stream running over the pebbly plain. It was much smaller than the Yarkand was when we left it at Surakwat higher up, and, instead of being a muddy colour as it then was, was a clear blue, so I decided that it could not be that river, and that Chong Jangal must be on the other side of the next spur, several miles ahead. I was greatly delighted, therefore, when, on the baggage coming up, the Kirghiz guide said that this really was the Yarkand River after all, though very much diminished since we last saw it, because the melting of the snows had almost ceased, and that the jungle ahead was Chong Jangal. I hurried on then to see if Turdi Kol had arrived, but was disappointed to find no traces of him.

Chong Jangal we found to be an extensive stretch of jungle for these parts, where the mountain-sides are nearly absolutely bare, and only a few patches of brushwood, generally dwarf willows and juniper, are to be found in the valley bottom. This jungle was two miles long and half a mile broad. Some of the willows were from fifteen to twenty feet high, and there was plenty of good grass. There were, too, the remains of houses, and the spot had been inhabited and cultivated at one time, and, now that the raids from Hunza have been put an end to by the Indian Government, there is no reason why it should not be so again.

On October 6, a Kirghiz came riding into camp with a very welcome post, the first I had received for a month since leaving Shahidula. He had followed our tracks all round. By this post I heard from Colonel Nisbet that the Hunza chief, Safder Ali, had been very truculent on Captain Durand's visit, and I was warned to be careful about entering the country; but a subsequent letter said that the chief had apologized for his rudeness, and promised to allow me to go through. With such a man I could not, however, be very sure of my reception, and was all the more keen to reach his country and test his feelings as soon as possible.

But the second instalment of supplies had not yet arrived, and each day I looked anxiously up the valley of the Yarkand River for signs of Turdi Kol, as I was beginning to fear some mishap, and to imagine that we would be stranded in the middle of these mountains without anything to eat. At last, on October 10, Turdi Kol arrived with the long-expected supplies, and we then retraced our steps to the junction of the Shimshal River, and ascended the valley through which it flows. Up this valley, at five miles from its junction with the Oprang, is a Kanjuti outpost called Darwaza, or "the gate." It was from this place that the raiders started on their expeditions, and as we ascended the wild, narrow mountain valley in which it is situated, we wondered what sort of reception we should meet with from these robber bands. Rounding a spur, we saw in the distance a tower erected on the top of a cliff, and approaching nearer we saw that the whole line of the cliff, where it was at all accessible, was covered by a loop-hole wall, at the upper end of which was a second tower. The cliff formed the bank of a deep ravine, which cut transversely across the main valley. Looking up the valley on the right was the unfordable Shimshal river; on the left were precipitous mountains, and in front this deep ravine. The only possible way up the valley was by a difficult zigzag path up the side of this ravine, and that was guarded by the two towers. Some smoke was curling up from these towers, so we knew that they were tenanted, and the exciting moment had now arrived when we should have to beard these raiders in their very den.

I carefully reconnoitred the position with my field-glasses, so as to be able to decide on our best plan of action in case of a hostile reception. The path zigzagged down one side of the ravine, which was about two hundred feet deep, and up the other, and passed immediately under the wall and through a gateway in the tower. It would have been impossible to effect an entrance if the Kanjutis chose to be hostile, for even if they did not fire at us, they could have annihilated us by hurling down stones. I thought, therefore, that my best plan would be not to commit my whole party to such a risk, but to go on with an interpreter, and leave the Gurkhas on the top of the cliff on our side of the ravine, to cover the retreat in case the Kanjutis proved hostile. Having made these dispositions, I set off down into the ravine accompanied by Ramzan, the interpreter, and Shahzad Mir, the orderly, who spoke Persian. We had not gone very far, when the Gurkha naik came running after us and said that at Shahidula I had promised that he should be allowed to go first. The reader will remember that the timid Kirghiz had prophesied that whoever should appear first before this Kanjuti outpost would certainly be killed, and I had in chaff said to the Gurkha naik that he should be sent on first, and now, taking my word seriously, he had claimed this as a privilege.

We had descended to the bottom of the ravine, and climbed halfway up the opposite bank. The door through the tower was still open, and no one could be seen about, when suddenly the door was banged, the wall was manned by wild-looking Kanjutis, shouting and waving us back, and pointing their matchlocks at us. We were not fifty feet from them, and I expected at any moment to have bullets and stones whizzing about our ears; so I halted and beckoned to them, holding up one finger and signing to them in this way to send one man down to us. Gradually the hubbub ceased; they still kept their matchlocks pointed at us, but the door was opened and two men came down to us. We had a long parley together, and I told them who I was, that I was coming to visit their chief, and that Captain Durand had already spoken to Safder Ali about my coming. They said they had heard of this, but they wished to make quite sure that I had not an army with me, so I sent them to count for themselves exactly how many men I had. The Gurkhas then joined me, and we passed through the tower together; but just at the entrance, which was lined with Kanjutis in a double row, a man rushed at my pony and seized the bridle. I thought for a moment there was treachery. The Gurkhas sprang forward, and in half a second there would have been a scrimmage, when the man let go, and laughed, and said he had only intended it as a joke.

We then all gathered together round a fire on the inside of this line of wall, and now fresh difficulties arose. The Kanjutis said that all the Kirghiz with me must go on to Hunza; but this I could not agree to, as Turdi Kol had to return with the camels I had hired. So, being now on the right side of the position, with the Gurkhas round me, instead of the wrong side of the wall with the Kanjuti matchlocks pointed at us, I was able to take up a high tone, and tell these men that I did not intend to be dictated to what I was to do or what I was not to do. The Kirghiz were to go back, and they, the Kanjutis, would be held responsible if they were molested in any way.

Another difficulty was in regard to Turdi Kol, the Kirghiz chief, who was standing with us round the fire. The Kanjutis, not knowing who he was, said to me that their chief, Safder Ali, particularly wanted to get hold of Turdi Kol, as he had shot one of the Kanjutis in the raid of the previous year, and they asked me where he was. Turning to Turdi Kol, but addressing him by a hypothetic name, I said to him, "Sattiwal, do you know where Turdi Kol is?" Turdi Kol replied, "Yes; he is behind with the camels." And we kept up this deceit the whole time, though a little Gurkha as nearly as possible spoilt everything through calling Turdi Kol by his right name, and then, discovering his mistake, correcting himself and going off into a loud laugh. Gurkhas are brave, cheery little men, but they have not the wits of a hog.

We stood together for a long time round the fire, a curious

group—rough, hard, determined-looking Kanjutis, in long loose woollen robes, round cloth caps, long curls hanging down their ears, matchlocks slung over their backs, and swords bound to their sides; the timid, red-faced Kirghiz; the Tartar-featured Ladakis; the patient, long-suffering Baltis; the sturdy, jovial little Gurkhas; the grave Pathan, and a solitary Englishman, met together here, in the very heart of the Himalayas, in the robbers' stronghold. It is on thinking over occasions like this that one realizes the extraordinary influence of the European in Asia, and marvel at his power of rolling on one race upon another to serve his purpose. An Asiatic and a European fight, the former is beaten, and he immediately joins the European to subdue some other Asiatic. The Gurkhas and the Pathans had both in former days fought desperately against the British; they were now ready to fight equally desperately for the British against these raiders around us, and their presence had inspired so much confidence in the nervous Kirghiz that these even had summoned up enough courage to enter a place which they had before never thought of without a shudder.

I now found that the Hunza chief really meant to receive me, and the man in charge of the outpost informed me that an official would meet me on the other side of the Shimshal Pass to welcome me in the name of the chief. So we marched on towards the pass for another three and a half miles, to a camping-ground called Afdigar, where grass and low willows and other scrub for firewood were plentiful. A number of small side nullahs were crossed, and each was lined with a wall of defence. Seven Hunza men came on with us, and the Gurkhas quickly fraternized with them, winning their hearts by small presents of tobacco. I also gave them a good dinner, and their tongues were gradually loosed, and on that and other nights that they were with us they told us many interesting things about their country. They complained much of the hardships they had to suffer on the raids, and the little benefit they got from them. Everything they took, they said, had to be handed over to the chief, and all the raids were organized by him. If they were suspected of not having given up all they had, or if the chief wanted to squeeze more taxes out of them, they were stripped naked and kept for hours in a freezing glacier stream. They were in abject terror of their chief, and during their conversation they were constantly discussing the probabilities of their heads being cut off. If they did this or that they would lose their heads, and they would illustrate the action by drawing the edge of their hands across their necks. They wore always a grave, hard look, as of men who lived in a constant struggle for existence, and were too much engrossed by it to think of any of the levities of life. I afterwards found that down in the lower valleys of Hunza the people are fond of polo and dancing, but these I first met were men from the upper valleys, where the struggle is harder, and where they were frequently turned out for raiding expeditions.

On the following day, October 15, we at last crossed the Shimshal Pass, for which I had been seeking during so many weeks. The ascent was steep for a mile and a half, but not really difficult, and afterwards the road gradually ascends to the pass, which is a *pamir*, as the Kanjutis called it, that is, a nearly level plain or very shallow and wide trough between high mountains on either side. A mile from the summit we passed a collection of shepherds' huts, used in the summer; at the summit, which was fourteen thousand seven hundred feet above sea-level, there were two small lakes. There was no snow at all on the pass, which was a most unexpectedly easy one. We had been anticipating struggles with glaciers and climbs up rocky precipices, but here was a pass which we could have ridden ponies over if we had wanted to do so.

This Shimshal Pass forms one of those remarkable depressions which are here and there met with in these mountains. Up to this point the Mustagh Range is lofty and rugged in the extreme. Everywhere it is covered with snow and ice, and peaks of great height rise along it. There are within the neighbourhood of the Shimshal Pass many of these peaks, twenty-three and twenty-four thousand feet in height. But here it suddenly drops down to fifteen thousand feet, and the summits on the northern side of the pass, though still lofty, are smooth and rounded instead of sharp and ragged. The explanation that suggests itself to me is that the mountains on the south side of the pass are of more recent upheaval than those on the north, that the latter have been longer exposed to the wearing action of the snow and ice, and that consequently peaks which may formerly have been as lofty and rugged as those still standing to the south have now become worn and smoothed down. And though the *watershed* of the Mustagh Range runs across the pass and away in a northerly direction through the crests of these rounded mountains, I think that it would not be right to call this the *main axis*, for that, as it seems to me, runs away in a more westerly direction from the south side of the Shimshal Pass, and passes along a few miles above Hunza. This line passes through a series of peaks, more than one of which are over twenty-five thousand feet in height, and looked at either on the spot or on the map this appears to be the true axis of the range, while the watershed to the north seems merely a subsidiary offshoot.

Descending by a steep zigzag from the Shimshal Pass, we encamped near a second collection of shepherds' huts, to which the Hunza men come in the summer with their flocks. There were patches of good grass both here and on the flat surface of the pass, but no trees, and only low dwarf bushes. On the next morning, leaving my party behind here, I went on with a few men to examine the country a little further in the direction of Hunza, though it was my intention to return over the Shimshal Pass, and go up on to the Pamirs, before finally proceeding to the capital of the country. The valley we were in soon narrowed to a precipitous gorge, and Lieutenant Cockerill, who explored it three years later, confirmed the stories of the Kirghiz, and indeed of the Hunza men themselves, that the road along it is quite impracticable for ponies, and even very difficult for men.

An official, with a letter from Safder Ali, the chief of Hunza, came into camp this day. Captain Durand had duly impressed him with the necessity of seeing me through his country, and he accordingly extended a welcome to me. I wrote him back a letter thanking him for his welcome, and saying I wished to travel on the Pamirs first, and would do myself the pleasure of paying him a visit a few weeks later. I then returned with my party across the Shimshal Pass, and rejoining Turdi Kol and the Kirghiz, who had been left behind with the camels, again descended the Oprang River to its junction with the Yarkand River, or Raskam River as it is known locally, at Chong Jangal.

CHAPTER XII.

BY THE SKIRTS OF THE PAMIRS TO HUNZA.

THE Raskam River is what is usually considered the main branch of the river which flows by Yarkand, but till now the Oprang branch of this river had not been explored, and this latter certainly has a claim to be considered the main branch. The Raskam is the longer branch of the two, being about a hundred and eighty miles from its source, which was explored by Hayward to its junction with the Oprang at Chong Jangal; while the Oprang, as now explored by me from near its source throughout its course, is not more than a hundred and fifty miles. But the Oprang, in the month of October at any rate, has quite twice the volume of water—a fact which is easily understood when it is considered what a vast area of glaciers along the main range it drains.

Between these two branches of the Yarkand River lies a range which, so far as I could learn, can only be crossed at the Aghil Pass. It runs in a general north-west direction, parallel to and intermediate between the Mustagh Range and the western Kuen-lun Mountains. It is a hundred and twenty miles in length, and is broken up into a series of bold upstanding peaks, the highest of which must be close on twenty-three thousand feet. Near its junction with the Mustagh Mountains there are some large glaciers like those which fill the valleys leading down from the main watershed, but towards its western extremity these vast *mers de glace* are not seen, and only the lesser glaciers are met with on the higher slopes. The mountain-sides are perfectly bare, and only the scantiest scrub is found in the valley bottoms.

Akal Jan, a Kirghiz who belonged to the Tagh-dum-bash Pamir, but whom I had met at Shahidula, while we were exploring the passes, had gone to his home on the Pamir and collected camels and yaks, which he now of his own accord brought to Chong Jangal. He was also the bearer of a letter from Lieutenant Bower, who, with Major Cumberland, had made his way on to the Tagh-dum-bash Pamir by way of Shahidula, Kugiar, and Sarikol. In this letter was the information that Captain Grombtchevsky, the well-known Russian traveller, who had in the previous year found his way into Hunza, was now travelling towards Ladak, and would probably meet me on the way. Being anxious to see Lieutenant Bower, I despatched an urgent message to him to try and meet me at Tashkurgan, and set out from Chong Jangal on October 21, descending the Yarkand River towards the Tagh-dum-bash Pamir.

We saw many signs of cultivation, and were told by the Kirghiz that down to about forty years ago this valley was well populated, and that even now Kirghiz from the Tagh-dum-bash occasionally cultivate some of the ground in the side valleys, where they are well hidden in case of Kanjuti raids. Trees, too, are here met with, and in the Uruk valley there are still a few apricot trees.

The ponies had now become completely knocked up, and although the road here is good, even the unladen animals could not keep up with the loaded camels. The camels and yaks which Akal Jan had brought were sufficient to carry the whole of our baggage, so I discharged the ponies and sent them back to Ladak. Working at high altitudes among these mountains, where the road is always difficult, and grass at the camping-grounds very scarce, it is impossible to keep ponies going almost continuously, as I had been obliged to do, and in future explorations of a similar kind, it would be advisable, if possible, to arrange for changes of transport.

At the camping-ground near the junction of the Ilisu with the Yarkand River, I received a letter from Captain Grombtchevsky, written in Turki, and saying that he had halted at Khaian-aksai and was anxious to meet me. I answered, in Persian and English, that I was very glad to have the opportunity of meeting so distinguished a traveller, and would arrange to encamp with him the next day.

On October 23 we marched to Khaian-aksai, leaving the valley of the Yarkand River and ascending a narrow valley whose bottom was almost choked up with the thick growth of willow trees. Rounding a spur, we saw ahead of us the little Russian camp, and on riding up to it a fine-looking man dressed in the Russian uniform came out of one of the tents and introduced himself as Captain Grombtchevsky. He was about thirty-six years, tall, and well built, and with a pleasant, genial manner. He greeted me most cordially, and introduced me to a travelling companion who was with him, Herr Conrad, a German naturalist. We had a short talk, and he then asked me to have dinner with him. This was a very substantial repast of soup and stews, washed down with a plentiful supply of vodka.

This was the first meeting of Russian and English exploring parties upon the borderlands of India, and there was much in each of us to interest the other. Captain Grombtchevsky had already been to Hunza, having made a venturesome journey across the Pamirs into that country in 1888, that is, the year before we met. It had on the present occasion been his intention, he informed me, to penetrate to the Punjab through Chitral or Kafiristan, but the Amir of Afghanistan had refused him permission to enter Afghan territory on his way there. He had accordingly come across the Pamirs, and was now hoping to enter Ladak and Kashmir, for a permission to do which he was writing to the British Resident in Kashmir.

Captain Grombtchevsky's party consisted of seven Cossacks, a munshi who accompanied him to Hunza in the previous year, and one servant. He lived in a small light tent of umbrella-like construction; Herr Conrad, the naturalist, lived in another; the Cossacks lived in a very flimsy tent d'abri, with both ends open, which must have been an uncomfortable arrangement when the bitter winds of these high lands were in full force; and the servants lived in a fourth tent. Such was their little camp. The Cossacks appeared to do all the work; they scoured the mountain-sides for the ponies in the morning, fed them, and saddled and loaded them for the march; they formed a guard during the march, and at night Captain Grombtchevsky always had a sentry over his tent. For all this work they appeared to be indifferently equipped. Their wretched apology for a tent has already been described; their food seemed poor and insufficient, as they lived almost entirely on mutton, and ate even the entrails of the sheep, and seldom had any flour, as there was only ninety pounds in camp for the whole party for three months. The liberality of our Government, indeed, was very apparent on this occasion, for the contrast between the parties was remarkable. The Gurkhas had two snug little tents, with waterproof sheets, and numdahs, and everything that could be done to make them comfortable, and, as I had been given a liberal allowance of money for the expenses of the expedition, my men had as much and even more than they wanted of mutton, flour, rice, tea, and sugar, although we had then been travelling for seventy-one days from the last village where supplies were obtainable, and all we had with us had had to be brought from Chinese territory, where the rulers might have stopped our supplies. But, although the Cossacks did not strike me as being well cared for, they were good, sound, hardy fellows, who looked well able to stand the rough work they had to do. They were small, but thick-set men, averaging about five feet six inches in height, fair in complexion, thoroughly European in appearance, and resembling very much our English country labourers. They were clothed in khaki jackets, tight pantaloons, and high boots reaching above the knee; over this they wore a long brown great-coat, and at night a heavy sheepskin coat reaching to the ankles. The arms consisted of a rifle and sword. On the whole, the term "rough and ready" would summarize the general impressions left upon me by them.

Captain Grombtchevsky expressed his opinions freely on many subjects, and was enthusiastic in his description of the Russian army. He said that the Russian soldier went wherever he was ordered to go, and did not think about such things; that he looked upon the general of an army as his father, who would provide all that was possible, and if at the end of a hard day's march he found neither water to drink nor food to eat, he would still not complain, but would go on cheerfully till he died, and when he died there were many more Russians to take his place. Grombtchevsky quoted many instances from the Central Asian campaigns to illustrate this statement, and it is undoubtedly true that the Russian soldier is brave, enduring, cheerful, and uncomplaining; but it is equally true that Russian generals and their staffs have often shown themselves incapable of organizing large forces properly, and that the knowledge that there are always plenty of men behind has caused them to be so negligent that many a Russian soldier's life has been sacrificed through want of necessary arrangements. This may matter little in wars close at home; but in an expedition where each man has to be transported for hundreds of miles through countries where nearly all the food for him has also to be transported, a general cannot afford to have his men dropping off from neglect.

In the afternoon Captain Grombtchevsky asked for an

opportunity of inspecting the Gurkha escort, and I had them drawn up for the purpose. The Russian officer looked at them and then made a remark to me. The Gurkha non-commissioned officer, thinking that Captain Grombtchevsky must necessarily be remarking on their small size, whispered to me to tell him that these Gurkhas I had with me were unusually small, but that the rest of their regiment were much bigger than Captain Grombtchevsky himself. The Russian officer was well over six feet in height, and the average of a Gurkha regiment must be a good six inches lower, for Gurkhas are a small, thick-set race; so I could not commit myself to quite so flagrant an "exaggeration," but I told Captain Grombtchevsky how the Gurkha had wanted to impose upon him, and he was immensely tickled. Altogether he was very much taken with the appearance of the Gurkhas, and with the precision and smartness of the few drill exercises they went through. He said he had thought the native troops of India were irregulars, but he now saw that they were as good as any regulars. I think the Gurkhas were equally impressed with the soldierly bearing of the Russian officer; but I was surprised to see that they did not fraternize with the Cossacks, as they are noted for doing with British soldiers, and I found the reason to be that they rather looked down upon the Cossacks, on account of their being less well paid and equipped than themselves. This is a thoroughly Oriental way of regarding things; but for my own part I was much struck with the many excellent qualities of the Cossacks, and no officer could wish for any better material for soldiers than they afford.

Finding Captain Grombtchevsky's company so agreeable, I halted a day with him, and on October 25 set out again towards the Tagh-dum-bash Pamir. On leaving camp I made the Gurkha escort salute the Russian officer by presenting arms, and Captain Grombtchevsky returned the compliment by ordering his Cossacks to "carry swords." We then parted,

Captain Grombtchevsky saying to me that he hoped we might meet again, either in peace at St. Petersburg or in war on the Indian frontier; in either case I might be sure of a warm welcome. I thoroughly enjoyed that meeting with a Russian officer. We and the Russians *are* rivals, but I am sure that individual Russian and English officers like each other a great deal better than they do the individuals of nations with which they are not in rivalry. We are both playing at a big game, and we should not be one jot better off for trying to conceal the fact.

On the following day, October 26, we crossed the Kurbu Pass on to the Tagh-dum-bash Pamir. The pass is an easy one, fourteen thousand seven hundred feet high, and is quite practicable for laden animals. The change of scenery now was very striking. In place of the deep ravines and precipitous mountain-sides that we had hitherto been accustomed to in the valleys of the Yarkand and Oprang Rivers, we now found great open, almost level plains, some four or five miles broad, running down between ranges of mountains only a few thousand feet higher than the valleys. Grass, too, was plentiful, and there was no need for laboriously seeking good tracks for the ponies, as on the Pamir you could go anywhere. But the wind was bitterly cold, and although the temperature at night did not usually descend below zero (Fahrenheit), yet it was very much more trying than the cold which we had been experiencing lately on the Yarkand River. There, indeed, the thermometer was quite as low as on the Pamir, but the air was generally still, and there was no wind to drive the cold right into the marrow of one's bones.

Our first encampment was at a place called Ilisu, where one of the felt tents of the Kirghiz had been prepared for me, and where the headman of the Pamir, Kuch Mohammed Bey by name, had arrived to meet me. He was not very prepossessing in appearance, and had a bad reputation for giving the

Kanjuti Raja information to enable him to carry out his raids successfully; but he was friendly enough to me, and gave me all the assistance which I required. And this was a satisfactory thing, for he was really under the Chinese, and might have made difficulties here, as I had with me no Chinese passport, and had to trust to establishing friendly relations with the inhabitants to enable me to get through the country without hindrance.

The next day I left my escort, and set out to meet Major Cumberland and Lieutenant Bower at Tashkurgan, some seventy miles distant. This place I reached on the following day, and found them encamped a few miles lower down. The pleasure of meeting Englishmen again, and being able to talk in my own language, may well be imagined.

They had set out from Leh about two weeks before me, and, accompanied by M. Dauvergne, had travelled by Shahidula to the Kilian Pass, and from there had struck westward to Kugiar, near which place they had met with Colonel Pieotsof, the Russian traveller, who had succeeded the late General Prjevalsky in command of the expedition to Tibet. They say that this party had from eighty to one hundred camels, besides about twenty ponies. The guard consisted of twenty-five Cossacks, and they had no native servants whatever, the Cossacks doing the whole of the work. They lived in felt tents, and were apparently travelling very leisurely and comfortably. From Kugiar, Major Cumberland had made his way across the Tisnaf valley, which he describes as being very beautiful and abounding in fruit, to the Yarkand River, and from there up the valley of the Tung River, also a very fruitful one, to Tashkurgan. This road has never been traversed by Europeans, and, from Major Cumberland's account, it would appear to be not an easy one, by reason of the succession of passes over the spurs running down from the big ranges which had to be crossed.

They had also met Captain Grombtchevsky, and had been as much struck as I was with his genial manner, though they had warned him of the difficulties he would be likely to meet in gaining permission to enter Ladak, accompanied as he was with an escort of Cossacks.

The winter had now fairly set in, and as two passes on the main range had still to be explored, it was necessary for me to return quickly to my party. I accordingly had to leave Major Cumberland again on October 30, and retrace my steps down the Tagh-dum-bash Pamir.

The Sarikolis seemed very friendly disposed, and as I was passing through Tisnaf, a small walled village a mile or two north of Tashkurgan, the headman met me and pressed me to come in to breakfast, a request which I was very glad to accept. He took me to a small house, and brought me bread and tea, which he ate with me.

I was told that this year many fugitives from Shignan had been driven here by the Afghans, but most of them had been sent back by the Chinese, after they had received an assurance from the governor of Shignan that no harm should be done to them.

Tashkurgan and its neighbourhood was visited by Colonel Gordon, with some members of Forsyth's Yarkand Mission, in 1874, on their way to Wakhan and the Great and Little Pamirs, and there is nothing which I need add to the description of it which will be found in the report of the Mission.

The Tagh-dum-bash Pamir, of which Tashkurgan may be said to be the northernmost limit, had not been visited by Colonel Gordon's party, and a short description of it may therefore be interesting.

The Pamir may be said to commence, one branch at the Khunjerab Pass, and another at the Wakhujrui Pass, and to extend northwards to Tashkurgan, where the district of Sarikol begins. The Pamir is inhabited chiefly by Kirghiz, but there are also a few Sarikolis. All of these keep large flocks and herds, but cultivation and houses are not seen beyond Tashkurgan. The Pamir itself is a plain four or five miles broad, rising very gently on both sides to the mountain ranges by which it is enclosed. It gives one the impression of formerly having been a deep valley between two mountain ranges, which has now been filled up by the *débris* brought down by former glaciers.

On account of the insufficient rainfall, this valley has not been washed out and cleared of the *débris*, and consequently is now a plain at a high elevation. The Pamir rises from ten thousand feet at Tashkurgan, to fourteen thousand three hundred feet at the Khunjerab Pass. It is mostly covered with coarse scrub and gravel, but there are also some fine stretches of good grass. Fuel is very scarce, and the inhabitants generally use dung for their fires.

The total number of inhabitants, including women and children, probably does not exceed three hundred. They are a somewhat rough lot, and mostly bad characters, who have fled, for some reason, from Shahidula, the Alai, or the Tagarma Pamir. The headman, Kuch Mahommed, really belonged to the Kirghiz of Andijan, but had been placed here by the Chinese, and was in charge of the frontier in this direction; he, however, was also in the pay of the chief of Hunza, and seemed to have a good deal more respect for him than for the Chinese.

On October 30 I rejoined my escort on the Karachukur stream, and the following day set out for the Khunjerab Pass, which had just been explored by Lieutenant Bower. On the way I passed an encampment belonging to a Sarikoli, who very kindly asked me to have some refreshment; his son had passed through India on his way to Mecca, and could speak a little Hindustani. He was delighted to find an Englishman to speak to, and he talked over all his experiences of India.

Heavy clouds had been collecting for the last few days,

and during the night, which I spent in a yurt set up for me by Akal Jan, it snowed heavily. Yurts are generally constructed with a large hole some two and a half feet in diameter in the top, to allow the smoke from the fire going out. On this occasion, when I woke in the morning I found the floor of the yurt covered with snow, which, when the fire had gone out, came in from the opening. It was now falling heavily outside, and the whole country was covered with it, so the prospect for the exploration of the pass was not very promising.

However, I set out with two good men, leaving the rest of the party behind, and, marching through the snow, reached the summit of the pass at midday. The route was perfectly easy, so that we could ride the whole way to the summit. On the other side, however, the road could be seen running down a narrow gorge; and beyond this there is a pass over a secondary range, which at this time of the year is impracticable. The mountains here seemed to be of no great height compared with the mountains to be seen further east. There is another pass called the Oprang Pass, up a side valley, which leads down a valley to the Oprang River at Shor-Bulak, thus forming an alternative route to that by the Kurbu Pass; this road, however, is said to be very difficult and now out of use.

Ovis poli are said to abound in this part, and Bower had told me that he had shot six near the Khunjerab Pass; but to-day it was snowing so heavily that nothing could be seen of them, and I only saw a few wolves, which prey upon these *Ovis poli*, and catch the old rams when their horns have become so heavy as to retard their progress.

While descending from the pass to the small camp which had been brought to the foot of it, the snow ceased, the wind dropped, the sun came out, and the whole air became glistening with shining particles. This is a very curious phenomenon. I had at first thought that it was the sun shining on minute particles of snow, but I soon found that no snow at all was falling, and I am quite unable to account for these glistening particles. The Kirghiz informed me that it usually occurred after a fall of snow, and was a presage of great cold hereafter. The thermometer indeed went rapidly down, and at six o'clock in the evening was five degrees below zero (Fahrenheit); but then a wind sprang up, which immediately brought the thermometer up to zero, and during the night it never fell below that, though the thermometer of one's senses would have registered it very much below zero.

There was now only one more pass to explore, and I hastened back to get round the Mintaka Pass, for I was beginning to fear that I might perhaps be prevented by the snow from getting across the range into Hunza. Marching down to Akal Jan's camp, I had the good fortune to see a herd of *Ovis poli* in the distance; I managed to get fairly close to them, but not near enough for a shot, and by the time I had reached a rock from behind which I had hoped to bag one, I found they had disappeared right up the mountain-side, and were only just distinguishable through a telescope, looking down disdainfully at me from the top of the highest crag. This stalk after the *Ovis poli* showed me how much my strength had been reduced lately, from being so long at great elevations; and, moreover, owing to my having had no proper cook, my appetite had also gradually fallen away, and I had become too weak for any great exertions. But, fortunately, the Tagh-dum-bash Pamir is so easy that one can ride everywhere.

On November 4 I rejoined the Gurkha escort at Karachukur, where they had remained while I was exploring the Khunjerab Pass. They had now been halted for ten days, and were glad enough to get on the move again.

On the following day we marched up the Karachukur to Mintaka Aksai, where the stream from the Mintaka Pass joins the Karachukur, which flows from the Wakhujrui Pass, leading over to Wakhan. A road also leads from the valley of the

Karachukur by the Baijih Pass to Aktash, on the Little Pamir. This is practicable for ponies, and was crossed this year by Captain Grombtchevsky.

On this march Kuch Mahommed asked me in to breakfast at his camp, which is situated close to the road; and I there found two Kashgaris who were officials sent by the Chinese Taotai of Kashgar to inquire into affairs on this frontier.

After breakfasting, I again set out, but was passed on the road by these two Kashgaris, who arrived at the Mintaka Aksai camp shortly before me. They here found a tent set apart for some one, and, on asking Kuch Mahommed whom it was for, were told that it had been prepared for me. On hearing this they were furious, and demanded why a tent had not been prepared for them also. Kuch Mahommed tried to smooth them down, but he did not offer them the tent, and I was glad on my arrival to find it still kept for me, though, when I heard the circumstances, I was surprised at his having done so, as I was really on Chinese territory, and these were Chinese officials, while I was simply an English traveller. The Kashgaris were only given a place with the Kirghiz in one of their tents, and soon after my arrival, I heard that they had summoned a levée of all the Kirghiz in the place, and had warned them to be careful what they were doing. They also got hold of my interpreter, and began questioning him about my doings, and asked for my passport. On hearing this, I sent them a message requesting them not to interfere with my servants, and saying that if they wanted any information about my doings, I should be perfectly ready to give it them, and that when I had leisure I would send for them, and they might ask me any questions they wished.

Next morning I sent to them to say that I was at leisure, and would give them all the information they wished. They came over to my tent, and, after giving them tea and treating them politely, I told them that I was now returning to India by Hunza, and was merely crossing the Tagh-dum-bash Pamir on my way there. I told them that China and England were friendly with each other, and that, though I had not now a passport, as I had not been aware that I should have to cross a portion of Chinese territory, I had travelled, two years ago, from Peking, the capital of China, with a passport from the Emperor, right through to Yarkand and Kashgar. The Kashgari officials, on hearing this, said they were perfectly satisfied; that the Chinese and English were always friends; but that they should like me to put down what I had said in writing, that they might show it to the Taotai at Kashgar.

This I readily consented to do, and, after more tea-drinking and polite speeches, we parted in a very friendly manner, and soon after the Kirghiz came in to say that the Kashgari officials had given orders that I was to be given every assistance.

This would be my last day amongst the Kirghiz, and it was necessary, therefore, to pay them up, and give them presents for the service they rendered me. I accordingly paid them very liberally for the hire of camels, yaks, etc., and also gave each of the three headmen some presents. They, however, had heard exaggerated reports of the presents which I had given to the Shahidula Kirghiz, and expected to receive more than I had given them, and one of them, Juma Bai, was impertinent enough afterwards to send back my present, saying it was insufficient. I immediately sent my interpreter with a sheep, which Juma Bai had given me on the previous day, and with my presents which he had returned, back to the Kirghiz, and told him to throw away the tea and cloth, etc., which I had given him, before his eyes, to turn the sheep loose in the valley, and to express my extreme displeasure at being insulted in the way I had been.

Juma Bai happened to be living with the two Kashgaris, and when they saw all this occur, the Kashgaris turned on him and abused him roundly for insulting a guest like this, and the rest of the Kirghiz, taking the cue from them, set upon the unfortunate Juma and beat him.

The other two Kirghiz headmen then came and apologized profusely to me, hoping that I was not displeased with them also, and the next morning, when we parted, they were very friendly and full of expressions of good-will.

On November 8 we crossed the Mintaka Pass; the ascent for about a thousand feet is very steep, and near the top there was a considerable amount of recently fallen snow. Snow, indeed, was even now falling on the mountains all round continuously, but during our passage it remained clear, and though the snow was soft and we sank into it up to our knees, yet the yaks carried the baggage over without much real difficulty. The height is fourteen thousand four hundred feet, though the mountains near it must rise to fully twenty-two thousand feet. The descent is also steep, leading down a rocky zigzag on to the moraine of a glacier; but, after passing over this for about a mile and a half, all difficulties are over, and the route descends a stream to Murkush. Here we met Kanjuti officials, sent by the chief to await our arrival, with twenty coolies to carry my baggage, and I was therefore able to despatch the Kirghiz with the yaks which had brought our baggage over the pass.

But the Kirghiz are not a race with many good qualities; they are avaricious, grasping, and fickle, and I parted with them without regret, or any special desire to renew my acquaintance with them.

We were now safely on the southern side of the Indus watershed once more, and our explorations were over, for Colonel Lockhart's Mission, in 1886, had passed up the Hunza valley on their way to the Kilik Pass. But this valley we were now entering was full of interest, both as the abode of a primitive, little-known people, and from the grandeur of its scenery. As we marched down from Murkush, which was merely a camping-ground, to Misgah, the first village, we passed through gorges with rocky precipices of stupendous height on either side. The mountains seemed to almost rise perfectly sheer from the bed of the river for thousands of feet, till they culminated in snowy peaks, to view whose summit we had to throw our heads right back in looking upwards.

As we descended the valley the air became warmer and warmer, the marrow-freezing blasts of wind were left behind, and the atmosphere became less and less rarefied as we left the high altitudes of the Pamirs and came down again to parts where cereals could be cultivated. As we breathed the fuller air, with more life-giving properties in it, fresh strength seemed to come into us, and the feeling of languor which the cold and the rarefaction of the air together had produced, slowly disappeared.

Near Misgah we were met by the *Arbap*, or governor, of the upper district of Hunza, who professed himself very friendly, and evidently intended to be so; but on the next morning, when it came to producing men to carry our loads, as the chief had said he would arrange to do, difficulties immediately arose. The independent Kanjutis did not at all like having to carry the loads, and I could quite sympathize with them. Having to carry sixty or seventy pounds for a dozen miles over any sort of country must be unpleasant enough, but to have to do it over Hunza mountain-tracks affords a very intelligible cause of complaint, and I can well understand how galling these wild people of the Hindu Kush must find our calls upon them to act as beasts of burden. However, the call had to be made, whether I or they liked it or not, and after a delay of half a day the necessary number of men were produced.

Then arose another difficulty. The arbap, on the previous evening, had sent me over a present of a sheep and some eggs, and now he asked payment for them, saying he could not afford to give presents for nothing. I told him that our customs were different from his, and that I was going to follow out our own custom, which was to accept a present as a present, and not pay for it. These men of Hunza were a curiously uncouth people in those days of their first contact with Europeans. They thought they had a perfect right to fleece any stranger who entered their country, and I had heard from Captain Gombtchevsky of the demands they had made upon him, and from the Kirghiz of how they practically robbed the Chinese officials who occasionally visited the country.

By midday coolies and a few ponies were collected, and a start was made for Gircha. The track was rough and difficult, and in one or two places led along the sides of cliffs into which planks had been fastened, and a rude gallery constructed in this way. The valley was very narrow, and the mountains bare, rugged, and precipitous. At Gircha was a small fort, near which we bivouacked round a fire, waiting for the baggage, which did not appear till six o'clock the next morning, as the men had been benighted on the road, and dare not, laden as they were, pass along the cliffs in the dark.

Here at Gircha we halted for a day, and were visited by Wazir Dadu, the "prime minister" of the country, and Mohammed Nazim Khan, the present ruler of Hunza, and a half-brother of Safder Ali, the then ruler. Wazir Dadu was an interesting character, as he was afterwards the leader of the opposition to the British in the Hunza campaign, which took place two years after my visit. At the close of my journey I described him in the following terms: "The Wazir is a handsome-looking man, with good features and a very fine beard. He strikes one as being a clever, shrewd man, with plenty of common sense about him; and, from what I saw, I should think he had considerable influence with the chief. He is a keen sportsman and a good shot." Next to his half-brother Humayun, the Wazir of the present ruler of Hunza, he was the most capable man I have met upon the frontier, and one for whom I entertained a considerable respect on account of his manly qualities; and it is to be regretted that ignorance led him into committing his master to a course of policy which ended in the overthrow of both. Wazir Dadu eventually died in imprisonment in Chinese Turkestan.

Now, however, on his visit to me, he appeared in gorgeous robes, which had been presented to Ghazan Khan, the chief of Hunza, at the time of Colonel Lockhart's visit, in 1886. He brought very friendly messages from Safder Ali, and said he had been sent to accompany my party down to Gulmit, where the chief was at present residing. This place I reached two days later. We passed a few small, dirty villages on the way, and the valley opened out only very slightly, stupendous mountains rising as before on either hand.

Hearing that Safder Ali wished to receive me in state on my arrival at Gulmit, I put on my full-dress dragoon uniform, and the Gurkha escort also wore their full dress. We had to cross a nasty glacier at Pasu, and I did not find spurs and gold-laced overalls very appropriate costume for that kind of work. Then, as we neared Gulmit, a deputation was sent by the chief to say that I must not be frightened when I heard guns being fired, as they were intended for a salute, and not offensively.

Amid the booming of these guns I rode up through the village lands towards a large tent, in which the chief was to receive me. Thirteen guns were fired as a salute, and when they ceased a deafening tomtoming was set up. Hundreds of people were collected on the hillside, and in front of the tent were ranged two long rows of these wild-looking Kanjutis, armed with matchlocks and swords. There was no fierce look about these men, but they had a hardy appearance which was very striking. At the end of this double row of men I dismounted from my pony, and advanced between the lines to meet the chief, who came outside the tent to receive me. I was astonished to find myself in the presence of a man with a complexion of almost European fairness, and with reddish hair. His features, too, were of an entirely European cast, and, dressed in European clothes, he might anywhere have been taken for a Greek or Italian. He was now dressed in a magnificent brocade robe and a handsome turban, presented by Colonel Lockhart. He had a sword and revolver fastened round his waist, and one man with a drawn sword and another with a repeating rifle stood behind him.

He asked after my health, and as to how I had fared during my journey through his country, and then led me into the tent, which was a big one presented to him by Captain Durand. At the head of the tent was a chair covered with fine gold-embroidered velvet cloth. This was the only chair the chief possessed, or rather had in Gulmit, and it was evident that he intended to sit in it himself, and let me kneel upon the ground with the headmen of the country. I had, however, foreseen such an eventuality, and had brought a chair with me on the march, ahead of the baggage. So I now sidled in between Safder Ali and his chair, and whispered to my orderly to get mine, which, when produced, I placed alongside his, and we then sat down together. We then carried on a short complimentary conversation, in which I thanked him for the arrangements he had made for my reception, and the cordiality of the welcome he had offered me. In the tent all the principal men of the country were kneeling in silent rows, with solemn upturned faces, hanging upon each word that was uttered as if there was the profoundest wisdom in it, but never moving a single muscle of their features. The conversation was carried on through two interpreters, and the compliments dragged themselves out by slow degrees. At the close of the interview I again thanked the chief, and as I left the tent the Gurkha escort, by previous arrangement, fired three volleys in the air, a form of salute which is ordinarily only given at funerals, but which served the purpose of making a noise and consequently of pleasing these people.

As there is nothing but small dirty houses at Gulmit, I lived in a tent there, and on the day following my arrival paid another visit to the chief. The first question he asked me was, why I had entered his country from the north, when no other European had ever done so. I told him that I could not claim the honour of being the first European to enter his country across the passes on the north, for it so happened that I had just met a Russian officer who had himself informed me that he had crossed into Hunza from the north. I then explained to him that I had been sent by the Government of India to inquire into the cause of the raids on the Yarkand trade route, and was now returning to India through his country.

On the following morning, during a long visit Safder Ali paid me in my tent, I entered upon this question rather more fully. I reminded him that the raids were committed by his subjects upon the subjects of the British Government, and if he wished to retain the friendship of the British Government, as he professed to do, he should restrain his subjects from carrying on such practices. Safder Ali replied, in the most unabashed manner, that he considered he had a perfect right to make raids; that the profits he obtained from them formed his principal revenue, and that if the Government of India wished them stopped, they must make up by a subsidy for the loss of revenue. There was no diplomatic mincing of matters with Safder Ali, and this outspokenness did not come from any innate strength of character, but simply because he was entirely ignorant of his real position in the universe. He was under the impression that the Empress of India, the Czar of Russia, and the Emperor of China were chiefs of neighbouring tribes; but he had been accustomed to levy blackmail upon all the peoples round him, and he looked upon the various British officers who had visited his country, Captain Grombtchevsky, and the Chinese official who occasionally came to Hunza, as envoys from England, Russia, and China, clamouring for his friendship. He and Alexander the Great were on a par. When I asked him if he had ever been to India, he said that "great kings" like himself and Alexander never left their own country!

The difficulty was, therefore, to know how to deal with such a man as this. I told him, however, that I could not think of recommending that he should be subsidized to stop raids; that I had left some soldiers armed with rifles on the trade route, and I would recommend him to try another raid and see how much revenue he obtained from it. The discussion, in fact, became somewhat heated at one time; but the effect was none the worse for that, for these untutored people like to speak out their minds freely, and it is a good plan to allow them to do so. Safder Ali told me afterwards that he was astonished at my having refused the request he had made; for he said that all the men he had to deal with would, at any rate at the time, promise to do a thing asked of them, but they never said straight out to his face that they would not do what was asked of them.

Thinking it necessary to impress him in any small way I could with our strength, I now suggested to him that he should see the Gurkhas perform some drill exercise and fire at a mark. I accordingly had the men drawn up in line facing towards the inside of the tent where Safder Ali and I were seated. They then went through the movements of the firing exercise. One of these exercises consisted in bringing the rifles up to the present, and as the Gurkhas were facing the interior of the tent, the muzzles of the rifles were directed straight on Safder Ali and myself. This was too much for the successor of Alexander; he said he would see no more drill exercises, and he could only be induced to permit firing at the mark to proceed when he surrounded himself with one ring of men and placed another cordon round the Gurkhas who were firing. A guilty conscience was pricking him, for he had murdered his own father and thrown two of his brothers over a precipice, and he now feared that similar treachery might be played upon him, and that the Gurkhas might despatch him with a bullet. Under these excessive precautions the practice proceeded, and volleys were fired at objects far across the valley, the people being duly impressed both by the excellence of the shooting and by the sturdy character of the Gurkhas.

I had several interviews with Safder Ali, but on one occasion he was so rude that I had afterwards to tell the Wazir that I could neither receive visits from him nor pay visits to him while he spoke as he did. He caused me incessant annoyance, too, by sending down messengers to ask for various things in my possession. I had given him a handsome present, but he would send and ask me for my tent, my mule-trunks, and even some soap for his wives. Among my presents to the Wazir had been a few tablets of soap wrapped up in "silver" paper; these had excited the admiration of the ladies of the "king's" household, and they wanted some for themselves. All these requests I refused on principle, for if one thing had been given, more would be demanded, and every article of my kit would be taken from me. Of this Captain Grombtchevsky had good-naturedly informed me, and he had warned me to be firm from the first.

Balti coolies, to carry my baggage down to Gilgit, having arrived, I left Gulmit on November 23. On the morning of my departure, Safder Ali came down on foot to my tent and apologized for any annoyance he had given me, saying his only intention was to give me a suitable reception, *and* he wished a subsidy from Government! Safder Ali struck me as being a weak character, and the opinion I recorded of him at the time was that he was too childishly obstinate and too deficient in shrewdness and far-sightedness to appreciate the advantages of keeping on good terms with the British. I am the last European who has seen him; two years later he was forced to flee from his country, and he is now an exile in Chinese territory, while his half-brother, Mohammed Nazim, rules Hunza in his place.

This same Mohammed Nazim was now deputed by Safder Ali to accompany me as far as Gilgit. On the day after leaving Gulmit we reached Baltit, the chief place in Hunza, where the chief's palace and fort are situated. I now had to hurry through, for winter was fast approaching, and as I was able three years afterwards to make a stay in the country, I will describe it more fully later on, and merely state here the opinion which I formed, during my two weeks' journey through the country, that "once the chief had been brought under control, there would be little difficulty with the people, who are of a far less warlike character than the Afghans, and would probably gladly welcome a more settled state of affairs, in which they would not be continually liable to be employed in petty wars got up between rival chieftains." When, two years afterwards, Safder Ali was forced to flee from the country, the people showed no regret; and now, under Mohammed Nazim, a prince who understands that the time for truculency is past, it is acknowledged by every one who visits the country that these quondam-raiders are become a settled and contented people.

Pushing on ahead of my escort, I passed through Nilt, to which the next visitors were the gallant little force under Colonel Durand, who, at the end of 1891, conquered Hunza and Nagar. Two days from Baltit—after passing over sixty-five miles of most execrable roads, by paths climbing high up the mountain-sides to round cliffs or pass over rocks and boulders, and by galleries along the face of a precipice—I reached Gilgit, and was welcomed by Captain Durand and Lieutenant Manners-Smith, who had a few weeks before arrived to establish a British Political Agency there. To be once more free from anxiety, to be among my brother officers, to sit down to a meal prepared by some other than that most faithful of servants but worst of all cooks, Shukar Ali, the Ladaki, and to feel that the task which had been set me had been successfully accomplished, was satisfaction indeed, and that night of my arrival in the Gilgit Agency was another of those times the recollection of which is impressed indelibly upon my memory.

After staying a few days at Gilgit, we set out again for Kashmir. The season was now late, and the Burzil Pass, thirteen thousand four hundred feet, and the Tragbal Pass, eleven thousand two hundred feet, had to be crossed. On December 13 we crossed the former, and three days later we descended from the Tragbal into the valley of Kashmir once more. The round had been completed; we had crossed seventeen passes, and attempted two more, and had travelled through as rough a country as any that could be found. I now parted with my Gurkha escort, and they told me for the first time that, before leaving the regiment, their head native officer had told them that if anything happened to me on the journey we were to undertake, not a single one of them was to return to disgrace the name of the regiment to which he belonged. They must not come back without their officer. The Gurkha havildar, as he told me this, said they had all been ready to make any sacrifice for the success of the expedition; but they had had no hardship whatever, and he thanked me for all the care I had taken of them during the journey. These Gurkhas were splendid little men; I felt all through that I could have trusted them in anything, and it was hard to part with men who had been ready to lay down their lives for me at any moment, who were my only companions for many months together, and for whom I had come to feel so strong a personal attachment.

They returned to their regiment; the havildar and the naik were promoted, and they all received substantial money rewards and a certificate of commendation from the Government of India.

The Pathan orderly also returned to his regiment, where he was promoted, and received a money reward and a similar certificate, which was presented to him, at a parade of the whole regiment, by his commanding officer.

This was the first occasion on which I had had under me men of the native army of India, and my respect for their endurance, their devotion and loyalty, and discipline, was founded then, and has only increased as I have had the opportunity of knowing them better. Gurkhas, Pathans, or Sikhs, they are all ready to stand by a British officer to the last, and they are men of whom any leader might be proud.

CHAPTER XIII.

TO THE PAMIRS—1890.

THESE explorations, in 1889, had extended on to the edge of the Pamirs, and in the following year I was commissioned to travel round the whole of the Pamir region. At that time, though Russian parties had frequently toured through them, only one Englishman, Mr. Ney Elias, had travelled across the Pamirs since the time of Forsyth's Mission, when Colonel T. E. Gordon led an expedition through the Little and back by the Great Pamir. This was in the time of Yakoob Beg, before the Chinese had re-established themselves in Eastern Turkestan, and since then the state of affairs had very materially altered. The Pamirs form a sort of no-man's-land between the British dependencies on the south, the Russian on the north, the Chinese on the east, and the Afghan on the west. The waves of conquest which surged all round had not yet thoroughly immersed them, and the state of this meeting-place of the three great empires of Asia was, therefore, of interest and importance.

At the end of June, 1890, I left Simla for this remote region. No escort accompanied me, as on my former journey, but I was fortunate enough to have as a companion Mr. George Macartney, a son of Sir Halliday Macartney, the well-known Secretary of the Chinese Legation in London. Mr. Macartney spoke Chinese fluently and accurately, and his services as an interpreter would therefore be of the greatest value. Together we proceeded to Leh, and joined there two other travellers,

Messrs. Beech and Lennard, who were, for sporting purposes, also proceeding to the Pamirs and Chinese Turkestan. I again had to make those long dreary marches across the Karakoram Mountains which I have already described. It would be difficult to imagine anything more utterly desolate and depressing than these bare plains and rounded hills, and it was accordingly with an immense feeling of relief that we descended into the plains of Turkestan at the end of our six hundred miles' march through the mountains from the plains of India. On the last day of August we reached Yarkand, which, it is needless to say, showed no signs of change since my visit to it three years before. It is doubtful, indeed, whether these Central Asian towns *ever* change. Their dull mud walls, mud houses, mud mosques, look as if they would remain the same for ever. In most climates they would, of course, be washed away, but in Central Asia there is hardly any rain, and they remain on for ages. There are a few well-built brick mosques and some good houses. The Chinese, too, in their separate town, have substantial buildings; but the native town leaves a general impression of mud-built houses and sleepy, drowsy changelessness. "As it was in the beginning, is now, and ever shall be," would be a particularly appropriate motto to place over the gateway of a Central Asian town.

A few days after we had reached Yarkand, Captain Grombtchevsky, whom I had met in the previous year, also arrived there. I was going over to visit him, when he sent a message insisting upon calling upon me first, and shortly afterwards he appeared, dressed in uniform, with his decorations on. It was a great pleasure to me to meet him again, and to hear from him an account of his wanderings since we had parted near the borders of Hunza nearly a year ago. He had had a trying time since then, and must have suffered considerable hardships, for he had attempted the Karakoram Pass in the middle of December, and then passed on eastward to the edge of the high Tibetan tableland in the depth of winter. When I recall how inadequately he and his party were supplied with camp equipage, and how roughly altogether they were travelling, I cannot help admiring the stolid perseverance of this Russian explorer in ever attempting the task he did.

Captain Grombtchevsky dined with us, and we dined with him, and then we all dined with one of the principal merchants of the place. This last dinner was an event in Yarkand, and it is curious to think of a Russian and an English officer dining with a Turki merchant midway between the Russian and Indian Empires in the heart of Central Asia. The dinner was given in a house in the native city, and was a very sumptuous repast; course after course of stews, pillaos, and roast meat were served up, and the old merchant was profuse in his hospitality.

Grombtchevsky, after spending a few days in Yarkand, went off into the mountains to the westward, to work his way homeward to Russia through some new ground; and on September 15 Macartney and I also left Yarkand on our way to the Pamirs; while our companions, Beech and Lennard, remained on for a time, and then went eastward to shoot in the jungles of the Yarkand River.

The Pamirs are now a well-known region, and much has recently been heard about them, but at the time of our visit there was still a remnant of the mysterious attaching to them, and we set out with a good deal of enthusiasm to visit the Roof of the World. We had first to make for Tashkurgan, the principal place of Sarikol, and to reach there we had to cross ridge after ridge of the outlying spurs of the range which forms the buttress to the Pamirs. Here and there we passed a small village, but the country was mostly uninhabited, and the hills bare and uninteresting. By the end of September we reached Tashkurgan, and were on the borders of the Pamirs. Tashkurgan looks an important place, as it is marked in capital letters on most maps, but it is in reality merely a small fort built at the entrance to the Tagh-dum-bash Pamir. There are several small hamlets near it; but, being ten thousand feet above the sea, cultivation is, of course, not very productive, and the district can therefore support only a small population.

Above Tashkurgan is seen the wide Pamir of the Tagh-dum-bash, down which I had ridden to this place on the previous year, and overhanging it on the west was a rugged range of snowy peaks, which part the waters of Asia, those on the west flowing into the Oxus, and destined to mark the dividing-line between spheres of influence of two great empires, and those to the east flowing into the Yarkand River, and ending their career in Lob Nor. Behind this range were the chief Pamirs—the Little, the Great, and the Alichur Pamirs—which it was now our special object to visit.

On October 3 we left Tashkurgan to ascend the gorge which leads up to the Neza-tash Pass. The way was rough and stony, and the last part of the ascent steep, but we took our ponies over without any serious difficulty, and from the other side of the pass looked down upon a succession of bare, rounded, uninteresting spurs and barren valleys running towards the Little Pamir. After descending one of these, we found ourselves on what might almost be called a plain; it was flat and level, four or five miles broad, and extended for many miles on either hand, till the border of the mountain ranges hid it from view. This was the Little Pamir. On the side by which we had entered it, it was bounded by high snow-clad mountains, but opposite us were low rounded spurs, hardly high enough to be dignified with the name of mountains or to be covered with permanent snow.

The other Pamirs which we visited differed but very slightly, so that some detailed description of this one will suffice. We have, then, a level plain bounded by ranges of mountains of varying height on either side; and perhaps the best idea of what this is like will be gathered from an account of how it is formed. We must therefore look back some hundreds of thousands of years, to the time when these mountains were first upheaved. Whether that upheaval was sudden, as Sir Henry Howorth supposes, or gradual, as seems to be generally the case in the formation of mountains, there would in either case be clefts and hollows between the unevennesses which formed the various ranges of the mountain chain. Snow would fall in the upper parts, collect in masses in the hollows, and gradually form into glaciers. Then these glaciers, each with its burden of *débris* of rocks and stone from the mountain-sides, would come creeping down and gradually fill up the bottoms of the valleys parting the various ranges. In former times, on these Pamirs, glaciers descended much lower than they do now, and in all parts of them the moraines of old glaciers may be seen down in the valley bottoms to which no glaciers now descend. All these Pamirs were therefore in former times filled with vast glaciers, and as the ice of them melted away the stony detritus remained and formed the plains which are seen at the present day. If the rainfall were more abundant, this detritus would of course be washed out by the river flowing through the valley; but in these lofty regions, where the very lowest part of the valleys is over twelve thousand feet above sea-level, the rivers are frozen for the greater part of the year, they are unable to do the work that is required of them, and the valleys remain choked up with the old glacier-borne *débris* of bygone ages. Lower down, however, in the states of Wakhan, Shignans and Roshan, where the rivers have reached a level low enough to remain unfrozen for a time sufficiently long to carry out their duties properly, the valleys have been cleared out, the Pamir country has disappeared, and in place of the broad flat valley bottom, we see deep-cut gorges and narrow defiles.

I hope this description will have enabled my readers to understand that the Pamirs do not form a high plateau or tableland, as has often been supposed, but a series of valleys of a type common in very elevated regions where the winter is long and the rainfall in summer small, but not elsewhere. Tibet is a collection of Pamirs on a large scale, for there, too, there is not sufficient water to wash out the valleys down to their bottoms, and in many parts of the Himalayas, the Karakoram Mountains, and the Hindu Kush, where similar conditions exist, there are regular pamirs. And by this time the reader will have gathered that the word "pamir" is merely the distinctive name of this particular kind of valley. The Shimshal Pass into Hunza is called by the people of that country the Shimshal Pamir, though it is far away from the regions which we mark on our maps as "The Pamirs."

This, then, is the physical formation of the Pamirs. Of their outward clothing many conflicting accounts have been given. One traveller, going to them in the late autumn, when everything living has been nipped by frost, says that they are an utterly desolate region. Another, seeing portions of them in the summer, says that they are covered with the most splendid grass. My own experience was that, though grass of a close, good quality was to be found in certain places, the greater part of the valley bottoms is covered with coarse wormwood scrub only. Patches of rich pasture are to be found here and there, but no one must imagine rolling grassy plains on the Pamirs. This is what I had expected, and I thought the ponies of my caravan would have an abundance of rich pasture to graze on; but I was sadly disappointed to find that only in a few favoured spots could they obtain this, and that, for the greater part of the way, they had to content themselves with picking about among scrub.

Trees, of course, are never seen, and even shrubs and bushes in a few places only. Consequently fuel is scarce, and the inhabitants and travellers have to content themselves with the roots of the wormwood.

The climate, as might be imagined, is very severe. I have

only been there in the late summer and early autumn; but I found ice in the basin inside my tent in August, the thermometer at zero (Fahrenheit) by the end of September, and eighteen degrees below zero at the end of October. Lord Dunmore found his thermometer at five degrees below zero *inside* his tent in November. Strong winds, too, are very frequent, and increase the discomfort arising from the cold very considerably, and this is further augmented by the lassitude and weakness brought on by the elevation. So that the cold, the winds, and the elevation together, render life on the Pamirs anything but cheering.

In spite of this severity of the climate, however, the inhabitants of the Pamirs remain there the whole year round. They are almost entirely Kirghiz, with a few refugees from Wakhan. These Kirghiz are a rough, hardy race, as they must necessarily be; but they have little character, and no aptitude for fighting. They are avaricious and indolent, and possess few qualities which would attract a stranger to them. They live in the same felt tents which I have already described in the account of my journey from Peking.

At Aktash we found three or four tents and a "beg" or headman appointed by the Chinese. He was very civil to us, and made no difficulties whatever about our proceeding round the Pamirs, which at that time were considered Chinese territory. We accordingly struck off almost due west across the range on the western side of the Little Pamir to the valley of Istigh River. In all this eastern part of the Pamirs the mountain ranges are low and easily crossed. No snow-peaks, like those to the west of the Victoria Lake, or the Lake of the Little Pamir, are to be seen. They appear to have all been worn down and rounded off. We had no difficulty, therefore, in crossing first into the valley of the Istigh, and then from there to Chadir Tash, on the Alichur Pamir. On the way there, at a place called Ak-chak-tash, we found some hot springs, the temperature of which exceeded one hundred and forty degrees, the highest point to which my thermometer reached. The occurrence of these hot springs is not at all infrequent in these parts.

In the Ash-kuman, Yarkhun, and Lutku valleys of Chitral there are similar springs, which are much used by the people, and are believed by them to contain valuable medicinal properties.

At one spot before reaching the Alichur Pamir, I counted seventy *Ovis poli* horns within a quarter of a mile. This, of course, was an unusually large number to meet with, but everywhere on the Pamirs these fine horns are seen lying about the valleys and hillsides. The Pamirs, as is well known, are the home of these magnificent *Ovis poli* sheep, as big as donkeys, with horns measuring frequently sixty inches, and in one known case seventy-three inches, round the curve. The animal stands over twelve hands in height, and the weight of the head alone, even when skinned, is over forty pounds.

The Alichur Pamir we found to be an open valley, from four to five miles in width, and bounded on either side by barren brown hills. At the time of our visit, grass at the head of the valley was very scanty; but lower down towards Yeshil-kul there were some good pasturages, and a few Kirghiz encamped by them. It was now our intention to visit a spot which has since become historic, and indeed was already historic, though its name had not before been known to the European world. This was Somatash. Mr. Ney Elias, who had travelled in this, as he has in almost every other part of Asia, though the record of most of his travels has never been published, had heard rumours of the existence of a stone monument with an inscription on it erected on the shores of Lake Yeshil-kul (or Lake Yeshil, as one ought really to call it, the word *kul* itself meaning "lake"). My Kirghiz friends corroborated these rumours, and Macartney and I rode off from Bash Gumbaz to have a look at the stone. We had a long day's ride, passing by several small lakes in the hollows of the moraines of ancient glaciers, and at night we halted just at the point where the Alichur River enters the Yeshil-kul. Our baggage, including our bedding and cooking things, was brought on more slowly, and we spent the night cold and hungry in a yurt, which had been sent on for us, but we were delighted the next morning to find the stone. It was the broken remains of a large tablet mounted on a pedestal, and placed about a hundred feet or more above the river, on its right bank, a few hundred yards before it flowed into the lake. The inscription was in Chinese, Manchu, and Turki, and evidently referred to the expulsion of the Khojas in 1759, and the pursuit of them by the Chinese to the Badakhshan frontier. Above this ancient monument, on the left bank, was a ruined Chinese fort, built many years before.

The place is of historic interest, as it is the scene of the conflict between the Russians and the Afghans in 1892. An account of this has been given by Lord Dunmore, who visited the spot only a few weeks after the event, and found the dead bodies of the Afghans lying there. The Afghans appear to have sent a small outpost of about fifteen men to this place. A Russian party, under Colonel Yonoff, making its annual promenade of the Pamirs, came up to them, fired on them, and killed every single man.

After taking a rubbing of the inscription on the monument, which has, by the way, been since removed by the Russians and placed in the museum at Tashkent, we rode back to Buzilla Jai, and the following day retraced our steps up the Alichur Pamir. I do not think there is anything special to record about this Pamir. It is of exactly the same description as all the rest. The principal routes leading to it are: (1) that leading right along it from the valley of the Aksu River to Shignan; (2) that from Sarez on the west by the Marjunai Pass, a somewhat difficult one, which has, however, repeatedly been crossed by Russian military parties; (3) by the Bash Gumbaz and Khargosh Passes—both practicable for ponies to the Great Pamir; and (4) that by the Kokbai Pass to Shakhdarra. All these passes have been crossed and recrossed repeatedly by Russian military parties. They are most of them between fourteen thousand and fifteen thousand feet in height, and consequently about two thousand feet above the valley bottom.

The Neza-tash Pass, which we now crossed on our way eastward to the valley of the Aksu, is about fourteen thousand two hundred feet in height, and on the west side is very easy of ascent. The descent is more difficult, and is steep and stony. It led us down the Karasu stream to the Aksu River, just before that enters the gorges which henceforth confine it. At the point where we struck it the valley was flat, and more than a mile in width, and covered with good grass, and I was informed by the Kirghiz with me that this spot was called Sarez. It must be distinguished from the Sarez a little lower down, but this is probably the part which the "Sarez Pamir" marked on so many maps is meant to indicate. It might be said to extend from the vicinity of the mouth of the Karasu stream to near the junction of the Ak-baital with the Aksu.

At this latter point, on the right bank of the Aksu, is Murghabi. At the time of my visit there was nothing here but four or five Kirghiz tents among the pasturages by the river, and some old tombs on the high ground above, but there is now a Russian outpost permanently established. It is a dreary, desolate spot, twelve thousand four hundred feet above sea-level, with a certain amount of grassy pasture and a few scrubby bushes by the river, but surrounded by barren hills, and bitterly cold. How these Russian soldiers can support existence there is a marvel, but they can hardly do so without frequent relief. I can well imagine the joy it must be to them to return to more genial quarters. One can imagine that they must often long, also, to push on down to more hospitable regions *in front* of them. An officer shut up in these dreary quarters, with nothing whatever to do—week after week and month after month passing by in dull monotony, only the same barren hills to look at, the same stroll about the fort to be taken—must long to *go on*. "What's the good of staying here?" one can imagine his saying. "Why don't Government send us on to a proper place, a place worth having?" It is only human nature that he should wish so, and when he is in this frame of mind it obviously requires a very little inducement to move him on, and a pretty tight rein from behind to keep him still.

However, at the time of my visit to Murghabi, no Russian soldier had yet suffered exile in that spot. We only found a few Kirghiz, and after spending a night there, we pushed on up the course of the Ak-baital (White Mare) River to Rang-kul. The Ak-baital now, at the end of October, had no water in it. The valley was two or three miles broad and very barren. No water was to be found nearer than Rang-kul, so we had to make a long march of it to that place. We kept along the shores of the lake for several miles, and on the way passed an interesting rock called the Chiragh-tash, or Lamp Rock. It stands out over the lake at the end of a spur, and at its summit is a cave with what the native thought was a perpetual light burning in it. This light was variously reported to come from either the eye of a dragon, or from a jewel placed in its forehead. On coming up to this rock I asked to be shown the light, and there, sure enough, was a cave, in the roof of which was a faint white light, which had the appearance of being caused by some phosphorescent substance. I asked if any one had ever been up to the cave to see what was inside in it, but the Kirghiz said that no one would dare to do so. I fancy, however, that laziness and indifference, quite as much as fear, was the cause of their never having ascended to the cave, for Orientals seldom have any curiosity to discover the reason of phenomena. I was more curious, so I ascended the spur with my Pathan servant, and, reaching the rock, clambered up that, the last twenty feet in cat-like fashion, without boots, and clinging on with toes and fingers only; for the rock, just for that final bit, was almost perpendicular. We entered the mouth of the cave. I looked eagerly round to discover the source of the light, and, when I had got fairly on my legs, found that the cave was simply a hole right through the rock, and that the light came in from the other side. From below, of course, this cannot be seen, for the observer merely sees the top of the cave, and this, being covered with some white deposit, reflects back the light which has come in from the opening on the other side. This, then, was the secret of the Cave of Perpetual Light, which I am told is mentioned in histories many hundreds of years old.

We encamped that night by a few Kirghiz yurts, in an extensive grassy plain to the east of Rang-kul, and away at the end of the plain could be seen the magnificent snow mass of the Mustagh-ata, the Father of Mountains, twenty-five thousand feet in height.

The ordinary route to Kashgar, to which place we were now making, leads on eastward from Rang-kul over the Ak-berdi Pass, and down the Gez River. But I was anxious to visit the Great Kara-kul Lake, so I pushed northward through the depressingly barren hills which bound the Rang-kul Lake, and encamped the first night at the foot of the Kizil Jek Pass. Up till now we had been fortunate enough always to have yurts put up for us at each halting-place, and these thick felt-walled tents, with a fire inside them, can be made really very comfortably warm. At any rate, you have the fire, and can warm yourself thoroughly when you want to. But a thin canvas tent, in which a fire cannot be lighted, is a very different thing, and henceforward we had it piercingly cold. All the country between Rang-kul and Kara-kul is barren in the extreme. Cold wind used to rush down the valleys, and the night before we crossed the Kizil Jek Pass the thermometer fell to eighteen degrees below zero Fahrenheit —just fifty degrees of frost.

The Kizil Jek was quite an easy pass—merely a steep rise up one valley, over a saddle, and down another. On the northern side we found the country as inhospitable as it had been on the southern, and on the day after crossing the pass we encamped in a barren plain on the shores of the Great Kara-kul. This is a fine lake more than a dozen miles in length, and the day on which we reached it it presented a magnificent spectacle. A terrific wind was blowing, lashing the water into waves till the whole was a mass of foam. Heavy snow-clouds were scudding across the scene, and through them, beyond the tossing lake, could be seen dark rocky masses; and high above all this turmoil below, appeared the majestic Peak Kaufmann, twenty-three thousand feet in height.

I boiled my thermometer very carefully, to ascertain the difference of level between the Rang-kul and this lake, and then we turned off sharp to the eastward, to hurry down to the warmer regions of Kashgar. Winter was fast coming on, and we required little inducement to push rapidly on to the plains. We crossed out of the basin of the Kara-kul by the Kara-art Pass, fifteen thousand eight hundred feet. It is well known that the lake has no exit. No water flows out from it. There is very little indeed that flows into it, and it can well be kept at its present level by evaporation only. But there are evident signs all round the lake that in former times it reached a much higher level than it does at present. On the other hand, the Kara-art Pass may have been lower; for the neck which forms the pass is composed of old moraine and *débris*, which might have accumulated after the lake had fallen. There is a possibility, therefore, that in former times the waters of the lake may have flowed out over where the Kara-art Pass is now.

Following down the bed of the Kara-art stream, on the northern side of the pass, through rugged, bare mountains, we struck the Markan-su, followed that river for one march, and then, turning off eastward, passed along the spurs which form the northern declivity of the buttress range of the Pamirs to Opal. We were off the high ground now; the climate was milder, and both in the valley of the Markan-su and along these spurs patches of jungle were seen, and dwarf pine on the hillsides.

At Opal we were again in the plains of Turkestan, and on November 1 reached Kashgar, where my official duties kept me for the winter.

We were to make Kashgar our winter quarters, and we found a native house prepared for us on the north side of the old city. It was pleasantly situated on some rising ground, and looked out to the north over the cultivated and tree-covered plain round Kashgar to the snowy peaks of the Tian-shan. From far away on the east, round to the north, and then away again on the east, these snowy mountains extended; and from the roof of our house we could see that magnificent peak, the Mustagh-ata, rising twenty-one thousand feet above the plain. About the house was a garden, which gave us seclusion, and in this garden I had pitched a Kirghiz yurt, which I had bought on the Pamirs. One night up there we had found an unusually large and very tastefully furnished yurt provided for us. It was quite new, was twenty feet in diameter, and about fourteen feet high in the centre, with walls six feet high all round. But what surprised us most was to find it most elegantly decorated. The walls were made of a very handsome screen-work, and round the inside of the dome-like roof were dados of fine carpeting and embroidery. I was so taken with this tent, that I persuaded the owner to sell it to me, and carried it off to Kashgar on a couple of camels, and lived in it the whole winter. With good carpets on the ground, and a stove to warm it, it made a very comfortable place to live in, and, personally, I preferred it to a house.

This tent I found ready pitched on my arrival in Kashgar, and it was very delightful to feel myself comfortably settled down again after our rough and constant travelling. It was curious, too, to note the change from the lonely mountains to this populous town. On the Pamirs at night all had been as still as death, but here we felt the town beside us; the great gongs of the Chinese guard-houses beat the hours through the night, and at nine o'clock a gun was fired and trumpets were blown. The Chinese are always good at effect, however bad they may be in practice; and as, in countries like Turkestan, a good deal may be done by effect alone, I think this noisy parade of watchfulness must make no small impression on the people. The deep booming of the gongs through the stillness of the night, the blaring of the trumpets, and the noise of the cannon, nightly remind the inhabitants of these towns of Turkestan that the conquerors, who have returned again and again to the country, are still among them and still on the watch.

The day following our arrival, we called on M. Petrovsky, the Russian consul, whom I had met here, in 1887, on my way to India from Peking. He and Madame Petrovsky, their son, M. Lutsch the secretary, and a Cossack officer in command of the escort, made up a very pleasant little Russian colony here in Kashgar, and it was a comfort to think that during the winter we should not be thrown entirely upon our own resources, but would have the advantage of intercourse with other Europeans.

CHAPTER XIV.

A WINTER IN KASHGAR.

DURING the first days of our stay in Kashgar, we had a round of visits to make on Chinese officials. Kashgar is the principal town of the western part of Chinese Turkestan, and there is here a Taotai in civil charge of the Kashgar, Yarkand, and Khotan districts, as well as of the Kirghiz along the frontier. There is also, at Kashgar, a general in command of the troops in these districts, who lives in the new town, about two and a half miles to the south of the old town of Kashgar, in which the Taotai lives. Of these two functionaries, the civil governor is the most important, and he is surrounded with a good deal of state. His official residence is of the usual Chinese type, with fine rooms and courtyards, and the massive gateways so characteristic of these places. Here he receives visitors of distinction with considerable ceremony; but it is when he goes out that he appears in greatest pomp. Then men with gongs and trumpets go in front, a large procession is formed, and both on leaving and returning to his residence a salute is fired. He is carried along in a handsome sedan chair, and every sign of respect is paid to him. Here again the Chinese show their skill in the art of impressing those they govern, for the sight—not too common—of their governor parading through the streets of the city in this ceremonial manner undoubtedly has its effect. I do not say that this ruling by effect is a good way of ruling, and as a good deal of the effect is obtained by keeping the rulers aloof and inaccessible, it *is* in that respect bad. But *in* this particular line of governing the Chinese certainly are at the top of the tree.

The Taotai and I performed the usual civilities to each other. I called on him first, of course, and he returned my visit, accompanied by his usual procession. The visits of Chinese officials are always of considerable length, and the Taotai would remain for a couple of hours or so talking away upon any subject which cropped up. He was an old man, who had done much good service in Chinese Turkestan during the Mohammedan rebellion, but he was now weak and past his best. When we had become more intimate, he told me that he had no very high idea of European civilization, for we were always fighting with one another. We were not bad at inventing machines and guns, but we had none of that calm, lofty spirit which the Chinese possessed, and which enabled them to look at the petty squabbles between nations with equanimity and dignity. We spent all our time in matters which should only concern mechanics and low-class people of that sort, and gave ourselves no opportunity for contemplating higher things. These were the Taotai's ideas on Europeans, and it was interesting to see the calm air of superiority with which these views were given.

The Taotai's secretary—a thorough scamp, who was subsequently removed for gross bribery—was another official with whom we had a good deal of intercourse at Kashgar. He had been at Shanghai, and had some knowledge of Europeans. He used to say that the Chinese could never understand why the Russians went to all the trouble and expense of keeping a consulate at Kashgar to look after the trade there, when in a whole year only as much merchandise was brought into the country as is imported into Shanghai by a single British steamer.

The official, however, whom we came to know the best, was the general in command of the troops quartered in the old or native city, near which our house was situated. Old General Wang was very friendly, and used to get up dinner-parties for us in his barracks, and insisted upon calling me by my Christian name. Like all Chinese military officials, he was very indifferently educated, and having learnt the art of writing long scrolls with quotations from classics, he was very proud of it. The barracks in which his men lived were really extremely comfortable. Chinamen—at any rate the inhabitants of North China—seldom live in squalor, and these barracks were well constructed, roomy, and comfortable. The officers houses were really very neat. The only things that were badly looked after were the arms. The Chinese never can look after their guns and rifles properly; and although there were many good breech-loading rifles in the hands of these men, they would probably be perfectly useless on account of the rust. I think what chiefly struck me about the arrangements of these barracks was the family-party air which pervaded the whole. Here was the comfortable old general, only bent on taking things as easily as possible, and the officers and men appeared to be merely there to attend to his wants. They had to look after him a little, and hang about him generally; but they might be quite sure that he would not trouble them with any excess of military zeal, and they might go on leading a quiet, peaceful existence till their turn for command came round. The men worked hard at their vegetable gardens outside the barracks, and we had opportunities of testing the excellent quality of the vegetables which they turned out; but drill and rifle-practice were very seldom carried on. As far as our personal comfort was concerned, this was lucky, for one day when rifle-practice *was* going on, I had just turned the corner of a wall when a bullet came whizzing close by my head; the troops were at rifle-practice, and firing right across a public way, without taking any precaution to warn people.

But my intercourse at Kashgar was not only with the

Chinese; I also saw there men from nearly every part of Asia. It is a curious meeting-ground of many nationalities from north and south, and from east and west of Asia; from Russian territory and from India, from China, and from Afghanistan and Bokhara, even men from Constantinople. With all of these I had from time to time opportunities of speaking. Ethnologically they differed greatly, but they were all Asiatics, and nearly all traders, and their general characteristics, in consequence, varied but little. The effect of Central Asian listlessness had made itself felt on all. The wild fanatical Pathan from the Indian frontier allowed his ardour to cool down here till he became almost as mild as the comfortable merchant from Bokhara. All were intelligent men who, in their wanderings, had picked up much useful knowledge; and as a rule the constant rubbing up against their neighbours had produced good manners in them. They were seldom anything else but courteous, if they knew that courtesy would be shown to them, and a visit from any of them was always a pleasure. They discussed politics constantly, as their trade depended so much upon the political situation; and the man in all Asia whom they watched with the keenest interest was Abdul Rahman, the Amir of Kabul. On him and on his life so much of their little fortunes depended. He was credited with boundless ambitions. At one time he was to attack the Chinese in Kashgar, and turn them out; at another he was to invade Bokhara; and four times during our stay in Kashgar he was dead altogether. These Central Asian traders speculate freely on what is to happen when he dies. If a son of his is to rule in his stead, then Afghanistan will remain as much closed for them as it is now, and the trade of Central Asia will be strangled as before by the prohibitive tariffs, and other obstacles to it which are imposed by the ruler of Kabul. But if Afghanistan is swept away as an independent state, and the Russian and Indian frontiers coincide either on the Hindu

Kush Mountains or the river Oxus, then trade will increase, railways and good roads will be constructed, and oppression by petty officials be unknown. The Central Asian question is therefore one of great interest to them; every move in the game is watched with keenness, and the relative strength and probable intentions of the two great powers, whom they regard as struggling for the supremacy of Asia, are freely discussed by them.

It is naturally difficult for an Englishman to get at their real opinions as to the respective merits of British and Russian rule; but, as merchants, I think they highly appreciate the benefits which are conferred by an administration which makes such efforts to improve the communications of the country, by the construction of railways, roads, and telegraphs; which adds so greatly to the production of the country by the cutting of irrigation canals; and which encourages trade by removing all duties that are not absolutely necessary, as the British do. They hate the system of law in India, though they believe in the justice of the individual officer, and I am not altogether sure that they do not prefer administrations where the decision of law may be less just, but will probably be less costly, and will certainly be more rapid. But they consider that, on the whole, their trade interests are furthered more under British than under any other rule.

In regard, however, to the comparative strength of the two rival powers of Asia, there is not a doubt that they consider the Russian more powerful than the British. Even if they have not really got the greater strength, the Russians succeed better in producing an impression of it than do the British. Their numbers in Central Asia are really very small, but they are much more numerous in proportion to the number of natives than are the British in India. Then, again, the Russians, when they strike, strike very heavily; and when they advance they do not go back, as the British generally find some plausible reason for doing. Moreover, they have subjugated people who were easy to conquer, and the general result of all this, and of the rumours of untold legions of soldiers stationed in Russia proper, is to impress the Oriental mind with the idea that the Russians have a greater strength in comparison with the British than they perhaps actually have. Some English writers argue that the retirement from Afghanistan, in 1881, has had no effect upon British prestige. That retirement may have been wise on financial grounds, but that it did effect our prestige in Central Asia there can, I think, be little doubt. If we had gone to Kabul and Kandahar, and remained there, our prestige, for whatever it is worth, would certainly have stood higher than it does now, when it is perfectly well known throughout Asia that the Amir of Kabul practically closes Afghanistan to every Englishman. To keep up this prestige may not have been worth the money which it would have been necessary to expend in order to do so, but it is false to argue that the prestige is just as high after retirement as it was before. We cannot save up our money and expect the same results as if we had expended it. The shrewd native observers of our policy in Central Asia see perfectly well that we did not hold Afghanistan, because we had not sufficient men to do so. The Russians, chiefly because they have only had very unwarlike people to conquer, have never yet in Central Asia been put in the position of having to withdraw after a conquest.

Among other interesting features of my stay in Kashgar were my conversations with M. Petrovsky. He was a man with a large knowledge of the world, who had lived many years in St. Petersburg, as well as in Russian Turkestan and Kashgar. He had read largely on subjects connected with India and Central Asia; he had a number of our best books and Parliamentary Reports, and, like all Russians, he talked very freely, and, on subjects not connected with local politics, in which of course we were both concerned, very openly.

Hence I had an opportunity of seeing ourselves as others see us.

M. Petrovsky had read the report of the Sweating Committee, our Factory Legislation Reports, accounts in our newspapers of the strikes which continually occur. All this had produced on his mind the impression that we were in a bad way. Forty thousand men hold all the riches, and the rest of the thirty-six millions were just ground down to the last penny. This was his idea of the state of things in England; and he compared it with the condition of Russia. In Russia there was no great gulf between rich and poor. Strikes, which he looked upon as mild revolutions, were unknown, and all lived together in peaceful contentment under the Czar.

When I found an intelligent Russian taking this distorted view of the condition of England, and holding such optimistic opinions of the state of Russia, it often struck me that perhaps our own views of Russia were not always so true as they might be.

But it was in his criticisms of Indian and Central Asian affairs that I found M. Petrovsky most interesting, and, perhaps, more sound. One of the points upon which he was very insistent was our treatment of the natives. He thought that we held ourselves too much aloof from them, and that we were too cold and haughty. Here, I think, we must plead guilty; though if we had the faculty of getting on closer terms with those whom we rule, in addition to our other good qualities, we should be well-nigh perfect. When Englishmen are working hard together with natives, as on active service in the field, for instance, or surveying or exploring, the two nationalities become very firmly attached to each other. But ordinarily an Englishman finds great difficulty in "letting himself out" to strangers of any description. Very few, indeed, have that genial manner which draws people together. But as soon as the Englishman in India gets out of his wretched office, and away from all the

KASHGAR.

stiffness of cantonment regularity, and is really thrown with the natives, so that he can see them and they him, the coldness thaws, and the natives see that in reality there is much warmth of heart inside the cold exterior. Offices and regulations are evils which apparently are necessary for effective administration of our civilized type, but if we shut ourselves up too closely behind these barriers, and lose touch with the people, then the Russian consul's fears as to the eventual result of our coldness will undoubtedly be realized.

Of the Chinese, M. Petrovsky held a very poor opinion. He looked upon them with contempt, and had hardly a good word to say for them. Their administration was corrupt, the army badly officered and badly armed, and the empire generally honeycombed with secret societies. M. Petrovsky's practical acquaintance with the Chinese Empire was, however, entirely confined to Kashgar, and he had not been a hundred miles into the country, even into this outlying dependency, much less into China itself. I was surprised, too, to find that neither he nor any of his staff spoke Chinese, though they had been many years in Chinese Turkestan, and that they were dependent for their interpretation upon a Mussulman. Every English consul in China can speak Chinese, he is compelled to pass an examination in it, and even for a temporary stay in Turkestan I had been furnished with a competent English interpreter and a Cantonese clerk. In this important particular of acquiring a knowledge of the language of the people with whom we had to deal, it appeared, therefore, that we took far greater pains than the Russians did.

This is not the only case in which the Russians show themselves careless in learning the language of a country. In Turkestan it is the exception, and not the rule, for a Russian officer to speak the language of the people, and of six Russian officers whom I afterwards met on the Pamirs, only two could speak Turki, though they were permanently quartered in

Turkestan. Those Russians who speak a foreign language, speak it very well indeed; but, contrary to the general belief in England, the majority of even Russian officers speak Russian only.

Enlivened by these conversations with Central Asian merchants and with the Russian consul and his staff, the winter at Kashgar passed more quickly than it might be expected to do in so remote a corner of the world. We were fortunate, too, in having several visitors from Europe. The first of these was M. E. Blanc, a French traveller, who, having spent a few months in Turkestan, was perfectly willing to put both the Russian consul and myself right upon any point connected with Central Asia. The next visit was from the young Swedish traveller, Doctor Sven Hedin, who impressed me as being of the true stamp for exploration—physically robust, genial, even-tempered, cool and persevering. He only paid a hurried visit to Kashgar from Russian Turkestan, but he had already made a remarkable journey in Persia, and has since travelled much on the Pamirs, in Tibet, and Chinese Turkestan. I envied him his linguistic abilities, his knowledge of scientific subjects, obtained under the best instructors in Europe, and his artistic accomplishments; he seemed to possess every qualification of a scientific traveller, added to the quiet, self-reliant character of his Northern ancestors.

Later on, again, we had a visit from M. Dutreuil de Rhins and his companion M. Grenard, who did me the honour of staying with me during their fortnight's halt in Kashgar, preparatory to their three years' wandering in Tibet, which ended so disastrously in the murder of De Rhins by the Tibetans. M. de Rhins was a man of about forty-five, who had served the principal part of his life in the French navy and mercantile marine. He had already devoted his time for some years to the study of Tibet, and was most thorough and methodical in all his arrangements, and especially in his astronomical observations. We had many long conversations together, and I remember being particularly struck with a remark of his regarding the feeling between the French and the Germans. He said that neither he nor the majority of Frenchmen desired to bring on a war with Germany, but that if the Germans ever brought a war on he would at once enlist as a private soldier. In the Franco-German war he had served as an officer.

Having secured the necessary transport, M. de Rhins, with his companion, set out for Tibet. Macartney and I rode out of the town with them, and we parted with many assurances of goodwill, and after making arrangements to meet one day in Paris. I afterwards received a couple of letters from M. de Rhins, from Tibet; but he never returned from there. He was attacked by Tibetans, his arms were bound to his body with ropes, and he was thrown into a river and drowned; and so died one of the most hardy, plucky, and persevering of explorers whom France has sent out. Three years after leaving Kashgar his companion, M. Grenard, returned to Paris, and is now engaged in publishing the results of the journey.

These were our visitors, but we had also the company of a permanent European resident in Kashgar, Père Hendriks, the Dutch missionary, whom I had met here in 1887, and who still remains there. Regularly every day he used to come round for a chat and walk with us, and even now he writes to me every few months. His is lonely and uphill work, and he often appeared pressed down by the weight of obstacles which beset his way. But his enthusiasm and hopefulness were unbounded, and no kinder-hearted man exists. Many of his methods of conversion used to surprise me, and he certainly was not viewed with favour by the Russian authorities; but he was a man who had travelled much and studied much, and he was ready to talk in any language, from Mongol to English, and upon any subject, from the geological structures of the Himalayas, to his various conflicts with the Russian authorities. It would astonish people at home to see in what poverty this highly educated man lived, and to what straits he put himself in the exercise of his calling. Soon after we arrived he was dining with us, and the next morning when he came to see us he said he had slept much better that night. I asked him how it was he had done so, and he replied he thought it must be from having had some meat to eat at dinner with us. Then it was we found out that he lived on bread and vegetables only, for he had not more than ten or twelve rupees a month to spend, and lived in the merest hovel, which the Chinese had lent him. Of course, after that he always had one, and generally two meals a day with us, and we were delighted at the opportunity of having his company.

Beech and Lennard returned from a trip to Maralbashi before Christmas, so we were able, with them and with the Russian consul, his secretary, his son, the Cossack officer of the escort, and Père Hendriks, to have a good-sized dinner-party on Christmas Day. Beech had a wonderful tinned plum-pudding, which went off with an explosion when it was opened on the table, and I had another, which a kind friend in India had sent up, and which arrived on Christmas Eve, so we were able to show our Russian friends what "le plum-pudding anglais," which they had heard so much about but never seen, was really like.

Beech soon set off to Russian Turkestan, and was most hospitably entertained there by the governor-general and every other official whom he met, and came back in April much impressed with his reception. Then he and Lennard departed for the Pamirs to shoot *Ovis poli*, seventeen head of which magnificent animals they managed to bag.

At this time my life was saddened by two of the hardest blows which can befall a man. Both of them were sudden and unexpected, and in that far-away land letters from my friends took many months to reach me, and only came at intervals of weeks together. I longed to be home again once more, and those at home were needing me only a little less than I did them. But three more months I had still to remain stationary in Kashgar, the long days slowly dragging by with never-varying monotony.

At last, at the beginning of July, a man appeared one evening at our house, laden with a huge bag. This was a post from India. None had arrived for nearly two months, and in this one the permission to return to India, which I had been so longing for, arrived at last. Another pleasure, too, awaited me. An official letter for me bore the letters C.I.E. after my name. I did not at first pay any attention, thinking it was a mistake on the part of the clerk. But in a newspaper I found the announcement that I had been made a Companion of the Order of the Indian Empire, and this recognition of my services could not possibly have come at a more welcome time.

Permission was given me to return to India by either Leh or Gilgit, whichever I preferred; but poor Macartney was to stay on in Kashgar, and he is still there. I chose to return by the Pamirs and Gilgit, as I had already twice traversed the desolate route across the Karakoram. So I proceeded to hire ponies for the journey, and to make other necessary arrangements.

In the meanwhile, news arrived from Yarkand that an English traveller had reached Shahidula from Leh, in an almost destitute condition, and had told the Chinese authorities that he wanted to come on to Kashgar to see me. I asked the Chinese to give him any assistance they could. This they did; and shortly after a roughly pencilled note arrived for me, saying that he was Lieutenant Davison, of the Leinster Regiment; that he had come from Leh with the intention of crossing the Mustagh Pass, explored by me in 1887, but he had been stopped by the rivers on the way, all his men but one had run away, and he had lost nearly all his ponies, kit, and money. He had, therefore, no means of returning to Leh, and was compelled to come on to me for assistance. He travelled up to Kashgar with astonishing rapidity, and wanted, after getting information and assistance from me, to start off back again the next day to tackle the Mustagh Pass once more. He was exactly like a bulldog—you could not get him off this pass. He had come out to get over, and it was hours before I could convince him that it was impossible to do so before September. But he had already had experience of the depth and rapidity of the rivers on the way to it, and he gradually saw that it was out of the question. I then asked him for an account of his adventures on the way to Kashgar. It appeared that he had been given two months' leave from his regiment. He had no time to get a proper map of the route he would have to follow; but he pushed on as hard as he could through Kashmir and Ladak towards the Karakoram Pass, from which point he imagined that he would merely have to "turn to the left" and he would see a long distinct range of snow-mountains, with a gap in them, which would be the Mustagh Pass. He had little idea of the pathless labyrinth of mountain that actually shut in this remote pass! Crossing his first pass between Kashmir and Ladak, he became snow-blind, and had to be carried across on a bed. At his second—beyond Leh—the Ladakis whom he had engaged struck work, and said the pass would not be open for ponies for weeks yet. But Davison, by measures more severe than diplomatic, managed to get both them and his ponies over. Then came the Karakoram Pass; and the only way to traverse this in the month of May, when the snow on it was all soft and yielding, was by tediously laying down felts and blankets in front of the ponies for them to walk over, picking them up as the ponies had passed over them, and again laying them down in front—and so on for mile upon mile. Those who have themselves had experience of trudging through soft snow at an elevation of eighteen thousand feet, can best realize what this must have been to a man who had come straight up from the plains of

India, and who had never been on a snow-mountain in his life before. Now came the crisis of the journey. Davison had no map to show him the way to the Mustagh Pass, and, still worse, he had no guide. He had not been able to find a single man who had been a yard off the beaten track to Yarkand; but he had a rough map which gave him the relative position of the Mustagh and Karakoram Passes; so he plotted those two points on a piece of paper, and then started a prismatic compass survey, which in future he plotted out regularly on the same piece of paper, and by these means he hoped to be able to make out his way to the goal he had before him. With this intention, he followed down the stream which flows from the Karakoram Pass past Aktagh. But the further he advanced the more rugged and impracticable became the mountains which bounded in the valley in the direction of the Mustagh Pass. He could see nothing of that great snowy range which he had expected to find standing up conspicuous and distinct from all the rest, and with the Mustagh Pass forming a landmark which he could make out from any distance, and steer for without difficulty. Instead of this, he found himself shut in by rocky precipitous mountains, which forbade him following any other route but that which led down the valley he was in. He had lost three ponies on the Karakoram Pass. Two of his men now deserted with most of his supplies. But Davison still pushed on, in spite of the danger of doing so with his scanty stock of food, till— very fortunately for him—he was pulled up on account of the stream having increased so much in depth that it had become unfordable. This was at Khoja Mohammed gorge, about two marches below Chiragh Saldi. Davison tried to swim the river with a rope tied round his waist, but the stream was too strong for him. Finding it impossible to get down the valley at the time of year when the snows were melting and the rivers in flood, he reluctantly retraced his steps for a short distance and then turned north, crossed a pass (the Kokalang, if I remember rightly) which had not previously been explored, and then, finding ahead of him nothing but snowfields and impracticable-looking mountains in the direction of Yarkand, he made his way back again to the valley of the Yarkand (Raskam) River, with the intention of making for Shahidula, the nearest point at which he could hope to get supplies. He was now at the last extremity; he had but one man, one pony, and supplies for a day or two. He then fell sick, and could not move, and in this plight he had to send away his sole remaining servant to find Shahidula, and bring some supplies and help from that place. As it turned out, he was nearer Shahidula than he thought. His servant reached there the same day, and on the following returned with food and a pony. Davison's difficulties were then over, and, after resting a few days at Shahidula to regain his strength, he made his way rapidly to Kashgar. The ground that Davison covered had been previously explored by both Russians and English, but Davison had not the benefit of their experience; and the remarkable thing about his journey was that he accomplished it without any previous experience either of mountaineering or of ordinary travelling. A young subaltern, of only two years' service, he set out from the plains of Punjab, and by sheer pluck found his way, in the worst season of the year for travelling, to the plains of Turkestan, and this is a feat of which any one might feel proud.

I persuaded Davison to come back with me to India by the Pamirs, and our preparations for the journey were rapidly made. I called on all the Chinese officials, and received farewell dinners from them, and especially from old General Wang much hospitality. But it was a disappointment to me that I had to leave Kashgar without having the pleasure of saying good-bye to M. Petrovsky, the Russian consul. His dignity had been hurt because I took Davison to call upon him in the afternoon. He had refused to receive us, and afterwards informed Macartney that first calls ought always to be made in the middle of the day. I did my best to appease him by explaining by letter that we had only intended to do him a civility; that it was our custom to call in the afternoon; and that at Peking I had myself called upon his own official superior, the Russian minister, in the afternoon, and been called on in return by him. But M. Petrovsky replied that he was only concerned with Kashgar, and that at Kashgar the custom was to call in the middle of the day.

I regretted this misunderstanding with M. Petrovsky all the more because I felt myself indebted to him for many civilities during my stay in Kashgar. He had been most obliging in forwarding our letters through his couriers to Russian Turkestan; he had lent us numbers of books to read; and in many other ways had done us kindnesses for which I should have wished to show my gratitude. I had, however, the satisfaction of parting on very friendly terms with M. Lutsch, the secretary, and receiving from him a handsome present as a token of his regard.

CHAPTER XV.

KASHGAR TO INDIA.

> "And o'er the aerial mountains which pour down
> Indus and Oxus from their icy caves,
> In joy and exultation held his way;
> Till in the vale of Cashmere, far within
> Its loneliest dell, where odorous plants entwine
> Beneath the hollow rocks a natural bower,
> Beside a sparkling rivulet he stretched
> His languid limbs."
>
> SHELLEY.

WE left Kashgar on July 22, 1891, Macartney riding out a couple of marches with us, and then returning to Yarkand. We had been together for a year now, and the greater part of the time by ourselves. It does not always follow that two men who have never seen each other in their lives before can get on together for a year at a stretch without a break, and with scarcely a change of society. I felt myself particularly fortunate, therefore, in having for a companion a man who was not only a first-rate Chinese scholar, and extremely tactful in dealing with the Chinese, but who was also even-tempered, and willing to give and take, as travellers have to be. Mr. Macartney has since that time done very valuable service in arranging with the Chinese authorities for the release of slaves from states under the protection of the Government of India, who have been sold into Chinese territory. Many such have now been released, and have returned to their homes in Gilgit, Baltistan, and Chitral, and a good work has been successfully accomplished.

It was with little regret that I now turned my back on the plains of Turkestan, and ascended the mountains once more on my way towards India. Chinese Turkestan is an interesting country to visit, but a dreary place to live in. Even the air is oppressive; it is always "murky." For a few days one does not notice it particularly. There are no clouds; but when week after week goes by and the clear sky is never seen, then a feeling of oppression comes on. The air is always filled with this impalpable dust from the desert, and Chinese Turkestan is for ever shrouded in sand. And this not only leaves its mark upon the mountains, depositing on them layers of light friable soil, but also makes its impression upon the people of the country. To a traveller from the direction of China, who has become accustomed to the insolence of Chinese mobs, these submissive, spiritless Turkis appear a genial, hospitable people. And, similarly, when a traveller enters the country from the inhospitable regions over which the route by the Karakoram Pass leads, he is so thankful to be in an inhabited, cultivated country again, that everything to him seems rose-coloured. But when he has been resident for some months among the people, he finds them heavy and uninteresting. In only one respect do they show any enterprise, and that is in making pilgrimages to Mecca; hundreds of them do this, whole families of them—fathers, mothers, and children in arms, will set off across those bleak passes, over the Himalayas, through all the heat of India, and over the sea to Mecca. Numbers perish on the journey, but still, year after year, others follow in their track; and that so apathetic a people should go to such extremities, is one of the most remarkable instances I know of the stirring influence of religion.

The heat in the plains had now become very considerable, daily registering one hundred and two or one hundred and three degrees Fahrenheit, so we were glad to leave them behind, and find the road gradually rising towards the great buttress range of the Pamirs, which stood before us like a wall. We headed straight towards that glorious mountain, the Mustagh-ata, which rose twenty-one thousand feet above the plains on which we stood, and, three days' march from Kashgar, we entered the Gez defile, the road up which was rough and difficult and almost impractical for ponies. When the river, which runs through the defile, is low, ponies can be led up the bed; but now, in the summer-time, when it is in full flood, they have to be taken two and three thousand feet higher up, over a spur, then down again for a mile or two, along the valley bottom again, then once more over a hill, and so on for the whole way up. On the hillside there was seldom any path, and the ponies had to scramble about amongst the rocks and boulders, and up and down places not much less steep than the roof of a house. But, once through this defile, we found ourselves on an open plain, surrounded on all sides by mountains, but itself quite flat. To the left, as we emerged from the defile, was a large lake. This was not marked on any of my maps, though the district has been well surveyed, and I was further puzzled to see quantities of sand-drift covering the lower parts of the low, rounded mountains on the opposite bank. As the water of the lake came right up to the mountain-side, it was difficult to see where the sand could come from; but I found that the lake was only a few feet deep, and when the melting of the snows has finished, it dwindles to a mere marsh, exposing, at the same time, large deposits of sand, which the wind blows on to the mountain-sides. This lake was an extension of the Balun-kul.

The scenery now changed completely. Up the course of the Gez River, the valleys had all been deep and narrow, with precipitous sides, and at the head of the defile, on the left-hand side, the great mountain mass of the Mustagh-ata looked as if it had but just been rudely thrust upward, and the shattered sides of the mountain were exposed fresh from the upheaval.

But beyond the defile, looking toward the Pamirs, the mountains were all rounded, the main valleys were flat open plains, and even the side valleys were wide and shallow. No trees grew anywhere. The mountain-sides were brown, and only covered with coarse wormwood, but the valley bottom had a luxuriant growth of grass, which at this time of year was very rich and succulent.

At Lake Bulun-kul, Lieutenant Davison parted from me, and travelled westward to the Alichur Pamir, by the Ak-berdi Pass, which he was, I believe, the first European to cross. It is an easy one, as most of the passes on the Pamirs are, and leads down to the Rang-kul. Meanwhile, I travelled on to the Little Kara-kul, a lake with absolutely unique surroundings. No other lake in the world can boast of two peaks of over twenty-five thousand feet each, rising from its very shores. Here, on the edge of the Roof of the World, was this lovely sheet of clear blue water, with its grassy banks, and the two great mountains standing like two sentinels above its shores. These mountain peaks are the Mustagh-ata and another, which Mr. Ney Elias, who discovered it, named Mount Dufferin. They rise not as rugged pinnacles, but in huge masses, and so gradually and evenly that the ascent seems perfectly easy, and entices travellers to scale the icy summits, and from these to look out over the Roof of the World, far away to the Himalayas, and round over the vast plains of Turkestan to the Celestial Mountains, which divide Russia from China. No other mountain that I have seen seems easier of access, and from no other could such an extended view be obtained; Russia, India, and China, each presses round its base.

Near the Kara-kul there were several encampments of Kirghiz, with their numerous flocks feeding on the rich pasturage round the lake. Thence I crossed by the easy Ulugh Rabat Pass into the wide Tagarma plain, and passed on to Tashkurgan, which I now visited for the third time. After halting here for a day to collect supplies, I left on August 5, and marched up the Tagh-dum-bash Pamir, intending to proceed to Gilgit by the Baroghil or some other pass leading into Chitral territory. A considerable amount of rain fell at this time of year, and places which two years before I had seen dried up and parched by the November frosts, were now fresh with the summer green, and grass was plentiful.

All this time reports kept coming in that a small Russian force had entered the Pamirs, and proclaimed them Russian territory, and at the head of the Tagh-dum-bash Pamir I found several families of Kirghiz who had fled before the Russians. I crossed the Wakhijrui Pass, fifteen thousand six hundred feet, an easy pass, with a small lake on the summit, and the surface of the ground carpeted with gentians, edelweis, and yellow poppies. I then descended into the basin of the River Oxus, and passed along the Pamir-i-Wakhan, uninhabited at this season, but tenanted in the winter by Wakhis, to Bozai-Gumbaz, which I reached on August 10. So much has since been written about this place, that people might easily imagine it to be a town or large village, whereas the only building on the spot is the tomb of a murdered Kirghiz chieftain, and the only inhabitants occasional nomadic Wakhis. Here I found a party of ten Cossacks encamped. They formed a guard over the stores which had been left here by the main party of Russians, which had gone on to reconnoitre in the direction of the Baroghil Pass. There was no officer with this party of Cossacks at Bozai-Gumbaz, so I halted here till the officers returned, as I was anxious to meet them. Among the Cossacks of this party I recognized one who had been with Captain Grombtchevsky in 1889, and was able to show him a photograph of our combined parties which the Russian officer had taken, and of which he had sent me a copy from St. Petersburg, together with a very kind invitation to visit him in Margillan.

On August 13 the reconnoitring party returned. As I

looked out of the door of my tent, I saw some twenty Cossacks with six officers riding by, and the Russian flag carried in front. I sent out a servant with my card and invitation to the officers to come in and have some refreshments. Some of them came in, and the chief officer was introduced to me as Colonel Yonoff. He and all of them were dressed in loose "khaki" blouses, with baggy pantaloons and high boots, and they wore the ordinary peaked Russian cap, covered with white cloth. Colonel Yonoff also wore on his breast a white enamel Maltese cross, which I recognized as the Cross of St. George, the most coveted Russian decoration, and I at once congratulated him upon holding so distinguished an order. Colonel Yonoff was a modest, quiet-mannered man, of a totally different stamp to Captain Grombtchevsky. He had less of the bonhomie of the latter, and talked little; but he was evidently respected by his officers, and they told me he had greatly distinguished himself in the Khivan campaign. I gave the Russian officers some tea and Russian wine, which Mr. Lutsch, the consul's secretary, had very kindly procured for me from Margillan; and I then told Colonel Yonoff that reports had reached me that he was proclaiming to the Kirghiz that the Pamirs were Russian territory, and asked him if this was the case. He said it was so, and he showed me a map with the boundary claimed by the Russians coloured on it. This boundary included the whole of the Pamirs except the Tagh-dum-bash, and extended as far down as the watershed of the Hindu-Kush by the Khora Bhort Pass.

The Russian officers stayed with me for about an hour, and then went off to make their own camp arrangements, asking me, however, to come and dine with them that evening. When I went round to them, I found that they were doubled up in very small tents. Three of them lived in a tent which was not high enough to stand upright in, and at dinner there was just room for seven of us to squat on the ground, with a tablecloth spread in the middle—three officers on each side, and one at the head. No wonder these Russians thought my camp arrangements luxurious. I had what is known as a field-officer's Kabul tent, about eight feet in length, breadth, and height, and with a bath-room and double fly. I had, too, a bed, table, and chair. Such luxury filled the Russians with astonishment; but they were merely making a rapid raid, while I had set out from India to travel for more than a year. The whole tent and equipment of camp furniture was not a pony-load, and when there is no necessity to stint transport, as there is not on the Pamirs, for a small party, it it much better to take a whole pony-load, and make one's self comfortable, than to take half a load and be miserable. When there is any necessity for it, British officers go without any tent at all; but when they can make themselves comfortable, as a rule they do.

We squeezed into the little tent, and proceedings commenced with drinking the inevitable glass of vodka. Then followed a dinner, which for its excellence astonished me quite as much as my camp arrangements had astonished the Russians. Russians always seem to be able to produce soups and stews of a good wholesome, satisfying nature, such as native servants from India never seem able to imitate. The Russians had vegetables, too—a luxury to me—and sauces and relishes, and, besides vodka, two different kinds of wine and brandy. Though only one of the six Russians spoke French, they were all very hospitable and cordial, and at the conclusion of dinner Colonel Yonoff proposed the health of Queen Victoria, while I proposed that of the Emperor of Russia.

There were, besides Colonel Yonoff, a staff-officer from St. Petersburgh, two Cossack officers, a doctor, and a surveyor named Benderski, who had been to Kabul with the Russian mission of 1878, and had also surveyed the Pamirs with Ivanoff's expedition of 1883. Colonel Yonoff now showed me the survey which his party had just made, and the route they had followed across the Hindu Kush. They had proceeded from Bozai-Gumbaz to the Khora Bhort Pass (also called Baikra and Tash-kupruk, and now by the Russians the "Yonoff"). They had crossed this, and then turned westward up the head-waters of the Ashkuman or Karumbar River, and then across the lower watershed into the valley of the Yarkhun River, and from there up to the Darkot Pass, the summit of which they reached, and looked down into the valley of Yasin. Since crossing the Khora Bhort they were on the Indian side of the watershed, and in territory generally considered to belong to Chitral. From the Darkot Pass they turned north again, and crossed the Baroghil Pass, or rather another depression in the range within a few miles of it, and, passing by the Afghan post of Sarhad, returned up the valley of the Panja to Bozai-Gumbaz. The Cossacks were all mounted, and they had some difficulty in getting over the Khora Bhort Pass, but they seemed well satisfied with the results of their trip. They imagined, however, that the existence of the Khora Bhort Pass was unknown to the English, and were astonished when I showed them a passage in the French traveller Capus's book with this pass mentioned in it. It had, too, as a matter of fact, been thoroughly surveyed by the English Engineer officer, Captain Tyler.

We spent a long evening together, squatting on the floor of the little tent, and talking very freely upon subjects of mutual interest. The Russian officers were very anxious to know how near on the other side of the range supplies could be obtained, for along the four hundred miles up to it from their starting-point at Osh, nothing in the way of grain is procurable. They said, too, that they wondered at our stationing a political agent in Gilgit, and making that place an important military outpost, while we had no representative in Chitral, and appeared to pay no attention to that place. At that time, though British officers had visited Chitral on temporary missions, we had no agent permanently stationed there, and, curiously enough, I was myself, two years later, appointed the first permanent agent in that important place.

It was not till after midnight that the dinner broke up, and Colonel Yonoff and all the officers escorted me back to my tent, half a mile off, parting with many protestations of friendship. On the next morning they left for the Alichur Pamir. I waited on for a few days, expecting Davison to rejoin me, and we would then have proceeded together to Gilgit.

But three nights later, as I was getting into bed, I heard the clatter of horses' hoofs on the stones outside my tent, and, on looking out, saw, in the bright moonlight, about thirty mounted Cossacks drawn up in line, with the Russian flag in the centre. I hastily put on a great-coat, and sent my servant to ask the officer in command if he would come in. Two or three officers dismounted, and I found they were Colonel Yonoff and the same officers whom I had parted with three nights before. Colonel Yonoff said he had something very disagreeable to say to me. He then courteously and civilly, and with many apologies, informed me that he had that morning, while at Lake Victoria, on the Great Pamir, received a despatch from his government, in which he was instructed to escort me from Russian territory back to Chinese territory. He said he very much disliked having to perform such a duty, for I was a military officer and he was a military officer, and this was a duty usually performed by police officials; we had, moreover, met before on very friendly terms, and he had been in hopes that I would have already left Bozai-Gumbaz, and saved him from the necessity of carrying it out.

I told him that I did not consider I was on Russian territory at all, and that, in any case, I was returning to India; but Colonel Yonoff replied that by his maps Bozai-Gumbaz was included in the Russian territory, and his orders were to escort me back to Chinese, and not British territory. I then asked him what he would do if I refused to go, and he said he would, in that case, have to use force. There was, of course, no answering this argument, for he had thirty Cossacks, while I had not a single soldier with me. I therefore informed him that I should have, in these circumstances, to submit to any terms he might wish to impose, but I should do so under protest, and should report the whole matter to my Government. Beyond that I had, therefore, nothing further to say.

Colonel Yonoff again repeated his regrets at having to treat me as he had been instructed to do, and said that he would so far modify his action as to allow me to proceed by myself instead of escorting me. He then drew up, in French, a form of agreement, in which it was said that, acting under the *instruction* of the Russian Government, he was to cause me to leave Russian territory, and that I agreed, under protest, to do this, and undertook to proceed to Chinese territory by the Wakhijrui Pass, and not to return by any of a number of passes which he named, and which included every known pass across the watershed of the Pamirs from the vicinity of the Alai as far down as the Baroghil Pass. Having signed this agreement, and made a copy of it, I told Colonel Yonoff that I hoped he would consider that business over, and return to our former friendly relations, and have supper with me. His baggage was far behind, and it was now nearly midnight. We accordingly all sat down to a rough supper; and the Russian officers afterwards went off to their own encampment and left me alone once more. Next morning I packed up my things and started for the Wakhijrui Pass. As I rode past the Russians, Colonel Yonoff and his companions came out to wish me good-bye, and express their sincerest regrets at having to treat a friend as they had been obliged to treat me. They presented me with a haunch of *Ovis poli*, from an animal they had shot on the previous day, and we parted on as friendly terms as it was possible to be in the circumstances.

I, of course, at once reported the whole matter to my

Government, and thirteen days after the incident had occurred, far away on the Pamirs though it was, the British Ambassador at St. Petersburg had made a protest to the Russian Government, the upshot of which was that the Russian Ambassador in London apologized to Lord Salisbury for the illegal action of Colonel Yonoff, and the Russian Government has now declared, in the Pamir Agreement, that Bozai-Gumbaz the place which Colonel Yonoff had stated to be Russian territory, is beyond the sphere of Russian influence.

Meanwhile I recrossed the Wakhijrui Pass, and encamped for some weeks on the far side of it, at the mouth of the Kukturuk valley. This is immediately opposite the Kilik Pass into Hunza, and as these people of Hunza were showing signs of hostility to us, which a few months later resulted in the sending of an expedition against them; and as, moreover, they committed a raid on a Kirghiz encampment only ten miles below the spot where I was myself encamped, I had to take turns with my Pathan servants to keep watch during the night, till an escort under Lieutenant J. M. Stewart arrived from Gilgit for my protection. For six weeks I remained at this place, situated over fifteen thousand feet above sea-level. Even at the end of August there were sharp frosts at night, and the water in my basin would be coated over with ice in the morning, and by the end of September the thermometer went down to zero Fahrenheit. The patches of grass, so green and fresh in the summer months, now died down and withered, and the hills and valleys became bare and bleak as the winter cold closed on them. The mountains in that part were mostly rounded and uninteresting—ugly heaps of rock and earth, with no trace of beauty to attract attention, and life in Kukturuk was in the highest degree monotonous till Lieutenant Stewart arrived.

At last, on October 4, Lieutenant Davison rejoined me. He had been treated in an even more cavalier manner by the

Russians than I had, and been marched off back with them to Turkestan from the Alichur Pamir. As far as he personally was concerned, he seems to have enjoyed the trip; he found the Russian officers very cheery companions; he was asked to dinner by the Russian governor of Margillan, and altogether he had a much better time with them than he would have had with his regiment in the plains of India during the hot weather. He was able to do some useful work, too, for the Russians took him by a road which no British officer had traversed before. Having thoroughly satisfied themselves, the Russians escorted Davison to the Chinese frontier, and then let him go. But here a difficulty arose. Davison had with him no passport, and as he came from Russian territory, the Chinese frontier official naturally took him for a Russian and wished to stop him. But the want of such a trifle as a passport was not likely to stop Davison very long, and he and his man jumped up on their ponies while the Chinese official was vociferating, and they galloped off towards Kashgar, scarcely stopping till they reached the place, where Davison saw the Chinese officials who had known him before, and explained matters to them. He then came on to rejoin me on the Tagh-dum-bash Pamir. Away in the distance down the valley I saw a horseman approaching dressed in the peaked cap and high boots of the Russians, and I thought that another Russian was going to honour me with a visit. This proved, however, to be Davison. As was the custom with him, he had travelled with wonderful rapidity, and had only taken ten days to reach Kukturuk from Kashgar.

We now had to find our way back to India as originally intended. Colonel Yonoff had barred all the known passes to me, so our only resource was to discover an unknown pass —always an easy matter in those parts—for the mountains there are rarely too difficult for small parties to get over. On October 5 we set off, therefore, and instead of following up the main valley to the Wakhijrui Pass, we branched off from it about five miles lower down than the pass, and ascended a side valley. In this we found a glacier, up which we had to make our way, but it was easy enough to admit of our taking yaks up it, and just before sunset we reached the summit.

Then, indeed, a magnificent view presented itself. By Kukturuk the mountains had all been low and tame—I speak, of course, comparatively, for they were far higher even above the valley bottom than are any hills in the British Isles above the sea—but here we were among the real mountain monarchs once more. We saw before us an amphitheatre of snowy peaks glittering in the fading sunlight, and at their foot one vast snowfield, the depository of all their surplus snow and ice, and the first beginning of the great glacier which would bear the burden down the valley from it. This nook of mountains was the very Heart of Central Asia. One side of the amphitheatre was formed by the range of mountains which divides the waters of the Oxus, which flow to Turkestan, from the waters of the Indus, which make their way to India. Here was also the meeting-point of the watershed which divides the rivers flowing eastward into Chinese Turkestan from those flowing westward to Russian and Afghan Turkestan, with that other watershed which separates the rivers of India on the south from the rivers of Central Asia on the north. At the very point at which we stood those two great watersheds of Asia met; they formed the glittering amphitheatre of snowy peaks which we saw before us, and it was from the snowfields at the base of these that issued the parent glacier of the mighty Oxus.

Just below the pass we found a small lake, about three-quarters of a mile in length and width, fed by three glaciers. It was walled all round, except at one point, by cliffs a hundred feet and more in height of pure transparent ice. Its waters were of a deep clear blue, and overflowed at the one unguarded side in a small stream down the glacier in the main valley below.

We did not now descend into this main valley, which is that of the Panja River, the principal branch of the Oxus, but kept along high up the mountain-side, about fifteen thousand feet above the valley bottom. Darkness had come on, and I was unable to see how far down the valley the glacier extended; but at rather more than a mile above the point where the route by the Wakhijrui Pass descends into this same valley, we came down into the valley bottom, and found there no glacier, but a considerable stream—the Panja. The pass which we crossed was situated about eight miles south of the Wakhijrui. There are no signs of a path by it, and, as far as I could learn, not even a Kirghiz had been by it before. But it presents no particular difficulties, and we were able, as I said, to take yaks the whole way, and were generally able to ride them. The pass has, however, no importance, as the Wakhijrui is easier and more direct.

Arriving in the dark at midnight, and with the whole country deeply covered with snow, we could find no brushwood. We had, accordingly, to content ourselves with a few tent-pegs as fuel for a fire by which to heat up a little water for tea; and then, having pitched our tents on the snow, we turned in. Next day we marched down the Pamir-i-Wakhan, which, on account of its right bank facing south and so getting the sun, is much frequented by the Wakhi shepherds in the winter months; and on the day after passed by Bozai-Gumbaz. We now had to discover another new pass, for here again all the known passes were barred by my agreement with Colonel Yonoff. The range of the Indus watershed, the main ridge of the Hindu Kush, was likely to prove far harder to cross than had the last mountain barrier, and I had, therefore, for some time past taken pains to find out from the natives if any other pass than the known ones existed. It is of little use to ask the people straight out, "Is there a pass?" They would, of course, reply, "No, there isn't," and the conversation would end.

So I used to say that I was going by a pass to the right of such and such a pass, the latter being some well-known one. For a long time the men replied, one after another, that no such pass existed, but at last one man said that it was a very difficult one. Then I had the clue that there really *was* one, and matters after that were comparatively simple.

Two days after passing Bozai-Gumbaz, we reached the foot of the long-sought-for pass. But it was snowing hard, and had been snowing equally hard for some days. Lieutenant Stewart, who had preceded me by a few days, had crossed the Khora Bhort Pass with difficulty, according to our Wakhi guides. We were now well into October, and this heavy fall of snow had closed the pass for the year. I told the Wakhis that the weather would certainly clear on the morrow, and then we should find no difficulty, for I had crossed many passes before and knew how to tackle them. But when we rose at five the next morning it was snowing harder than ever, and the Wakhis said it was quite impracticable. I told them, however, that I wanted them to come with me to show me how impracticable it was, and then we started off, Davison and I riding yaks, and two Wakhis on foot. How thankful we in England ought to feel that the Oriental does not come raging round our country and insist upon turning us out to climb mountains in the depth of winter, and in the middle of snowstorms, while he rides comfortably along by our sides and tells us that there is no difficulty! The patient, submissive Wakhi consents to do this without a murmur—that is to say, without a murmur worth recording in these pages. And the result was that we were able to cross the pass successfully and without any serious inconvenience.

After ascending a rocky valley for three miles, we suddenly came on a glacier, up which we had to climb for about seven miles to the summit of the pass. The snowfall was so heavy, that when we were once on this glacier we could not see a trace of the mountains on either side. The only thing we saw was the billowy, snow-covered glacier, and up this we kept, knowing that it must necessarily lead to the pass. We, of course, had to proceed very slowly and carefully, for fear of crevasses hidden by the snow. But, like the elephant, which will not cross a shaky bridge, the yak knows by instinct the parts that will not bear, and, snorting and sniffing along, he finds his way unerringly up a glacier; and about four o'clock in the afternoon we reached the summit of the pass without experiencing any real difficulty. The pass was very narrow and deep-cut, and, on the opposite side, very abrupt; and the wind blew through it as through a funnel. I never experienced such an icy blast as that which met us as we reached the summit. It came concentrating down upon us with terrific force, and sharp as a knife. We only had its full force for a few minutes, for we quickly dropped down into comparative shelter, but during that short time our faces were cut across in slashes. Most of my face was protected, for I wore a thick beard; but Davison had no beard, and suffered very badly. His face did not recover for weeks after.

The descent from the pass for about a thousand feet was extremely rough and steep, and then we emerged on to a gentler slope, trending downwards towards the Ashkuman or Karumbar River. There was no sort of path, and, as the snowstorm was still raging, we had no means of discovering in which direction we should move, but wandered aimlessly about till we were suddenly brought up on the brink of a precipice. Here we had to halt, for it was dangerous to move when we could see little before us. But, fortunately, just before sunset the snowstorm cleared, and we looked down over the precipice into the valley of the Karumbar River far below. We followed along the edge of the cliffs till we found a way down into the valley, and, at about ten o'clock, reached a spot by the river where wood was procurable in plenty, and here we camped for the night.

We were now once more on the Indian side of the great watershed of Central Asia, and all we had to do was to push on as rapidly as we could to India. We reached Gilgit on October 13, and after a few days' halt with Colonel Durand, who was still carrying on his work there, pressed on to Kashmir. Two years before, I had crossed the passes in that direction in the middle of December, and it did not strike me that there could be any difficulty at this season, when we were not yet through October. But this year the winter had closed in unusually early; there had been very heavy snowstorms, and consequently, when we came to the Burzil, a pass thirteen thousand four hundred feet in height, we found that a detachment of Gurkhas coming over it had suffered very severely. The evening we arrived there this detachment of two hundred men was expected, and we prepared dinner for the officers. But it was not till nearly one o'clock at night that any arrived, and then we heard that the mules carrying their baggage had stuck in the snow; the officers and men had worked for the whole of the day and halfway through the night to get them along, but the poor animals and their unfortunate native drivers—all of them, animals and men, from the plains of India, and unacquainted with cold and snow—had not been able to perform the task. The animals had to be unloaded in the narrow path through the snow, and left there till morning, while the men got what shelter they could in the woods farther on, near the camping-ground. When Captain Barratt, the officer in command, arrived, he complained of a pain in his foot, and this proved to be a severe frost-bite, which laid him up for nearly six months, and through which he lost three toes. Altogether there were one hundred and thirty-two cases of frost-bite among the men and followers of that detachment, who, coming up suddenly from the heat of India, were unable to withstand the unexpected cold.

Next day Davison and I, with our sturdy Yarkand ponies now inured to cold and snow, crossed the pass without mishap, and, finding the ponies still had work in them, we were able to accomplish another march on the opposite side as well.

Two days later we crossed our last pass, the Tragbal, eleven thousand four hundred feet, and from the summit saw once again the lovely vale of Kashmir spread out at our feet, and looked out on the pine-clad slopes, the cultivated village lands, the placid lake, and the distant range of snowy peaks beyond. All was deep in snow at the summit of the pass, and the cold intense in the early morning, but at each step we descended towards the valley of Kashmir the air grew warmer. The icy blasts of the Pamir passes, and the gloomy frosts of the Burzil, were now left well behind us. We discarded our fur cloaks, and, as we approached the valley, even our coats also; and then, as evening was drawing in, we reached the shores of the lake and threw ourselves into one of the luxurious Kashmir gondolas which was awaiting us.

Another journey had been accomplished; all the difficulties and all the anxieties of it were now over. For seventeen months I had been away from civilization, and cut off from intercourse with my friends, and now once more I was returning to all the pleasures which that can give. As the sun was declining towards the horizon, and casting the long shadows from the mountains over the still waters of the lake, we pushed off from the shore, and were paddled smoothly and quietly over its unruffled surface. No more exertion on our part was now necessary; all we had to do was to recline luxuriously in the boat, while we were borne swiftly and easily over the water. The sun set in a glow of glory. The snows of the mountain summits were tinged with ruddy hues, the fleecy clouds overhead were suffused in ever-changing colours; then slowly the peaks in the distant east grew grey, the warm tints faded from the scene, one by one the stars pierced through the skies, and night settled down upon the mountains.

Then, as I lay back watching the enchanting scene of peaceful beauty, and as the sense of rest and quiet grew upon me and soothed away the feeling of stern resolve which settles on one through a journey, I thought over the long marches past, the many privations now at an end, and the difficulties overcome. I thought of these, and of those hard latter months of my stay in Kashgar, and I knew that the hardest must be past, and that a brighter time was nearing.

At Srinagar I parted with poor Davison, and never saw him again. Two years later he was ordered to the Gilgit frontier, but he caught a chill in crossing the Burzil Pass, and died of enteric fever a few marches beyond it. He had all the makings of a great explorer; he had unsurpassable energy, what one might almost call blind pluck, for nothing to him was dangerous, and he had an inexhaustible enthusiasm for travel. I may add that, though few of us who knew him suspected him of it, papers written by him, and found among his effects, showed that he thought very seriously upon many subjects not generally supposed to engage the attention of so young an officer as he was, and his loss must be deplored by all who can admire true manliness and resolution.

CHAPTER XVI.

CHITRAL AND HUNZA.

"A peace is of the nature of a conquest;
For then both parties nobly are subdued,
And neither party loser."

HENRY IV.

THE expedition recorded in the previous chapter was my last real journey, but for two years and more afterwards I was employed in the interesting and important states of Chitral and Hunza, and some account of these countries may be given as a fitting conclusion to the narrative of my travels on the northern frontier of India.

We may begin with Hunza, as we already have some acquaintance with that country. When I travelled through Hunza in 1889, the country, it will be remembered, was ruled by a certain Safder Ali. The Government of India found themselves compelled, in the winter of 1891–2, to make war upon this chief, and as the result of a brilliant and successful campaign, directed by Colonel A. G. Durand—a campaign remarkable for the gallantry displayed by individual British officers, and for the military efficiency of the newly trained Kashmir troops—Safder Ali was forced to flee from the country, and Hunza was brought more directly under the control of the Maharaja of Kashmir and the Government of India. This country of marauders was henceforth to be duly, though not too severely, controlled, and both people and rulers made to understand that in this latter end of the nineteenth century the time had passed when they could raid with impunity, and without ever considering the other side of the question.

It might be imagined that after a war with them, and after the flight of their ruler, the people would be anything but friendly with the British, but eight months later, when I again visited the country, to relieve Captain Stewart, the political agent, upon whom had devolved the task of superintending the affairs of the country at the conclusion of the campaign, the people were quiet and peaceful, as if they had been born and bred under British administration; officers were able to travel anywhere through the country without an escort, and were always treated with respect. As I have already intimated, these people had no rooted antipathy to the British Government, and they form a remarkable instance of the good effects which come of following up a successful campaign by assuming a permanent control. Had we given these people a hard knock and then retired, as we so frequently do, and as we are always recommended to do by certain people, these men of Hunza, like children, would have forgotten the lesson that had been taught them, and in a few years would have committed some act of folly—a raid, an attack upon a Kashmir outpost, or some other aggression—which would have necessitated another invasion of their country, and bad feeling would gradually have grown up between us and them, as it has between the Afghans and the British, though originally the Afghans were well disposed towards us. The theory that if the troops were entirely withdrawn after a campaign, and the people left quite independent, they would be more friendly, is not to be trusted. It sounds very well, but it is not borne out by facts. There are other ways of preserving such amount of independence as a semi-barbarous state situated between two great civilized Powers can have, besides withdrawing all troops from the country, and as an instance of the way in which this may be done, the state of affairs in Hunza may be described.

What these rough hill-men like above everything else is being ruled by their own rulers—that is, by members of their own reigning families—and having their customs kept up without innovation. In Hunza the people are now ruled by a member of the family which has sat on the throne for probably hundreds of years—at any rate, as long as tradition goes back—and not by the murderer who brought their country into trouble, but by another son of the murdered father, by a man liked and respected by them. And not a single custom, unless raiding can be called a custom, has been interfered with. In their internal affairs the people are in much the same condition as when I first passed through the country in 1889. All cases are brought before the chief now, as then, and the British officer who resides in the country is only too glad to be free from the responsibility and trouble of having to deal with them. In only one respect is control exercised by the agent of the Government of India, and that is in regard to the foreign relations of the state. In that one single respect this country must lose its independence, but that is inevitable. Even the larger state of Afghanistan has to this extent been compelled to lose its independence. And little states like Hunza no longer can remain entirely independent as regards their foreign affairs. A wise ruler, however, would recognize the altered conditions which the spread of two great civilized Powers through Asia has produced, and would seek to form his relations with the suzerain power as much as possible on the basis of an alliance, and this the new chief of Hunza has informally done. On two occasions he has been asked by the political agent to give aid to Government. On the first occasion I was told by Colonel Durand to ask him and his neighbour, the chief of Nagar, to give, each, twenty-five men, trained in the use of rifles, to do the advance guard and scouting work of a small force which was moving towards Chitral. Both chiefs immediately agreed to the proposal, and the Hunza chief said he would not send twenty-five, but fifty men, or, as far as that goes, a hundred or two hundred, if so many were necessary, and he would send his Wazir—his chief adviser—with them. In 1895 he again sent men with Colonel Kelly's force to the relief of Chitral, and Colonel Kelly has placed on record how useful these men were in scaling the heights and turning the enemy's position. In this manner the chiefs, recognizing that their interests are bound up with those of the British Government, have definitely thrown in their lot with the British, and by so doing have not diminished their dignity and importance nor lessened their independence, but, on the contrary, increased this independence, and placed their relations with the supreme power more on a basis of alliance with than of dependence on it. And the history of British rule in India shows that states which act on this principle most consistently retain their independence longest. The Sikh state of Patiala, in the Punjab, from the very first assisted the British Government, and there is now not even a British Resident in it. Lahore, on the other hand, attacked the British even after the state had once been defeated. It had, therefore, of necessity, to be subdued, and it is now British territory, and administered by British officials.

In the hands, then, of the rulers and people of little states, such as Hunza, lies the decision as to whether they shall remain dependent or be absorbed, and those officers who have had dealings with these states recognize best how much to the interest, both of the British Government and of the people, it is that they should be allowed to retain the amount of independence which Hunza, for instance, still possesses. Even from the point of view of picturesqueness, it would be a thousand pities to destroy the freedom of these mountain peoples; to break up those primitive courts where the ruler meets his people face to face, and knows each man among them as they know him; and to wither their simple customs, as the grass is withered by the frost, by introducing the cold system of British administration, the iron rules and regulations, and all the machinery of an empire into this little state. But when Government can see that the ruler is ready to help them when aid from him is required; when they see that he recognizes how essential to his very existence as ruler of the state it is that he should have dealings with no other than the British; when they note that he governs his people without oppression; and when ruler and people realize that Government has no wish to destroy their independence, or to interfere with their customs;—then it is evident that satisfactory relations have been established, and that Government is in a far better position than if the country were governed directly.

In Hunza there are now rather less than a hundred Kashmir troops, connected by small posts with the garrison at Gilgit, sixty-five miles distant. There is also a British officer to conduct the relations of Government with this state and with the neighbouring state of Nagar across the river. Hunza is ruled by a half-brother of the late chief Safder Ali, named Mohammed Nazim, a pleasant-mannered, intelligent man, about thirty-four years of age. He and the successive British officers who have represented the Government of India in his state have always been on very intimate terms, and the duties of the latter have become so light that, since the end of 1894, no special political officer has been deputed, but the military officer attached to the Kashmir troops stationed in the country has been instructed to carry on the little political work that has to be done. The presence of just a few troops in the country, and the certainty of Government support, serve to keep the ruler and people steady, and the British officer is able to exercise a useful influence for good throughout the country, not by any direct interference, but by simple daily intercourse with the chief and his people. And no more enjoyable appointment than that at Hunza could be imagined. I remember on a stifling day in August, 1892, at that season of the year when the sun beats down upon its bare rocks more like the interior of an oven than what one would expect of a mountain valley five thousand feet above the sea, riding up from the Gilgit valley, out of all this heat into the freshness of the Hunza valley, and, as I came round a spur of the hills, suddenly encountering Rakapushi Peak rising sheer nineteen thousand feet from the place where I stood. I had seen this mountain before in my journey down the valley in 1889, and had borne away no humble impression of it. I have often seen it since, but it is a remarkable fact about this and other great mountains, that each new sight of them seems to impress itself more deeply than the one before. I came now with a vivid recollection of the splendour of Rakapushi, the towering mass of mountain rising directly from the valley bottom, the glittering snowfields, and the proud cold summit soaring right into heaven. But as I once again turned the corner of the spur, and this wonderful sight suddenly came full upon me, I involuntarily pulled up. It far exceeded all that I had remembered.

We followed the valley sometimes along the bare hillside, but more often through pretty village lands, first by the fort of Nilt, the position so gallantly captured by Colonel Durand's troops, when the gateway was blown up by Aylmer; by the rocky mountain-side—up which Manners-Smith and Taylor clambered with their handful of men, and so outflanked the enemy's breastwork, built all along the edge of precipitous cliffs —till Nilt is left behind and other forts reached, near the gates of which are sitting groups of the very men who fought us only a few months before; past these and the shady apricot orchards and waving cornfields, now galloping along the level cultivated land, now descending to the rocky bed of a glacier torrent, then on to more village lands again, till the valley widens out and the towers of the chief's palace at Baltit are seen in the distance.

Here, a few miles from his capital, I was met by Mohammed Nazim and all his principal men, dressed up in the gorgeous Indian robes presented to them on various former occasions by British officers. We both dismounted and came forward on foot to greet each other, and I was able to recall to the chief how he had accompanied me through Hunza to Gilgit in 1889, and how we had met in Sarikol in the following year. Then we all mounted again and rode into Baltit, the capital of Hunza, a hundred or so of these rough picturesque fellows riding and running along by our side, and a band marching in front. It was a bright clear day of early autumn. Behind Baltit was a row of rocky peaks like the spires of a cathedral, and immediately overhanging the fort-palace was a rugged mass of mountain rising in a succession of precipices fifteen thousand feet above it.

My tent was pitched in an orchard of apricot trees, on a cool grassy plot, by the encampment of the detachment of a hundred Kashmir troops under Captain Bradshaw, who now preserved order in Hunza. This little camp was situated at the end of a spur facing down the valley, and from it we looked out over orchards and terraced fields to the great Rakapushi Peak filling up the end of the valley with a wall of snow. Away to the right was the fort-palace perched on an outstanding rock, and above it the peak, twenty-three thousand feet in height, whose summit seemed almost to overhang the fort. Then to the left was the Nagar valley, with snowy peaks, twenty-three and twenty-four thousand feet high, guarding it on all sides. No more romantic spot than this could be imagined.

The people, too, as I came to know them, proved to be particularly attractive. They are a manly race, with a hard, resolute look about them, and they are devoted to games and sport. They play polo with extraordinary zeal and energy, their chief being one of the best and keenest players, and they love dancing and music. At the same time, there is none of that aloofness and sullen hidden suspicion and hatred which often characterizes Pathan tribes, and they are ready and willing to attach themselves to British officers. They are undoubtedly the pick of the frontier, and every officer who has lived amongst them likes them.

For about two and a half months I lived in this delightful country, till the winter was approaching, and the beauties of the place were day by day increased by the wonderful autumn tints which the apricots and poplars take on, and the warm hues of red and yellow and gold contrasted with the glittering white of Rakapushi and the deep clear blue of the sky above. Then, as I was engaged in building rough quarters for the troops and myself for the winter, and converting the piles of old matchlocks, which had been collected after the war, into rude hoes and spades for the people, turning their swords into ploughshares, news arrived that trouble had occurred in Chitral, and Colonel Durand wrote to say that the Mehtar had been killed, and that he wished me to come at once to Gilgit with some Hunza levies.

On the frontier "at once" means at once, and in a little more than two hours after receiving Colonel Durand's letter I had packed up my things; handed over what little "office" there was to Lieutenant Gurdon; arranged for the Hunza levies to follow, and started on my ride of sixty-five miles to Gilgit. During daylight there was little difficulty, but after the sun had set, and when no stars appeared, and the night was pitch dark, the task of finding my solitary way along a mountain path by the side of steep cliffs and over troublesome rocks was no easy one. But at one o'clock that night I arrived without mishap, and at ten o'clock the next night the Hunza levies arrived also. They had traversed the sixty-five miles on foot in thirty-six hours, starting on the war-path at a moment's notice. And these the men that not a year before had been fighting against us!

Chitral, the country where the trouble had arisen, lies to the west of, and is a considerably larger and more important state than Hunza. Its population is estimated at about eighty thousand, and it is roughly about two hundred miles in length and one hundred and twenty in breadth. It is mountainous throughout, and only special parts of the valley bottom, where water can be laid on to the land, are inhabited. This state was ruled, till the close of 1892, by an astute old chief named Aman-ul-Mulk, who had welded together Chitral proper and Yasin into one state. Aman-ul-Mulk was over seventy years old in 1892. He had seventeen sons, and at his death it was known that there must be a scramble among these for the throne. At the end of August, 1892, he died, and the long-expected scramble began. The second son, Afzul-ul-Mulk, was in the fort at Chitral at the time of the death of his father, and he, of course, seized all the arms and treasure stored there, murdered those of his brothers whom he feared, collected an army, and set off to fight his elder brother, Nizam-ul-Mulk, who was away in Yasin. Nizam had little stomach for fighting, and, without much ado, ran away to Gilgit. Afzul was then recognized by the Government of India as *de facto* ruler of Chitral.

But a few weeks later another claimant for the throne appeared. This was Sher Afzul, a half-brother of the old Mehtar's, who had been driven from Chitral by that chief many years before, and who had ever since lived in exile in Afghan territory, almost forgotten. He now suddenly appeared upon the scene. He crossed into Chitral from Afghan territory by the Dorah

Pass, only forty-seven miles from the fort at Chitral, rode rapidly down the valley with a hundred or so of his adherents, collected others as he went along, and, on the following night, reached the fort. Afzul-ul-Mulk, hearing a noise, appeared upon the walls, and, in exposing himself, was shot dead on the spot. Had this unfortunate accident not occurred, he would, in all probability, have been able on the following day to have expelled Sher Afzul, but, now that he was dead, the people of Chitral eagerly gathered round Sher Afzul, who proclaimed himself their Mehtar. It was the news of this event that had reached Colonel Durand in Gilgit.

Nizam, the eldest son of the old Mehtar, and the rightful heir to the throne, was in Gilgit at the time the news of his brother's death reached that place. He at once signified to Colonel Durand his intention of moving against Sher Afzul, and started off towards Chitral with all the men he had with him and with some others of his adherents who had now come into Gilgit. Colonel Durand, at the same time, despatched two hundred and fifty rifles, two guns, and the Hunza and Nagar levies into Yasin, to strengthen his own position in the event of it becoming necessary to treat with Sher Afzul, and to preserve order in the western part of the district and in Yasin. Nizam was entirely successful in his move. He had one small skirmish with Sher Afzul's troops, and then Sher Afzul fled back to Afghan territory as rapidly as he had come. Nizam marched into Chitral and placed himself on the throne, being its fourth occupant within a space of a little over three months.

Nizam-ul-Mulk's first act, on ascending the throne, was to request Colonel Durand to send a British officer to him. He well knew the value of such an outward and visible sign that he was closely allied with the British Government, and he believed that the presence of a British officer in the country would prevent the recurrence of disturbances such as had already occurred. Accordingly, on January 1, 1893, a mission, under Dr. Robertson, left Gilgit. It consisted, besides Dr. Robertson, of Lieutenant Gordon and myself, and we had with us an escort of fifty Sikhs. To reach Chitral we had to cross the Shandur Pass, twelve thousand four hundred feet high, and it was now midwinter. Even near Gilgit snow fell frequently, and on the whole march of two hundred and twenty miles to Chitral it was only in very few places that the snow was not lying deep. At Ghiza, the last village at which we halted before crossing the pass, twenty-four miles from it, and situated at an elevation of ten thousand feet above sea-level, the thermometer was below zero, and the whole country, of course, deep in snow. Through this snow we made our way to the camping-ground of Langar, at the foot of the pass, where we spent the night before crossing it, the Sikh escort in some rough shelters which had been erected for them, and the officers in tents. We were fortunate in only having one or two frost-bites in our party, and these Bruce at once tackled, rubbing the men's feet till they said they would much rather have the frost-bite than the rubbing. A lanky Indian cook of mine, who had never seen snow in his life before coming to this frontier, was the worst, and implored Bruce and me to let go of him, as we rubbed the skin off his feet. We were fortunate in having a cloudy night, and it was consequently less cold than it would have been had the sky been clear; and the following day we plodded through the snow over the pass and down to Laspur, the first village on the Chitral side. Here we were met by the governor of the district and a number of notables, and two days later we reached the fort of Mastuj, where a year later I had to spend a dreary winter. Here we made our first halt, and even here the thermometer fell to three degrees below zero, and a bitter wind blew down the valley, which, like the valleys we had passed along the whole way from Gilgit, was narrow and hemmed in by lofty rocky mountains, now covered with snow, but generally bare and desolate looking. On January 25 we reached Chitral, the valley up to within a few miles of that place narrowing to little more than a gorge, with occasional open spaces where villages had been built. But about three miles above the fort of Chitral the valley widens out, and is here about two miles in width. The weather, too, in the lower parts was considerably milder, and we were able to ride into Chitral in our uniforms, without great-coats. The new Mehtar, Nizam-ul-Mulk, met us about three miles above Chitral, with a great cavalcade of his principal men, and we all rode in together. This was my first acquaintance with the prince, at whose side I was to remain for nearly two years. I found him to be a handsome man of about thirty-four years of age, very European in appearance, intelligent, and well-mannered; of medium height, thick-set, and strong. He was dressed in a suit of clothes intended to represent a British uniform, and he wore on his head the round cloth cap common in the country. About a mile outside Chitral the whole cavalcade halted, and we were shown some firing at a popinjay. At the top of a high mast an earthenware pot had been hung, and men galloped past firing at it. As we reached the fort, a salute was fired. The Mehtar, having accompanied the mission to the quarters which it was to occupy, then took leave of them, after declaring how warmly he desired to welcome them.

We had now had some opportunity of observing the Chitralis, and I cannot say that my own impression, at any rate, was a very favourable one. They seemed a gloomy and depressed people. They had about them none of the hard, determined look which the men of Hunza have; and, after coming from Hunza, I felt little attraction towards these rather sulky-looking Chitralis. These first impressions I had afterwards to modify, as I shall relate further on; but I record them, as they serve to show that the first impressions of these people are not always what will be subsequently proved correct. The country, too, now in the depth of winter, was as depressing as the people.

Except when crossing the Shandur Pass—and even that was not very exhilarating—we were always at the bottom of narrow valleys, with lofty mountains overhanging and enclosing them in. Not a blade of anything green was to be seen, for all that was not buried in snow was withered by the frost. All the trees were bare and sombre-looking, and the mud-built villages damp and cheerless. Chitral itself we found to be, not a town or even a large village, but a collection of little hamlets scattered over a stretch of cultivated land about three miles in length and a mile and a half in width, at the northern end of which, close by the river, stood a small fort, which formed the residence of the Mehtar. This was Chitral, a place at that time almost unknown to English people.

Our first month or two in Chitral was certainly not enlivening. We lived in a native house, without windows or chimneys, and with only a hole in the roof by which to let in the light (and the snow and the cold) and to let out the smoke (and the heat) of a fire lit in the middle of the floor. There was little to do out-of-doors, except to take a walk one day up and the next day down the valley, and the weeks wore by with monotonous regularity. But as spring came on the whole aspect changed. Through January and February we had frequent falls of snow, and the thermometer at night ranged from twelve degrees Fahrenheit to the freezing-point. But in March the snow cleared away from the valley bottom and the lower hillsides, the new grass began to sprout, the young corn-shoots appeared in the fields, little purple primulas and a beautiful yellow and crimson tulip bloomed out on the river-banks; then the willow trees were tinged with green as the young leaves budded out. By the beginning of April the apricot trees burst into blossom, and the valley was covered with clouds of white bloom, and then, as day by day the sunshine grew warmer, every tree—the magnificent planes, the poplars, the drooping willow, and the orchards of apricots, peaches, pear and apple trees—came into full leaf, and spring in all its freshness of beauty had blossomed into life.

With the spring the looks of the people lost their winter gloom. It would be hard for these mountain people to be anything but gloomy, or think of anything else than "stratagems and spoils," when all their surroundings, indoors and out, are so depressing as they are in winter, when there is no outdoor work to be done, and they can only brood and contemplate. But everything is different when spring comes on. Then they have to go out to work in the fields; they have the warm bright sunshine, and growing crops, and blooming orchards, and the fresh green of the trees to cheer them. During the winter we had had more than one scare of attacks and conspiracies and plots of various kinds. But as the people found more to occupy their minds, and as they saw the Mehtar establishing his position in the presence of the British mission in the country, these ugly rumours grew less frequent, and the disposition of the people more favourable.

We were now able to make little excursions, and Bruce and I had a very delightful climb up the ridge of mountains behind Chitral. Bruce had with him four Gurkhas from his regiment. Two of these had been with him on Sir William Conway's explorations and climbs in the Karakoram Range. He had also the appliances of Alpine mountaineering—ice-axes, ropes, climbing-irons, etc. So, for the first time in my life, I was able to do a climb in the orthodox Alpine-club manner. Our first night we spent on a grassy patch, high up the mountain-side, at the edge of a pine forest, and we immediately felt a sense of relief at having some breadth of view before us, something to look out upon instead of being cooped up in the narrow valley below. The next day we made our way along a ridge through deep snow, and bivouacked directly under the peak we were going to attack. Then, on the following morning, the ice-axes and ropes came into play, and Bruce and

VALLEY IN THE HINDU KUSH.

his Gurkhas showed their mountain craft. I was then able to realize how valuable is a training in mountaineering, and how useful are the Alpine appliances. Bruce took me up places which I should, of course, have attempted if I had been obliged, but which I should certainly not have cared to ascend in cold blood like this without the aid of rope and ice-axe. We finally reached a very narrow rock arête or ridge, and, climbing thence to its summit, found ourselves sitting astride of a razor-like ridge of limestone, with our legs on each side dangling over nearly sheer precipices. Just at the summit the rock was so sharp that it was impossible to stand up, and I doubt if we could even have sat except astride. We were at no great height, for the summit, according to our aneroid, was only thirteen thousand five hundred feet above sea-level; but this was the highest point in the immediate vicinity, and we were able to get a magnificent bird's-eye view of the Chitral valley and a good part of the country.

It is from a height like this that one can best appreciate what Chitral really is. It is just a sea of mountains. The peaks stand all round like the crests of a wave, sometimes of the same dull colour as the general mass, sometimes breaking upwards in crests of white snow. Ridge behind ridge the mountains rise, like the waves of the sea, and they finally toss themselves up into one great towering mass, and we saw straight before us, and only a few miles distant, the Tirich Mir, twenty-five thousand four hundred feet in height. For the most part these mountains are absolutely bare, and the whole country appears to be nothing but rock, till far down in the valley bottoms, at places where the water from some mountain torrent can be led on to cultivable ground, patches of green are seen. Even of the valley bottoms the whole lengths are not cultivated, and it is only where suitable soil has been washed down from the mountains and deposited in the valley, and when water can be brought on to this, that any cultivation is possible. So, of the whole floor of a valley, perhaps from one-eighth to one-sixth is all that would be cultivated. The valley bottoms form but a small proportion of the whole country, for they are generally mere gorges, and seldom widen out to a breadth of a mile. It may be imagined, therefore, that Chitral is not a rich or productive country.

CHAPTER XVII.

CHITRAL AND HER RULERS.

At the end of May Mr. Robertson and Lieutenant Bruce returned to Gilgit, and I was left in Chitral with Lieutenant Gordon and his fifty Sikhs. During the summer months, when we could meet at polo and in various out-of-door amusements, I was able to see more of the Mehtar and his people than had been possible during the winter. Three or four times a week the Mehtar and his principal men used to come to our house and sit out under the great plane trees in the garden for a good two hours, talking over every kind of subject. In our garden, as in most other gardens in Chitral, an earthen platform had been made under the shade of the plane trees. Here we spread carpets, and placed chairs for the Mehtar and ourselves; twenty or thirty of the chief men were allowed to sit round on the carpets, and the Mehtar's guards and servants stood about in the garden. Then tea, biscuits, sweetmeats, sherbet, and ices were served round to the Mehtar and his principal men, and conversation was carried on upon any topic which might happen to arise. I could not speak Chitrali sufficiently well to converse in that language, so the native political assistant, Jemadar Rab Nawaz Khan, a native officer in the Bengal cavalry, who had been resident in the country for nearly eight years, used to interpret. Generally I brought down illustrated newspapers or books, passed them round, and talked upon the various subjects which were suggested by the pictures.

Chitralis are quite illiterate, and certainly not a dozen in the country can either read or write. Even the Mehtar could not read; and I do not suppose there has ever been a Mehtar of Chitral who could. But these Chitralis could perfectly well understand pictures, not of things which they had never seen, such as ships, but pictures of men, animals, and natural objects, with which they were acquainted. When Colonel Lockhart's Mission visited the country in 1885-86, Dr. Giles took several photographs of the people, and other photographs had been taken of Chitralis who had travelled down to India. When I showed these photos to my visitors, I found that they could readily say who each man in the photo was; and when they saw photos of British officers who had visited Chitral, they were able to put the correct names to them. They had their own very definite ideas about beauty. In the illustrated papers, and in advertisements, there would often be fancy pictures or portraits of princesses or actresses, over which they would grow very enthusiastic, and they would generally select as the most beautiful very much the same types as a European would. But there was one very pretty picture in the advertisement of a soap-maker, who shall be nameless, which I thought they would certainly like; yet they said the lady in question was not worth looking at, and the reason they gave for this was because she had grey hair! There was no intention of the artist to give her grey hair, but in our prints we have what is really nothing more than a conventional sign for indicating the light falling on a subject, and they thought this light falling on the hair was grey hair.

The Mehtar used to grow very enthusiastic over some of the advertisements. One, in the *Field*, of an incubator for hatching eggs, excited his special curiosity, and when I explained to him that it was a machine for turning eggs into chickens, he wanted me to write off at once for one for him. A picture of a collapsible boat also won his admiration, and he told me if only he could have a boat like that he would take it every summer to the lake at the top of the Shandur Pass, and shoot ducks there. From the pictures, he and those of his men who had been down to India were led on to talk of the various wonders which they had seen there, and I used to encourage them to talk of such things, for it gave them an opportunity of appealing to me to corroborate, before their fellow-countrymen, the truth of their description. The Mehtar had himself been down to Calcutta, and he complained that when he came back nobody would believe the stories he told them. His old father, Aman-ul-Mulk, had believed him up to a certain point; he had believed about the railway and the telegraph, for he thought it might be possible that men who could make such good rifles as the English did, might also be able to invent some arrangements for sending men and messages rapidly along; but when his son told him that the English made ice in the middle of the hot weather, he said he could not possibly believe that, for God only could do such a thing. He said he drew the line there, and told his son he need not tell him any more of his stories!

When, however, the Mehtar or his men told such stories before me, and I corroborated them, the Chitralis gradually came to believe they were true; and, both for the sake of enlightening them about India, and of seeing what had specially struck those men who had been there, I used to encourage the Mehtar to talk of his experiences. I am inclined to think that what he liked best was driving about in a "buggy" in Calcutta. He was allowed the free use of an open victoria with a pair of horses, and he liked to drive about all day long, lying back in it and enjoying himself. He said he thought one day of making a road in Chitral, on the three or four miles of flat by the fort, and getting a carriage up in pieces and driving in it. The Mint, and the rows upon rows of guns laid up in the arsenal at Calcutta, 'also struck his imagination. Chitralis who have heard of the mint can never understand how it is we can ever refuse to give them as many rupees as they like to ask for. They are told that we have a machine which turns out rupees in bucketsful without ever stopping, and they think that this stream of rupees is like a stream of water which never stops. They never consider that the silver for the rupees must be found first of all, and their only idea is that when we want money we have only to take a bucket down to the Mint and draw off rupees like water from a fountain. Chitralis have just the same ideas on the subject of money as children have on the riches of their parents. A boy at school cannot understand why his father, who has ever so many hundreds of pounds, is so chary about giving him even one; and the Chitralis, when they know that the Government of India has this fountain of wealth down at Calcutta, do not understand why British officials should refuse to give them the few rupees they ask for. It may well be imagined, therefore, how indignant the Mehtar was when, on taking with him down to Calcutta thirty-three instead of the thirty men he had arranged for, he was asked to pay the railway fares for the additional three men.

There is no doubt that the Mehtar derived very great advantage from his visit to India, and my task in dealing with him was very considerably lightened from his possessing some idea of what the power and resources of the British Government really are. An intelligent prince, like Nizam-ul-Mulk, who visits India, recognizes how backward his country is. He sees the advantage to be gained from the improvement to be seen in India, and he knows that the arguments of the old-fashioned party, who say that things have done very well all these years and that there is, therefore, no need for change, are not sound. He was, therefore, always wishing to make improvements in his country—most, it is true, for his own, and not for his people's, benefit, for Nizam, like most Oriental rulers, was a very selfish man; but even then their adoption would have done much good in the country, by showing the people some higher standard, either of comfort or convenience, to which they might aspire. He had already begun to improve his house, and he was most anxious to get a few native masons up from India to teach his people to build properly, and, with the marble which is to be obtained within a few miles from Chitral, to build a good house for himself. He wanted his men taught blasting, too, so as to be able to construct watercourses by which new lands could be irrigated, and he was always asking me if I could not have up some one to drive artesian wells to irrigate a large plain above Chitral. With a British officer beside him, therefore, to advise him, and keep him from branching out into any useless expenditure, he might have done much good work.

In dealings between him and the British Government much good accrued from his visit to India. The great art in dealing with these wild chiefs is to guide them and make use of them without actually employing force. The British Government does not wish to destroy their independence, and, in fact, would be only too pleased if they were really strong enough to be absolutely independent. But they are not, and never could be, strong enough for this; and, as they are the neighbours of a great empire, the rulers of that empire have to ask certain things of them, the chief of which, as I stated above, is that they should place their foreign relations under the control of the suzerain Power. Nizam had been to India, he knew the resources of Government, and he knew that his interests lay in the preservation of a close alliance with the British. He, therefore, always acted with that object. By far the larger number of his people did not, however, know the real strength of Government, and when Nizam was murdered at the beginning of 1895, they rashly plunged their country into a war with the British, and, of course, suffered for it. A number of them, whom I met in Chitral just after the war was over, told me that, had they known that we were so powerful, they never would have thought of fighting us. But they did not know, and both they and we had to suffer the consequence of their ignorance. I always think these chiefs are rather in the position of children. We do not want to beat them or cow them. We want them rather to grow up strong and vigorous, and, perhaps, to become eventually able to look after their own affairs themselves. But we have to keep them straight, and, when they run crooked, we have to punish them. To have an effective influence over them it is necessary that we should make our resources known to them, that they may be fully aware of the advantages of keeping on friendly terms with us, and the evil effects which are likely to follow from their going astray.

With Nizam-ul-Mulk I never found any difficulty in the discharge of my duties, and, as by his astuteness and common sense I was saved from the necessity of ever having to make any disagreeable demand upon him, when the British agency was subsequently withdrawn from Chitral to Mastuj, he kept repeatedly asking that it might be sent back to Chitral again, so that he might have a British officer at his side.

But while Nizam and his men interested themselves with what we did in India, I was no less interested in noting how they lived in Chitral, and one of the points which I most carefully observed was their system of government. This system is absolutely despotic. There could scarcely be a greater despot than a Mehtar of Chitral. Nominally, everything in the country—man, women, child, and beast—belong to him, and the whole of the land, and every house as well. He can take away one man's wife and give her to another. He can dispose of the daughters to whom he likes. He can give away a man's house or his land just as he wishes. And he can, of course, administer any sort of punishment that may please him. In addition to this, he may call upon any men to serve him, and he may summon the whole country, if he so wishes, to go to war. All this he may do theoretically. Practically, of course, by custom and by public opinion, he has to keep the exercise of this authority within reasonable bounds. Still I have known cases of wives being given away when the husbands have committed some offence, this being considered a punishment to the husband alone, and the woman being supposed to have no feelings.

The method by which the Mehtar carries on his government is by durbars, and as this is a very interesting form of government, and one of which the original simplicity is likely to disappear as the country comes in closer touch with British method, I wish to draw especial attention to it. Twice every day the Mehtar holds durbar; the morning durbar is at about eleven or twelve o'clock, and a second is held at ten o'clock at night. In the summer-time the morning durbar was regularly held under the huge plane trees round the fort, but frequently Nizam-ul-Mulk held them somewhere along the river-bank where he was hawking or shooting. The evening durbar was held in a hall or room inside the fort. At these durbars the Mehtar sat with his legs crossed on a broad low seat, which serves as a sort of throne, the members of his family sat near him, and the other principal men range themselves in a semi-circle in front of him, every one except the Mehtar squatting on the floor. A few guards and servants were stationed behind the Mehtar. There are no very formal proceedings, though very strict etiquette is observed in many particulars. The Mehtar comes out of his private apartments, and is followed to the durbar hall by his attendants; then he seats himself, the people squat down after him, and informal conversation commences. Perhaps some one has come in from the frontier or the provinces, and the Mehtar asks what the news is. Whatever news there may be the Mehtar discusses with the principal men, and they give their opinion about it. Then some one who has a case to bring before the Mehtar for his decision will advance, kiss his feet, and state his case. The people at the upper end of the watercourse of his village have taken all the water, and left none for his lands in the lower part of the village. The Mehtar turns to the durbar and asks if any one knows about this. Some men from the village will then say what they know; a conversation about the matter will follow; then the Mehtar will give orders as he thinks fit, and the matter is there and then disposed of. No record of any case is kept, but, as every case is decided in full durbar, there is generally some one present who remembers former decisions; and, cases being usually simple and not very numerous, it is possible to administer justice satisfactorily on these primitive lines, both civil and criminal cases being disposed of in this manner.

While these conversational trials are being carried on, dinner is brought in on a number of trays and dishes, some special dishes being laid before the Mehtar, and the remainder being placed before the men in durbar. Just a few members of the Mehtar's family, whose rank is undeniable, are permitted to eat from the same dish with him; the rest eat out of the common dishes placed round the durbar. The meals consist of bread, rice, and stews of meat; in the summer fruit is served round, and the Mehtar and a few principal men have tea. No spirituous liquor of any kind is served, for the people are Mohammedans. The food is taken up with the fingers, water being handed round before and after the meal for washing the hands.

All the time the dinner is being eaten, the Mehtar is quietly disposing of affairs; conversation about the cases before him is kept up, and, perhaps with his mouth full, he will give his decision in the matter. Often, when Nizam-ul-Mulk held his durbars by the river, or on a shooting-expedition, a man would rush up to say there were some duck by the water, or markhor on the mountain-side, and the Mehtar and his men would jump up in wild excitement and go off with their hawks and their rifles, and leave the affairs of state to look after themselves.

All this seems very irregular, but the system has many good points about it, the chief of which is that the ruler and people see each other face to face, and know each other man to man. There is an excellent custom in Chitral, by which every man of importance in the country is expected to come down to the capital to attend these durbars for at least a couple of months every year, and each village has to send a contingent to serve the Mehtar, either in his guard or in some household capacity. An ebb and flow of men from the provinces to the capital is thus set up, and every man of any note becomes intimately acquainted with the Mehtar and the Mehtar with him, and the greater number of the lower classes also come to know their ruler personally. So intimately, indeed, does the Mehtar in this way become acquainted with his men, that I found Nizam-ul-Mulk knew the name, the personal history, and the character of nearly every man in his country. Since he was a small boy he had attended his father's durbars, and so, seeing year after year the relays of men coming to attend them, he had got to know every man of any position, and most of the common people as well. This personal intimacy between the ruler and the ruled, and the method by which the ruler administers justice and governs his country face to face with his people, and not by deputy and by paper, are really good points in the system of government in Chitral. I have related how despotic is the authority of this Mehtar, but the reader will see that by this system of durbars the people also have a voice in the conduct of the affairs of the country, and it would be impossible for a ruler to go far against the wishes of his people.

Though the Mehtar has so absolute authority, he is bound to consult, and perhaps even defer to, the wishes of the Adamzadas, or nobles, for he is not so much the ruler over a number of inferior people as the chief of a number of chiefs, who have each their own train of followers. In old days Chitral was split up into a number of little chieftainships. The villages are all separated from each other by strips of barren land, and nearly every village, and, at any rate, every valley, had its separate chief. In the course of time these were federated together under the chief of the village of Chitral. He was to be the head chief, and would lead them all in war, for instance; but it was understood that each separate chief had rule over his own followers. Gradually, however, the power of the lesser chiefs dwindled, and that of the Chitral chief, or Mehtar, increased. But even now there are traces of the original state of affairs, and the Adamzadas, the descendants of these minor chiefs, are very jealous of the remnants of authority still left them, and often oppose the orders of the Mehtar. They are now, indeed, a very unsatisfactory element of the Chitral state. They have little authority, but an immense idea of their importance, and they consider it necessary to stand upon their dignity on every possible occasion. They are sullenly hostile to every Mehtar, and jealous of his authority, and I have even known some of them refuse to turn their men out to resist an invasion of the country. The greater part of them are thoroughly hostile to the British alliance, because they have heard that the British treat rich and poor, small and great, exactly alike, and attach no importance to rank. They therefore fear that, as British influence increases in the state, their power will still further diminish, and they especially fear that their followers, who are on much the same footing as the serfs were in Russia, will, under the pressure of British influence, gain more freedom, till they become independent of them. However much, therefore, the Mehtar may realize that his position depends upon the closeness of his alliance with the British Government, he has always to contend against the sullen opposition of these effete remnants of a bygone age.

I have said that the Mehtar has to consult the feelings of these Adamzadas. On all important occasions, beside those who may happen to be in Chitral at the time, the principal Adamzadas throughout the country, and perhaps also the governors of the various districts (except the distant districts of Yasin) are summoned to Chitral, and the Mehtar holds a general council of state. Such councils are held when an invasion takes place, or when it is proposed to attack some neighbouring country, or when questions of foreign policy arise, such as whether the state should ally itself with the British Government or with Afghanistan. On occasions like these, all the chief men in the country would be asked down to Chitral, and the matter discussed in durbar. I was particularly struck by the openness with which the affairs of the country are discussed. While we make a great mystery of our policy, and conduct our business by confidential correspondence, the members of one department of Government not letting even the members of another department know what is taking place, in Chitral the affairs of state are discussed openly in durbar, and it is only very confidential matters that the Mehtar talks over separately with a few of his most trusted advisers. So little indeed do the Chitralis resort to secrecy, that several times I have known the Mehtar, when a letter has been brought him, and his own clerk was not present, hand it over to my native assistant, and ask him to read the contents to him.

Out of the general assembly the Mehtar naturally, and as it were involuntarily, selects certain men whom he trusts and consults more than the rest. If they live at a distance from Chitral, he will summon them oftener, and keep them longer. If they live at Chitral, he will have them repeatedly by his side. An informal cabinet council thus exists, and these men might be called "his Majesty's advisers." It is possible to trace in the council of Chitral, as in councils of men of every kind, the progressive and the stationary parties; the men who wish to see improvements brought in—who would, for instance, like to have roads made through the country, the telegraph brought in, and the men properly armed and drilled; and the men who, arguing that what was good enough for their fathers is good enough for them, are opposed to innovations of every kind. These latter, in Chitral, are in the majority. A shudder of horror went through the country when the late Mehtar, Nizam, one day took it into his head to give his wives and female relations a treat in the country, and had a picnic for them up the river. "No Mehtar had ever done such a thing before!" the people said. "So why should this one make such a change?"

We see, then, a state with the fully developed system of government of modern European countries here still in embryo. The control is imperfect. Governors are appointed to the outlying provinces of the state, and these exercise a very independent authority. There is no elaborate system of reporting to the central authority, and very little reference to it. As I have said, few men in the country can read or write, so correspondence is reduced to a minimum. For several months the Governor of Mastuj, where I was stationed, had no one by him who could read, and on the few occasions on which he did receive letters, he brought them round to my clerk to read for him. It might be imagined that, where there is so little connection with the central authority, the outlying provinces would gradually drop off and become independent. But there is in Chitral an excellent method by which just sufficient touch is kept up between the capital and the provinces to ensure the integrity of the country. Every now and then the governors have to come in to Chitral itself, to pay their respects to the Mehtar, and in this way, and in the manner already noticed, by which all the notables and a certain number of the poorer classes have to come in to Chitral every year, the Mehtar is kept in touch with all parts of his dominion.

This, briefly, is the system of government in Chitral as

NIZAM-UL-MULK, MEHTAR OF CHITRAL.

I knew it, and I think a very remarkable point to note in the practical working of the system is the rapidity and directness with which affairs are carried on. This, to an official working under the ponderous Government of India, seems as remarkable as the deliberate movements of the elephantine British Government appear to the Chitralis. The largest question that affects their state they can settle in a few days. Though they have no telegraphs, they can, in cases of urgent importance, send messages at the rate of sixty miles a day. The whole country can spring to arms at a moment's notice, and hundreds of men be moving to the frontier at twenty miles and more a day, a few hours after they receive the order. I have known a governor more than sixty years of age ride his sixty-five miles into Chitral with a large following on foot, in a couple of days. No time is wasted in useless correspondence; there are no records to be referred to; the matter is discussed and settled there and then, man to man, and action immediately follows. People accustomed to rapid decisions and immediate action of this kind are unable, therefore, to understand why the British Government, with its telegraphs and its thousands of troops kept permanently ready for action, should be so slow moving. A question arises upon which the decision of Government is required, the agent in Chitral says he will refer it to the agent in Gilgit, the agent in Gilgit refers to the Resident in Kashmir, he again to the Government of India, and they to the Secretary of State; and back through all these channels comes the answer, months after the question first arose. "With all your telegraphs, why cannot you get answers quicker?" is what the Chitralis were always saying to me. And then the action seems so slow to them. They are astonished at the force of the blow when it does come, but if a blow is to come at all, why does it not come sooner? If, for instance, Government did not intend to allow Umra Khan to take Chitral in the winter of 1894–95, why did not they oppose him at once, in January, when he first invaded the country, instead of months later, in April? With all their organization and rapid means of communication, their telegraphs, railways, and roads, Government, as the Chitralis think, ought to be more, not less, prompt in decision and rapid in action than themselves; and it is not to be wondered at, therefore, that they fret and chafe under the indecisive answers which British officers often have to give them, and that they sometimes go running off with the bit between their teeth.

Fuller knowledge modified my first impression of the character of the Chitralis. On first entering the country in the depth of winter, and when the people were panting after the recent struggles for the Mehtarship, I found them, as I have already stated, anything but attractive. They then had a gloomy, depressed appearance, which repelled one from them, and it was not till the spring and summer came on that they showed any brightness at all. But I saw them at their best, and, as I believe, in their natural state, in the autumn of 1893, when I went for a tour through the country with the Mehtar. I then took no escort with me, and travelled with him more as a private guest than as a Government official. We rode along together the whole of each march, which, with halts for hawking, occupied the entire day, and in the evenings, after I had had my dinner, the Mehtar would come to my tent and talk sometimes till midnight. The Mehtar was accompanied by a large number of followers, and was met at each village by every man in it; in the country, moreover, much of the formality and etiquette of the capital wore off, and I was able to see the ruler and his people in their natural life.

The Mehtar was on this occasion in the very best of spirits. No man could more thoroughly enjoy himself than Nizam-ul-Mulk. He had little courage or strength of character, but he at any rate knew how to enjoy life, and I picture him now riding along on a comfortable, easy-going pony, with his leg thrown lazily over the high peak of the saddle, as he grew tired of riding astride, his falconers all about him ready to fly a hawk at anything which might appear, while he now and then turned round to his brothers, saying, "See how lucky I am! I have all that my father had, and have no trouble in looking after it, for Government sees that I am not attacked. I can go out hawking and shooting just as much as ever I please, and enjoy myself as I like." He was passionately fond of sport of all kinds, and as we rode through the country together he was constantly pointing up the hill-sides and telling me how he had shot ibex or markhor there. "A *splendid* day I had there!" he would say, and give a story of some great shoot he had had. He was also about the best polo-player in the country. All day long he used to talk of his shooting experiences, and then he would tell us that in the following year he was going to take me to another part of his country, and then I must take him to England. He said he would like to go as the guest of Government, as he was when he went to India; but, anyhow, he meant to go, and if Government would not invite him, he would save up money and go himself. Then, in the evening, as he sat in my tent with a few of his most trusted men, he would talk on every possible subject, and I was astonished to note his quick intelligence, his receptive memory, and his insatiable curiosity. He used to ask about our system of government, and I would tell him of Parliament and of the two great parties in the state; how Mr. Gladstone would be in power at one time, and Lord Salisbury at another. He at first thought this was a bad system, as it looked as if the country was split into two; but when I explained to him how the two parties kept balancing each other, the one preventing things going too fast, and the other seeing that they went fast enough, then he said he understood why it was we kept progressing so steadily. Asiatics have only one idea of greatness: to them that country is the greatest which conquers most; and he knew the history of how we had advanced up from Calcutta and gradually conquered the whole of India.

In regard to the people, I found them as gay and cheerful as could be, now that their harvest was in, and the question of the Mehtarship was apparently settled. At each village we arrived at, crowds would come out to meet the Mehtar, a band played in the cavalcade, and, if a halt was to be made, there would certainly be polo, firing at the popinjay, or dancing. The Chitralis love amusement. Gloominess is not their natural trait at all; and, when they can be seen free from restraint, there is something very attractive about them. All day, as we rode along on the march, they used to be chaffing and laughing, and they are then as wild and simple and careless as children. We were crossing a pass one day; it was over thirteen thousand feet high, and snow was falling heavily the whole way over; but when a man came up to say there were some ibex (wild goats) in a neighbouring valley, they all wanted to go off after the ibex, although doing so would have meant sleeping out on the pass without tents. Whenever news of any sport like this reaches them, they all shout with excitement, and become as keen about it as a boy. On this occasion the ibex disappeared before we got up to them, so we proceeded over the pass, and waited at the foot of it, on the opposite side, for the baggage to come up. The Mehtar had a couple of hundred men with him, but only he had a tent, and as there was no village, they had to sleep in the open. A huge fire was lighted, and we all sat round in a circle till the Mehtar's and my tent arrived, and, in spite of the snow and the cold, I never saw men more cheery. Then, as we marched on down the Turikho valley the next few days, at each village, as we approached, the heights were lined with matchlock-men firing a rude *feu de joie*, and all the principal men and the Mehtar and I would join in a wild game of polo, every one galloping furiously about, quite regardless of everybody else, shouting with excitement, reaching far out of the saddle to hit the ball, running into each other, and enjoying themselves thoroughly.

In camp, and on the march, these men used often to talk over British officers, and I was astonished to note the keen interest they took in everything a British officer did, and whatever he did was always reported in exaggerated terms. Men would come in who had seen the British officers at Gilgit, or at the posts on the road between Chitral and Gilgit, and they would be questioned closely as to what they were like, and what they were doing. If they had done anything to the satisfaction of the Chitralis, these impressionable people would become excessive in their praises of the officer. If the officer had done something to offend them, they would unreasonably denounce him. Chitralis are always in extremes, never in the middle. They are a people eminently needing and liking a *leader*. They hate—and this is a very common characteristic of Asiatics—to have to act for themselves. They want some one to tell them what to do, and they will be only too glad to follow him. In the recent campaign they got in a huff with the English, and rushed off in their extreme impulsive way against them. They thought they saw in Sher Afzul a man who could lead them; they swarmed round him, begging to be led. Such people it ought not to be difficult for us to deal with. They have no inherent love of fighting merely for fighting's sake, as the Afghan tribes have. They fight when their country is attacked, and they fight in a desultory, half-hearted sort of way, in the usual fratricidal struggles for the throne which regularly occur on the death of a Mehtar. But they would much prefer stopping at home, eating fruit in their shady orchards, playing polo, and watching dancing. And as long as their old and cherished customs are not interfered with, and as long as they are not too much worried to carry loads and furnish supplies, they will remain contented.

But one innovation must certainly come with the presence of the British in the country: they will be taught the value and the need of money. I once asked a Chitrali why all the men of a certain valley, in a remote part of Chitral, were so much better, more loyal, and of simpler manners than the other Chitralis. He replied that they were so because they were off the main line of traffic, and no strangers and traders from outside came to corrupt them, make them buy things they did not want, and cause them to be discontented because they had not the things the traders brought round. In other parts of Chitral the people were exposed to all these temptations, and were corrupted by them. It seems hard to break in on the simplicity of such a people, and teach them a lust for wealth. But if a desire for money may bring with it some disadvantages, it cannot but contribute also to the strengthening of the character of the people. In some of these upper valleys the inhabitants had, until recently, no idea of the use or value of money. They had few wants. Their fields produced what they required in the way of food, and the wool from their sheep supplied them with material from which they could weave their clothing. If a man had need of a coat, he would give another a sheep or some corn for it. What, therefore, did they want with the round pieces of silver called rupees? They could use them as ornaments, but for anything else they were useless. But they have gradually been learning that with these rupees they can buy cotton goods, salt, looking-glasses, matches, iron implements, knives, scissors, needles, etc., from traders; and so they begin to want rupees.

A man walked more than sixty miles once to see me, and sat down on the ground while I was at breakfast in the garden, and then suddenly jumped up, kissed my feet, and said he had come all the way to ask me for five rupees. I said I would be very glad to give him five rupees, if he would go up the hillside and cut some firewood for me. He said he could not stay away from his home, and had to go back the next day. I told him that in that case I would give him the five rupees, but when I came to his village in a month's time, I should expect him to do work for me there, in return for the money. He went off with the rupees, delighted. But, an hour or two afterwards, returned with them, gave them back to me, and said he would not take them, as he did not like to have to do the work. That is just the fault of the Chitralis—they hate work. They love to enjoy themselves, but they hate having to exert themselves. And if the introduction of trade into their country can induce them to want rupees, and if they can appreciate that to get rupees they have to work, a stimulus will have been given them which must be beneficial. One of the greatest difficulties which British officers, in countries like Chitral, have to contend with is this lack of inducement to work. Roads have to be constructed, supplies have to be carried, work of all kinds has to be done, but the difficulty is to obtain the workers. There are numbers of men about, but they do not want to work, they much prefer being left alone; and in many cases they have to be compelled to work, even though they are liberally paid for what they do. Among people of this disposition it is absolutely necessary to instil a wholesome love of money, and as they come to appreciate its value and its uses, they will work more readily, become less lazy, and obtain the means of clothing and feeding themselves better, and of improving their houses. And this incentive to work, and the improvement of their environment, cannot fail to have some good effect upon their characters. As they come to work harder and more regularly, it may be expected that they will become less impulsive and more steady and trustworthy. And if this much can be obtained, good, and not harm, will have resulted from instilling into these simple people the love of money.

Every one who has seen them in their present primitive

state, however, must hope that it may never fall to their lot to be swallowed up in the flood of British administration, and that they may have rulers of sufficient ability to preserve to the country its independence. While the state is ruled by one of the old reigning family, the British officers can exercise over it a useful and beneficial influence, give character to the people, and infuse vigour into them.

In October of the year 1894, after making a tour down from Mastuj, which had then become my head-quarters, to Chitral, in the company of Mr. George Curzon, I left the country thinking never to see it again. Nizam-ul-Mulk, the Mehtar, had given Mr. Curzon and myself the warmest possible welcome at his capital. We had played polo together, and dined together, and he rode up some miles with us to say good-bye. Everything seemed as quiet as it ever can be in these volcanic countries of Central Asia. But not three months had passed when Nizam was murdered by his own half-brother, and trouble after trouble followed, till the British agent was besieged in Chitral fort, two detachments sent up, and a relief expedition on a large scale had become necessary. I again visited Chitral, this time as special correspondent of the *Times*, and arrived there a week after the siege had been raised. But the history of these events has been treated of separately, and I will here close the narrative of my travels, adding only a chapter or two on a few general impressions I formed in carrying them out.

CHAPTER XVIII.

THE MISSIONARY QUESTION IN CHINA.

> "I venerate the man whose heart is warm,
> Whose hands are pure, whose doctrine and whose life,
> Coincident, exhibit lucid proof
> That he is honest in the sacred cause."
>
> COWPER.

BEFORE recording the general impressions formed in my mind in the course of my travels, I am anxious to say something on the subject of missionary enterprise in China, because I have thought that a few words on this question from one who has seen missionaries at work in the remotest corners of the Chinese Empire may be of interest to readers in England at the present time, when the recent massacres in China have directed marked attention to the matter. I do not think that a mere casual traveller like myself ought to presume to judge in too assured a way the many really earnest men who, taking their lives in their hands, have gone out to impart to the Chinese a religion which they believe would help to elevate and rouse those ignorant of its blessings. Many of these men have devoted years to the study of the question, and they have had practical experience in dealing with the Chinese. It would ill befit a passing traveller, therefore, to undertake to say whether this or that method of proselytizing was good or the reverse, or to judge whether the missionaries have been successful or not.

But it is part of the duty of a traveller to observe and

record his observations for what they are worth for the benefit of those who are not so fortunate as himself in being able to penetrate to little-visited regions. And perhaps the impressions formed by one who has now had a varied experience of dealing with peoples of other religions than his own may not only be of interest to the people at home, but may also prove of some help to the workers on the spot. These latter will, at any rate, know that interest is taken in their work, and if criticism is sometimes hostile, they will remember that it is only by criticism and opposition that high standards ever are kept up. If no interest was shown in the work, if the traveller merely passed by on the other side, and never recorded a single impression of it, and if no criticism were ever offered, assuredly the standard would lower, the zeal would flag, and listlessness come on.

I may say at once, then, that my sympathies are entirely with the missionaries, and having seen the noble men I have met with in the far interior of China, and realized the sacrifices they have made, I say that the hearts of all true Englishmen and of all true Christian nations ought to go out to encouraging and helping those who have given up everything in this life to do good to others. I only wish that those who from the prosperous, comfortable homes of their native country so severely criticize missionary enterprise, could see one of those splendid French missionaries whom I met in North Manchuria, and who had gone out there for his life and would never see his home again. I feel sure that any fair-minded Englishman would see that this was a real man—a man to whom his sympathies might truly go out, and who was really likely to contribute to the elevation of the human race.

All missionaries are not of this same high standard. But because some missionaries have found their strength inadequate for the task before them, and have discovered that the fire of enthusiasm has died out in the clear light of everyday life, till they remain but burnt-out lamps by the way, it does not follow that the great Christian work of helping others is to be abandoned, and hundreds of English men and women asked to return home and acknowledge that the work to which they had devoted their lives, and for which their fathers before them had spent and often sacrificed their lives, was not worth doing.

Surely the true spirit of the English nation is one of sympathy with brave men who risk their lives as freely and fearlessly as any soldier for what they believe to be the good and right. Turn away those who have flagged by the wayside, and show the contempt for them that they deserve; but do not let the work of the *true* missionaries be allowed to suffer and be despised because of these. Readers who have followed me through these pages will have seen that good work is being done by the missionaries in some places at least, and let missionary enterprise be judged by the achievements of such men as these, and not simply of those who, living on the fringes of civilization, enjoying all its luxuries and comforts, and devoting but a fraction of their time to true missionary work, have deserved the sneers which have been thrown at them. These latter are the men who are most commonly met with, and the real workers are usually only seen by the few travellers who penetrate inland. But it is no more right to judge by these faint-hearted ones of the whole work done by missionaries, than it is to judge of an army in the field by the men who, from physical unfitness or known lack of energy, have been left behind at the base.

Nor should the work of missionaries be judged of by statistics of converts. Statistics are utterly valueless in cases of this sort. It is impossible to define, in the first place, what a convert is. The usual idea is that a man becomes a convert when he is baptized; but I have known a dying man baptized without his knowing anything about it, and surely he could not be claimed as a convert! Conversion means the changed state of the whole person; and the whole person, especially when he is a stolid Chinaman, changes very slowly indeed, so that it is impossible to say exactly when and where he has become a new man. I think, then, that those who have had most to do with peoples of other religions than the Christian, and have realized how difficult and slow the change from one state to another must be—and how valueless, if ever it is effected rapidly—will have the least faith in any mere statistics of converts to Christianity.

But, on the other hand, men who have studied the whole effect of Christianity upon European civilization, and have traced the first germ, planted nearly two thousand years ago, growing and expanding, till it influenced all the nations of Europe;—those who compare the state of society before that germ was implanted, with the state of society at the present day, have recognized what marvellous good the Christian religion has done. Men may not agree as to the truth of many of the doctrines which have become encrusted on to the central truth and essence of Christianity, but all can see the truth and force of the primary Christian doctrine of love toward their neighbour. And the results of the infusing of this principle into the human race are evident in the increased amount of sympathy displayed by European nations.

A well-informed writer in the *Times*, in the winter of 1894-95, stated that in London alone the amount annually given for charity by contributions, by legacies, and by the interest on legacies, did not fall far short of twenty million sterling. Every Christian country has numbers of benevolent institutions for the sick, the aged, the orphans, the lame, the blind, the deaf, the dumb, the weak-minded, and the fallen. And not for men and women only, but for horses, dogs and cats, and other domestic pets. Contrasted with the state of feeling one notices in Asiatic countries at the present day, there is, too, among Christians, a markedly deeper sensitiveness to suffering or oppression in any form. Such barbarities as those of the recent Armenian atrocities are thought little of among Asiatics. Through the Christian nations in Europe and America they send a thrill of horror, and the sympathy evoked for the sufferers shows itself in the practical form of active measures for preventing such atrocities for the future. We have, again, the case of one Christian nation spending millions of pounds to release slaves owned by its subjects. Sympathy is, of course, not unknown in Asiatic countries, and the devotion with which the natives of India provide for their old or infirm relations is worthy of all praise. But I think that every one who looks at an Asiatic nation, as a whole, and at a Christian nation, will agree that, in the latter, the sympathetic feelings are far more highly developed generally.

If, then, European nations have in the main derived so much benefit from the adoption of the Christian religion from one of the peoples of Asia, surely they are justified in trying to impart it to peoples of another part of the same continent. And they are not only justified in doing so, but it is human nature that they should. Christians cannot help feeling, when they are brought in contact with men of other religions, that they have a higher and truer idea of the Deity, and of their relations to the Deity—which is religion—than have the devotees of any other religion. They see that that portion of the human race which has embraced the Christian religion has progressed more than any other, and they naturally desire to impart to others those doctrines which they feel have done so much good to themselves. This is a natural and reasonable feeling, and is the mainspring of all missionary enterprise.

It is, however, in the method of imparting their own convictions to those who profess other religions, that some missionaries may be criticized. There are some whom we might call fanatical missionaries, who imagine that the Christian religion, with all the doubtful doctrines which have been hung on to it—as such doctrines do hang on to religions of every type, as time goes on—is all right, and that every other religion is all wrong. In uncompromising language they denounce the religion which differs from their own, and all that is connected with it. They tell men who have been brought up from their childhood in it—and whose fathers, for hundreds, and perhaps thousands, of years before them, have believed the truth of it —that they are to be damned eternally; that all they believe is wrong; and that unless they can believe in doctrinal Christianity, they will not be saved. Assertions like this, delivered by men very often of little culture, and little knowledge of the world and of human nature, naturally invite hostility. Mohammedans, Buddhists, Confucianists, feel that there is some right in what they profess, and they resent a stranger, who very often is ignorant of what the tenets of their religion really are, denouncing them, and trying to force his own ideas so rudely upon them. And these "heathen" have reason. Students of their religions say that, in many points, these coincide with the Christian; and, from experience among Mohammedans and Buddhists, I can say that, practically, in their lives they often work on very Christian-like principles.

I have found, too, at least among Mohammedans, that such general principles as doing to others as one would be done by one's self, and the existence of a Deity ruling the universe, are thoroughly understood and appreciated, though the means for acting up to them are not always available.

Europeans who have lived in these strange lands, perhaps for years, away from their own church—among people of a different religion to their own; people whom they have been accustomed to hear spoken of as heathen, and, consequently, destined for eternal punishment—find themselves taking note of these men, observing their natures, and studying the kind of life they lead. And when it is found that the followers of one religion after another lead lives not so clearly worse than the lives led by Christians, as to merit all the distinction of punishment between hell and heaven; when it is found, too, that the follower of each of these religions is just as sure as the Chrisitian is that his particular religion is the true one, and all others false, then the Christian stranger begins to question whether he is wholly right in regarding the "heathen" as only destined for damnation, and their religion as so utterly wrong.

At the same time the truth gradually dawns upon him that religion is universal, and an essential part of human nature. Of the truth of this I have been deeply impressed upon my travels. I remember the rude Mongols, far away in the midst of the Gobi Desert, setting apart in their tents the little altar at which they worshipped. I recall nights spent in the tents of the wandering Kirghiz, when the family of an evening would say their prayers together; I think of the Afghan and Central Asian merchants visiting me in Yarkand, and in the middle of their visits asking to be excused while they laid down a cloth on the floor and repeated their prayers; of the late Mehtar of Chitral, during a morning's shooting among the mountains, halting, with all his court, for a few minutes to pray; and, lastly, of the wild men of Hunza, whom I had led up a new and difficult pass, pausing as they reached the summit to offer a prayer of thanks, and ending with a shout of "Allah!"

In all these there was a religious sentiment deeply rooted. They all shared the feeling that there was some Great Spirit or Influence guiding and ruling all things, and that in some indefinable way they were dependent on this Spirit. This feeling, which is religion, is universal, and has developed with the development of the human race. It seems to have been implanted in the mind of man as life was breathed into his body. And as I have watched the workings and the results of this feeling in its different forms, and examined the effects and tried to judge of the value of the different religions, I have come to look upon them as so many progressive steps in the development of the religious idea—that is, of the religious feeling in the human race; as so many steps in the development upwards, of which it is by no means certain that the highest has yet been reached.

If, then, we can argue, from the universality of the religious idea in man, that religion is essential to the human race; if we can trust the universal feeling that there is some Spirit—call that Spirit what we will—ruling the Universe and guiding the development of the human race;—then it is only reasonable to believe that, as the race grows older and accumulates experience, and as other faculties develop, so this religious feeling will develop also, and the conception of the Deity and of the relations of man to the Deity enlarge itself. The traveller through strange countries sees that the various forms of religion professed by separate peoples only differ in degree of truth, that none are wholly false, and that all have the same foundation of belief in a Power governing and influencing all men.

He can no longer believe that the Christian religion is so far superior to the Buddhist or the Mohammedan religion; that the Christian is to go to heaven, while the "heathen" is to go to hell. He cannot help recognizing that there is something in the Christian religion vastly superior to others, but he sees that these latter have much that is good and true in them also. The feeling, then, that is begotten from reflecting on all this, is that those who desire to be leaders in a religion, and to gain adherents to it, must study in a sympathetic manner the religions of others. They must do this, and it cannot be doubted that cultured men, living true and noble lives, must be able to influence those around them. Be they professed missionaries or be they simple Christian men and women, be they in their own or in a strange country, men of culture and learning, who do their best to carry out in their daily lives the precepts which they know to be good, will be able slowly to raise the moral standard of those among whom they live, and give those who are more ignorant a higher conception of the Deity and of the relation of man to the Deity. They will be able to disabuse the untutored of the gross ideas of God which are so often formed—of such ideas, for instance, as that of an inhuman monster who is prepared to consign to eternal torture of the most barbarous description those whose faults are so trivial as not to meet with special punishment even here on earth; and by the daily example of well-lived lives they will be able to afford an ideal which cannot but be helpful to those who would wish to practise the precepts which they know so well are true, but only so difficult to carry out in daily life.

This is what the best missionaries really are doing in China, and have been doing for years and years. Little effect may have been produced in so short a time as a couple of centuries upon over three hundred millions of the most stationary and unimpressionable race in the world. But that was to be expected. In the first two centuries after Christ only the most infinitesimal effect had been produced upon Europe, and it would have been perfectly marvellous if in so short a time any great effect had been produced upon so vast and hard a mass as China; but that some effect is being produced I can vouch for from personal experience. I can testify to the fact that, living quietly and unostentatiously in the interior of China, there are men who, by their lives of noble self-sacrifice and sterling good, are slowly influencing those about them; men who have so influenced not only a few, but many thousands of these unenthusiastic Chinese, as to cause them to risk life itself for their religion. And if this good work is going on, if Christians are willing to give up all they hold most dear in this life to help others forward, then is this not worthy of support?—not the support of force, for even the missionaries do not desire that, but the support to be afforded by the encouragement of their fellow-Christians. The slothful, the ignorant, and the foolhardy may well be criticized, and the missionary cause will only be advanced if such criticism has the effect of stirring them to increased and more discreet activity. But the true missionary, the man who devotes his life to the work of imparting to other races the religion from which his own has derived so much benefit; who carefully trains himself for this work; who sympathetically studies the religion, the character, and the peculiarities of the people he wishes to convert; and who practically lives a life which those about him can see to be good;—should be admired as the highest type of manhood, and it is he for whom I should wish to enlist the sympathies of my fellow-countrymen in this grave crisis of the missionary cause.

CHAPTER XIX.

IMPRESSIONS OF TRAVEL.

> "I have felt
> A presence that disturbs me with the joy
> Of elevated thoughts: a sense sublime
> Of something far more deeply interfused,
> Whose dwelling is the light of setting suns,
> And the round ocean, and the living air,
> And the blue sky, and in the mind of man:
> A motion and a spirit, that impels
> All thinking things, all objects of all thought,
> And rolls through all things."
>
> WORDSWORTH.

To have travelled among such varied descriptions of country as have been portrayed in this narrative—through desert, forest, mountain, plain—and to have been brought in contact with so many types of the human race, from the highly cultured Hindoo to the rough tribesman of the Himalayas, without forming some general impressions, would be impossible. When a European travels among uncivilized, ignorant people, he is constantly being asked questions about the natural phenomena around him. He is thus made to realize how advanced our knowledge of these phenomena is in comparison with that possessed by semi-barbarians; and in his solitary journeyings he is incited to inquire into the meanings of what he sees, and, looking backward from the starting-point of our knowledge, as marked in the untutored people around him, and so thinking of the store that has been acquired, his fancy inevitably wanders into the fields of discovery to come.

No one, indeed, who has been alone with Nature in her purest aspects, and seen her in so many different forms, can help pondering over her meanings; and though, in the strain and stress of travel, her deepest messages may not have reached my ear, now, in the after-calm, when I have all the varied scenes as vividly before me as on the day I saw them, and have, moreover, leisure to appreciate them and feel their fullest influence, I can realize something of her grandeur, the mighty scale on which she works, and the infinite beauty of all she does. These impressions, as I stand now at the close of my narrative, with the many scenes which the writing of it has brought back to my mind full before my eyes, crowd upon me, and I long to be able to record them as clearly as I feel them, for the benefit of those who have not had the leisure or the opportunity to visit the jealously guarded regions of the earth where Nature reveals herself most clearly.

Upon no occasion were the wonders of the universe more impressively brought before my mind than in the long, lonely marches in the Gobi Desert. For seventy days I was travelling across the desert, and, knowing that the marches would be made mostly by night, I had brought with me one of those popular books on astronomy which put so clearly before the reader the main principles of the working of the stellar universe. I used to read it by day, and in the long hours of the night march ponder over the meaning of what I had read. There, far away in the desert, there was little to disturb the outward flow of feeling towards Nature. There, before me, was nothing *but* Nature. The boundless plain beneath, and the starry skies above. And skies, too, such as are not to be seen in the murky atmospheres of the less pure regions of the earth, but clear and bright as they can only be in the far, original depths of Nature. In those pure skies the stars shone out in unrivalled brilliancy, and hour after hour, through the long nights, I would watch them in their courses over the heavens, and think

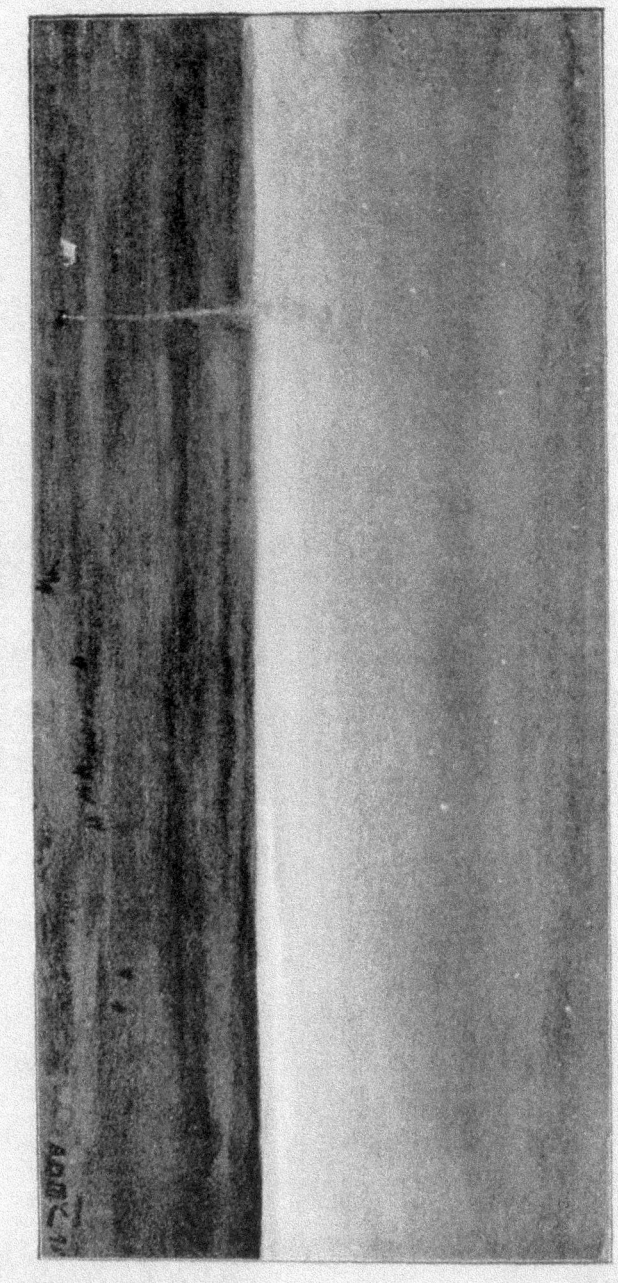

NIGHT SCENE IN THE GOBI DESERT.

on what they are and what they represent, and try to realize the place which we men hold in the universe stretched out before me.

In the busy world of civilization the truths of science seem to leave little impression. We have so much else to think of, so much beside to occupy our attention, that they excite only a momentary feeling of wonder, and we are inclined to think that, after all, it is a matter of small consequence what lies beyond our little world. But when we have been for months cut off from civilization, when there are none of the distractions of daily life to arrest our attention, then, in the midst of the desert, or deep in the heart of the mountains, these truths approach realities. Then it is that we think over the facts which the science of astronomy presents. The distance of the stars, so great in certain cases that the light from them, travelling at the rate of one hundred and eighty-six thousand miles in every second, must have started before the birth of Christ to reach the earth in our day; and their numbers, which are reckoned not by thousands, but by hundreds of millions, will furnish instances of the truths to which I allude.

Such, we are told, are the distances and number of the stars; and their size, and the speed at which they are travelling, are equally marvellous. But what is beyond them? Say we could travel to the very furthest star that is to be seen from the earth, what is beyond that? Is that star the limit of everything? is there yet another hundred million stars beyond? Then, again, when we learn that all this world, and the sun and the stars, came from a vast expanse of nebulous gas, where did that gas come from? And what will happen to all these myriads of worlds? It is said that the earth will become cold, barren, and lifeless as the moon, and then be drawn into the sun, which itself will have expended the last ray of heat it has been giving out for millions of years, and will go whirling through space, a cold, dead, lifeless star. Is every star to burn itself out like this, till the whole universe is a whirling vortex of dead worlds? or are life and heat to come to them again by impact with one another, or in some yet unknown manner?

Then, in the present, what is happening in these worlds around us? When I visited the secluded little state of Hunza, whose inhabitants were shut out by the mountains from contact with outside peoples and countries, I found they thought that the world only consisted of a few neighbouring valleys, and that no higher race than themselves existed. They could form no conception of such vast plains of cultivated land as are seen in India; they could imagine nothing like the ocean; a railway and a telegraph would have seemed supernatural to them, and men who could invent and work such things, as of an altogether superior order to themselves. We men on this earth are in as remote a corner of the universe as Hunza is in this world; and, among the millions of worlds around us, there must be living beings of some sort, and, among them all, may there not, perhaps, be some who are superior to ourselves? Man is the highest form of living being in this single little world of ours—this little speck, which is to the universe as the smallest grain of sand to the stretch of the seashore. But is he the highest in the whole universe? Are not the probabilities overwhelmingly in favour of his not being so? Would it not be the veriest chance, if, among all these millions of worlds, this one on which we live should have happened to develop the highest being? Thinking on all this, one cannot help believing that, in some few at least of those myriads of worlds, there may be more perfect beings than ourselves. There, there may be beings with the senses more highly developed, who could see, for instance, with the power of our telescopes and microscopes; beings, again, who had still other senses than we possess, who might have the power after which we seem to be dimly groping, of reading the thoughts of others, and directly communicating with others at a distance. Or, again, beings whose lives, reckoned by centuries instead of single years, could accumulate experience and knowledge such as we never can in our fleeting threescore years and ten. May we not, too, imagine in these stellar worlds, beings who would no more allow themselves to be bound down to their island worlds by mere space than we permitted ourselves to be confined to land by the ocean; beings, who, as Columbus crossed the ocean to discover a new world beyond his own, would set out through the depths of space to communicate with other worlds around them? And, lastly, amid all these millions of worlds, may we not conceive of societies as superior to our own as ours is to the savage tribes about us—societies where culture of the mind, where sympathy and love, and all that is noblest in man's moral nature, have attained their highest development, and are given fullest play?

In many such ways as these, may we not imagine beings more perfect than ourselves to exist in the realms of light above? And, fanciful as these conjectures may seem, they are in no way beyond the bounds of possibility, and indulgence in such fancies is of deep practical use in making us realize more clearly what our true position in the vast universe really is. The simple nomads, whom from time to time I used to meet in the desert, looking up into the heavens with a keenness of sight such as is only granted to these dwellers in the wilderness, saw only a number of bright specks, which one by one disappeared below the horizon, and reappeared in apparently the same places on the following evening. Towards morning they would see a round of light appear, which would slowly pass across the sky and disappear, like the stars, below the western horizon. Day after day, night after night, the same process would be repeated, the stars by night and the sun by day, coursing over the heavens.

And what did these children of the desert think of these phenomena? Simply this, that what they *seemed* to see was really what they saw—that the small ball of fire by day and these little specks of light by night, went round and round this great flat plain which constituted their world, appearing above it in the east, ascending high overhead, and then sinking beneath it once more in the west. They knew not that that ball of fire was made of the same materials as their desert tracts, or that, indeed, those very tracts were part of that ball of fire. They had no conception that this sun was a million times as far from them as the most distant hill they could see—a million times as far away as the longest day's march they had ever made. They had never supposed that that seemingly small ball of fire was millions of times as great as the round of their horizon, vast as that desert horizon appears. And in their highest flights of imagination they had never thought those little specks of light were greater worlds still—greater and infinitely more distant; or that, besides those few thousands which they could see with their eyes, there were millions and millions beyond.

And if we know so much more than these primitive peoples, it is simply because those who have gone before have thought, and reasoned, and given play to their imagination, and have recorded their thoughts to help on those who will follow after. It is not so many centuries ago that the most learned men in Europe would have told us that we could never hope to know what the sun was made of, still less what were the materials of the stars. And yet, little by little, these and other secrets have been forced out of Nature. Men have watched her, studied her every movement, marked each down, and thought over it, till Nature could no longer conceal what had been hidden in her breast during all the long ages of the past, and so it is we now know what we do know. So it is that the cultured European is able to realize so much better than these simple nomads what our true position in the universe is; and, realizing this, to have higher and more enlarged ideas of the character of its Creator and Ruler.

In the long night marches in the desert, my thoughts turned chiefly on the relations of this world with the worlds of space. Of the magnitude of this our own world, my best idea was formed from observation of high mountains. In the pages of this book I have described many a scene among the Himalayas where I stood spell-bound at the height and grandeur of the mountains. I see before me now the Tian-shan—the "Heavenly Mountains"—as I saw them from the Gobi Desert, their white summits forming part of heaven itself, and their base rooted in the broad bosom of the desert. I recall to my mind the sight of the Pamir Mountains, the outer wall of the "Roof of the World," viewed from the plains of Turkestan, and rising from them like one vast rampart. I think of the Mustagh—the "Ice Mountains"—rising tier upon tier before me, and the great peak K.2, the second highest mountain in the world, soaring above all the rest. I remember the Wanga Parbat—the "Naked Mountain"—seen across the lovely vale of Kashmir, or, again, from the banks of the river Indus, above which it rises for twenty-three thousand feet in one continuous slope. All these scenes I recall, and many others with them—the Rakapushi Peak in Hunza, and the Tirich Mir in Chitral, each of them twenty-five thousand feet above sea-level; and I think of the first sight I ever had of high snow-mountains, when from the Juras I looked across to the Mont Blanc range, and could not at first believe that the snowy summits were not clouds, so high above this earth did they appear. Mont Blanc was but a little mountain in comparison with the giants I afterwards saw in the Himalayas, and yet even these, we find, are mere roughnesses on the surface in comparison with the whole volume of the earth. Of such enormous size is this world—this world, which in proportion to the sun is as a pin's head beside an orange, and, in relation to the starry universe, but as a drop of water in comparison with the Atlantic ocean—that mountain heights which appal men by their magnitude are to it but as the roughnesses on the peel of an orange to the whole fruit. No wonder, then, that these minute excrescences, which we call mighty mountains, are soon washed down. To us they seem so immense as to be absolutely immovable and unchangeable. In comparison with the whole mass of the world they are nothing, and in a bird's-eye view of the entire earth they would be scarcely perceptible. Here, then, we have a scale upon which to base our views of the universe, and again we are reminded of its inconceivable proportions.

And from those cold mountain solitudes, from the lonely desert tracts, the thoughts are brought back to scenes of busy life—the crowded haunts of men, the teeming swarms of animal life, and the varied types of the vegetable kingdom; and I think of the forests in Manchuria, with all their numerous life crowded into the brief summer season—the huge oak trees, the tall elms; the birches, firs, and pines; and all the wealth of flowery beauty, the lilies, irises, and columbines, in sheets of colour: of the river-banks and waters of the lakes, teeming with animal life of every kind—the thousands of duck and geese and snipe, and every form of waterfowl in countless numbers; the swarms of insect life; the great droves of ponies on the steppes; and the herds of graceful antelopes:—I think of these, and of all the varied races of mankind with whom I have been brought in contact—the cold, unattractive, but intelligent and thrifty Chinamen; the dreamy, listless nomads of Mongolia; the lethargic men of Turkestan; the rough, hardy races of the Himalayas; the impressionable Chitralis; the trusty Sikhs; and the jovial little Gurkhas:—and there comes the remembrance of the latest scientific truth, that all this varied life, from the lowliest plant, from the minutest insect, to the sharp-witted Chinamen, and to the highest civilized races, are all but branches from the same original forms of life. While the mountains have been slowly raised from their birthplace in the ocean-beds, then washed down again and others raised in their place, during all these millions of years, animal and vegetable has been developing, first, like the mountains, beneath the waters of the sea, and afterwards in the continental tracts of land.

And with the idea of evolution thoroughly engrafted into the mind, as it must be on reading any of the books of science which a traveller naturally takes up, the observer of varied races of mankind finds himself considering how these races are developing, to what goal they are progressing, and upon what lines their evolution is taking place. And especially interesting is the question raised by the study of these various stages of human evolution; whether the race is developing intellectually, or whether its development, not being towards an increased intellectual capacity in the individual, is rather in the direction of a higher moral nature. And in this matter my observations seem to corroborate the views put forward by Mr. Benjamin Kidd, that the development now is not primarily intellectual, but rather moral and religious; that since man has become a social creature, the development of his intellectual character has become subordinate to the development of his religious character.

It is the privilege of a traveller to have opportunities of mixing, on and after his journey, with persons in every grade of the social scale, and of every degree of intellectual capacity. During his travels he frequently associates with men who are little better than beasts of burden, and on his return he meets with statesmen, men of science, and men of letters of the first rank in the most civilized countries of the world. He sees every step of the ladder of human progress. And, so far as I have been able to make use of my opportunities of observation, I have not been impressed with any great mental superiority of the most highly developed races of

Europe over lower races with whom I have been brought in contact. In mere brain-power and intellectual capacity there seems no great difference between the civilized European and, say, the rough hill-tribesman of the Himalayas; and, in regard to the Chinaman, I should even say that the advantage lay on his side. In the rude hill states of Hunza and Chitral, among men whose natural endowments I have had some means of judging, for I have been in contact with them for months, and engaged with them in the transaction of business where their intellectual capacity might well be observed, I have remarked that the average ability is certainly not inferior to the average of a European people. One meets there with shrewd, sharp, intelligent men who, with regard to any of their own concerns, or any subject with which they have some acquaintance, can grasp points quickly, and give their answers directly and comprehensively; men with excellent memories, and with a power of speech, and, amongst themselves, a quickness of repartee, certainly not inferior to that of a European. Amongst the races of India, and with the Chinese, this is still more noticeable. The European may feel his *moral* superiority over them, but in sharpness of intellect there seems little to choose between the two. The brain capacities of these less-civilized races is no smaller, and their mental abilities are no less.

On the other hand, no European can mix with non-Christian races without feeling his moral superiority over them. He feels, from the first contact with them, that, whatever may be their relative positions from an intellectual point of view, he is stronger morally than they are. And facts show that this feeling is a true one. It is not because we are any cleverer than the natives of India, because we have more brains or bigger heads than they have, that we rule India; but because we are stronger morally than they are. Our superiority over them is not due to mere sharpness of intellect, but to that higher moral nature to which we have attained in the development of the human race.

What, for instance, was the power by which six British officers, shut up in Chitral fort, hundreds of miles from the nearest British soldier, and with only native troops to rely on, were able to evoke such attachment from these men of the very same races who had, forty or fifty years before, fought desperately against the British, that those men stood by them for seven long weeks, against thousands of the enemy, till succour came? And how was it that the few British officers under Colonel Kelly were able, without the assistance of a single British soldier, and with none but these same men of India who had formerly opposed us so resolutely, to afford that timely succour to the Chitral garrison? Englishmen at home must often have wondered how this is done, and those who have been in the position of having to rely upon this power, whatever it is, have equally wondered what it can be.

It cannot be solely because he is more brave than the men he controls that the Englishman is able to carry on this work, for there are races in India scarcely less brave than the English. Few races on the earth can excel in bravery the Sikhs and the Gurkhas, and no amount of bravery alone would have preserved the British officers in the Chitral fort. Nor can it be because the Englishman is able to pay the men to do as he wishes; for he does not pay them; they pay themselves. He does not take a single shilling from England to pay the natives of India to fight for him; he, in fact, makes the natives of India pay him. Every English officer and soldier receives his pay from revenue drawn from the natives of India; so the Englishman does not pay the natives to fight for him, but they actually pay him to control them! There must, therefore, be some other means by which we in India are able to hold so great an empire by such apparently inadequate methods, and to my mind it seems that the chief, if it cannot be considered the only, power by which we do so, is the power of sympathy.

Let a stranger go anywhere outside the barracks of the seventy thousand British troops in India, and watch those Englishmen who are employed in direct dealings with the natives of India. Let him go to a native regiment, or to a civil district, or to a political agency in a native state, and watch the officer who is engaged on behalf of Government in dealing with the crowd of natives around him. If the stranger looks sufficiently carefully, he will see that, in spite of the Englishman's cold, "stand-offish" exterior, he has the interests of the natives under his charge very deeply at heart. He may not "fraternize" with the natives, and as likely as not he will tell the stranger that a native of India can never be trusted; but, in spite of that, he will trust those particular natives who are under himself, and will look very sharply after their interests. If they are attacked in any way, or any semblance of an injustice is attempted on them, he will stand up for them, often against his own Government; and many cases might be mentioned where he has even laid down his life in proof of his trust in them.

This regard for the interests of those whom he governs is one of the most characteristic features of the Englishman's rule in India. Wherever an Englishman is left long enough in the same position, it will nearly always be found that his sympathies go out to those under him, often to the extent of opposing his superiors. And we have recently seen an ex-Viceroy and a Secretary of State for India declaring, the one in the House of Lords and the other in the House of Commons, that even before our own interests the interests of those we govern must first be looked to. And that this same principle of showing sympathy to those we govern is not merely enunciated as an empty platitude by statesmen living here in England, but that it is actually carried into practice, every one must acknowledge who thinks of those men in the stirring days of the Mutiny, who showed to what extent they really believed in the native soldiers under them, by going amongst them while other regiments all round were in a state of mutiny, telling those who maligned their men that they would not believe a word that was said against them, and then going down to their men's lines, and, by their very display of trust and confidence, keeping their men in subordination. Death overtook these officers only too frequently. But that the principle on which they acted was a true one is shown by the multitude of cases in which it was successful, and by the fact that, in spite of experiences where officers have suffered for their confidence, we still find it successful, and at Chitral, in 1895, we have had, perhaps, the most remarkable instance on record of its inherent truth and soundness.

This, then, is the chief power by which we hold India, this power of sympathy, this deep-rooted tendency in us to watch over the interests of those whom we control. It is by using this to supplement mere physical courage that we are able to control the millions of India. We do still require physical force in addition, but the power of sympathy must always be the paramount influence; no weak sentimentality, but sympathy and moral courage, such as "our simple great ones gone" have practically shown in days gone by. It is because we have this as our ideal, and because in the history of India we have selected for dealing directly with the natives, not merely clever men any more than physically strong men, but good men, such as the Lawrences, Nicholson, and Edwardes, with unflinching moral purpose and capacity for sympathy, that we have gained the position we hold.

It is a well-recognized fact, too, amongst those Englishmen who have had dealings with Asiatics, that if once the European give up his higher moral standard, and descends to intriguing with Asiatics, and engaging with them in cunning intellectual fencing, the chances are very much in favour of his being worsted. It is not so in every case, for there are, of course, Europeans just as nimble-minded and subtle as Asiatics; but, in the overwhelming majority of cases, the sharp-witted Asiatic wins. On the other hand, where real influence has been gained by the European over Asiatics, it has been due to his straightness and strength of moral character, and not to any original intellectual superiority. The European shows his greater moral strength by his tenacity of purpose, his persistence in the object he has before him, his disregard of selfish interests in the advancement of that object, and his sympathy with those about him. These characteristics of a higher moral development enable him to win the day in his competition with men of natural capacity equal to his own, who fail in the struggle because they have not the same "grit" or resolution, and, above all, because they do not practise that abnegation of self in the interest of others, and that sympathy with those about them which have been inculcated into the European races by the teaching of the Christian religion. Europeans are anything but perfect in the practice of these principles, but when we hear of a wounded British officer* dismounting from his pony and insisting upon his wounded comrade, a native soldier, mounting it in his stead and riding back to safety, while he walked, although the enemy were firing from all sides, then we know that such principles are sometimes applied, and it is because they are more frequently and more thoroughly applied by the Christian than by the non-Christian races of the world that the former have been able to establish their superiority over the latter.

If this conclusion, based upon experiences with men of many different races, is right, it furnishes a strong argument in support of the opinion that the development of the human race is now, not towards bigger heads, with cold, subtle brains,

* Lieutenant Fowler, R.E., at Reshun, in Chitral.

but towards larger hearts, with warmer, fuller blood flowing through them. The development now is of man as a social being, and in the keen struggle of societies for existence, that society will win whose members are able to subordinate most thoroughly their own individual interests to the well-being of the whole society to which they belong. Nowhere has this principle been more deeply impressed than on the society formed by the Christian religion, and may we not then conclude that, if that society now finds itself foremost in all the societies of the world, it is so because of the inherent superiority of the principles which it professes?

These are the thoughts that fill me as I bring together in one focus the various impressions of Nature and of Man that have, during ten years' wanderings, formed themselves upon my mind. And here I will close this narrative, these last words of which I am writing on the Atlantic Ocean, far away from the scenes I have depicted, as I approach the shores of Africa, the field, maybe, of yet further explorations to come. Hardships I necessarily had in the course of those travels, and, to a certain degree, danger also, but never once now do I regret leaving those comforts of my native land, now more appreciated than ever, to wander amid the real haunts of Nature. Forgotten now are all the trials; dimmer and dimmer do they become as they recede into the background. But the keen pleasure of travel remains, and the impressions of Nature live and grow for ever. Nature, when once she has revealed herself, impresses herself more deeply on us with each succeeding year.

> " 'Tis her privilege,
> Through all the years of this our life, to lead
> From joy to joy : for she can so inform
> The mind that is within us, so impress
> With quietness and beauty, and so feed
> With lofty thoughts, that neither evil tongues,

Rash judgments, nor the sneers of selfish men,
Nor greetings where no kindness is, nor all
The dreary intercourse of daily life,
Shall e'er prevail against us, or disturb
Our cheerful faith, that all which we behold
Is full of blessings."

INDEX.

A

Abbottabad, 216
Adamzadas of Chitral, 365
Afdigar, 262
Afzul-ul-Mulk, ruler of Chitral, 349
Aghil Pass, 185, 237
—— Range, 233, 237
Akal Jan, a Kirghiz, 267
Ak-baital River, 301
Ak-berdi Pass, 302
Ak-chak, 159
Ak-chak-tash hot springs, 297
Aksakals, 164
Aksu, 154
—— River, 300
Aktagh Range, 232
Aktash, 278, 297
Alichur Pamir, 298; principal routes, 299
—— River, 299
Allen, Mr., British Consul at Newchwang, 7, 48
Altai Mountains, 100, 107
Aman-ul-Mulk, chief of Chitral, 349
Amur River, 14
Andijani merchants, 136; silk, 137
Aral, 156
Arbap, or governor, of Hunza, 281
Artysh, 163
Ashkuman River, 329, 337
Asia, Central, characteristics of the traders of, 309; their opinion of the respective merits of the British and Russian rule, 310; comparative strength of the two powers, 310
Askoli village, 170, 204
Avalanches, danger from, 242
Aylmer, 346

B

Bai, 154
Baijih Pass, 278
Baikra Pass, 329
Baltis, the, 207
Baltistan, 207
Baltit, 288, 347
Baltoro Glacier, 202
Barkul, 117
Baroghil Pass, 329
Baroso-khai Peak, 95, 100
Barratt, Captain, 338
Bash Gumbaz, 298, 300
Bautu, caravan from, 89, 93
Bazar Darra River, 234
—— valley, 181
Beech, Mr., 292, 316
Bell, Colonel, 58, 123, 213; his letter from the Karakoram Pass, 172
Bellew, Dr., 179
Benderski, 328
Blanc, M. E., 314
Bortson well, 92
Bower, Captain, 214, 226
——, Lieutenant, 267, 273
Bozai-Gumbaz, 326, 329, 335
Bradshaw, Captain, 347
Braldo River, 207
Brenan, Mr. Byron, Consul at Tientsin, 55
Brigands, resort of, 101
Bruce, Lieutenant, 351, 354, 357
Bulun-kul Lake, 325
Burzil Pass, 289, 338
Bu-yur, 149
Buzilla Jul, 299

C

Cairns, 102
Card, M., 26
Carey, Mr., 4, 173
Chadir Tash, 297
Chang-pai-shan, or "Ever-White Mountain," 5, 15
Chang-san, the interpreter, 78
Chapman, General, Quarter-Master General in India, 211
Charch, 149
Chê-ku-lu-chuen, 129
China, the Great Wall of, 51, 62; introduction of railways into, 54; the missionary question, 377-386
Chinese temples, 9; industry of colonists, 11, 18, 50; cooking, 19; characteristics, 20; carts and mules, 30; mode of levying troops, 71; intricacies of the language, 115; officials in Kashgar, 306
Ching-cheng, 121
Ching-shiu-kou, 143
Chiraghsaldi Pass, 179, 234
Chirag-tash, or Lamp Rock, 301
Chitral, 329, 349, 353; population, 349; claimants for the throne, 349; the Mehtar of, 352, 357; system of government, 362-368; durbars, 363; the Adamzadas, 365; councils of state, 367; rapidity of the administration, 369
Chitralis, 352, 358, 370, 372-376
Chong Jangal, 253, 258
Christie, Dr., 46
Chukshu, 235
Clarke, Mr. and Mrs. G. W., 70
Cockerill, Lieutenant, 265
Collins, Messrs. G. W., & Co., of Tientsin, 81
Conrad, Herr, 268
Conraux, Père, French missionary, 25
Conway, Sir William, 203, 354
Corea, 11
Cossacks, appearance, 34, 35; pay, 35, 269
Crevasse Glacier, 251
Cumberland, Major, 226, 267, 273
Curzon, Mr. G., 376

D

Dalgleish, Mr., 164, 172; murdered, 173; character, 173; memorial tablet, 226
Darkot Pass, 329
Darwaza, a Kanjuti outpost, 259
Dauvergne, M., 209, 226, 273
Davison, Lieutenant, 317, 325, 332; his attempt to cross the Mustagh Pass, 317-320; death, 340
Deer (huang-yang), herds of, 83
Depsang Plains, 225
Dharmsala, 1
Diament, Miss, 63
Doolans, 150
Dorah Pass, 349
Drogpa, 177, 198
Dufferin, Lord, 59
———, Mount, 325
Dunmore, Lord, 297, 299
Durand, Sir Mortimer, 214, 216
———, Colonel, 228, 260, 288, 338, 341, 346, 348
Dust-storm, 96

E

Edgar, Mr., commissioner of China customs, 48
Elias, Mr. Ney, 60 note, 75, 214, 291, 298, 325
Eurh-pu village, 126
Ever-White Mountain, The, 5, 15; its height, 15; meadows, 16; lake, 16

F

"Feng-shui," superstition of, 54
Forsyth, Sir Douglas, 152
——— Mission, 156, 174, 274
Fowler, Lieutenant, 400
Fulford, Mr. H., 5, 42, 49

G

Gad-flies, 13
Galpin Gobi, 89, 92
Gez River, 302, 324
Ghazan Khan, 283
Ghiza, 351
Giles, Dr., 358
Gilgit, 288, 338, 350

Ginseng plant seekers, 14
Gircha, 282
Glaciers, 191, 202, 205, 238, 241, 243, 246, 251, 283, 334, 336
Gobi Desert, 60; preparations for crossing the, 74-77; monotony of the marches, 86; dryness of the atmosphere, 87; temperature, 88; winds, 88
—— Hills, 112
Godwin-Austen, Colonel, 194
Gordon, Colonel, 274, 291
——, Lieutenant, 348, 351, 357
Gourbaun-Seikyn Mountains, 100
Grenard, M., 314
Grombtchevsky, Captain, 267, 268, 292; on the Russian army, 270
Guchen, 74
Gulmit, 283
Gurkhas, escort of, 216, 289; average height, 271
Gusherbrum Mountain, 238

H

Hajji, the Arab, 137
Hami, 60, 74, 123
Hayward, 1, 174, 180, 232
"Heavenly Mountains," 113, 115
Hedin, Dr. Sven, 314
Hendriks, Père, the Dutch missionary, 166, 315
Hillier, Mr. Walter, 56, 65
Himalayas, first tour through the, 2
Hindu Kush, 327, 329, 335
Ho-lai-liu stream, 85
Howorth, Sir Henry, 125, 295
Ho-ya-shan hill, 111
Hsiao Pachia-tzu, Roman Catholic mission, at 43
Hsi-yang-chê, 130
Hulan, 25
Humayun, 282
Hunchun, 32
Hun-kua-ling sandhills, 97
Hunza, raiders of, 215; campaign against, 341; under British rule, 342; internal and foreign affairs, 343; relations with the Government, 344
Hurka River, 29
Hurku Hills, 91, 100
Huru-su-tai, 95

I

I, General, 33
Ice-boat sailing, 55
Ilisu, 268, 272
In-shan Range, 297
Ivanoff, M., 63
I-wang-chuen, 128

J

James, Mr. H. E. M., 3, 42, 49; "The Long White Mountain," 5, 49
Jehol-Lamamian, 106
Jemadar Rab Nawaz Khan, 357
Jhelum valley, 217
Juma Bai, 279

K

K.2 peak, 186, 203, 238, 245
Kabul, Abdul Rahman, the Amir of, 309
Kaiping, 52; coal-mine, 53
Kalgan, 62; missionary station at, 63
Kalmaks, encampments of, 144
Kamesha hamlet, 142
Kangra valley, 2
Kanjut, 215
Kanjuti robbers, 179
Kanjuti's account of the raid on the Kirghiz, 227; outpost, 259; interview with, 260; appearance, 262; terror of their chief, 263
Kara-art Pass, 303
Karachukur stream, 275, 277
Kara-kara Pass, 159
Karakash River, 236
Karakoram Mountains, 185, 292
—— Pass, 225
Karakul Lake, the Great, 303; the Little, 325
Karashar, 143
Karash-tarim plain, 180, 234
Karasu stream, 300
Kargalik, 178
Karul, 236
Karumbar River, 329, 337
Kashgar, 164, 304; Chinese officials, the civil governor, 306; the general, 307; barracks, 308
Kashmir valley, 211, 289, 339

Kashmir, state of the army in 1889..221
Kaufmann Peak, 303
Kelly, Colonel, 344
Khatan-aksai, 268
Khal Chuskun, 232
Khardung Pass, 224
Khargosh Pass, 300
Khoja Mohammed gorge, 181, 236
Kholga, 147
Khora Bhort pass, 329
Khunjerab Pass, 275
Kidd, Mr. Benjamin, 395
Kieulung, Emperor, his poem on the Ever-White Mountain, 6
Kilik Pass, 332
Kinder, Mr., 53; introduces railways into China, 53
Kirghiz encampments, 157, 160; apply for protection against the Hunza raiders, 215; account of the raid, 227
Kirghiz Jangal, 233
Kirin, 18, 42; arsenal, 19
Kitai, the, 144
Kizil, 153
Kizil Jek Pass, 303
Kobdo, 75
Kokalang Pass, 235
Kokbai Pass, 300
Korlia, 148
Kotwal, the Turk, 152
Kuan-cheng-tzu, 43
Kuch Mohammed Bey, headman of the Pamir, 272, 275, 278
Kuche oasis, 150; town, 152
Kuenlun Mountains, 179, 233, 235
Kugiar village, 178
Kukturuk valley, 332
Kulanargu River, 235
Kulanuldi, 233
Kulu valley, 2
Kurbu Pass, 272
Kwei-hwa-cheng, 62, 73; China inland mission at, 70

L.

Ladak, 219
——, the kyang of, 106
Ladakis, 177
Lain-tung, 128
Langar, 351
Laspur, 351

Leh, 219
—— to Hunza, question of transport, 222; supplies, 223
Lennard, Mr., 292, 316
Liang-ko-ba, 107
Liang-lang-shan or Eurh-lang-shan Mountains, 84
Liang-ming-chung, 132
Litot, Père, 43
Little Pamir, 294
Liu-san, Chinese servant, 62, 213; his propensity for fibbing, 82, 83
Lob Nor, 294
Lockhart, Sir William, 3
Loess formation, 66
"Long White Mountain," by Mr. James, 5, 49
Lutsch, M., 166, 305, 321

M

Macartney, Mr. George, 291, 317, 322
Macgregor, Sir Charles, Quartermaster-General in India, 4
Man-chin-tol, 103
Manchuria, 5; climate 49; mineral products, 50; population, 50
Manners-Smith, Lieutenant, 288, 346
Mao-erh-shan, 12
Maralbashi, 316
Marjunai Pass, 299
Markan-su, 304
Masher-Brum Peak, 202
Mastuj fort, 351, 376
Ma-te-la, the Mongol assistant, 79; his work, 80; home, 110; wages, 110
Maviel, Père, 43
Meadows, Mr. Taylor, 50
Mecca, pilgrimages to, 323
Mehtar of Chitral, 357
Midges, scourge of, 13
Mintaka Aksai, 277
—— Pass, 277, 280
Misgah village, 281
Mission stations at Hsiao-Pa-chia-tzu, 43; Kaigan, 63; Kwei-hwa-cheng, 70; Mukden, 46; Pa-yen-su-su, 26
Missionary question in China, 377-386
Mist, a frozen, 45
Mohammed Nazim Khan, 282, 288, 345, 347
Moli-ho stream, 84

Mongul yurts or felt tents, 68; hunters, 83; temples, 83; encampments, 95
Mongolia, Plain of, 67; pasture lands, 81; camel wool, 82
———, steppes of, 23
Mongolian ponies and mules, 44
Morgai, a Turki house, 117
Mosquitoes, scourge of, 13, 23
Mukden, 7, 46; temples of, 9; Scottish mission at, 46
Murdock, Miss, 63
Murghabi, 300
Murkush, 280
Murree, 212, 217
Musa, the Kirghiz, 221
Mustagh-ata, the Father of Mountains, 302, 304, 324
Mustagh Pass, 188; description of the crossing, 188-200; the Old, 194; the New, 194, 205
——— Range, 185

N

Nagar valley, 347
Naked Mountain, 217
Nanga Parbat Mountain, 217
Nankon gate, 62
Newchwang, 5, 48
Neza-tash Pass, 294, 300
Nilt, 288, 346
Ninguta, 31, 42
Nisbet, Colonel Parry, 217, 258
Nizam-ul-Mulk, the Mehtar of Chitral, 349, 352, 360, 370; murdered, 376
Nonni, 23
Notovitch, M. Nicolas, 210
Novo-kievsk, 38
Nubra valley, 225
Nurhachu, tomb of, 8

O

Oases, 111, 132, 149, 150
Opal, 304
Oprang Pass, 276
——— River, 185, 186, 233, 237, 254, 266
Osh, 329
Ovis argali, size of the horns, 112, 119
——— *poli* horns, 114, 298
Oxus River, 294, 326, 334

P

Pakhpu race, 179
Pakhpulu, 234
Pamir Mountains, first sight of the, 163
Pamir-i-Wakhan, 326, 335
Pamirs, The, 291; the Little, 294; the Great, 294; the Alichur, 298; formation, 295; meaning of the word, 296; climate, 296; inhabitants, 297
Panja River, 335
——— valley, 329
Passes, 159, 179, 183, 188, 194, 205, 210, 218, 224, 225, 226, 227, 232, 235, 237, 241, 263, 272, 276, 277, 280, 289, 294, 299, 300, 303, 325, 326, 329, 332, 335, 338, 339, 351, 372
Pasu Glacier, 283
Pa-yen-su-su, mission station, 26
Peiho river, 55
Pei-lin-tzu, Roman Catholic mission at, 26
Peking, 56; British legation at, 57; Gazette, despatches of the Chinese commander in, 24
Petrovsky, M., Russian Consul at Kashgar, 166, 305, 311, 320; his view of the condition of England, 312; on the treatment of natives, 312; opinion of the Chinese, 313
——— Madame, 305
Petuna, 23
Pevstof, the Russian traveller, 100
Pi-chan, 131
Pieotsof, Colonel, 273
Pil, 235
Possiet Bay, 39
Prjevalsky, his description of the Mongolian camel, 82 *note*; the Galpin Gobi, 92
Punmah glacier, 205
Pyramids, compared with Great Wall of China, 52

R

Raguit, M., 26
Rahmat-ula-Khan, 155, 161
Railway, the first Chinese, 53
Rakapushi Peak, 346
Ramsay, Captain, 211, 220
Ramzan, the interpreter, 260

Rang-kul Lake, 301
Raskam, 181, 324
—— River, 266
Rawal Pindi, 212, 216
Religion, universality of, 383
Rhins, M. Dutreuil de, 314; murdered, 315
Riffard, M., 26
Roberts, General Sir Frederick, 165, 211
Robertson, Dr., 351, 357
Rockhill, Mr., 213
Rope bridge, crossing a, 206
Ross, Mr., 46

S

Sable-hunters' huts, 13
Safder Ali, the Hunza chief, 258, 283-287; letter from, 265; campaign against, 341
Saltoro Pass, unsuccessful attempt to cross the, 241
Sandhills, 89, 97, 132; formation, 99
Sang-ching-kou, 133
S'an-pu, 127
Sansing, 28; fort, 28
San-to-lin-tzu village, 128
Saram village, 153
Sarez, 300
Sarhad, 329
Sarikolis, The, 274
Sarpo Laggo River, 186, 190
Saser Pass, 225
Schlagentweit, 174
Scottish mission at Mukden, 47
Shahidula, 223, 226, 232
Shahzad Mir, 218
Shakhdarra, 300
Shaksgam River, 185, 186
Shandur Pass, 351
Shan-hai-kuan, the Great Wall at, 51, 62; forts, 52
Shaw, Robert, 1, 58, 156; Political Agent to Yakoob Beg, 174
Sheitung-ula Mountains, 84
Sher-Afzul, 349
Shigar valley, 207
Shi-ga-tai, 131
Shignan, 299
Shimshal Pass, 227, 263
—— River, 255, 259
Shor-Bulak, 276

Sho-shok, 146
Shukar Ali, 203, 219
Simla, 213, 216
Sind valley, 211
Skardu district, 189, 209
Skinmang, 205
Sokh-bulak Pass, 232
Sokolowski, Colonel, Russian Commandant at Swanka, 34; his hospitality, 36; on the Russo-Turkish war, 37
Somatash, 298
Sontash, 159
Sprague, Mr., 63, 65
Srinagar, 211, 340
Stewart, Captain, 332, 336, 342
Su-chow, 103
Suget Jangal, 186, 246, 252
Suget Pass, 226
Sung, Mr., 19
Sungari River, 14, 23, 28; source of the, 17
Surakwat River, 181, 236
Swanka, 34
Syrt country, 159

T

Tagarma plain, 325
Tagh-dum-bash Pamir, 267, 274, 294, 326
Takhta-kuran Pass, 235
Ta-pu-ma village, 126
Tash-kupruk Pass, 329
Tashkurgan, 273, 293, 325
Taylor, 346
Taylor, Mr. Hudson, 71
Tian-shan Mountains, 113
Tientsin, 55
Tirich Mir, 355
Tisnaf River, 235
—— village, 274
Toksun, 140
Tragbal Pass, 289, 339
Travel, impressions of, 387-402
Tsi-tsi-har, 24
Tuan-yen-kou, 130
Tumen River, 32
Tung River, 273
Tungani, 144
Tupa Dawan Pass, 179
Tu-pu-chi, a Mongol encampment, 97

Turdi Kol, 227, 259
Turfan, 135, 139
Turikho valley, 372
Turkestan, 116; appearance of the men, 117; the women, 118; the races of, 144; its physical features, 170; character of the people, 171
Tyler, Captain, 329

U

Ula-khutun, 111
Uliasutai, 75
Ulugh Rabat Pass, 325
Uruk valley, 267
Urumchi, 130
Ush-ta-le, 142
Ush Turfan, 156

V

Victoria Lake, 297

W

Wakhan, 277
Wakhijrui Pass, 274, 326, 332
Wali, the guide, 177, 208
Wall, the Great, of China, 51, 62; compared with the Pyramids, 52
Walsham, Sir John, 56, 59, 60
Wang, General, 308, 320

Wazir Dadu, the "Prime Minister" of Hunza, 282
Webster, Mr. and Mrs., 46, 47
Wells, number of, 134
Williams, Mr., 63
Wu-hau-pu-la inn, 142
Wular Lake, 217

Y

Ya-hu oasis, 111
Yakoob Beg, 151, 156, 171; his pillars, 153; canal, 163
Yalu River, 11
Yang-ho valley, 65
Yang-sar, 149
Yarkand, 168, 172, 176, 292; Chinese governor of, 175
—— River, 180, 230, 233, 255
Yarkhun River, 329
Yasin valley, 174, 329, 350
Yerum-kou, 149
Yeshil-kul, 298
Yonoff, Colonel, 299, 327; his instructions from the Russian Government, 330
Yu-fu-kou, 142
Yurts or felt tents, 68

Z

Zoji-la Pass, 210, 218
Zungari, desert of, 113

THE END.

LONDON: PRINTED BY WILLIAM CLOWES AND SONS, LIMITED,
STAMFORD STREET AND CHARING CROSS.

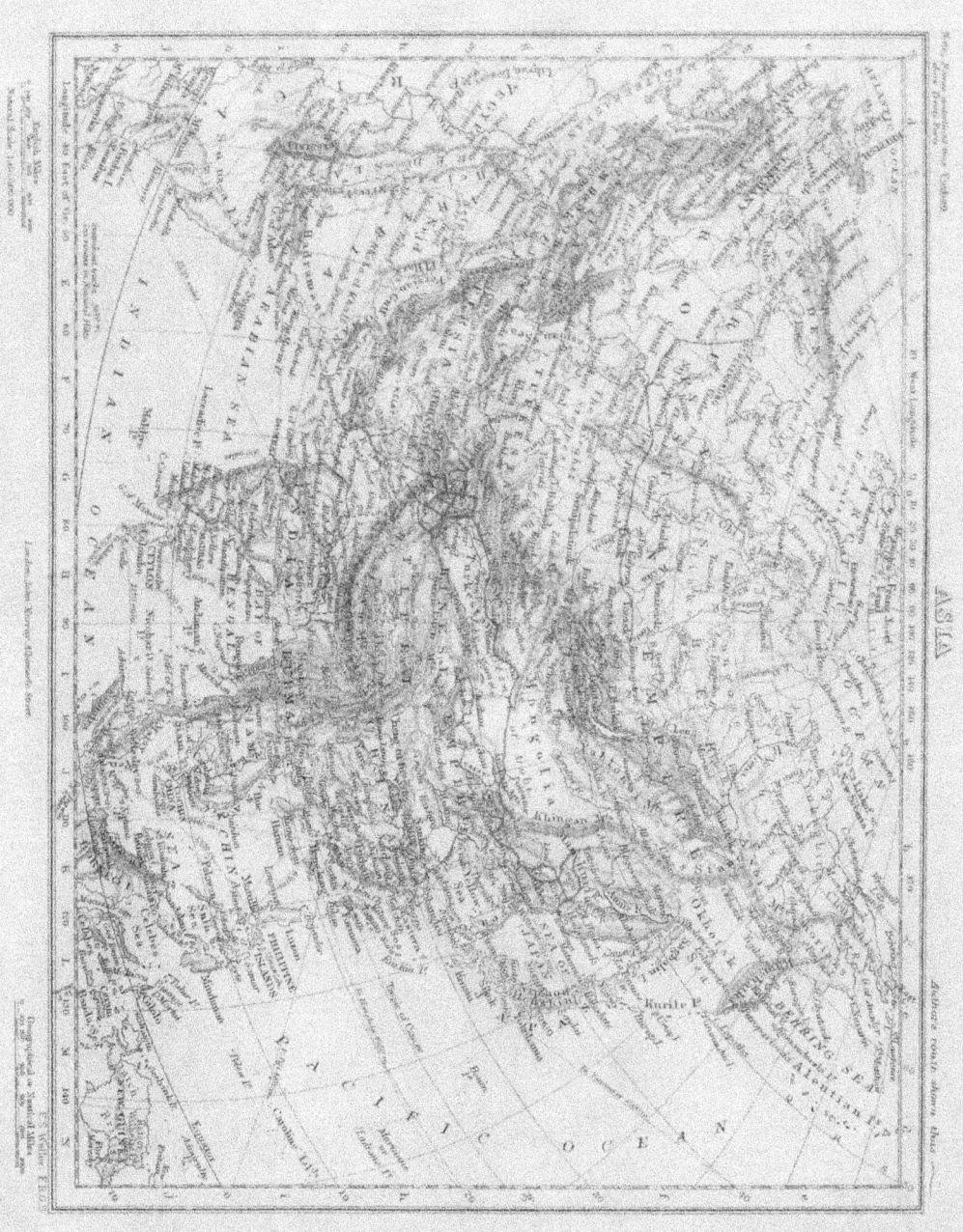

www.ingramcontent.com/pod-product-compliance
Lightning Source LLC
Chambersburg PA
CBHW080235170426
43192CB00014BA/2461